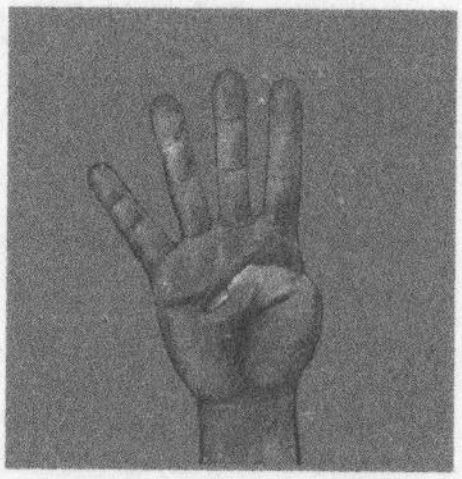

尾田栄一郎

Try making a four with your fingers! "Four!!"
Is it just me, or is your thumb bent way more than you expected?!
Okay, here comes Volume 85!! Let's go!!

-Eiichiro Oda, 2017

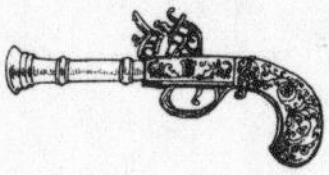

Eiichiro Oda began his manga career at the age of 17, when his one-shot cowboy manga **Wanted!** won second place in the coveted Tezuka manga awards. Oda went on to work as an assistant to some of the biggest manga artists in the industry, including Nobuhiro Watsuki, before winning the Hop Step Award for new artists. His pirate adventure **One Piece**, which debuted in **Weekly Shonen Jump** in 1997, quickly became one of the most popular manga in Japan.

ONE PIECE VOL. 85
NEW WORLD PART 25

SHONEN JUMP Manga Edition

STORY AND ART BY EIICHIRO ODA

Translation/Stephen Paul
Touch-up Art & Lettering/Vanessa Satone
Design/Yukiko Whitley
Editor/Alexis Kirsch

Printed in the U.S.A.

Published by VIZ Media, LLC
P.O. Box 77010
San Francisco, CA 94107

10 9 8 7 6 5 4 3 2 1
First printing, February 2018

www.viz.com

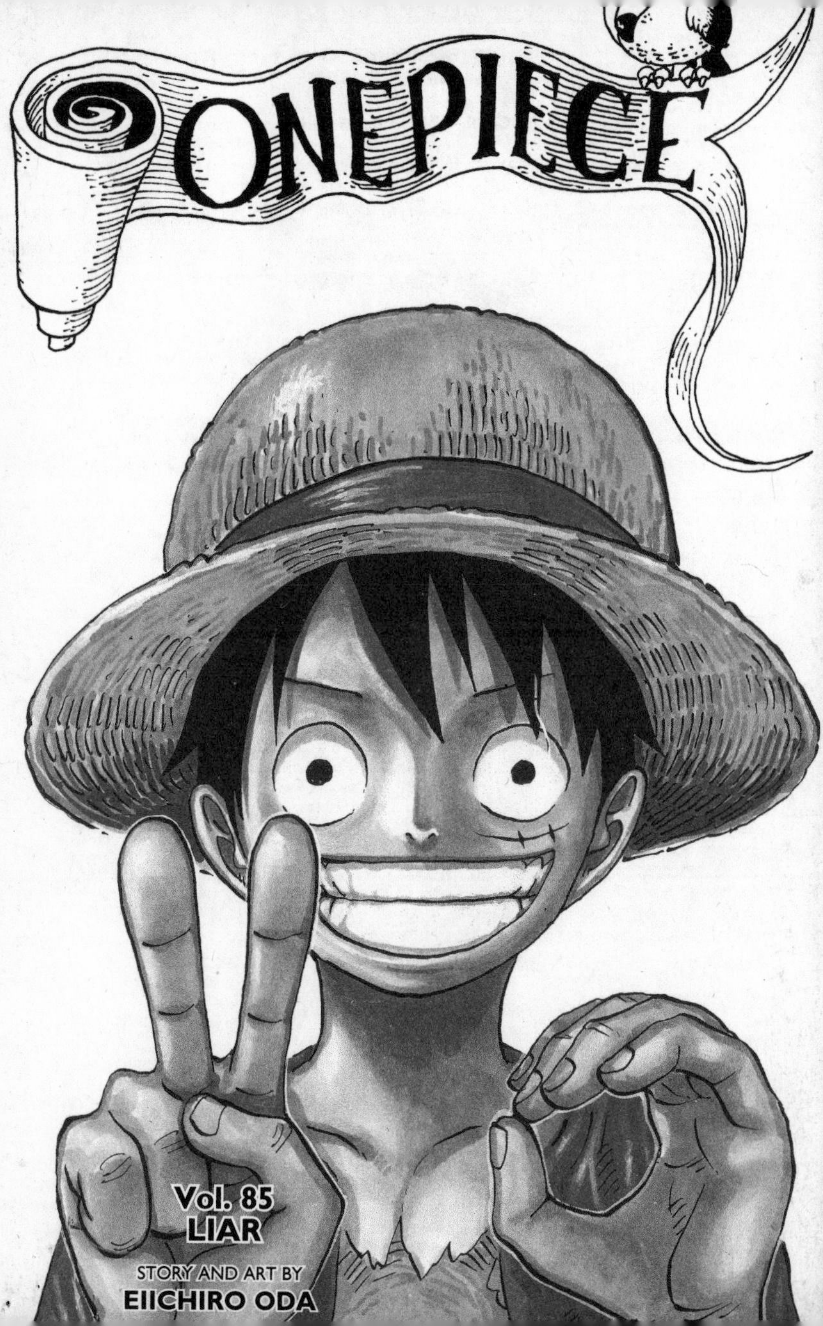
ONE PIECE
Vol. 85
LIAR
STORY AND ART BY
EIICHIRO ODA

The Straw Hat Crew

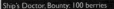

Tony Tony Chopper

After researching powerful medicine in Birdie Kingdom, he reunited with the rest of the crew.

Ship's Doctor, Bounty: 100 berries

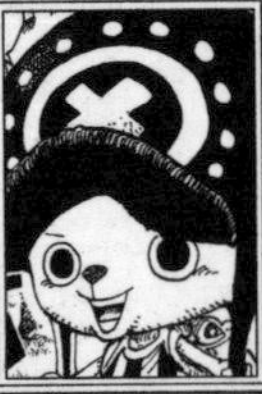

Monkey D. Luffy

A young man who dreams of becoming the Pirate King. After training with Rayleigh, he and his crew head for the New World!

Captain, Bounty: 500 million berries

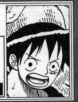

Nico Robin

She spent her time in Baltigo with the leader of the Revolutionary Army: Luffy's father, Dragon.

Archeologist, Bounty: 130 million berries

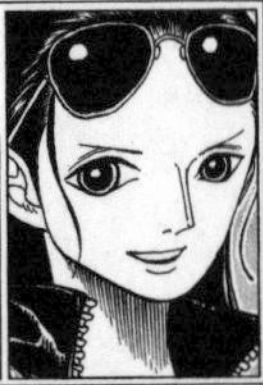

Roronoa Zolo

He swallowed his pride and asked to be trained by Mihawk on Gloom Island before reuniting with the rest of the crew.

Fighter, Bounty: 320 million berries

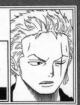

Franky

He modified himself in Future Land Baldimore and turned himself into Armored Franky before reuniting with the rest of the crew.

Shipwright, Bounty: 94 million berries

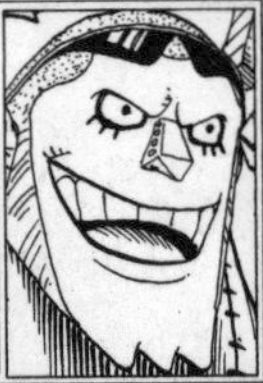

Nami

She studied the weather of the New World on the small Sky Island Weatheria, a place where weather is studied as a science.

Navigator, Bounty: 66 million berries

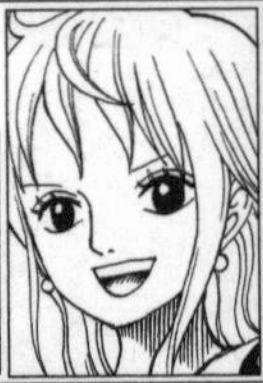

Brook

After being captured and used as a freak show by the Longarm Tribe, he became a famous rock star called "Soul King" Brook.

Musician, Bounty: 83 million berries

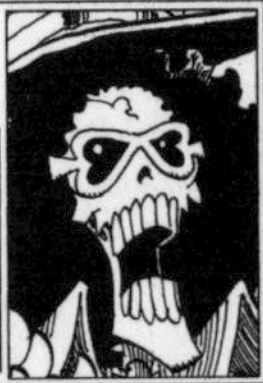

Usopp

He trained under Heracles at the Bowin Islands to become the King of Snipers.

Sniper, Bounty: 200 million berries

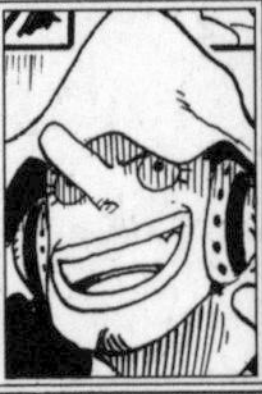

Shanks

One of the Four Emperors. Waits for Luffy in the "New World," the second half of the Grand Line.

Captain of the Red-Haired Pirates

Sanji

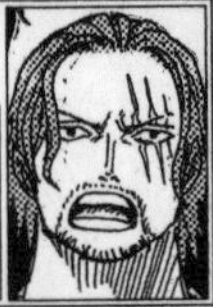

After fighting the New Kama Karate masters in the Kamabakka Kingdom, he returned to the crew.

Cook, Bounty: 177 million berries

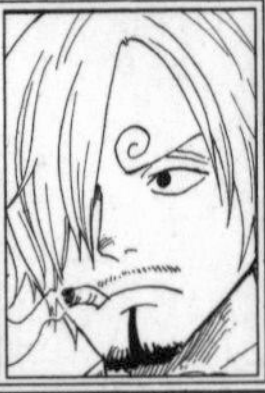

Wano Kingdom from his grasp. Meanwhile, Sanji is in terrible danger! His true father has arranged a political marriage for him with Big Mom's daughter. Sanji agrees to meet Big Mom in order to refuse the marriage, but they trap him and prevent his escape. Luffy's group rushes to save him, but Sanji refuses the help and clashes with his captain. Then Big Mom's forces capture Luffy...

Big Mom Pirates

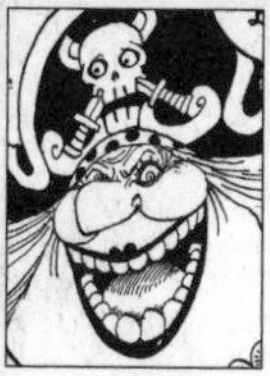
Charlotte Linlin
Captain, Big Mom Pirates

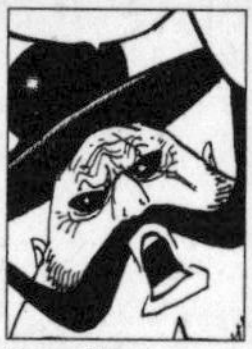
Baron Tamago
Fighter, Big Mom Pirates

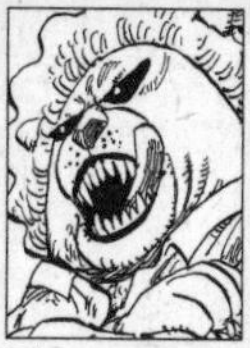
Pekoms
Fighter, Big Mom Pirates

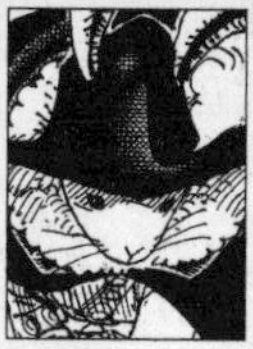
Randolph
Cranerider, Big Mom Pirates

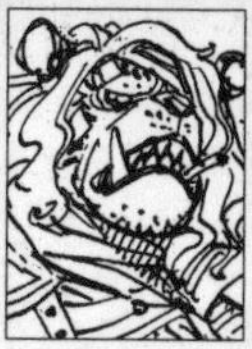
Treetop Pedro (Jaguar Mink)
Leader of the Guardians

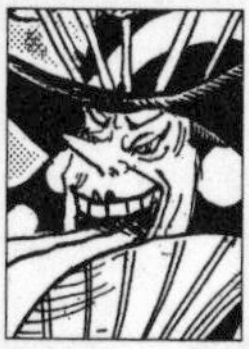
C. Perospero
1st Son of Charlotte

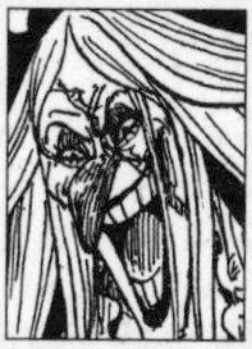
C. Brulee
8th Daughter of Charlotte

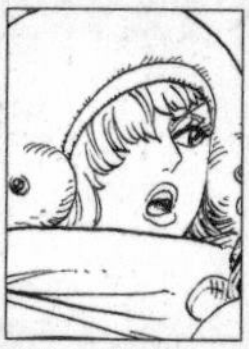
C. Smoothie (Sweet 3)
14th Daughter of Charlotte

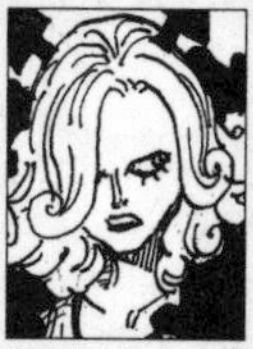
C. Galette
18th Daughter of Charlotte

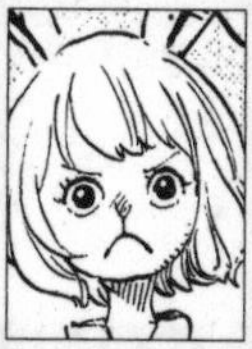
Carrot (Bunny Mink)
Battlebeast Tribe

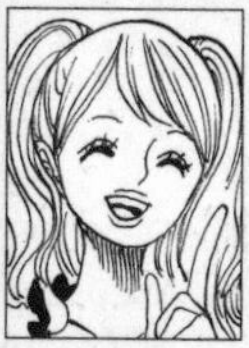
Charlotte Pudding
35th Daughter of Charlotte

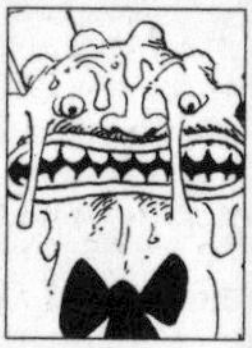
C. Opera
5th Son of Charlotte

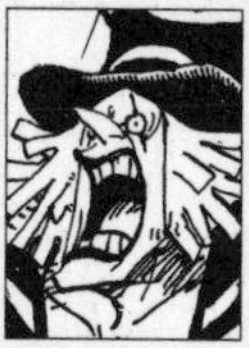
C. Montd'or
19th Son of Charlotte

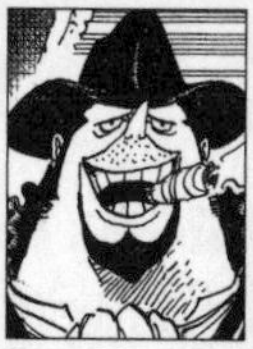
Capone "Gang" Bege
Captain of the Firetank Pirates

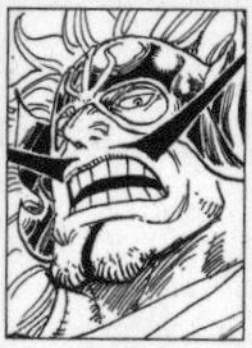
Vinsmoke Judge
King of Germa Kingdom

Germa 66

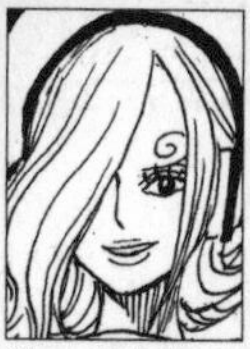
Vinsmoke Reiju
Eldest Daughter of Vinsmoke

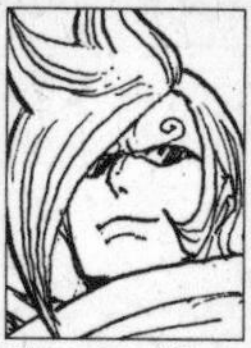
Vinsmoke Ichiji
Eldest Son of Vinsmoke

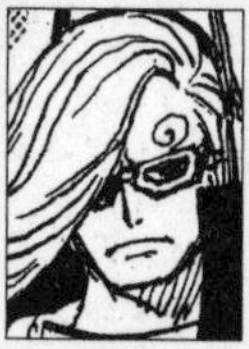
Vinsmoke Niji
Second Son of Vinsmoke

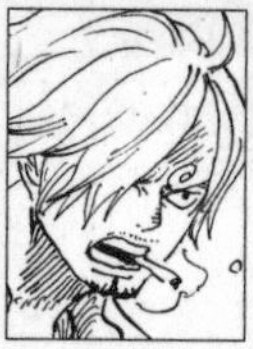
Vinsmoke Sanji
Third Son of Vinsmoke

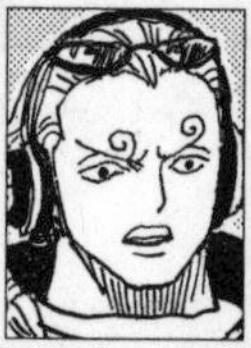
Vinsmoke Yonji
Fourth Son of Vinsmoke

Story

After two years of hard training, the Straw Hat pirates are back together, first at the Sabaody Archipelago and then through Fish-Man Island to their next stage: the New World!!

The crew happens across Law on the island of Punk Hazard, and they travel to Dressrosa to defeat Doflamingo. Next, the crew forms an alliance with the samurai and minks to topple Kaido, an Emperor of the Sea, and rescue

NEW WORLD

ONE PIECE

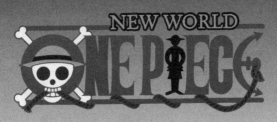

Vol. 85
LIAR

CONTENTS

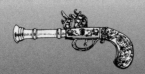

Chapter 849:
CHOBRO IN THE LAND OF MIRRORS

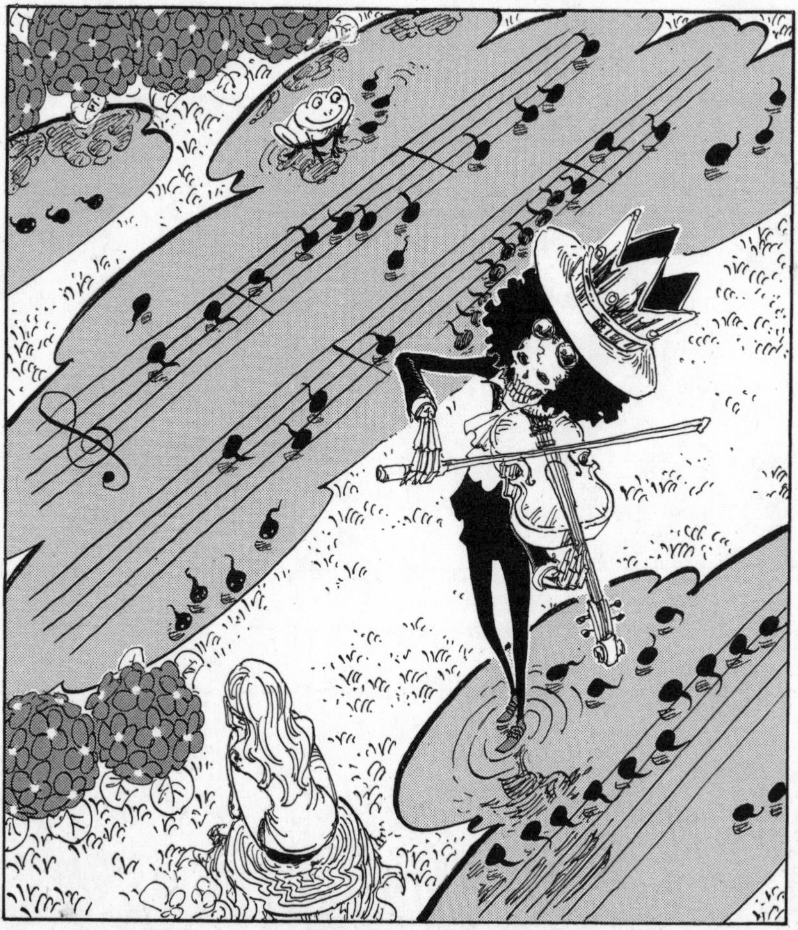

REQUEST: "BROOK COMPOSING WITH TADPOLE NOTES"
BY NODA SKYWALKER FROM OSAKA

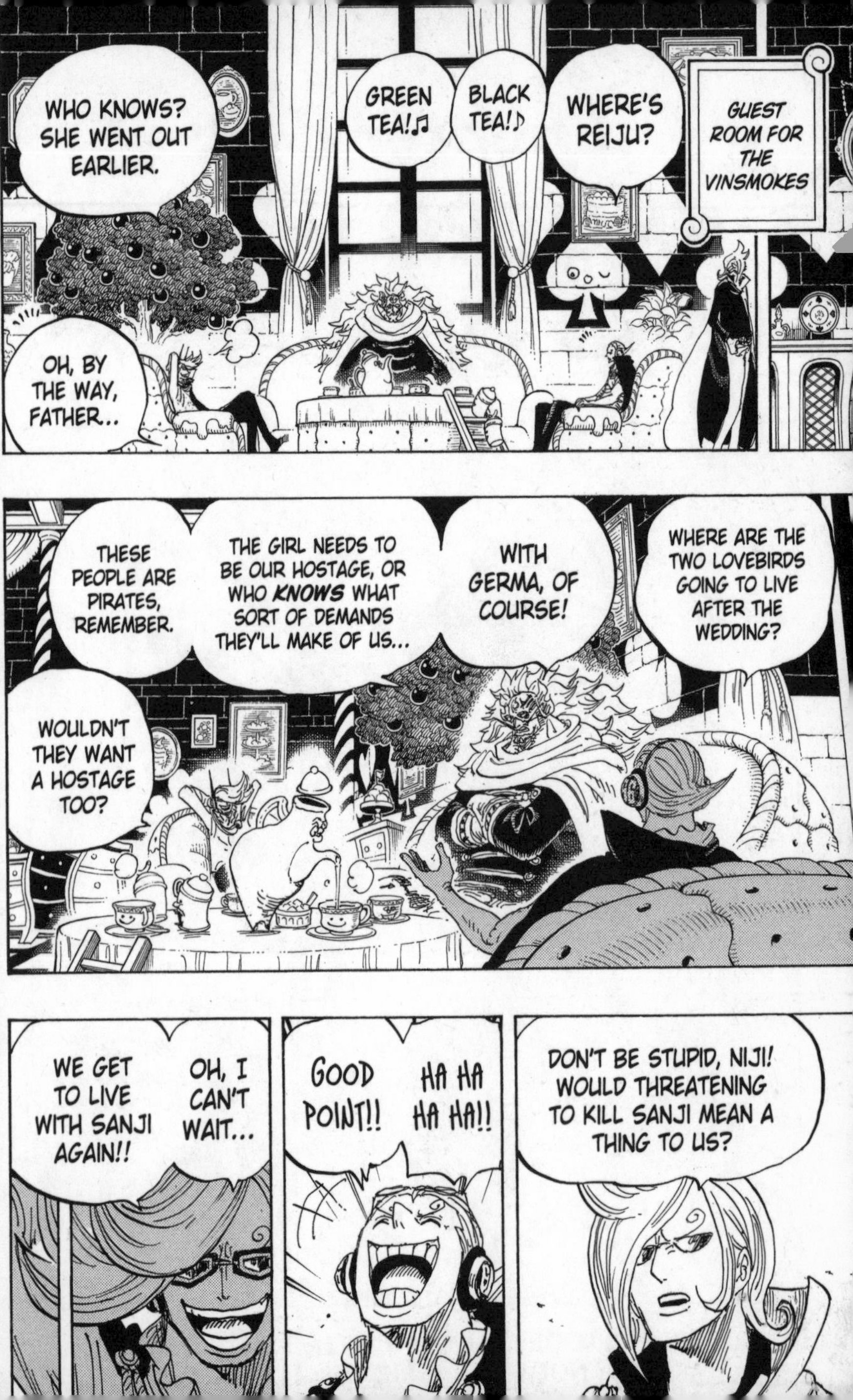
GUEST ROOM FOR THE VINSMOKES
WHERE'S REIJU?
BLACK TEA!♪
GREEN TEA!♫
WHO KNOWS? SHE WENT OUT EARLIER.
OH, BY THE WAY, FATHER...
WHERE ARE THE TWO LOVEBIRDS GOING TO LIVE AFTER THE WEDDING?
WITH GERMA, OF COURSE!
THE GIRL NEEDS TO BE OUR HOSTAGE, OR WHO ***KNOWS*** WHAT SORT OF DEMANDS THEY'LL MAKE OF US...
THESE PEOPLE ARE PIRATES, REMEMBER.
WOULDN'T THEY WANT A HOSTAGE TOO?
DON'T BE STUPID, NIJI! WOULD THREATENING TO KILL SANJI MEAN A THING TO US?
HA HA HA HA!!
GOOD POINT!!
OH, I CAN'T WAIT...
WE GET TO LIVE WITH SANJI AGAIN!!

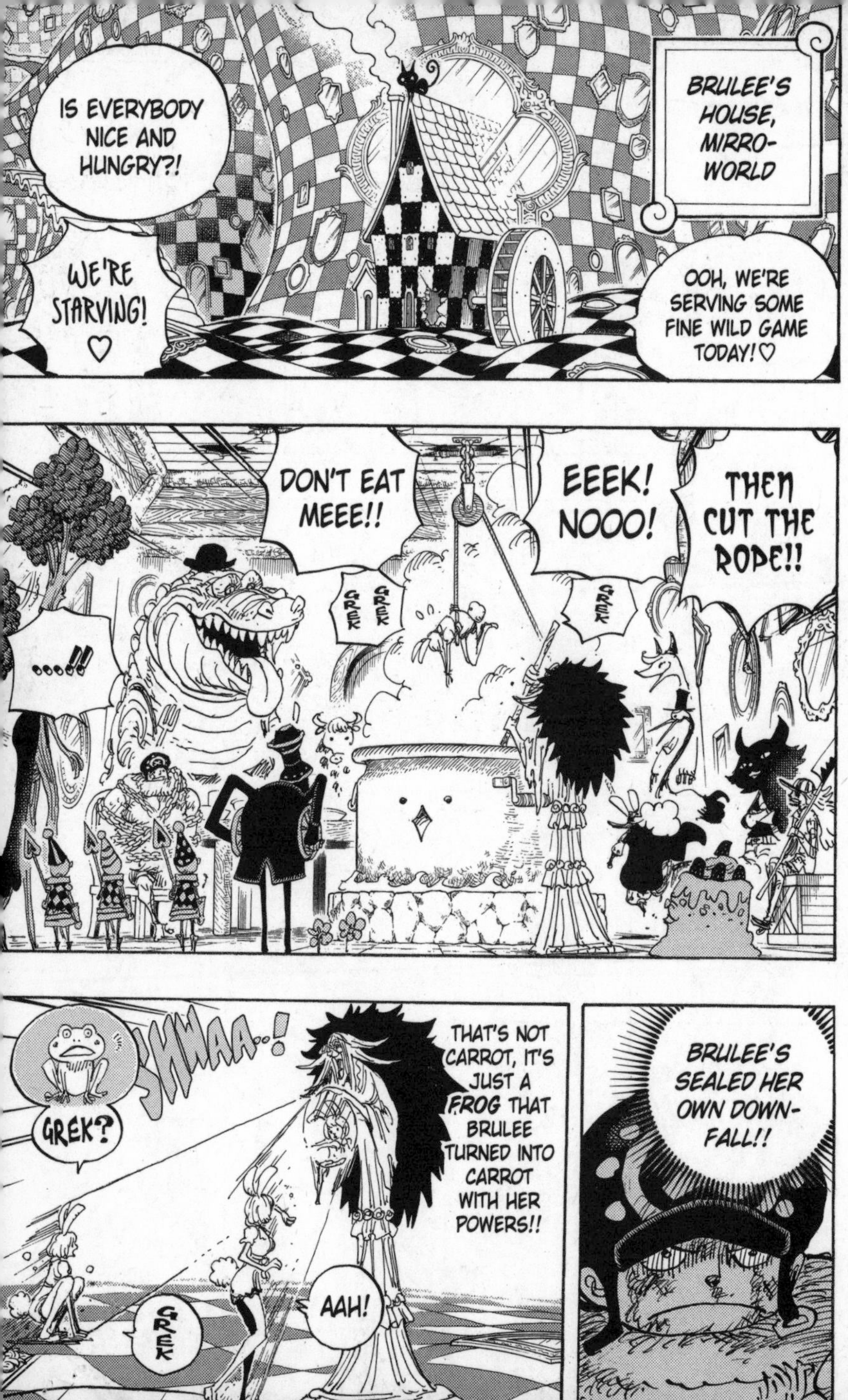
BRULEE'S HOUSE, MIRRO-WORLD
IS EVERYBODY NICE AND HUNGRY?!
WE'RE STARVING! ♡
OOH, WE'RE SERVING SOME FINE WILD GAME TODAY! ♡
THEN CUT THE ROPE!!
EEEK! NOOO!
GREK
DON'T EAT MEEE!!
GREK GREK
...!!
BRULEE'S SEALED HER OWN DOWN-FALL!!
THAT'S NOT CARROT, IT'S JUST A FROG THAT BRULEE TURNED INTO CARROT WITH HER POWERS!!
SHWAA..!
GREK?
AAH!
GREK

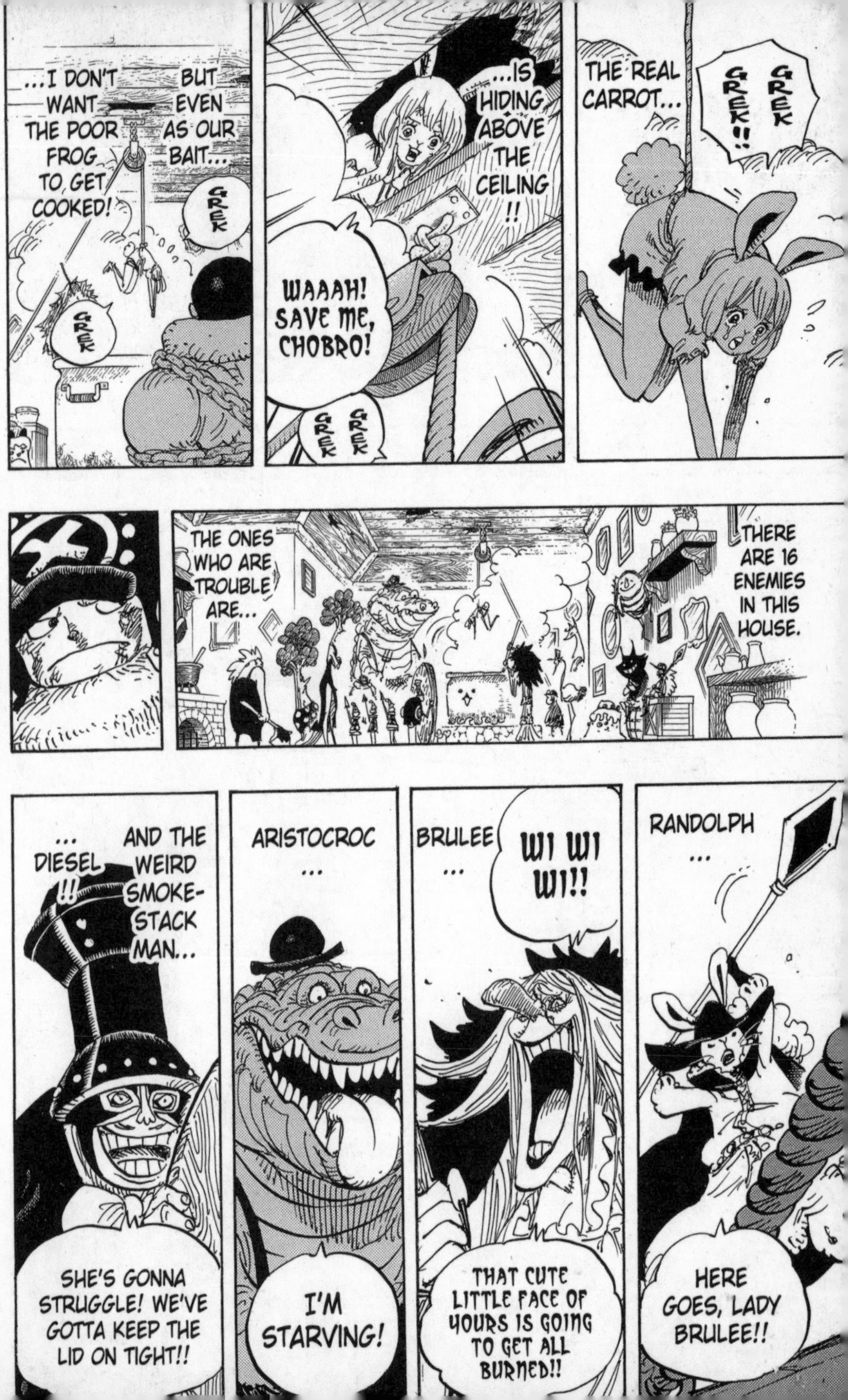
GREK GREK!!
THE REAL CARROT...
...IS HIDING ABOVE THE CEILING!!
WAAAH! SAVE ME, CHOBRO!
GREK GREK
BUT EVEN AS OUR BAIT...
...I DON'T WANT THE POOR FROG TO GET COOKED!
GREK
GREK
THERE ARE 16 ENEMIES IN THIS HOUSE.
THE ONES WHO ARE TROUBLE ARE...
RANDOLPH ...
HERE GOES, LADY BRULEE!!
BRULEE ...
WI WI WI!!
THAT CUTE LITTLE FACE OF YOURS IS GOING TO GET ALL BURNED!!
ARISTOCROC ...
I'M STARVING!
AND THE WEIRD SMOKE-STACK MAN...
... DIESEL!!
SHE'S GONNA STRUGGLE! WE'VE GOTTA KEEP THE LID ON TIGHT!!

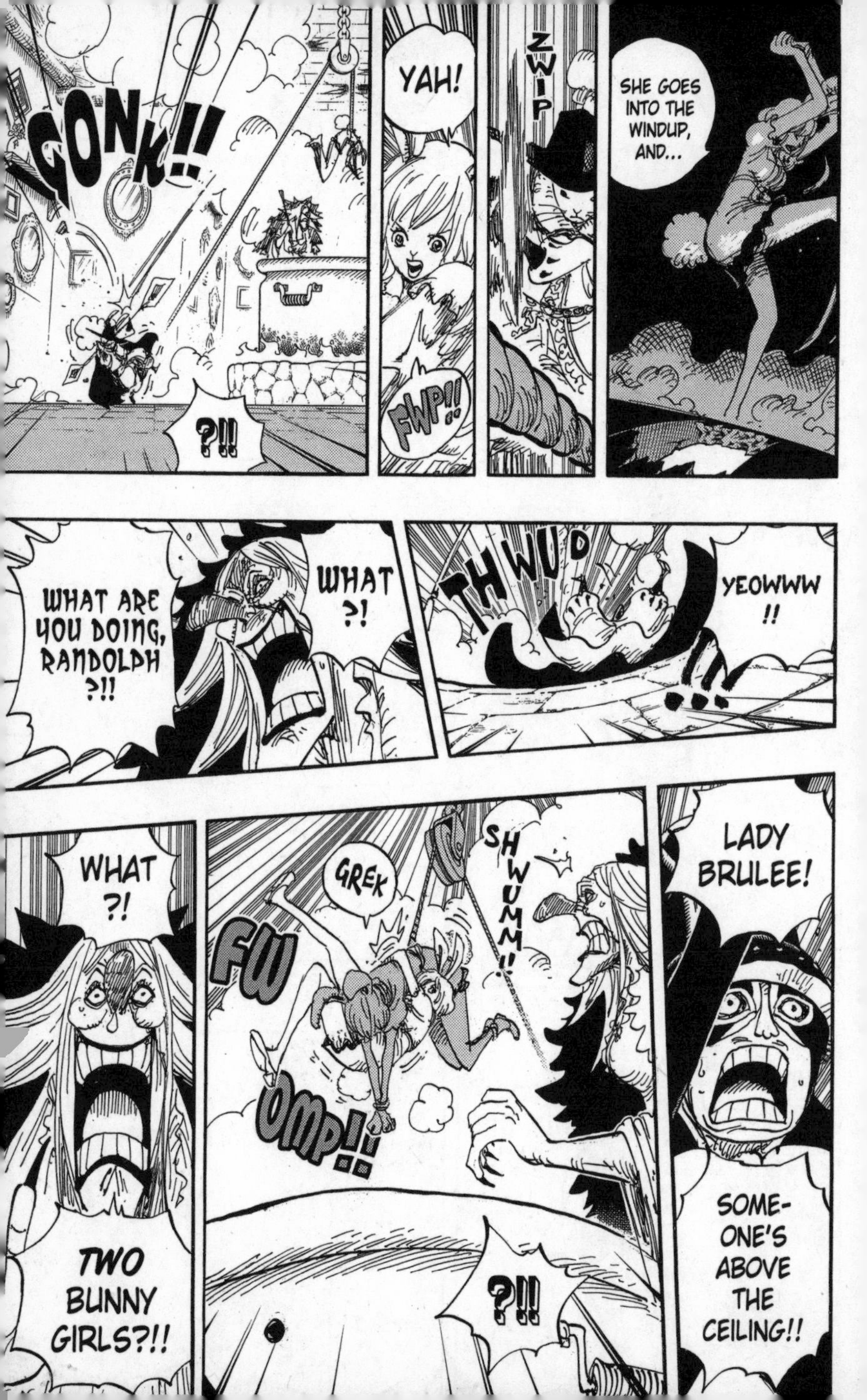
SHE GOES INTO THE WINDUP, AND...
ZWIP
YAH!
FWP!!
GONK!!
?!!
YEOWWW!!
THWUD
WHAT?!
WHAT ARE YOU DOING, RANDOLPH?!!
LADY BRULEE!
SOME-ONE'S ABOVE THE CEILING!!
SHWUMM!!
GREK
FW
OMP!!
?!!
WHAT?!
TWO BUNNY GIRLS?!!

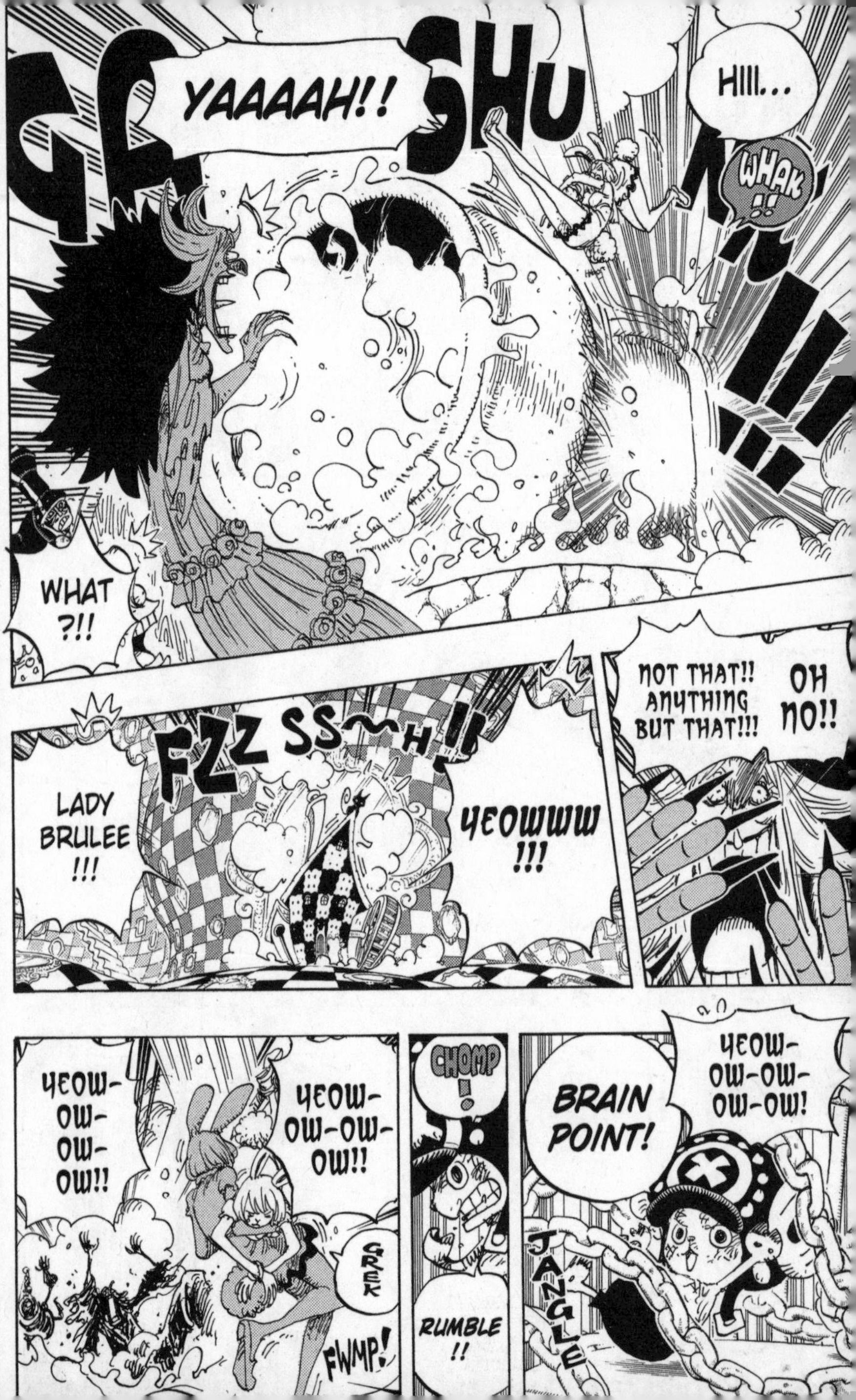
HIII...
WHAK!!
SHU
YAAAAH!!
WHAT?!!
OH NO!!
NOT THAT!! ANYTHING BUT THAT!!!
FZZ SS~H!!
YEOWWW!!!
LADY BRULEE!!!
YEOW-OW-OW-OW-OW!
BRAIN POINT!
JANGLE
CHOMP!
RUMBLE!!
YEOW-OW-OW-OW!!
GREK
FWMP!
YEOW-OW-OW-OW!!

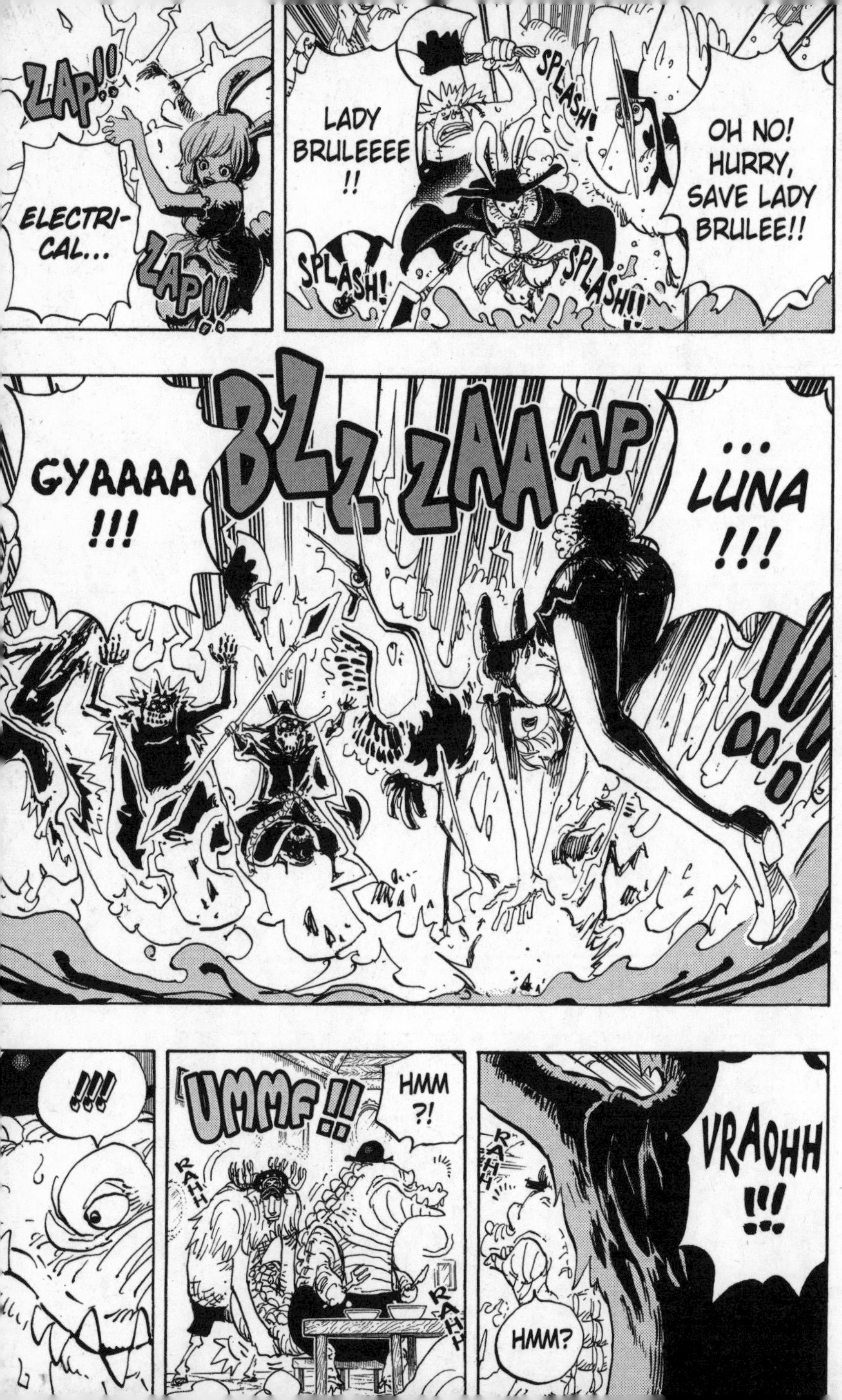
SPLASH!
OH NO! HURRY, SAVE LADY BRULEE!!
LADY BRULEEEE!!
SPLASH!!
SPLASH!
ZAP!!
ELECTRI-CAL...
ZAP!!
...LUNA!!!
BZZZAAAP
GYAAAA!!!
VRAOHH!!!
RAHH
HMM?
HMM?!
UMMF!!
RAHH
RAHH
!!!

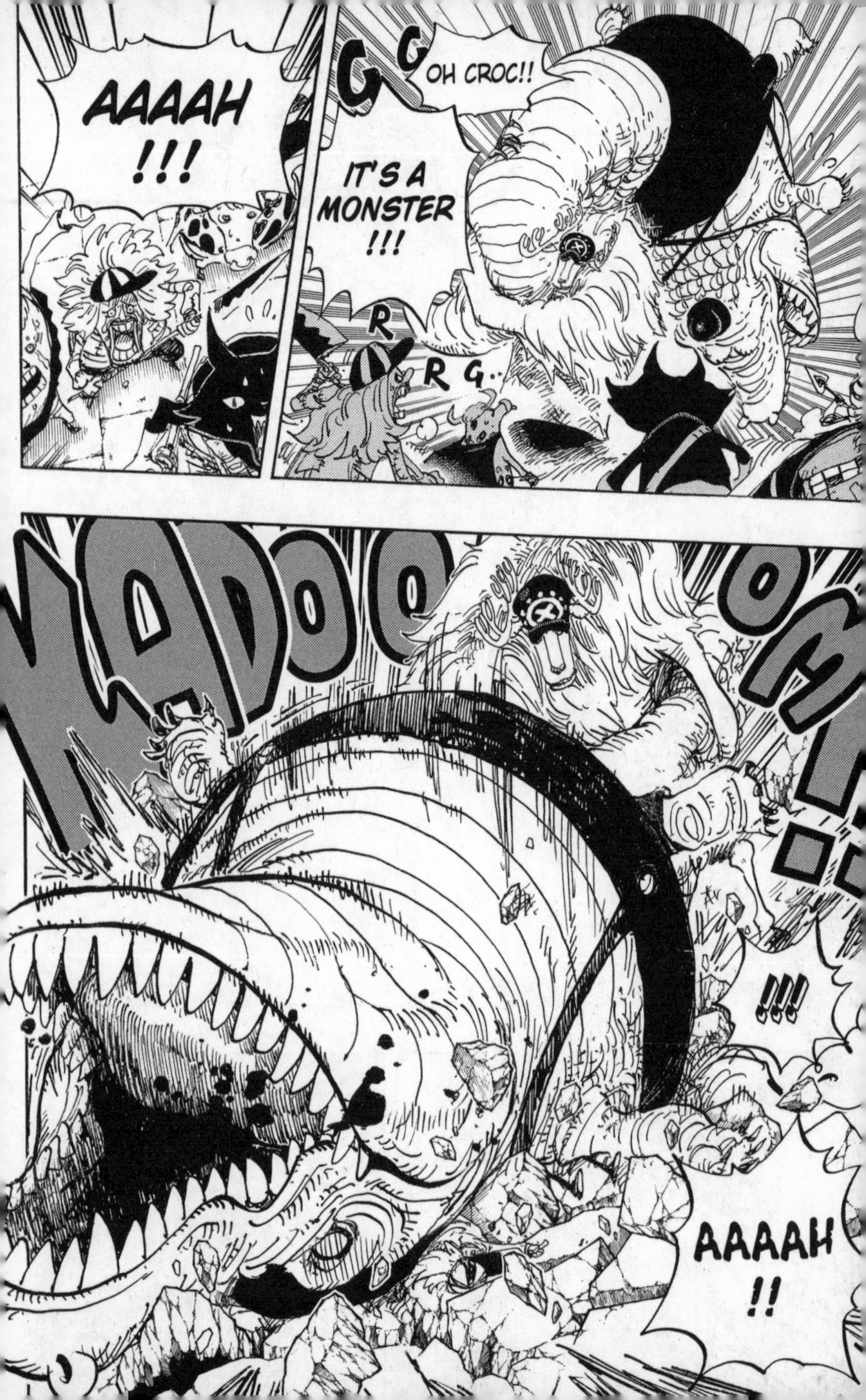
OH CROC!!
GG
IT'S A MONSTER!!!
R R G..
AAAAH!!!
!!!
AAAAH!!

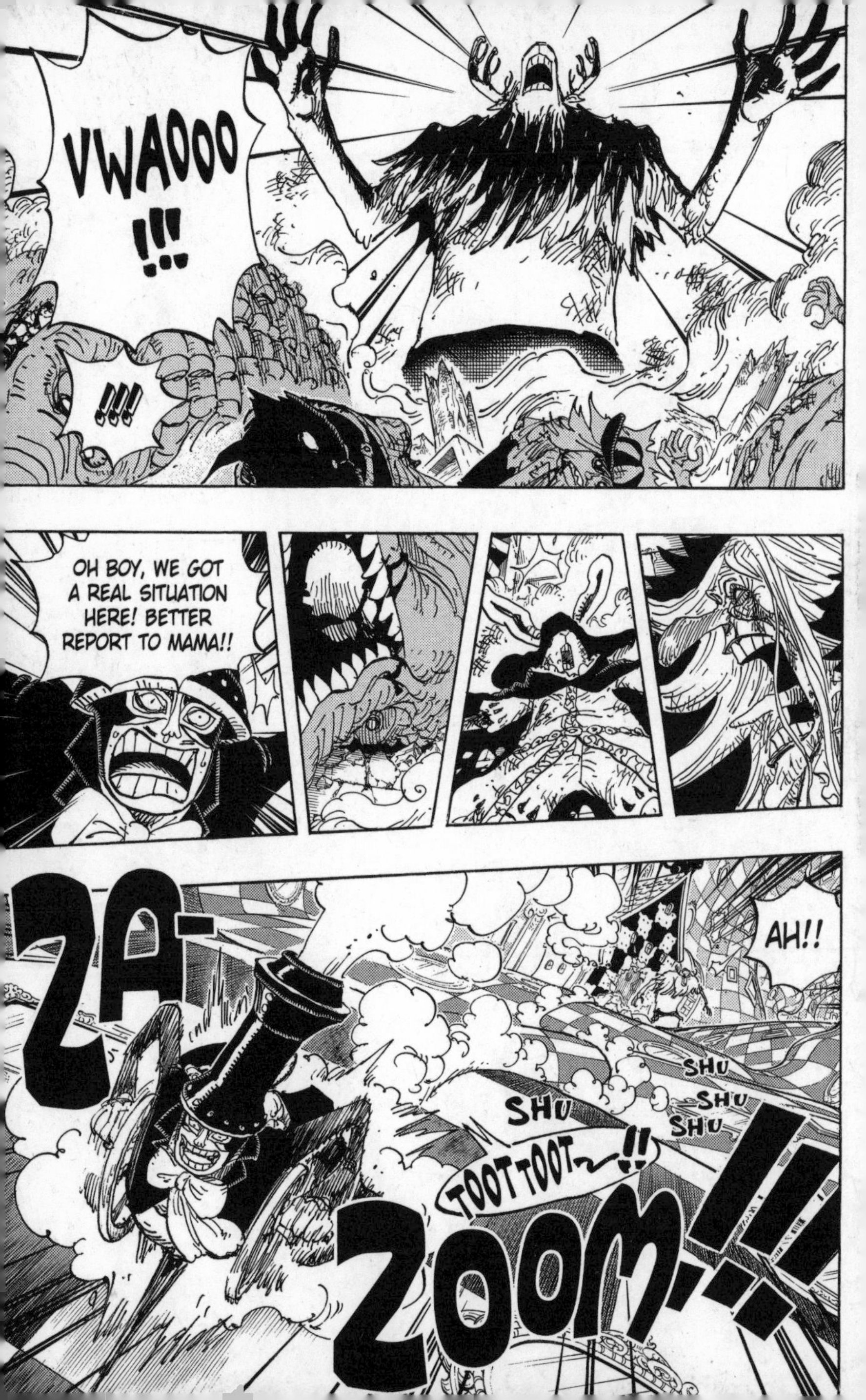
VWAOOO !!!
!!!
OH BOY, WE GOT A REAL SITUATION HERE! BETTER REPORT TO MAMA!!
AH!!
ZA-
SHU
SHU
SHU
SHU
TOOT TOOT~!!
ZOOM!!!

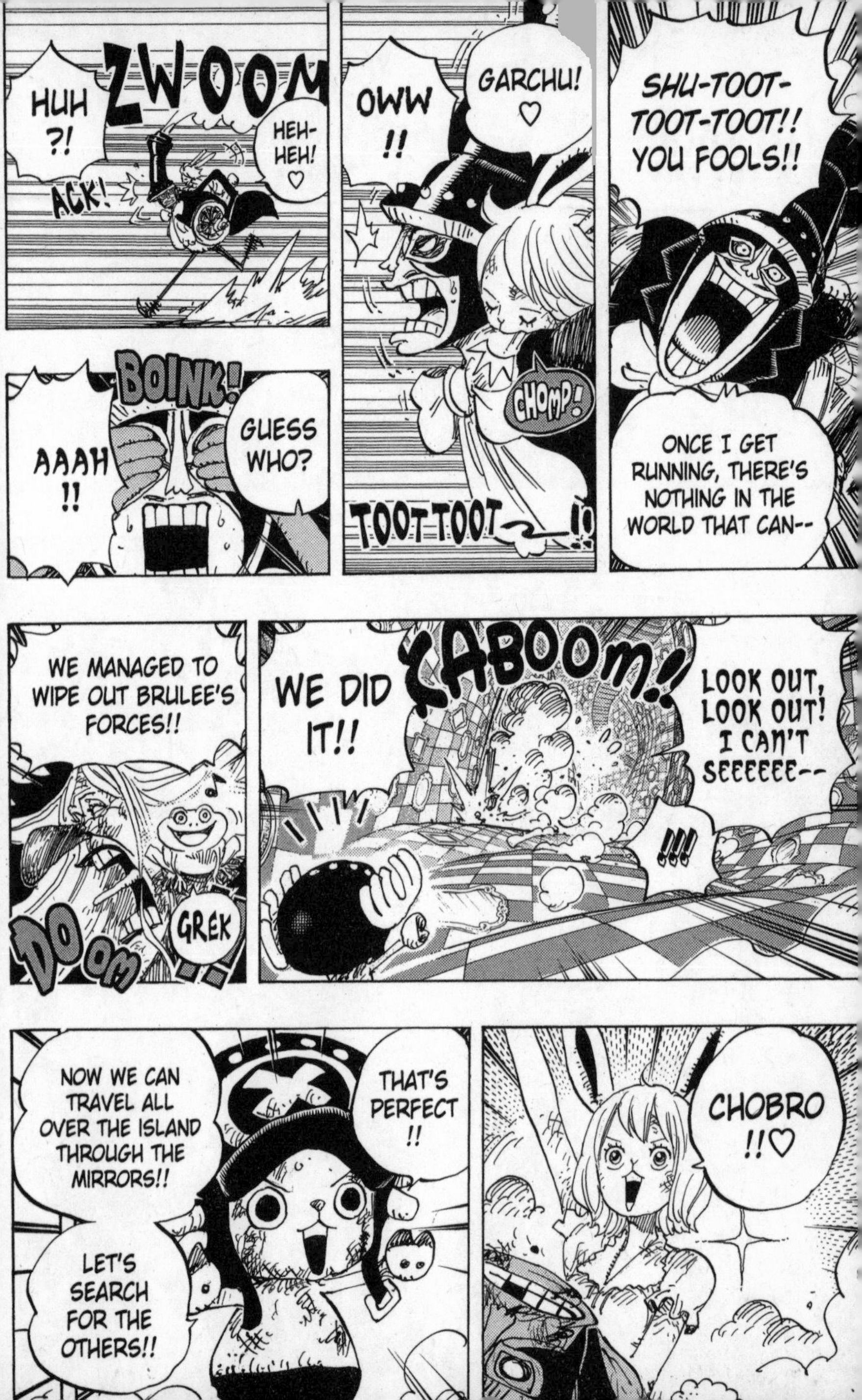
SHU-TOOT-TOOT-TOOT!! YOU FOOLS!!
ONCE I GET RUNNING, THERE'S NOTHING IN THE WORLD THAT CAN--
GARCHU! ♡
OWW!!
CHOMP!
TOOT TOOT
HEH-HEH! ♡
ZWOOM
HUH?!
ACK!
BOINK!
GUESS WHO?
AAAH!!
LOOK OUT, LOOK OUT! I CAN'T SEEEEEE--
KABOOM!!
WE DID IT!!
!!!
WE MANAGED TO WIPE OUT BRULEE'S FORCES!!
GREK
DOOM!!
CHOBRO!!♡
THAT'S PERFECT!!
NOW WE CAN TRAVEL ALL OVER THE ISLAND THROUGH THE MIRRORS!!
LET'S SEARCH FOR THE OTHERS!!

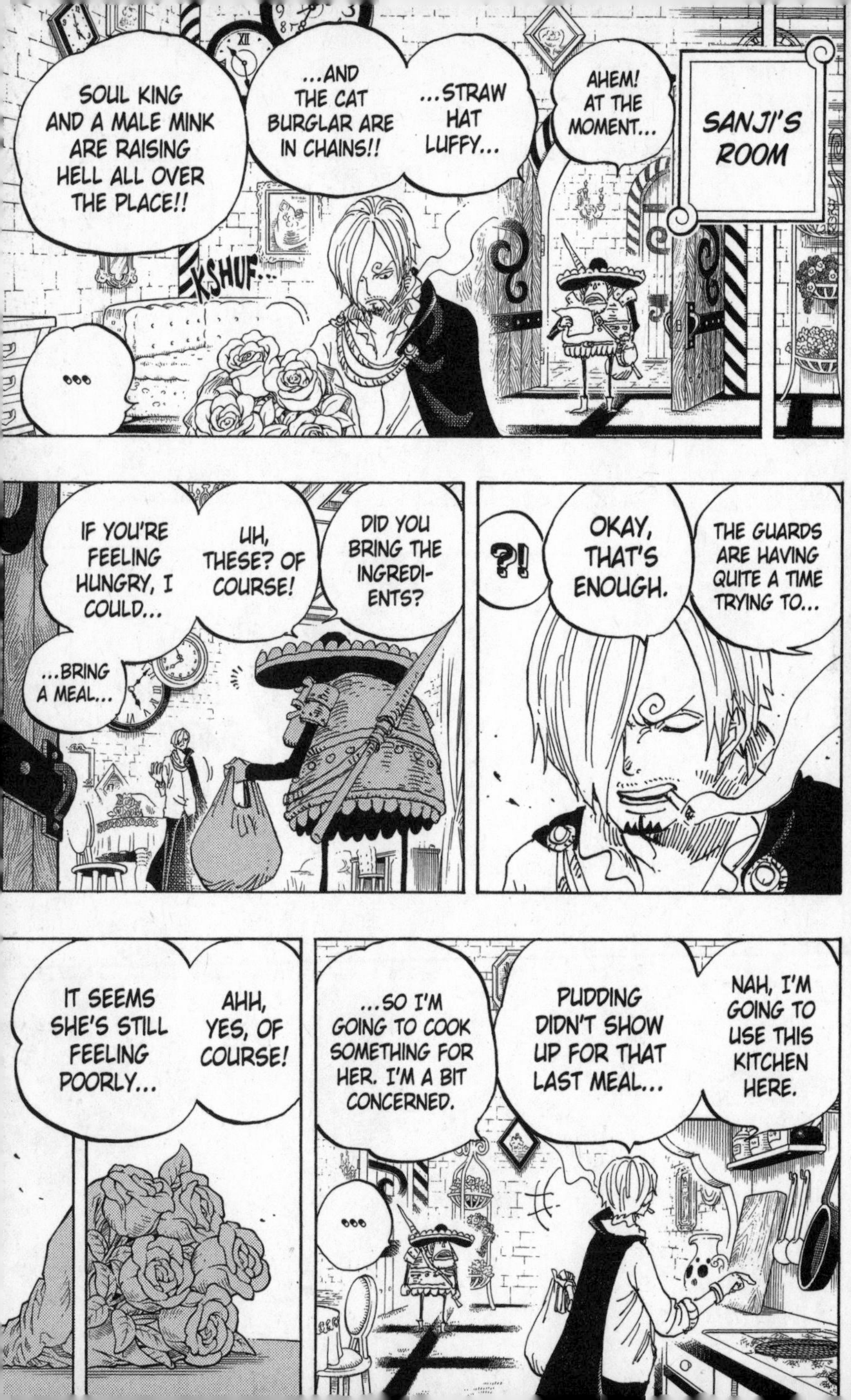
SANJI'S ROOM
AHEM! AT THE MOMENT...
...STRAW HAT LUFFY...
...AND THE CAT BURGLAR ARE IN CHAINS!!
SOUL KING AND A MALE MINK ARE RAISING HELL ALL OVER THE PLACE!!
KSHUF...
...
THE GUARDS ARE HAVING QUITE A TIME TRYING TO...
OKAY, THAT'S ENOUGH.
?!
DID YOU BRING THE INGREDI- ENTS?
UH, THESE? OF COURSE!
IF YOU'RE FEELING HUNGRY, I COULD...
...BRING A MEAL...
NAH, I'M GOING TO USE THIS KITCHEN HERE.
PUDDING DIDN'T SHOW UP FOR THAT LAST MEAL...
...SO I'M GOING TO COOK SOMETHING FOR HER. I'M A BIT CONCERNED.
...
AHH, YES, OF COURSE!
IT SEEMS SHE'S STILL FEELING POORLY...

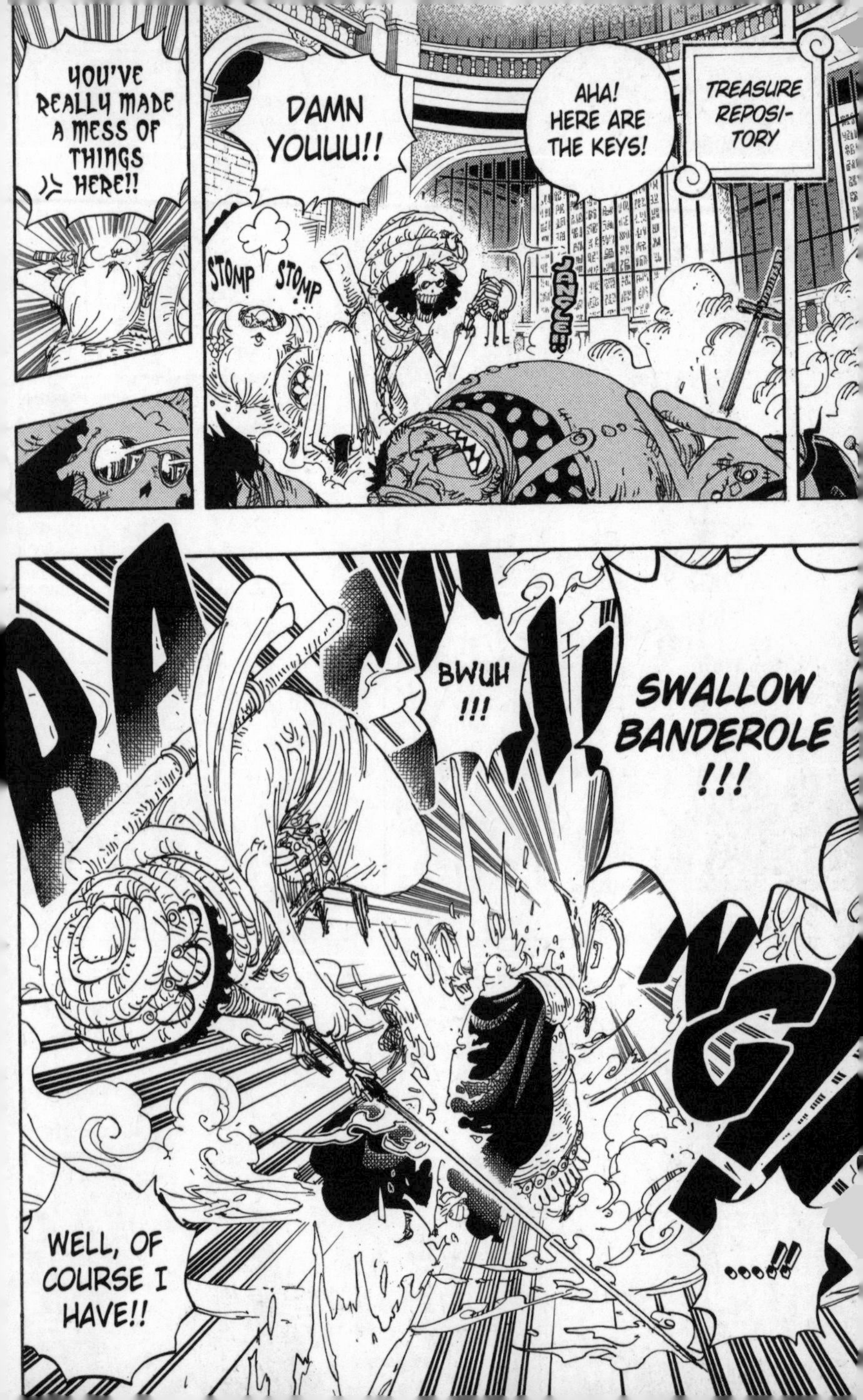
TREASURE REPOSI-TORY
AHA! HERE ARE THE KEYS!
DAMN YOUUU!!
STOMP
STOMP
JANGLE!!
YOU'VE REALLY MADE A MESS OF THINGS HERE!!
SWALLOW BANDERORE!!!
BWUH!!!
...!!
WELL, OF COURSE I HAVE!!

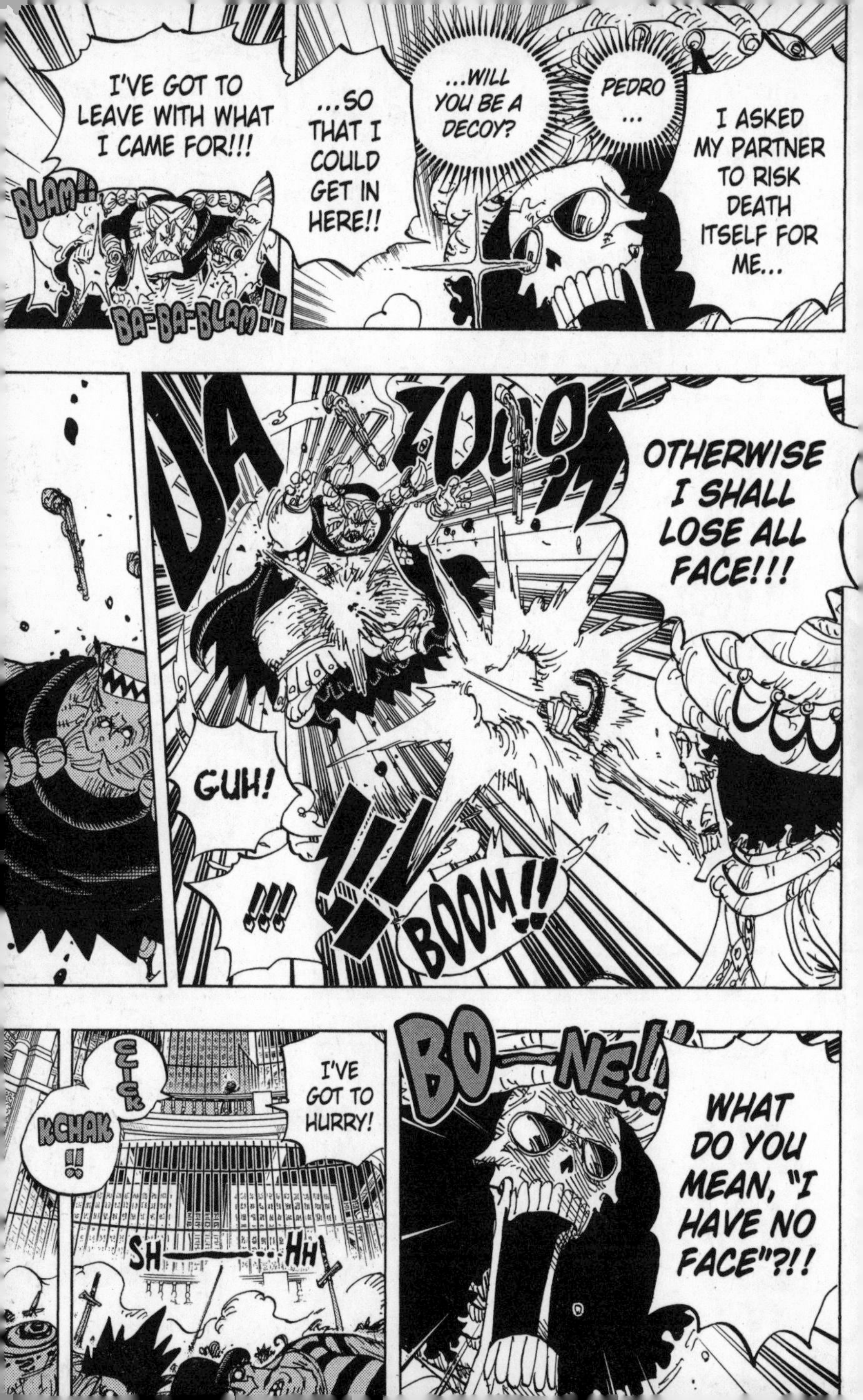

I ASKED MY PARTNER TO RISK DEATH ITSELF FOR ME...
PEDRO ...
...WILL YOU BE A DECOY?
...SO THAT I COULD GET IN HERE!!
I'VE GOT TO LEAVE WITH WHAT I CAME FOR!!!
BLAM!!
BA-BA-BLAM!!
OTHERWISE I SHALL LOSE ALL FACE!!!
DAZOOOM
GUH!
!!!
BOOM!!
BO—NE!!
WHAT DO YOU MEAN, "I HAVE NO FACE"?!!
I'VE GOT TO HURRY!
CLICK
KCHAK!!
SH——HH

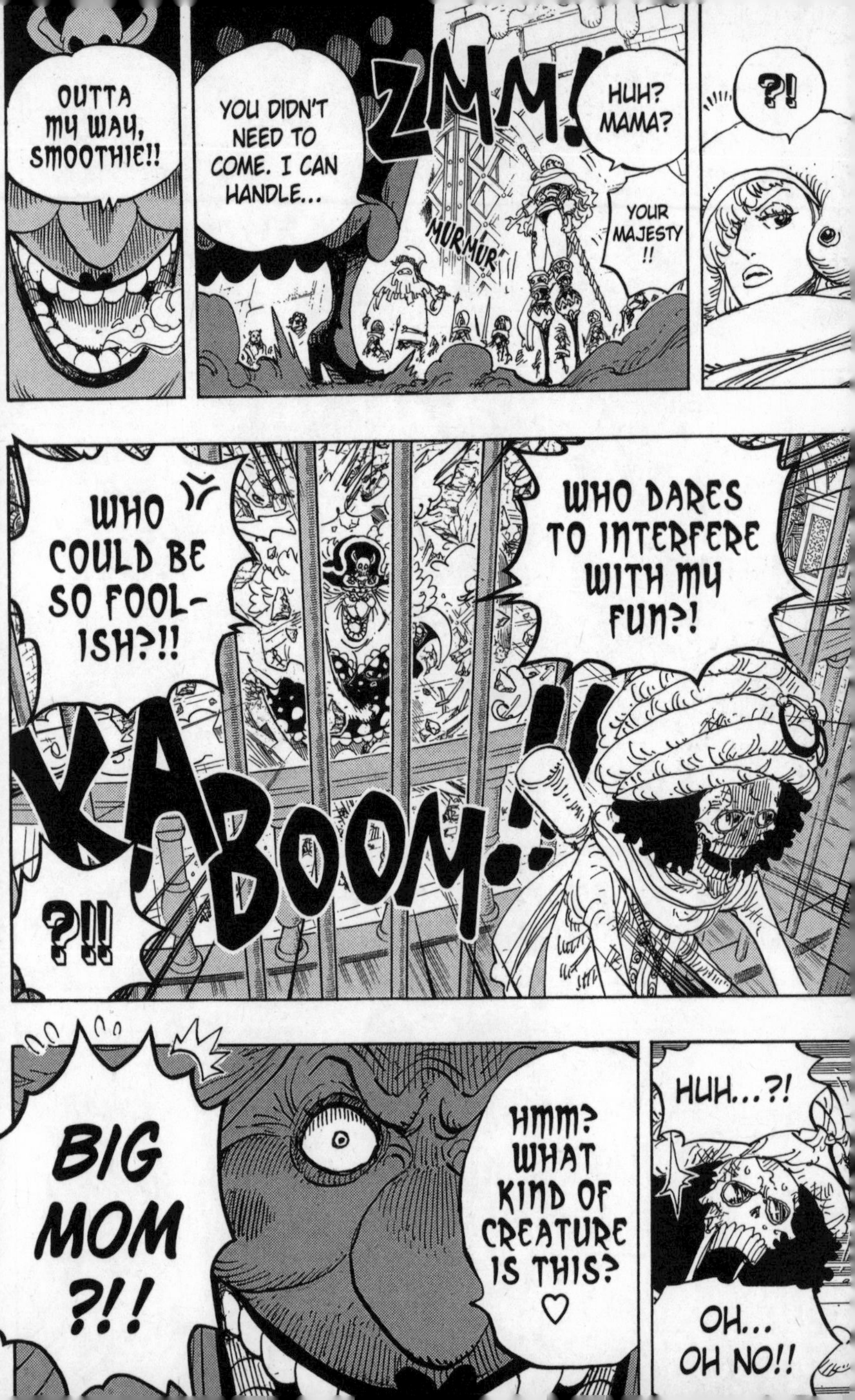
?!
HUH? MAMA?
ZMM!!
YOUR MAJESTY !!
YOU DIDN'T NEED TO COME. I CAN HANDLE...
MURMUR
OUTTA MY WAY, SMOOTHIE!!
WHO DARES TO INTERFERE WITH MY FUN?!
WHO COULD BE SO FOOL-ISH?!!
KABOOM!!
?!!
HUH...?!
OH... OH NO!!
HMM? WHAT KIND OF CREATURE IS THIS? ♡
BIG MOM ?!!

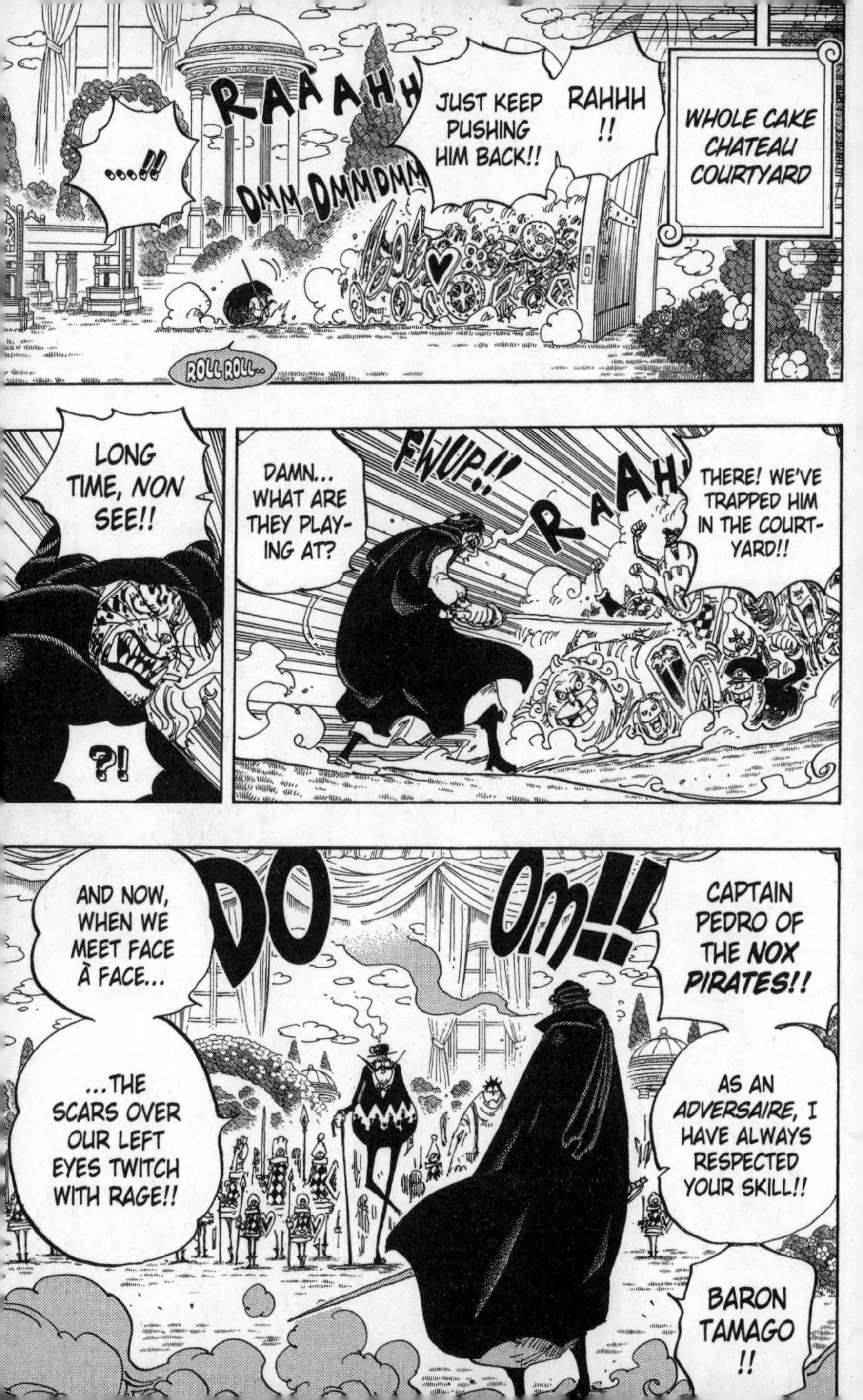
WHOLE CAKE CHATEAU COURTYARD
RAHHH !!
JUST KEEP PUSHING HIM BACK!!
RAAAHH
...!!
DMM DMMDMM
ROLL ROLL..
THERE! WE'VE TRAPPED HIM IN THE COURT-YARD!!
RAAH
FWUP!!
DAMN... WHAT ARE THEY PLAY-ING AT?
LONG TIME, NON SEE!!
?!
CAPTAIN PEDRO OF THE NOX PIRATES!!
DOOM!!
AND NOW, WHEN WE MEET FACE À FACE...
AS AN ADVERSAIRE, I HAVE ALWAYS RESPECTED YOUR SKILL!!
...THE SCARS OVER OUR LEFT EYES TWITCH WITH RAGE!!
BARON TAMAGO !!

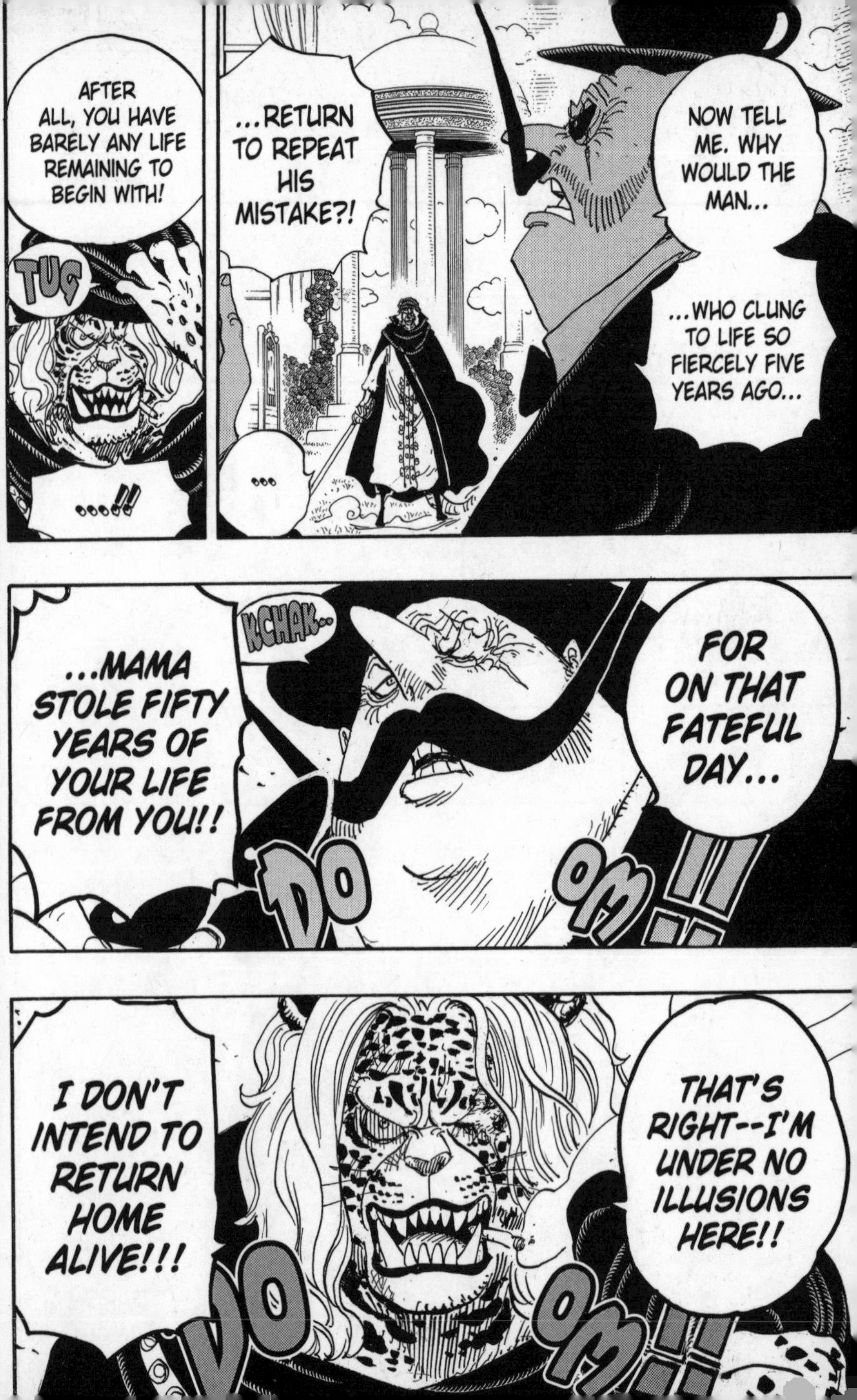
NOW TELL ME. WHY WOULD THE MAN...
...WHO CLUNG TO LIFE SO FIERCELY FIVE YEARS AGO...
...RETURN TO REPEAT HIS MISTAKE?!
...
AFTER ALL, YOU HAVE BARELY ANY LIFE REMAINING TO BEGIN WITH!
TUG
...!!
FOR ON THAT FATEFUL DAY...
KCHAK...
...MAMA STOLE FIFTY YEARS OF YOUR LIFE FROM YOU!!
DOOM!!
THAT'S RIGHT--I'M UNDER NO ILLUSIONS HERE!!
I DON'T INTEND TO RETURN HOME ALIVE!!!
VOOM!!

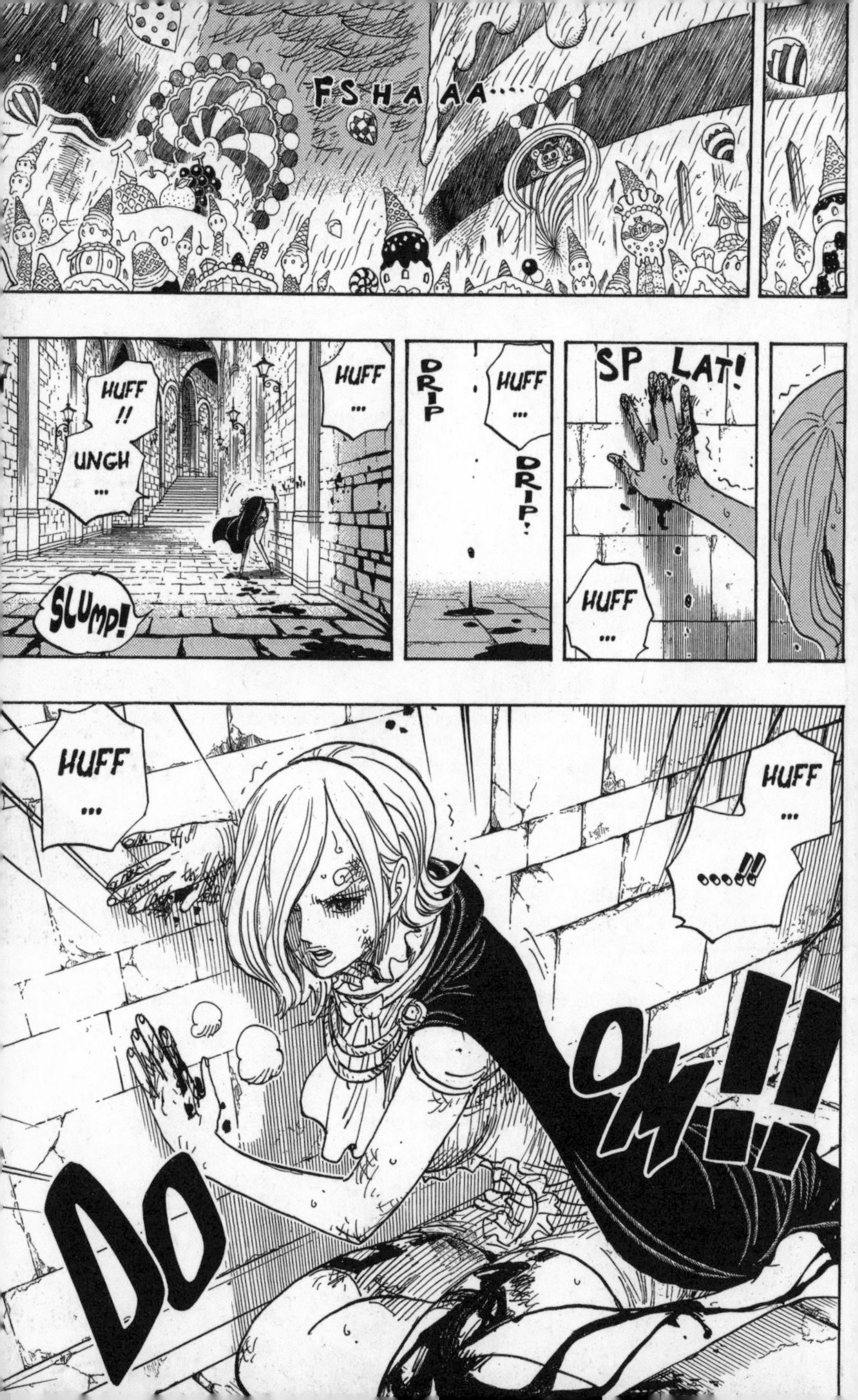
FSHAAA.....
SPLAT!
HUFF ...
HUFF ...
DRIP
DRIP
HUFF ...
HUFF !! UNGH ...
SLUMP!
HUFF ...
....!!
HUFF ...
DOOM...!!

SBS Question Corner

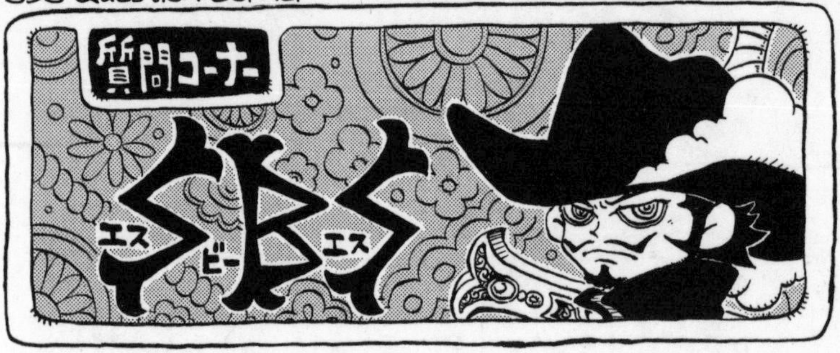
質問コーナー
SBS
エス ビー エス

(I ♡ OP, Ishikawa)

Q: Hi, Odacchi! I've been counting. Ever since that fateful day in volume 10 when Timmy Ueda first stole the SBS title call (which started in volume 4), readers have begun the SBS corner 60 times! (Doom!) I simply cannot believe that they would be shameless enough to steal your glory!! Go on, Oda Sensei. Scream those words as loud as you can today. Say the words, "The SBS has begun!!!"
And once again, the reader proudly proclaims, "Start the SBS!!!"
--Shokotan

A: The SBS has begun!!! I said it!! Thank you!!
Wait, noooo!!! This is not what I want!! (wailing)

Q: Would Heraclesun be really bad at *shiritori,* the word game where you have to start each word with the last letter of the previous word?
--Seikun

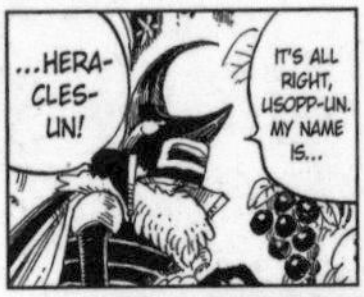
IT'S ALL RIGHT, USOPP-LIN. MY NAME IS...
...HERACLESLIN!

A: Well, since you lose by ending a word in "n," I'd say so.

Q: In chapter 840, "The Iron Mask," young Sanji was reading the storybook about Noland. But I'm more curious about that book of Devil Fruits sitting next to him! This must be the book he used to find out about the Clear-Clear Fruit in chapter 464!!
--Dorry

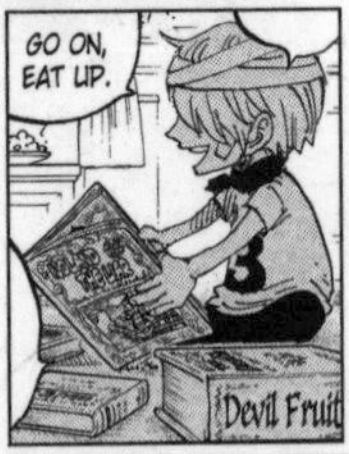
GO ON, EAT UP.
Devil Fruit

A: Well spotted. Sanji did indeed mention both books before in his travels.

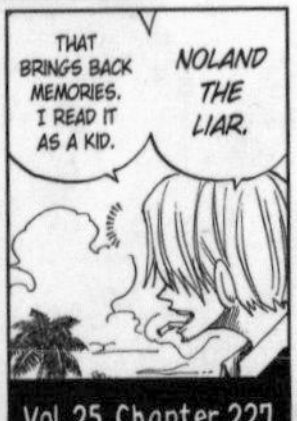
NOLAND THE LIAR.
THAT BRINGS BACK MEMORIES. I READ IT AS A KID.

Vol. 25, Chapter 227

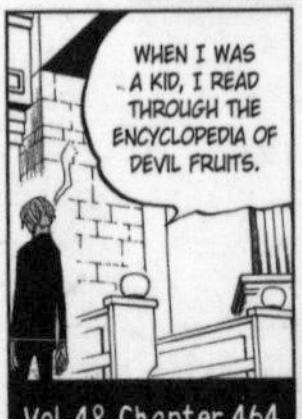
WHEN I WAS A KID, I READ THROUGH THE ENCYCLOPEDIA OF DEVIL FRUITS.

Vol. 48, Chapter 464

Chapter 850:
A RAY OF LIGHT

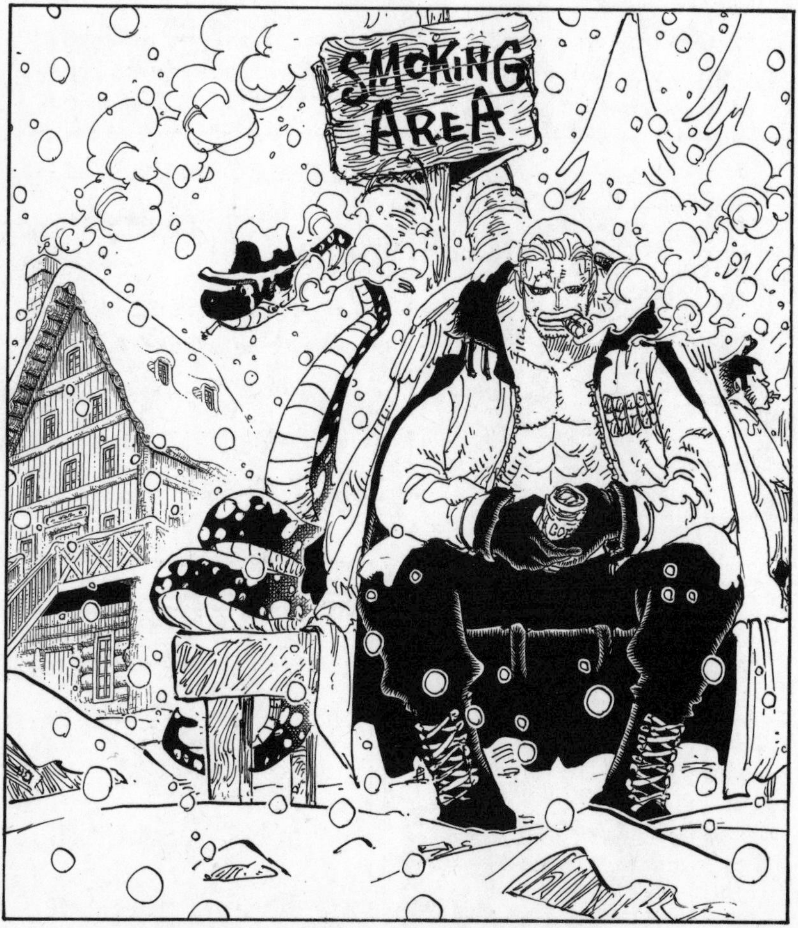
SMOKING AREA

REQUEST: "HEAVY-SMOKING SNAKE AND SMOKER SITTING IN THE SMOKING AREA" BY MICHI NAKAHARA FROM TOTTORI

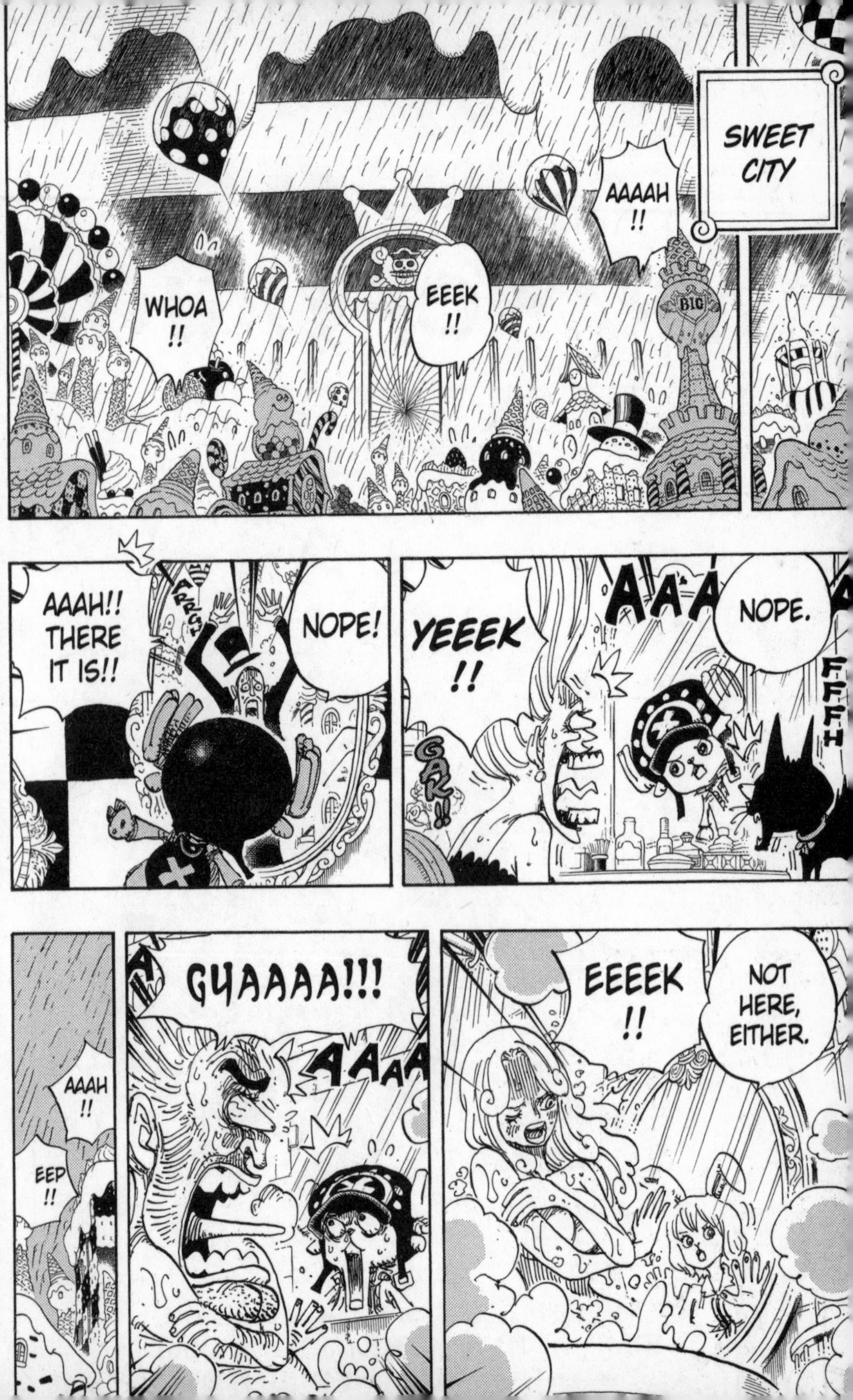
SWEET CITY
AAAAH!!
EEEK!!
WHOA!!
NOPE.
FFFH
AAA
YEEEK!!
GAK!!
NOPE!
AAAH!! THERE IT IS!!
NOT HERE, EITHER.
EEEEK!!
AAAA
GUAAAA!!!
AAAH!!
EEP!!

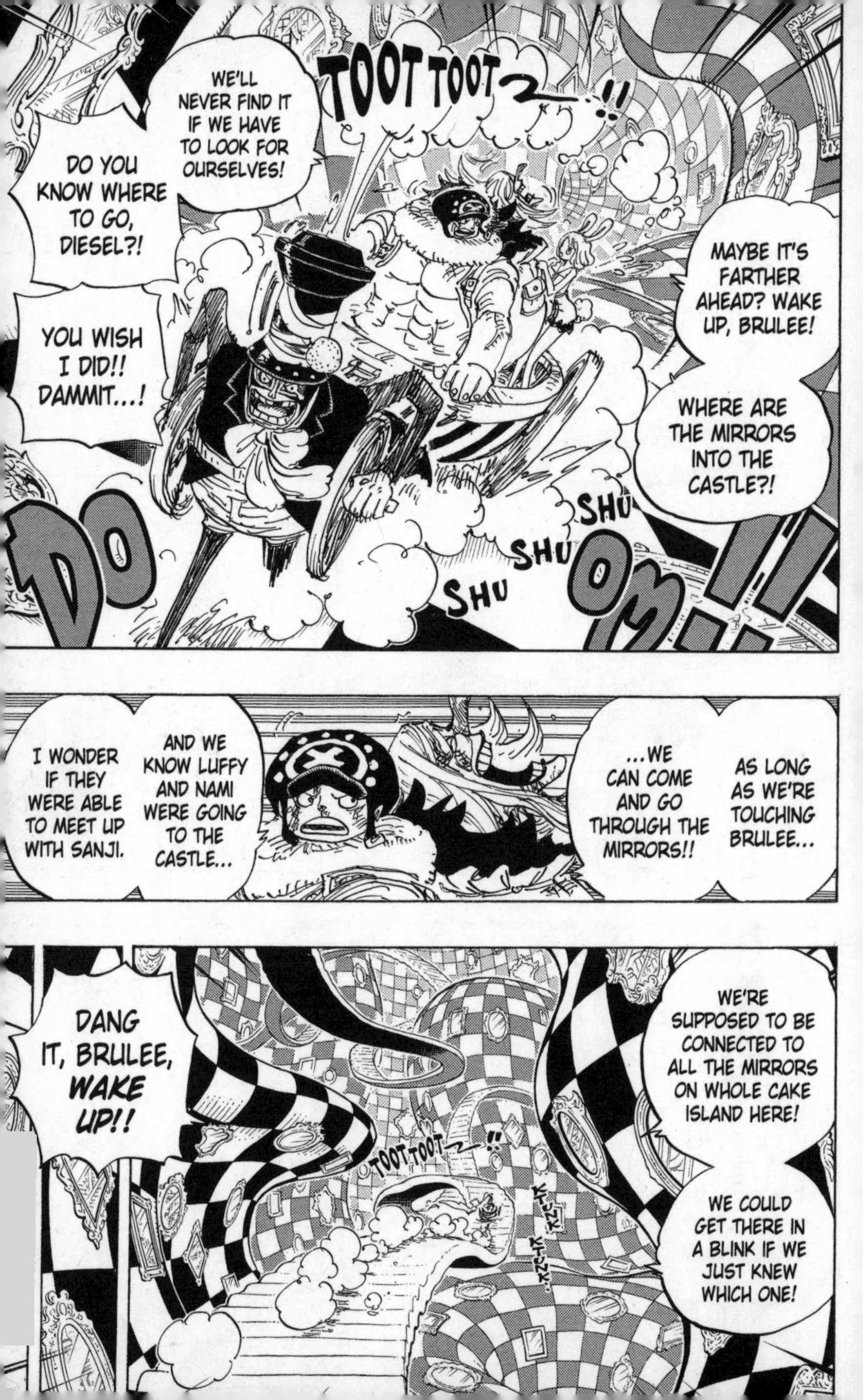
TOOT TOOT!!
MAYBE IT'S FARTHER AHEAD? WAKE UP, BRULEE!
WHERE ARE THE MIRRORS INTO THE CASTLE?!
WE'LL NEVER FIND IT IF WE HAVE TO LOOK FOR OURSELVES!
DO YOU KNOW WHERE TO GO, DIESEL?!
YOU WISH I DID!! DAMMIT...!
SHU
SHU
SHU
DOOM!!
AS LONG AS WE'RE TOUCHING BRULEE...
...WE CAN COME AND GO THROUGH THE MIRRORS!!
AND WE KNOW LUFFY AND NAMI WERE GOING TO THE CASTLE...
I WONDER IF THEY WERE ABLE TO MEET UP WITH SANJI.
WE'RE SUPPOSED TO BE CONNECTED TO ALL THE MIRRORS ON WHOLE CAKE ISLAND HERE!
WE COULD GET THERE IN A BLINK IF WE JUST KNEW WHICH ONE!
KTUNK
KTUNK
TOOT TOOT!!
DANG IT, BRULEE, *WAKE UP!!*

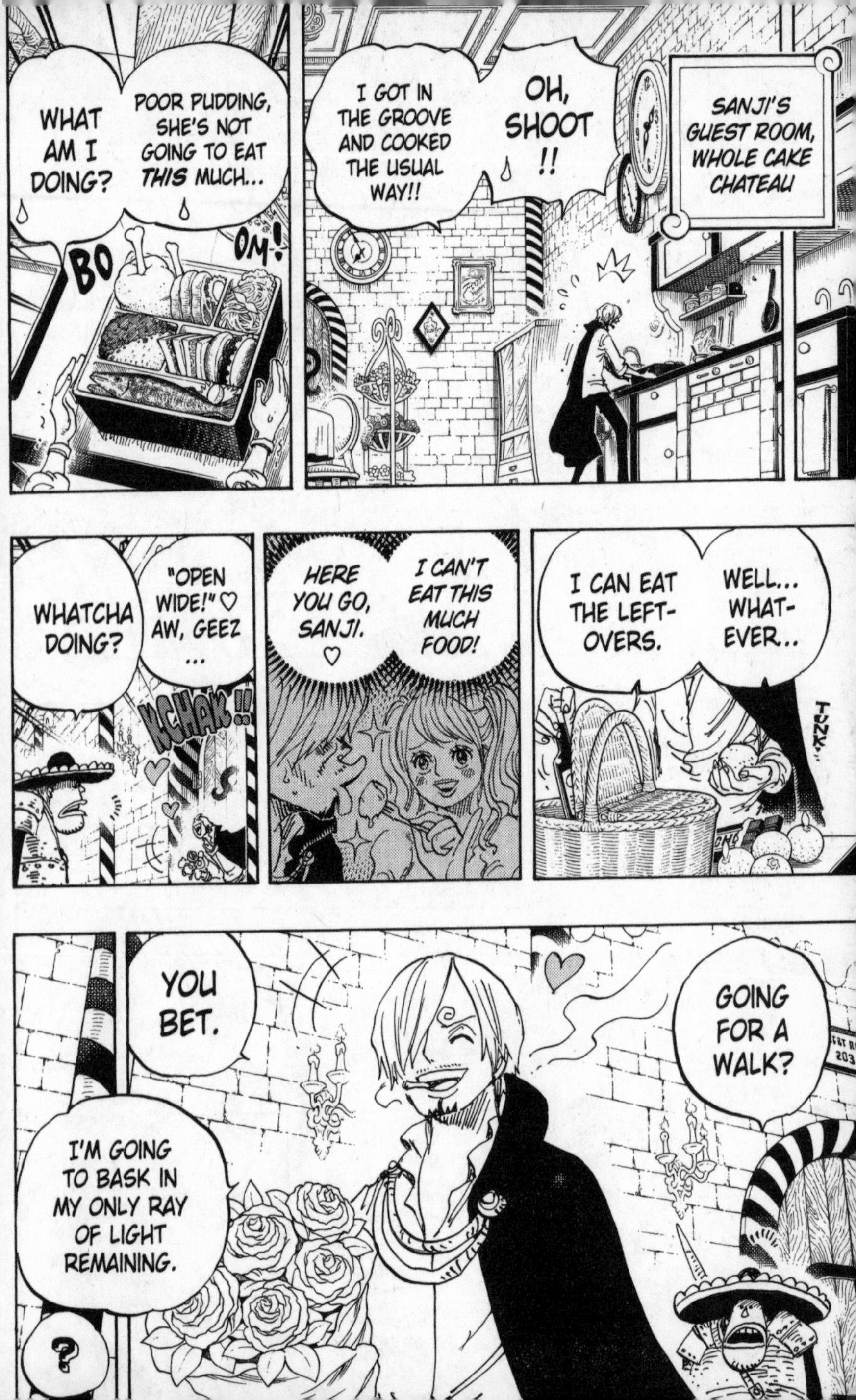
SANJI'S GUEST ROOM, WHOLE CAKE CHATEAU
OH, SHOOT !!
I GOT IN THE GROOVE AND COOKED THE USUAL WAY!!
POOR PUDDING, SHE'S NOT GOING TO EAT *THIS* MUCH...
WHAT AM I DOING?
BOOM!
WELL... WHAT-EVER...
I CAN EAT THE LEFT-OVERS.
TUNK
I CAN'T EAT THIS MUCH FOOD!
HERE YOU GO, SANJI. ♡
"OPEN WIDE!" ♡ AW, GEEZ ...
WHATCHA DOING?
KCHAK!!
GOING FOR A WALK?
YOU BET.
I'M GOING TO BASK IN MY ONLY RAY OF LIGHT REMAINING.
?

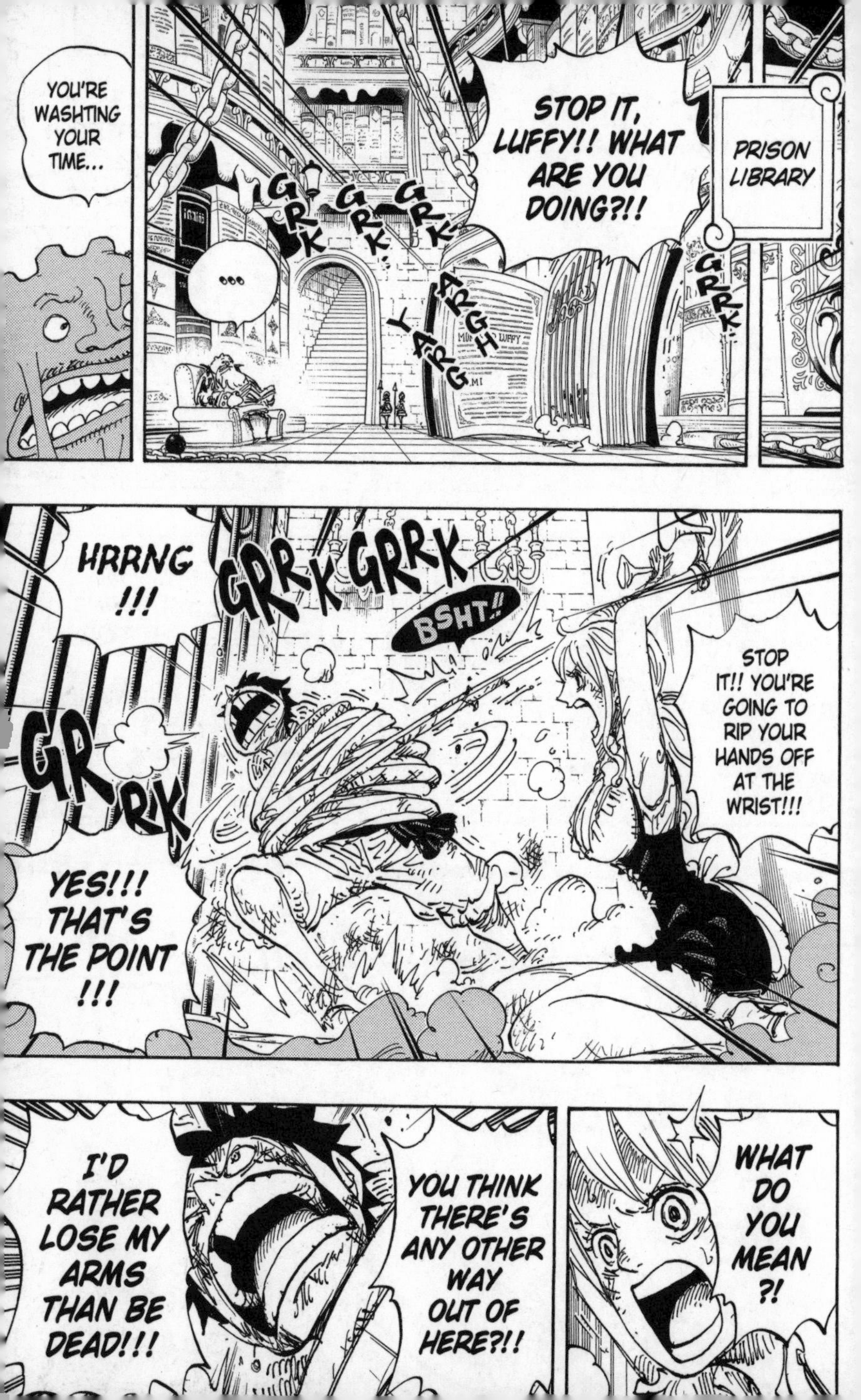
PRISON LIBRARY
STOP IT, LUFFY!! WHAT ARE YOU DOING?!!
GRRK
GRK GRK GRK
YARG ARGH
...
YOU'RE WASHTING YOUR TIME...
STOP IT!! YOU'RE GOING TO RIP YOUR HANDS OFF AT THE WRIST!!!
BSHT!!
GRRK GRRK
HRRNG!!!
GRRK
YES!!! THAT'S THE POINT!!!
WHAT DO YOU MEAN?!
YOU THINK THERE'S ANY OTHER WAY OUT OF HERE?!!
I'D RATHER LOSE MY ARMS THAN BE DEAD!!!

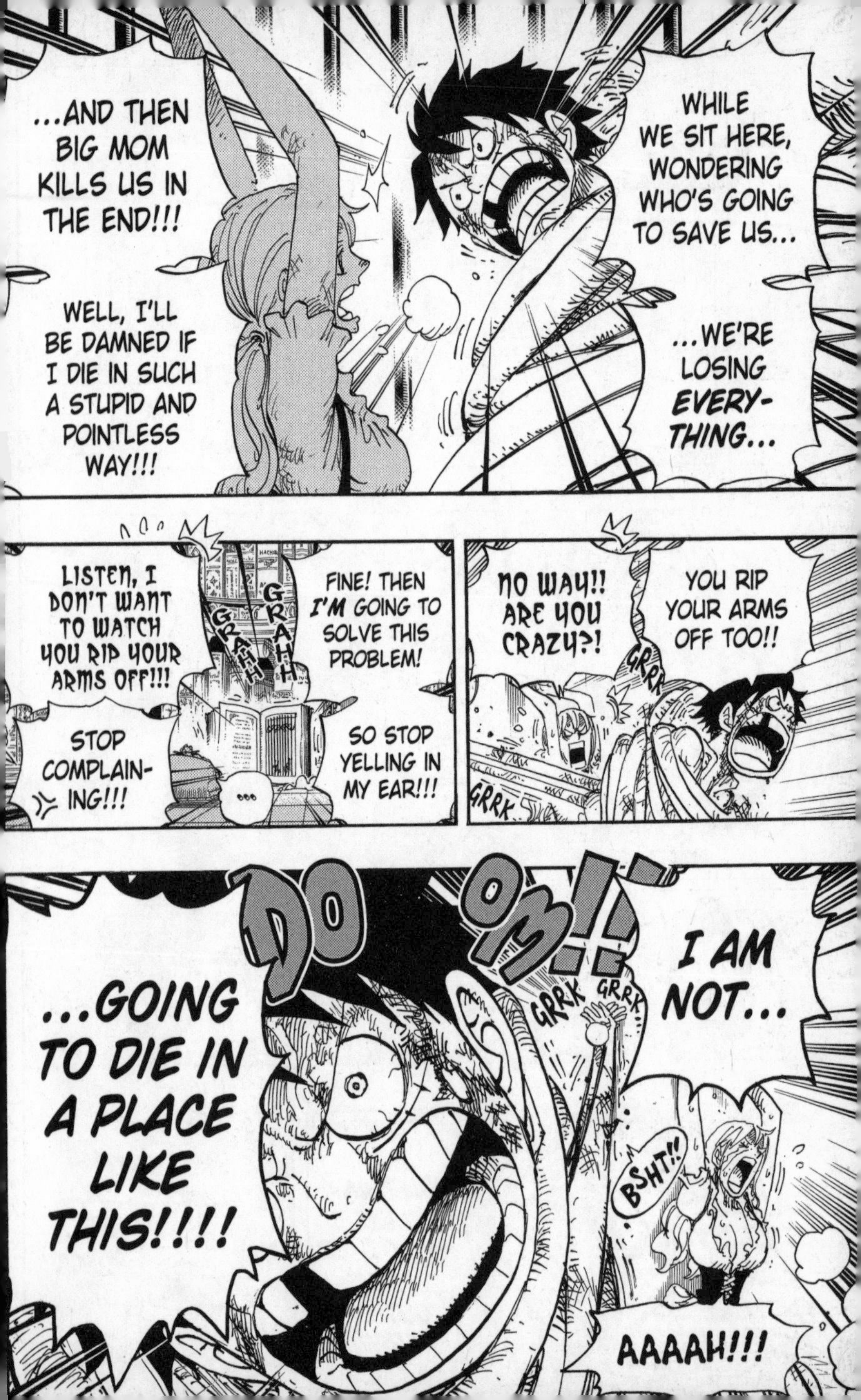
WHILE WE SIT HERE, WONDERING WHO'S GOING TO SAVE US...
...WE'RE LOSING EVERYTHING...
...AND THEN BIG MOM KILLS US IN THE END!!!
WELL, I'LL BE DAMNED IF I DIE IN SUCH A STUPID AND POINTLESS WAY!!!
YOU RIP YOUR ARMS OFF TOO!!
NO WAY!! ARE YOU CRAZY?!
GRRK
GRRK
FINE! THEN I'M GOING TO SOLVE THIS PROBLEM!
SO STOP YELLING IN MY EAR!!!
GRAHH
GRAHH
LISTEN, I DON'T WANT TO WATCH YOU RIP YOUR ARMS OFF!!!
STOP COMPLAINING!!!
...
DOOM!!
I AM NOT...
GRRK
GRRK
...GOING TO DIE IN A PLACE LIKE THIS!!!!
BSHT!!
AAAAH!!!

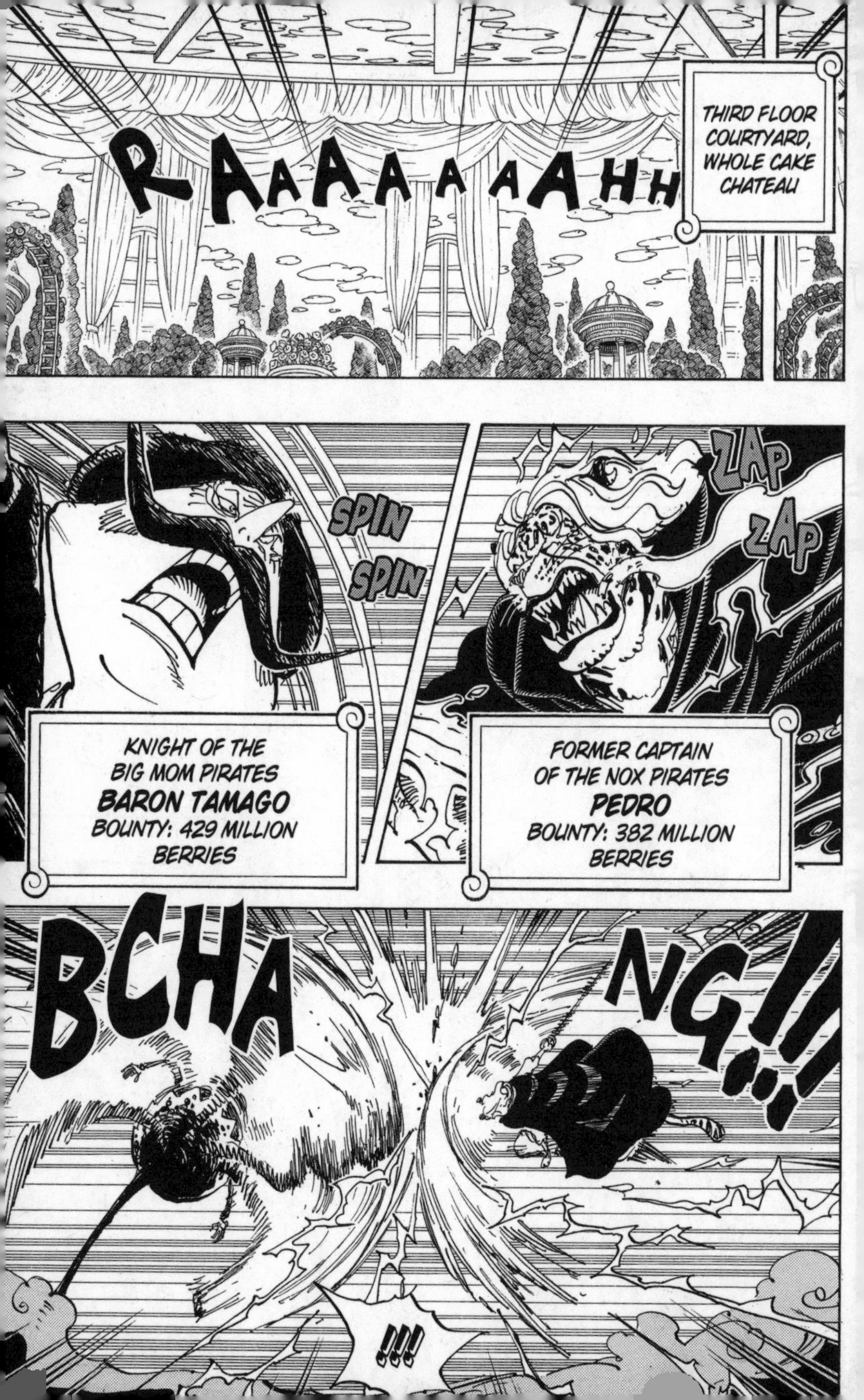
THIRD FLOOR COURTYARD, WHOLE CAKE CHATEAU
RAAAAAAAHH
ZAP
ZAP
FORMER CAPTAIN OF THE NOX PIRATES
PEDRO
BOUNTY: 382 MILLION BERRIES
SPIN
SPIN
KNIGHT OF THE BIG MOM PIRATES
BARON TAMAGO
BOUNTY: 429 MILLION BERRIES
BCHANG!!!
!!!

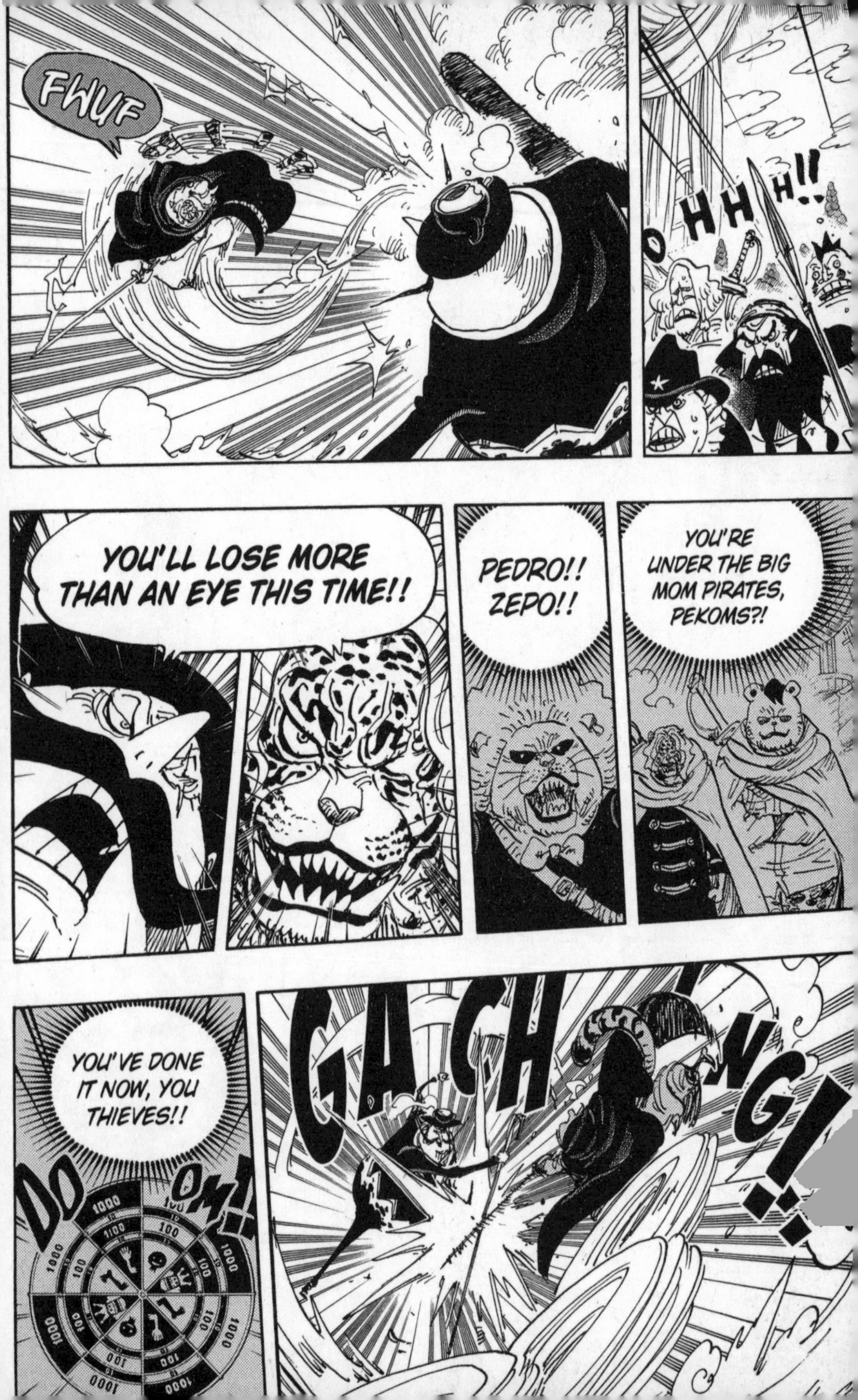
OHHHH!!
FWUF
YOU'RE UNDER THE BIG MOM PIRATES, PEKOMS?!
PEDRO!! ZEPO!!
YOU'LL LOSE MORE THAN AN EYE THIS TIME!!
GACH
NG!!
YOU'VE DONE IT NOW, YOU THIEVES!!
DOOM!!

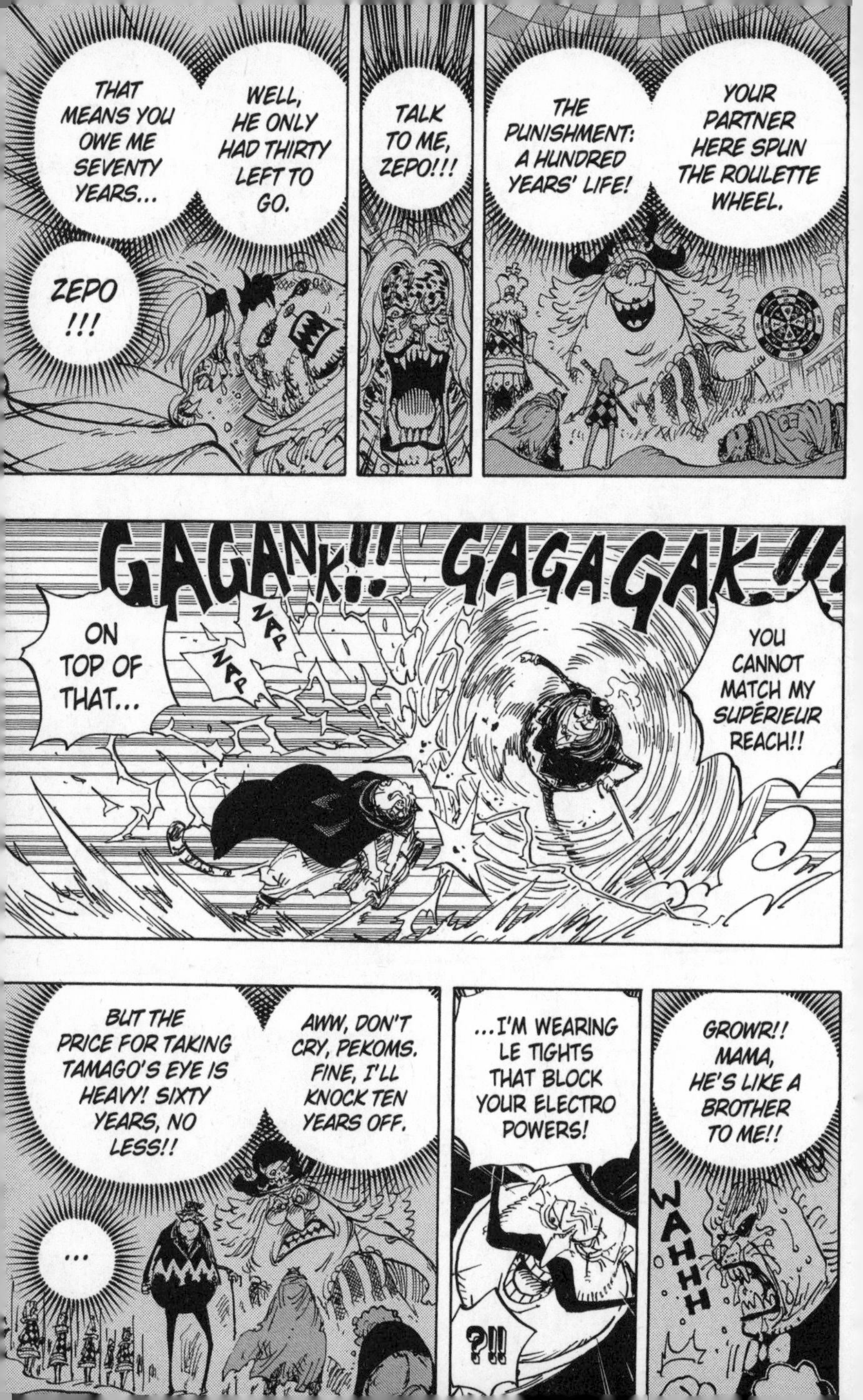
YOUR PARTNER HERE SPUN THE ROULETTE WHEEL.
THE PUNISHMENT: A HUNDRED YEARS' LIFE!
TALK TO ME, ZEPO!!!
WELL, HE ONLY HAD THIRTY LEFT TO GO.
THAT MEANS YOU OWE ME SEVENTY YEARS...
ZEPO!!!
GAGAGAK!!
YOU CANNOT MATCH MY SUPÉRIEUR REACH!!
GAGANK!!
ZAP
ZAP
ON TOP OF THAT...
GROWR!! MAMA, HE'S LIKE A BROTHER TO ME!!
WAHHH
...I'M WEARING LE TIGHTS THAT BLOCK YOUR ELECTRO POWERS!
?!!
AWW, DON'T CRY, PEKOMS. FINE, I'LL KNOCK TEN YEARS OFF.
BUT THE PRICE FOR TAKING TAMAGO'S EYE IS HEAVY! SIXTY YEARS, NO LESS!!
...

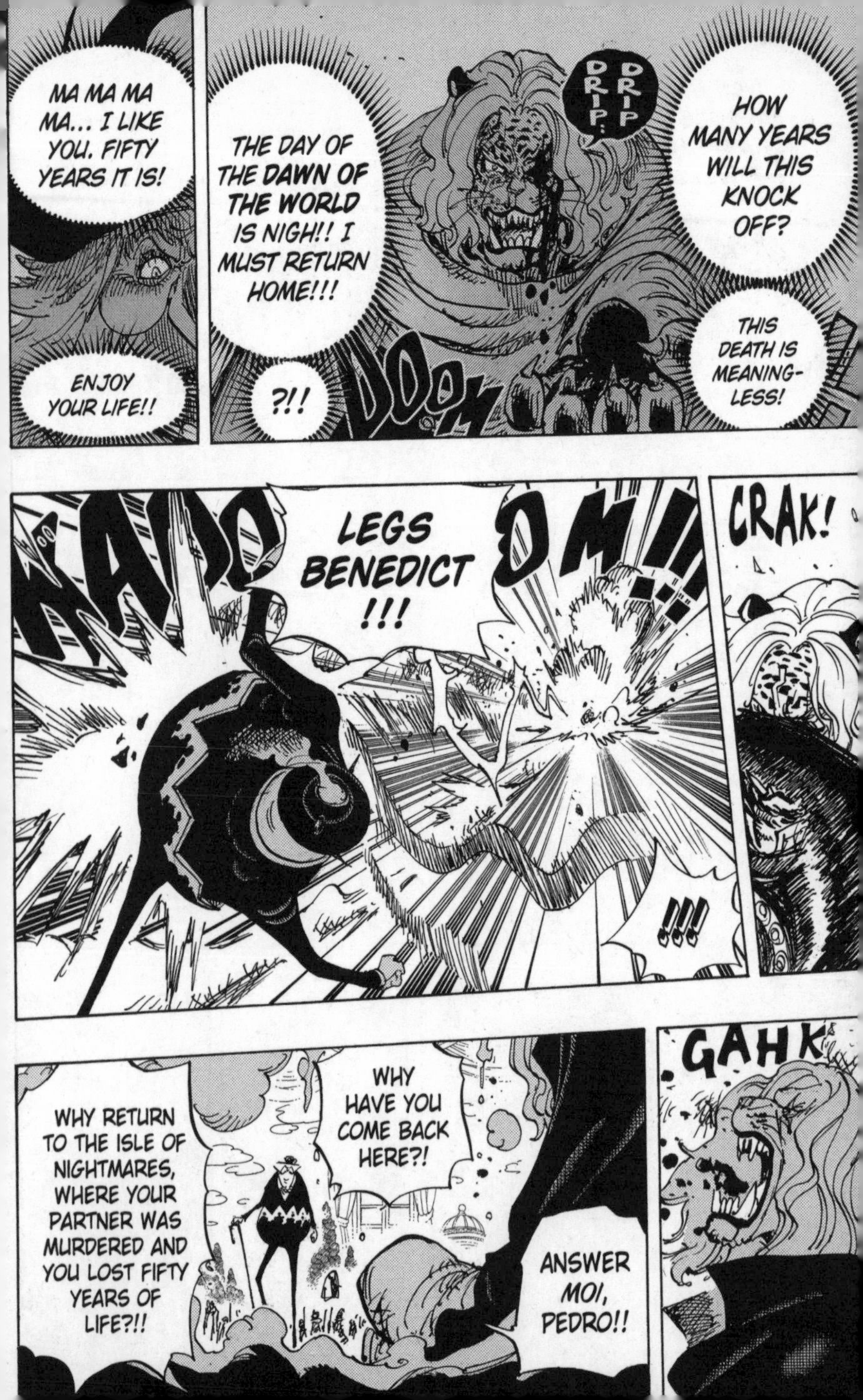
DRIP DRIP
HOW MANY YEARS WILL THIS KNOCK OFF?
THE DAY OF THE DAWN OF THE WORLD IS NIGH!! I MUST RETURN HOME!!!
THIS DEATH IS MEANINGLESS!
?!!
MA MA MA MA... I LIKE YOU. FIFTY YEARS IT IS!
ENJOY YOUR LIFE!!
CRAK!
LEGS BENEDICT !!!
!!!
GAHK
WHY HAVE YOU COME BACK HERE?!
WHY RETURN TO THE ISLE OF NIGHTMARES, WHERE YOUR PARTNER WAS MURDERED AND YOU LOST FIFTY YEARS OF LIFE?!!
ANSWER MOI, PEDRO!!

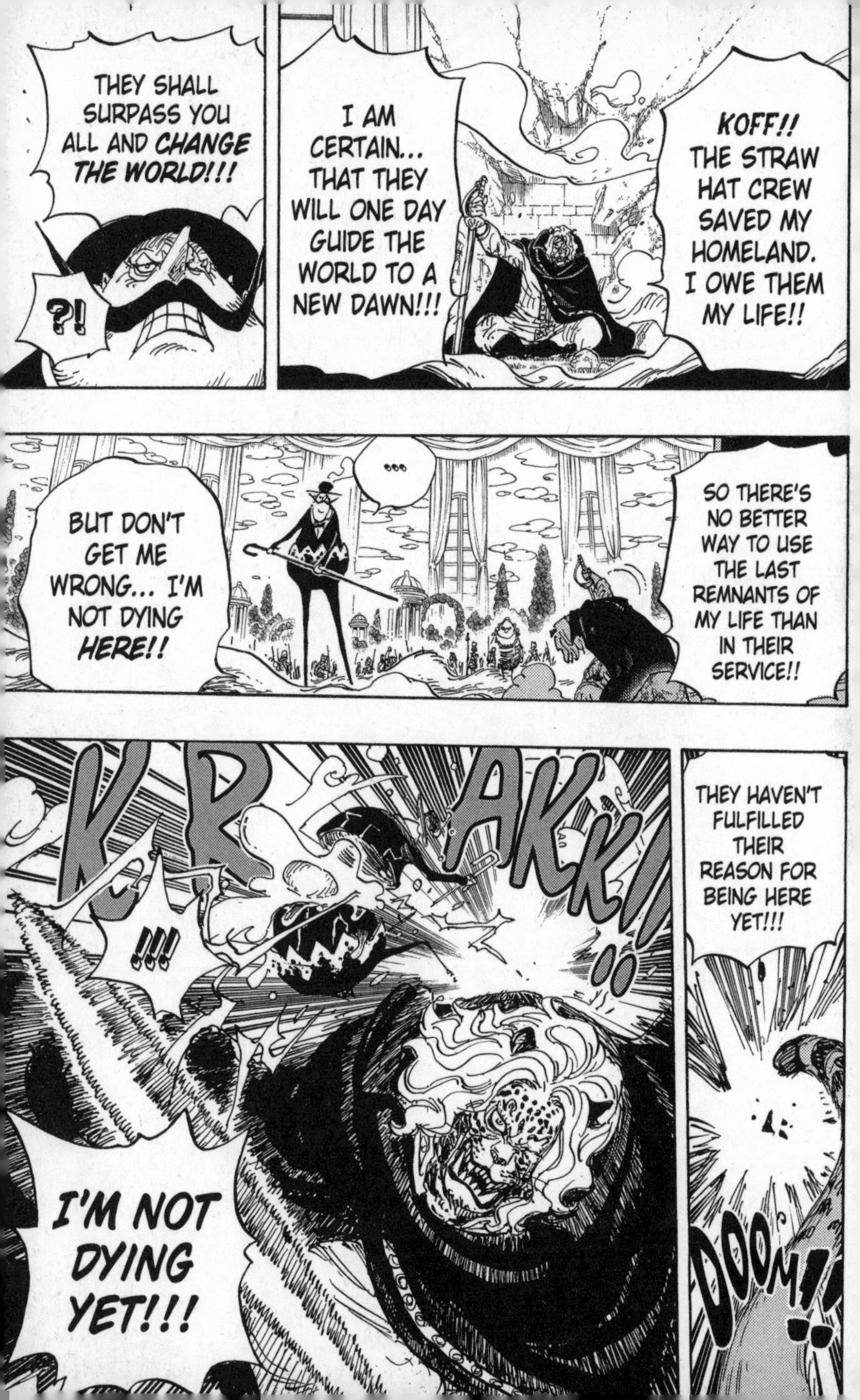
KOFF!! THE STRAW HAT CREW SAVED MY HOMELAND. I OWE THEM MY LIFE!!
I AM CERTAIN... THAT THEY WILL ONE DAY GUIDE THE WORLD TO A NEW DAWN!!!
THEY SHALL SURPASS YOU ALL AND CHANGE THE WORLD!!!
?!
SO THERE'S NO BETTER WAY TO USE THE LAST REMNANTS OF MY LIFE THAN IN THEIR SERVICE!!
...
BUT DON'T GET ME WRONG... I'M NOT DYING HERE!!
THEY HAVEN'T FULFILLED THEIR REASON FOR BEING HERE YET!!!
DOOM!!
KRAKK!!
!!!
I'M NOT DYING YET!!!

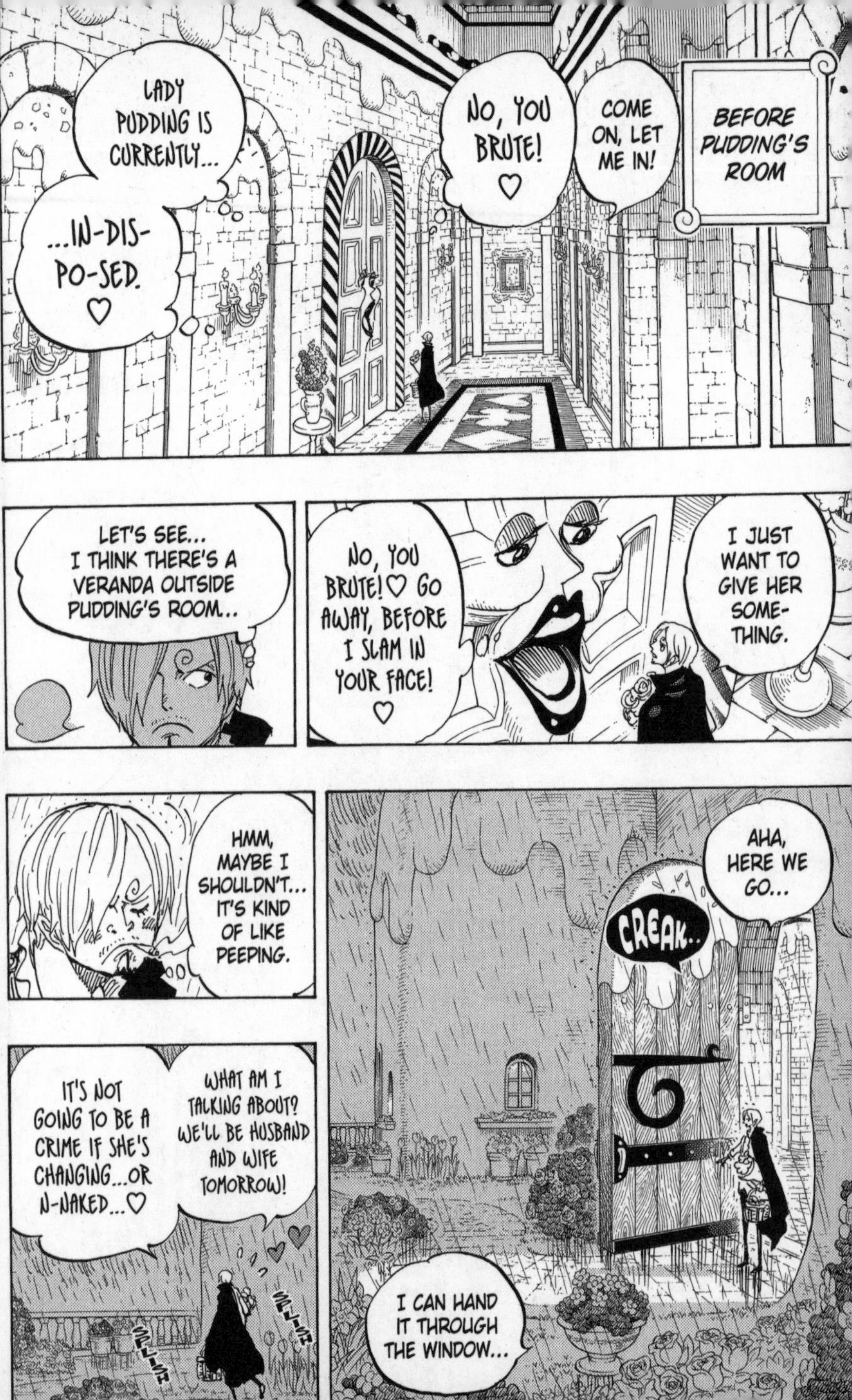
BEFORE PUDDING'S ROOM
COME ON, LET ME IN!
NO, YOU BRUTE! ♡
LADY PUDDING IS CURRENTLY...
...IN-DIS-PO-SED. ♡
I JUST WANT TO GIVE HER SOME-THING.
NO, YOU BRUTE! ♡ GO AWAY, BEFORE I SLAM IN YOUR FACE! ♡
LET'S SEE... I THINK THERE'S A VERANDA OUTSIDE PUDDING'S ROOM...
AHA, HERE WE GO...
CREAK..
I CAN HAND IT THROUGH THE WINDOW...
HMM, MAYBE I SHOULDN'T... IT'S KIND OF LIKE PEEPING.
WHAT AM I TALKING ABOUT? WE'LL BE HUSBAND AND WIFE TOMORROW!
IT'S NOT GOING TO BE A CRIME IF SHE'S CHANGING...OR N-NAKED...♡
SPLISH
SPLISH

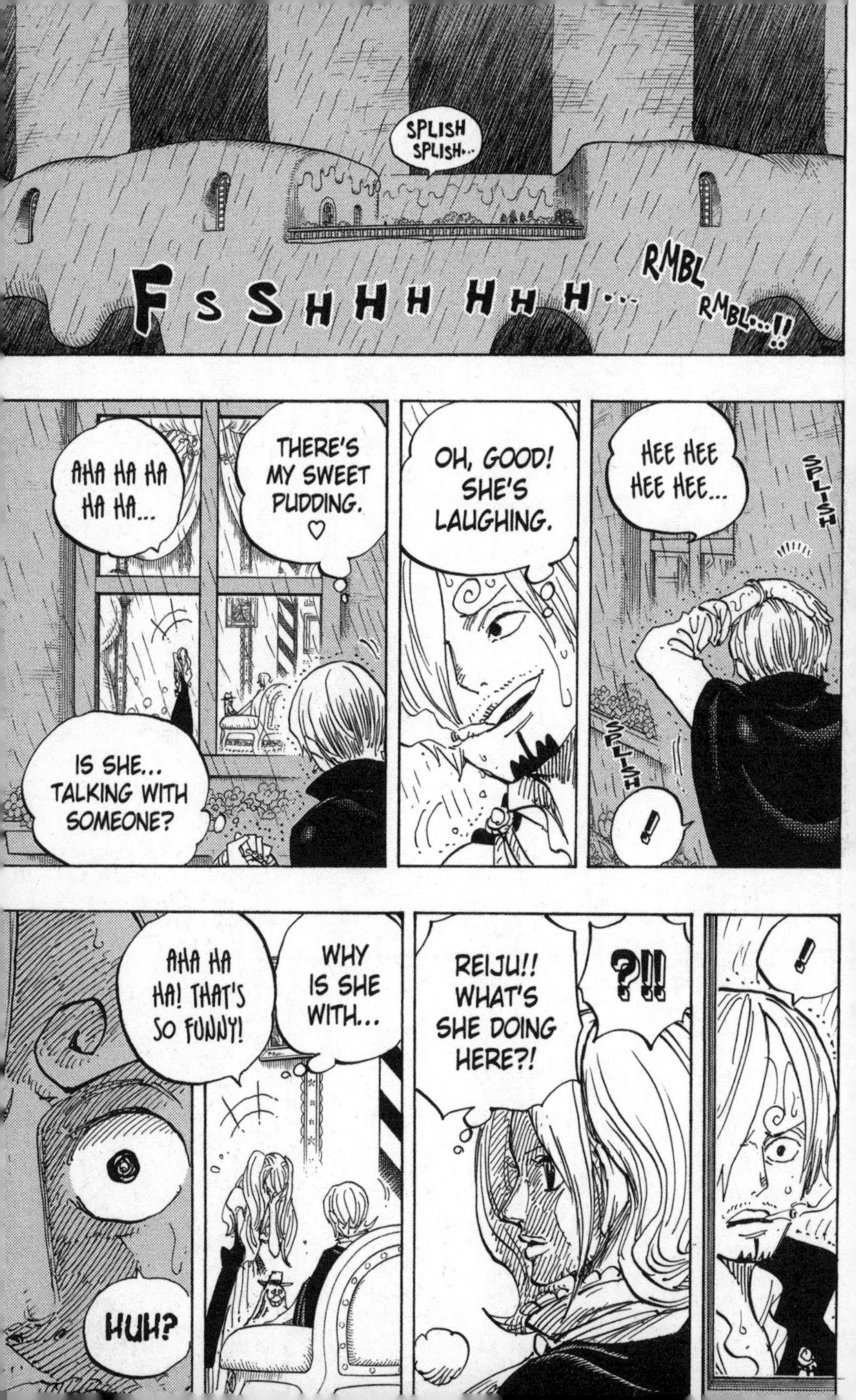
SPLISH SPLISH...
RMBL RMBL...!!
FSSHHHHHHH...
HEE HEE HEE HEE...
SPLISH
SPLISH
!
OH, GOOD! SHE'S LAUGHING.
THERE'S MY SWEET PUDDING. ♡
AHA HA HA HA HA...
IS SHE... TALKING WITH SOMEONE?
!
?!!
REIJU!! WHAT'S SHE DOING HERE?!
WHY IS SHE WITH...
AHA HA HA! THAT'S SO FUNNY!
HUH?

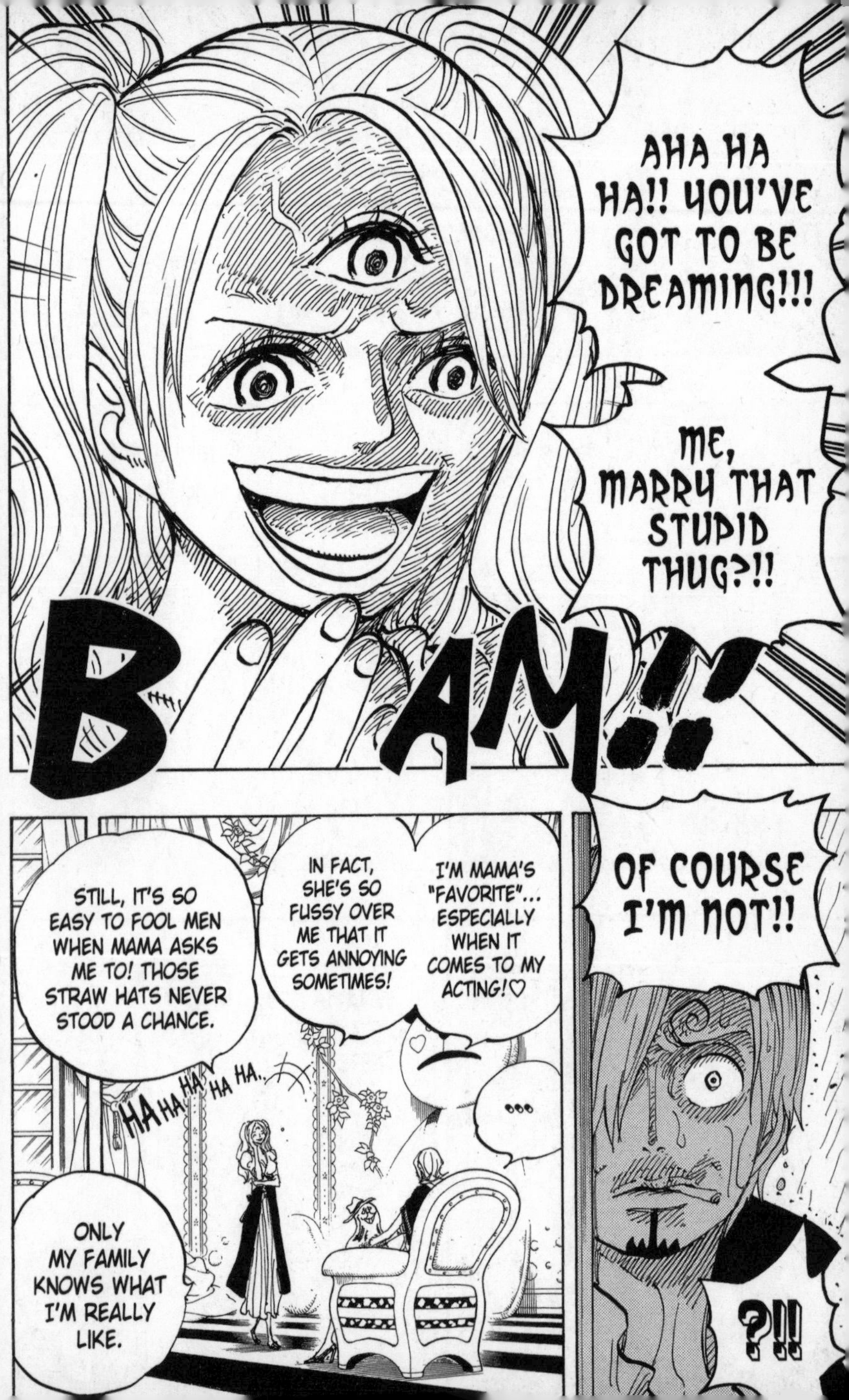
AHA HA HA!! YOU'VE GOT TO BE DREAMING!!!
ME, MARRY THAT STUPID THUG?!!
BAM!!
OF COURSE I'M NOT!!
?!!
I'M MAMA'S "FAVORITE"... ESPECIALLY WHEN IT COMES TO MY ACTING!♡
IN FACT, SHE'S SO FUSSY OVER ME THAT IT GETS ANNOYING SOMETIMES!
STILL, IT'S SO EASY TO FOOL MEN WHEN MAMA ASKS ME TO! THOSE STRAW HATS NEVER STOOD A CHANCE.
...
HA HA HA HA HA..
ONLY MY FAMILY KNOWS WHAT I'M REALLY LIKE.

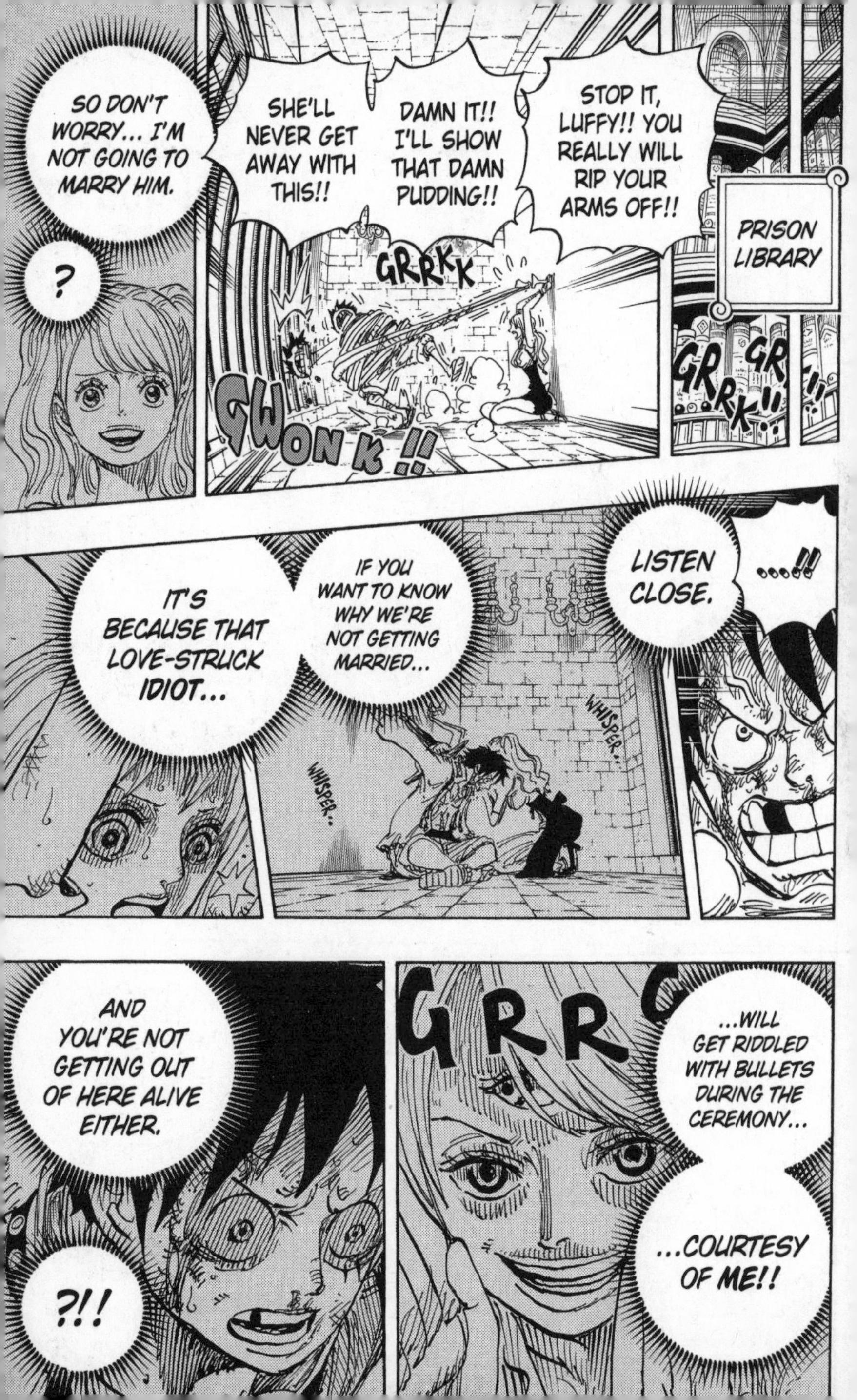
PRISON LIBRARY
GRRK!!
STOP IT, LUFFY!! YOU REALLY WILL RIP YOUR ARMS OFF!!
DAMN IT!! I'LL SHOW THAT DAMN PUDDING!!
SHE'LL NEVER GET AWAY WITH THIS!!
GRRKK
GWONK!!
SO DON'T WORRY... I'M NOT GOING TO MARRY HIM.
?
...!!
LISTEN CLOSE.
IF YOU WANT TO KNOW WHY WE'RE NOT GETTING MARRIED...
WHISPER...
WHISPER...
IT'S BECAUSE THAT LOVE-STRUCK IDIOT...
...WILL GET RIDDLED WITH BULLETS DURING THE CEREMONY...
...COURTESY OF ME!!
AND YOU'RE NOT GETTING OUT OF HERE ALIVE EITHER.
?!!

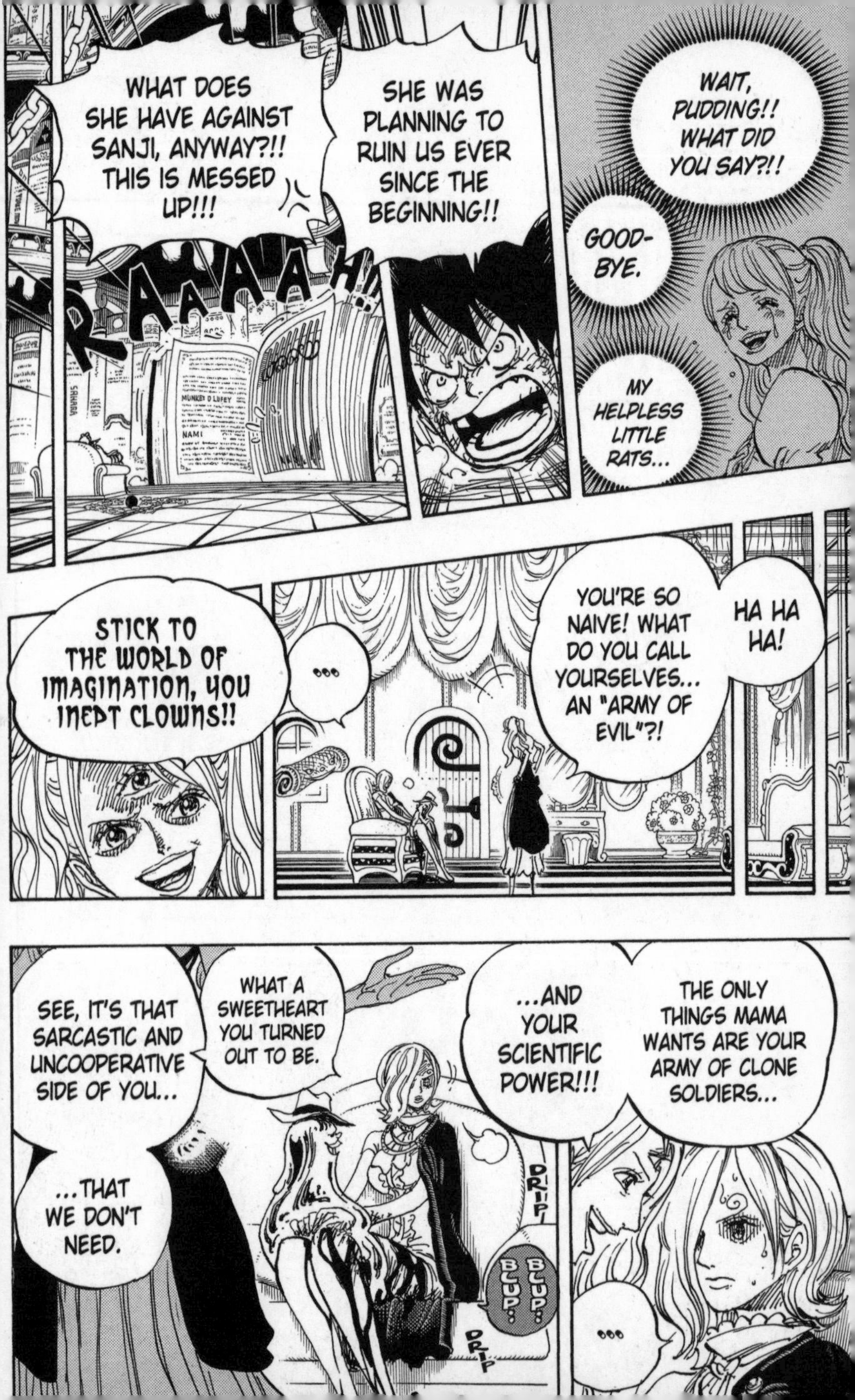
WAIT, PUDDING!! WHAT DID YOU SAY?!!
GOOD-BYE.
MY HELPLESS LITTLE RATS...
SHE WAS PLANNING TO RUIN US EVER SINCE THE BEGINNING!!
WHAT DOES SHE HAVE AGAINST SANJI, ANYWAY?!! THIS IS MESSED UP!!!
RAAAAH!!
MONKEY D LUFFY
NAMI
HA HA HA!
YOU'RE SO NAIVE! WHAT DO YOU CALL YOURSELVES... AN "ARMY OF EVIL"?!
...
STICK TO THE WORLD OF IMAGINATION, YOU INEPT CLOWNS!!
THE ONLY THINGS MAMA WANTS ARE YOUR ARMY OF CLONE SOLDIERS...
...AND YOUR SCIENTIFIC POWER!!!
...
WHAT A SWEETHEART YOU TURNED OUT TO BE.
SEE, IT'S THAT SARCASTIC AND UNCOOPERATIVE SIDE OF YOU...
DRIP
BLUP! BLUP!
DRIP
...THAT WE DON'T NEED.

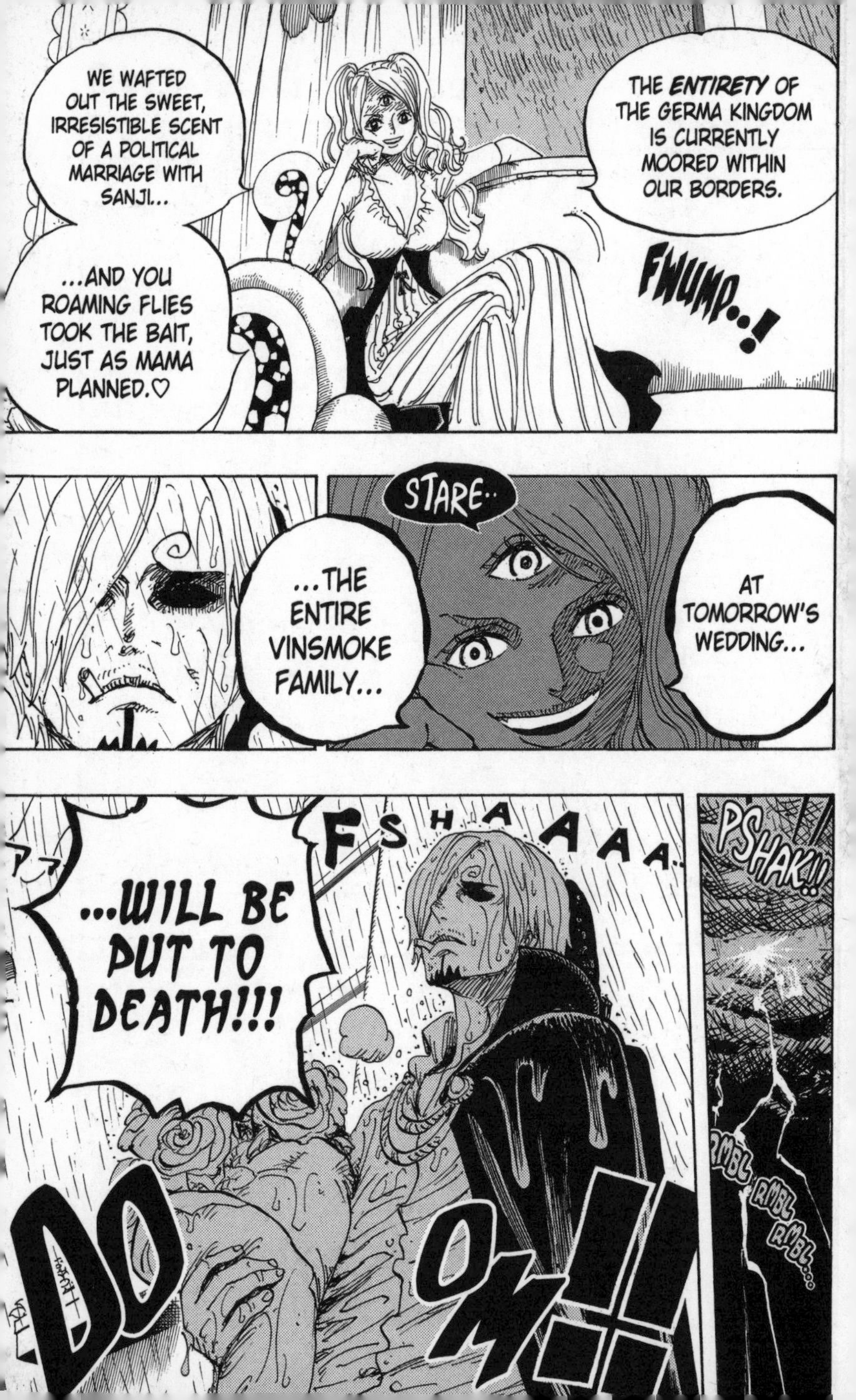
THE ENTIRETY OF THE GERMA KINGDOM IS CURRENTLY MOORED WITHIN OUR BORDERS.
FWUMP..!
WE WAFTED OUT THE SWEET, IRRESISTIBLE SCENT OF A POLITICAL MARRIAGE WITH SANJI...
...AND YOU ROAMING FLIES TOOK THE BAIT, JUST AS MAMA PLANNED.♡
STARE..
AT TOMORROW'S WEDDING...
...THE ENTIRE VINSMOKE FAMILY...
PSHAK!!
RMBL RMBL RMBL...
FSHAAAA..
...WILL BE PUT TO DEATH!!!
DOOM!!

Chapter 851: DOG-END

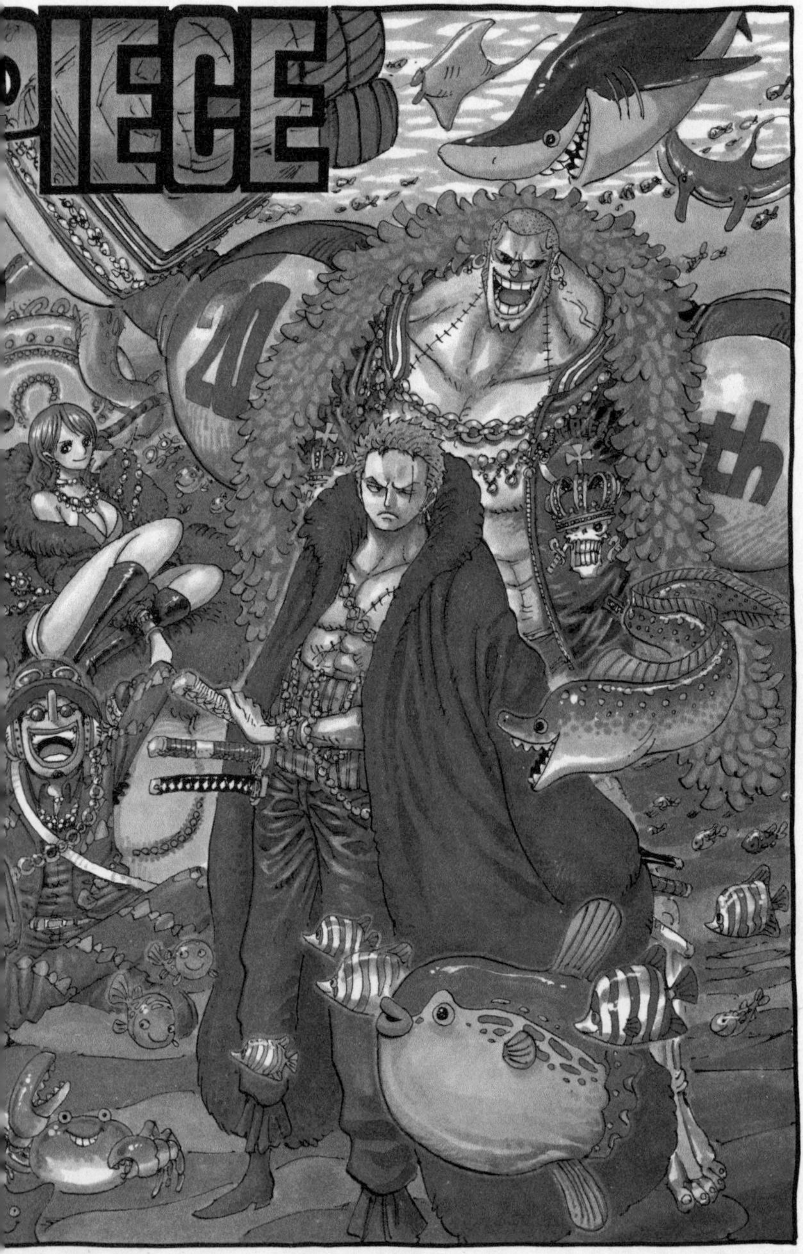
PIECE

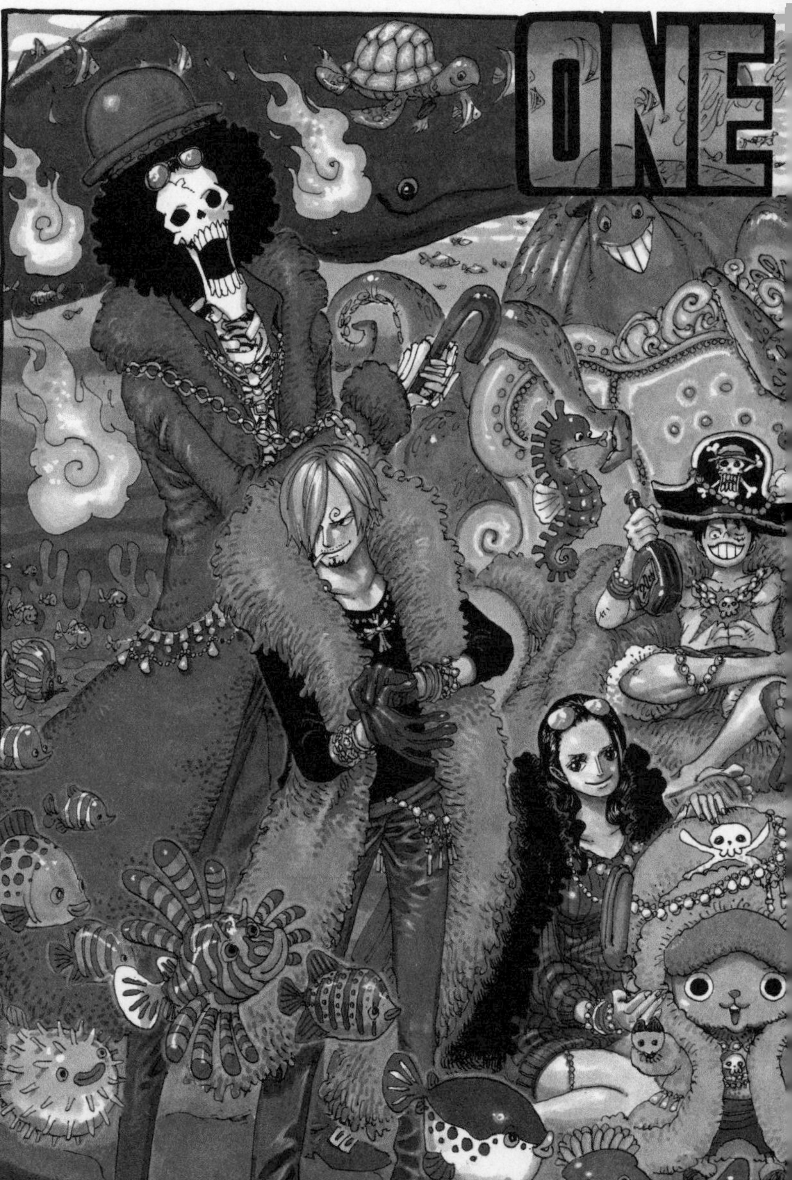
ONE

vol.85

ONE PIECE

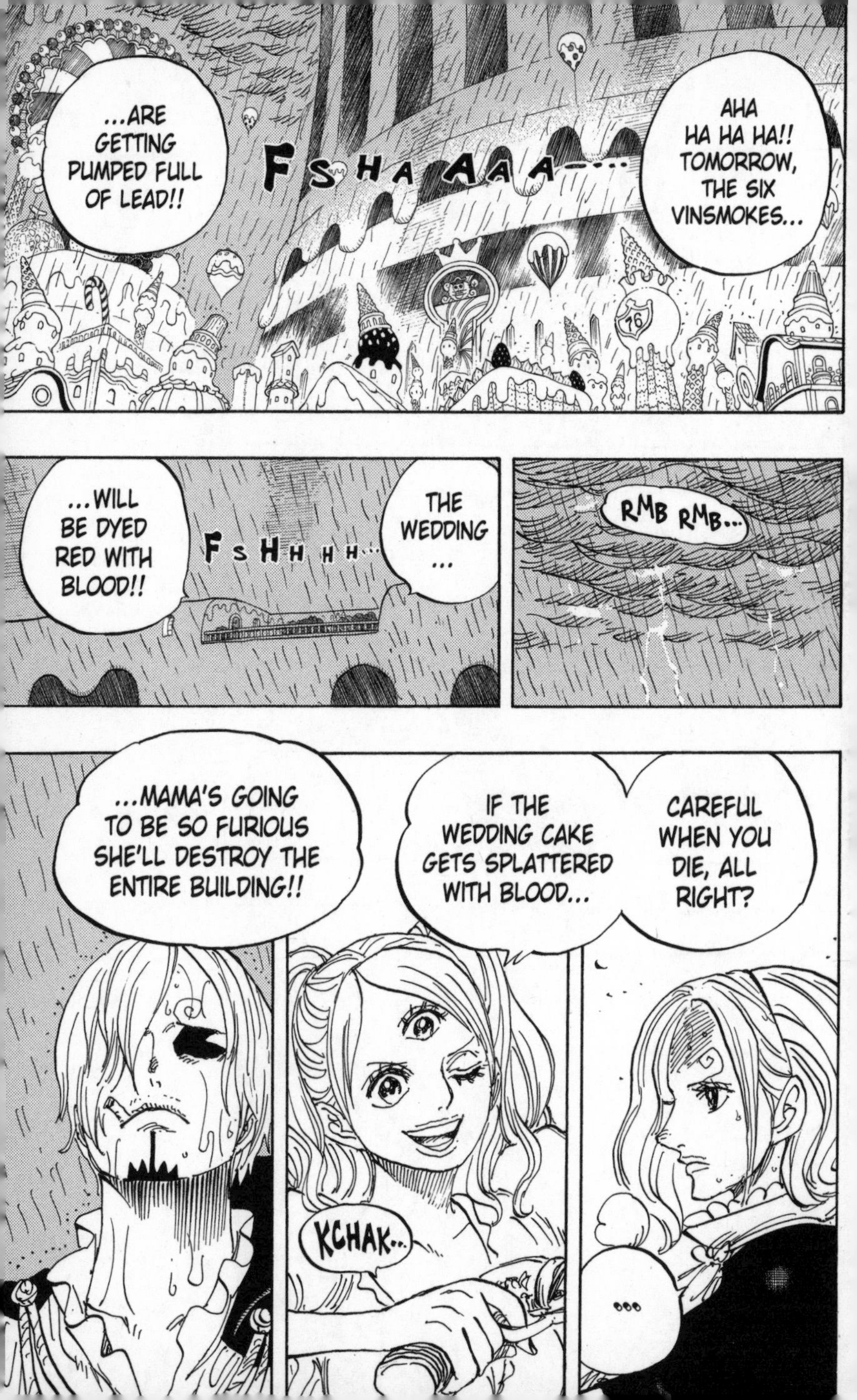
AHA HA HA HA!! TOMORROW, THE SIX VINSMOKES...
FSHAAAA-....
...ARE GETTING PUMPED FULL OF LEAD!!
RMB RMB...
THE WEDDING ...
FSHHHHH...
...WILL BE DYED RED WITH BLOOD!!
CAREFUL WHEN YOU DIE, ALL RIGHT?
IF THE WEDDING CAKE GETS SPLATTERED WITH BLOOD...
...MAMA'S GOING TO BE SO FURIOUS SHE'LL DESTROY THE ENTIRE BUILDING!!
...
KCHAK..

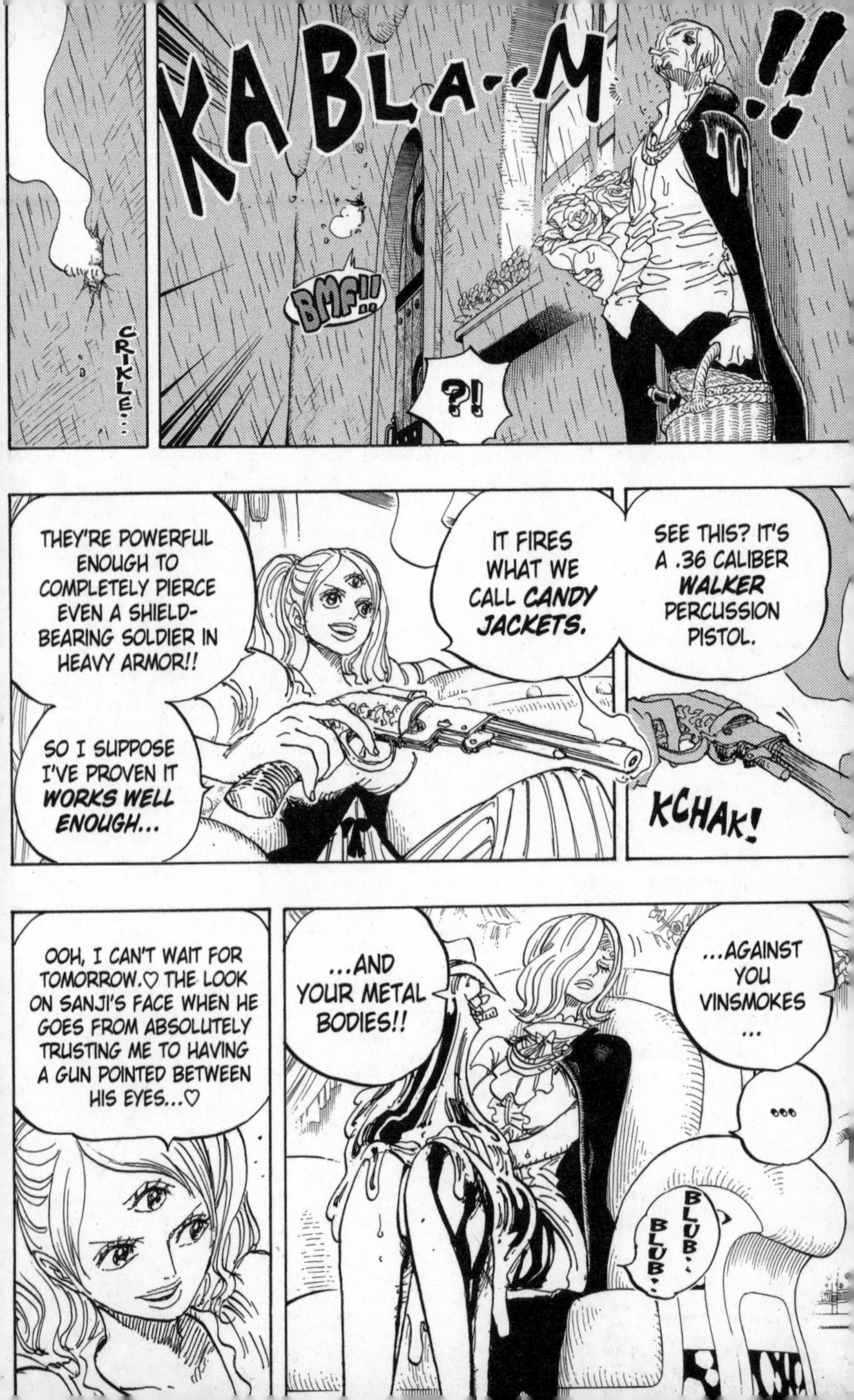
KABLA-M!!
BMF!!
?!
CRIKLE...
SEE THIS? IT'S A .36 CALIBER WALKER PERCUSSION PISTOL.
KCHAK!
IT FIRES WHAT WE CALL CANDY JACKETS.
THEY'RE POWERFUL ENOUGH TO COMPLETELY PIERCE EVEN A SHIELD-BEARING SOLDIER IN HEAVY ARMOR!!
SO I SUPPOSE I'VE PROVEN IT WORKS WELL ENOUGH...
...AGAINST YOU VINSMOKES ...
...AND YOUR METAL BODIES!!
...
BLUB. BLUB.
OOH, I CAN'T WAIT FOR TOMORROW.♡ THE LOOK ON SANJI'S FACE WHEN HE GOES FROM ABSOLUTELY TRUSTING ME TO HAVING A GUN POINTED BETWEEN HIS EYES...♡

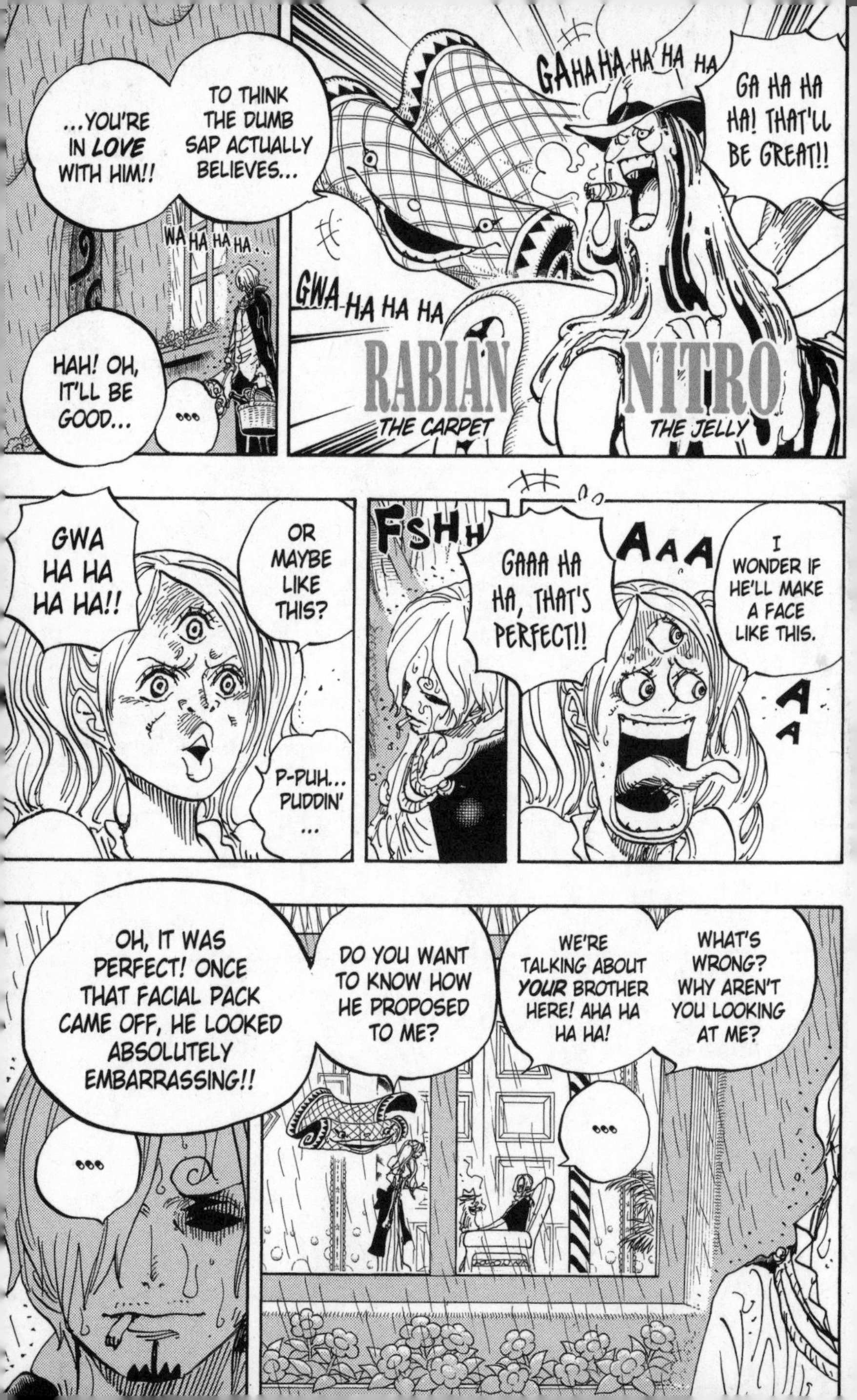
GA HA HA HA! THAT'LL BE GREAT!!
GAHAHA HA HA HA
GWA HA HA HA
NITRO
THE JELLY
RABIAN
THE CARPET
TO THINK THE DUMB SAP ACTUALLY BELIEVES...
...YOU'RE IN LOVE WITH HIM!!
WA HA HA HA...
HAH! OH, IT'LL BE GOOD...
...
I WONDER IF HE'LL MAKE A FACE LIKE THIS.
AAA
AA
GAAA HA HA, THAT'S PERFECT!!
FSHH
OR MAYBE LIKE THIS?
GWA HA HA HA HA!!
P-PUH... PUDDIN' ...
WHAT'S WRONG? WHY AREN'T YOU LOOKING AT ME?
WE'RE TALKING ABOUT YOUR BROTHER HERE! AHA HA HA HA!
...
DO YOU WANT TO KNOW HOW HE PROPOSED TO ME?
OH, IT WAS PERFECT! ONCE THAT FACIAL PACK CAME OFF, HE LOOKED ABSOLUTELY EMBARRASSING!!
...

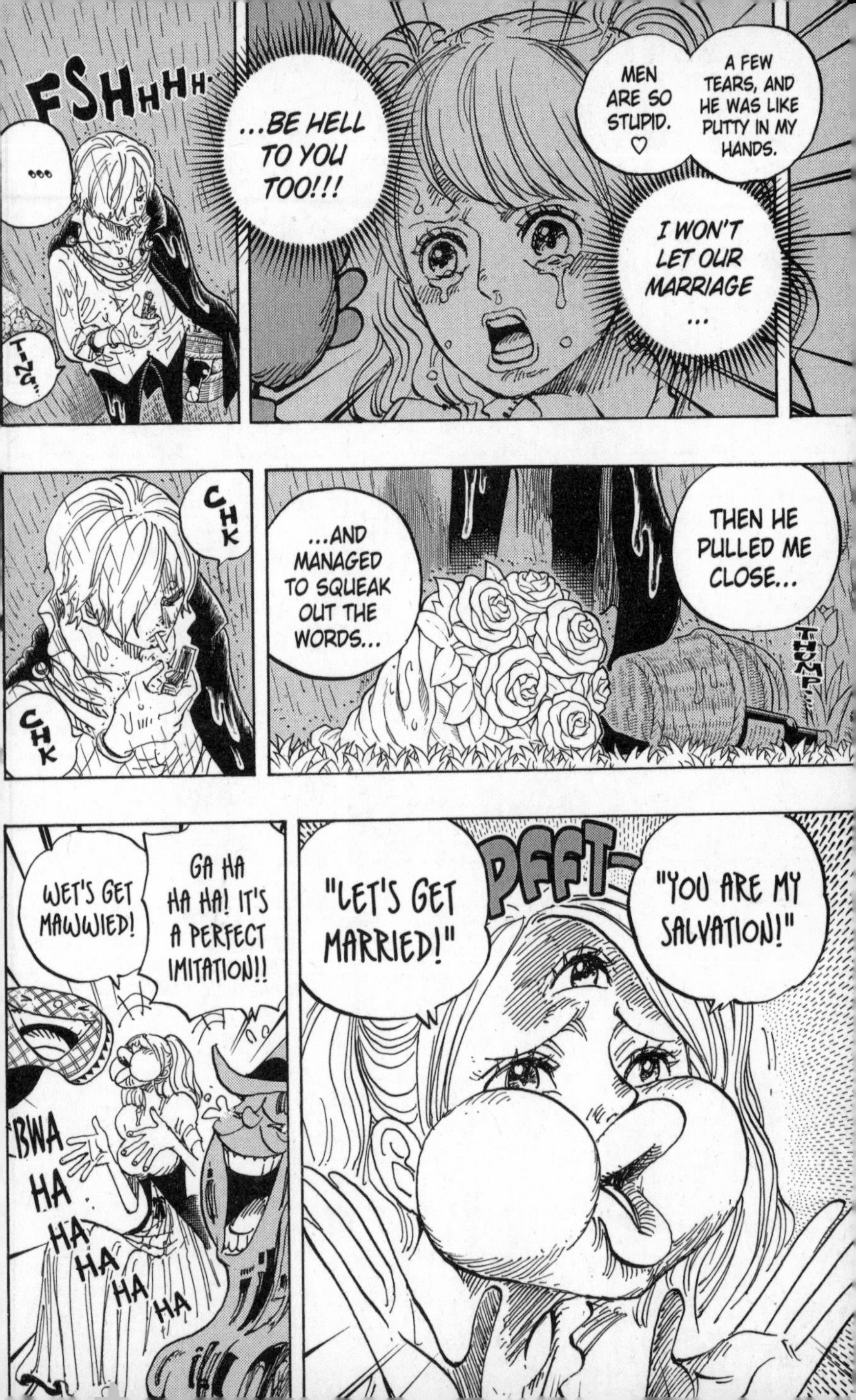
A FEW TEARS, AND HE WAS LIKE PUTTY IN MY HANDS.
MEN ARE SO STUPID. ♡
I WON'T LET OUR MARRIAGE ...
...BE HELL TO YOU TOO!!!
FSHHHHH
...
TING...
THEN HE PULLED ME CLOSE...
THUMP...
...AND MANAGED TO SQUEAK OUT THE WORDS...
CHK
CHK
"YOU ARE MY SALVATION!"
PFFT-
"LET'S GET MARRIED!"
GA HA HA HA! IT'S A PERFECT IMITATION!!
WET'S GET MAWWIED!
BWA HA HA HA HA HA

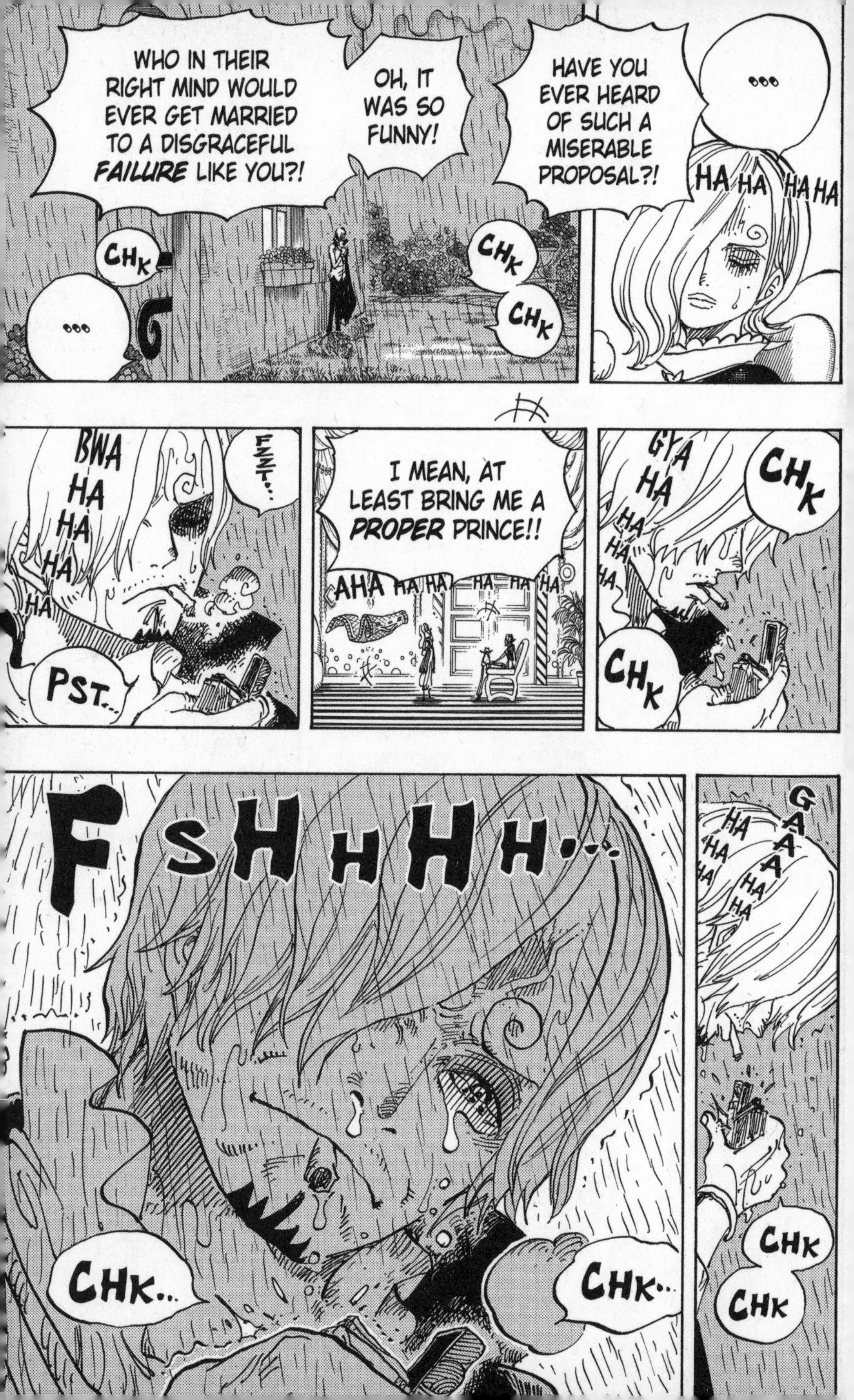
...
HA HA HAHA
HAVE YOU EVER HEARD OF SUCH A MISERABLE PROPOSAL?!
OH, IT WAS SO FUNNY!
WHO IN THEIR RIGHT MIND WOULD EVER GET MARRIED TO A DISGRACEFUL *FAILURE* LIKE YOU?!
CHK
CHK
CHK
...
CHK
GYA HA HA HA HA
CHK
I MEAN, AT LEAST BRING ME A *PROPER* PRINCE!!
AHA HA HA HA HA HA
FZZT...
BWA HA HA HA HA HA
PST...
GAAAA HA HA HA HA HA HA
CHK
CHK
FSHHHH...
CHK...
CHK...

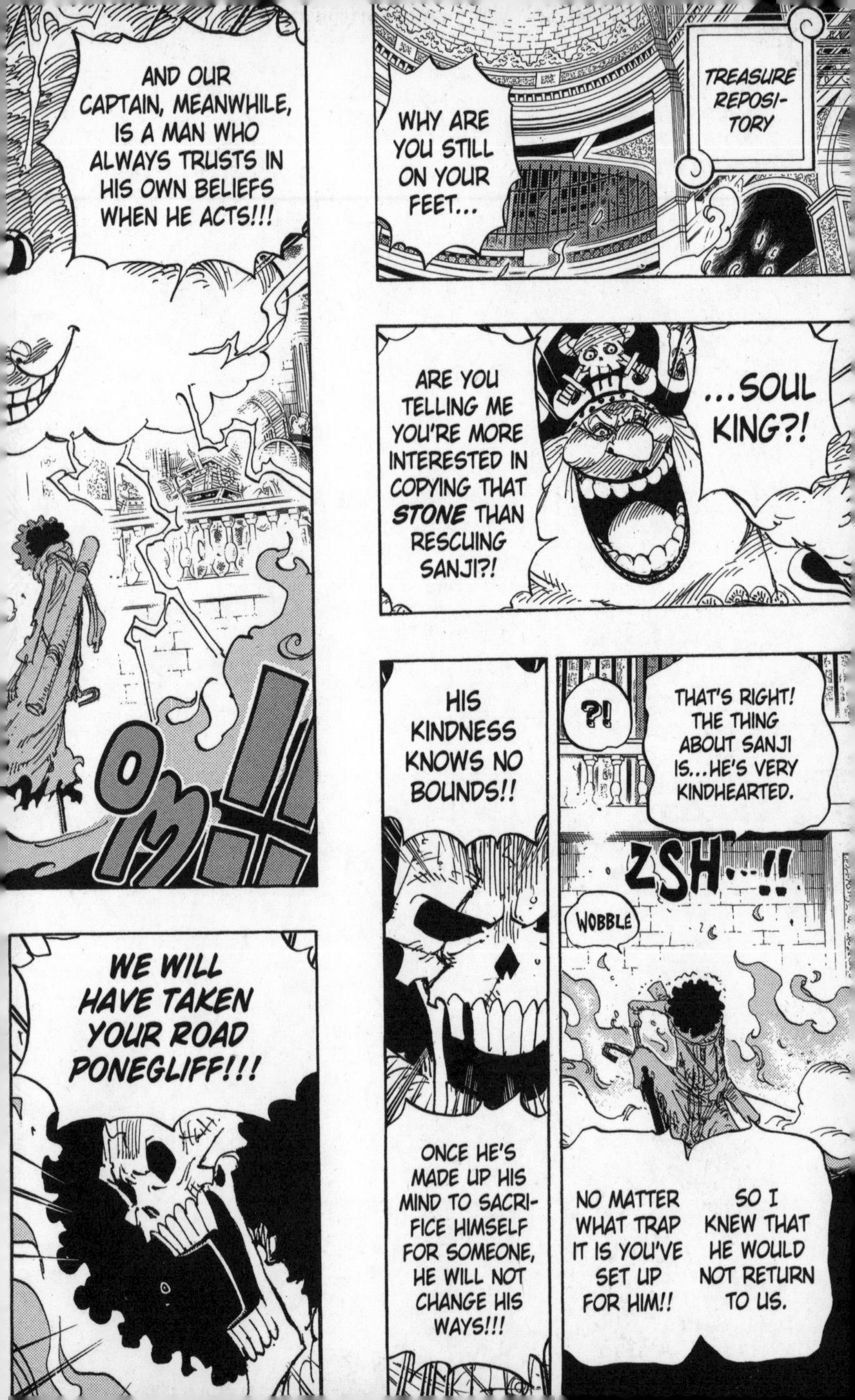

TREASURE REPOSITORY
WHY ARE YOU STILL ON YOUR FEET...
...SOUL KING?!
ARE YOU TELLING ME YOU'RE MORE INTERESTED IN COPYING THAT STONE THAN RESCUING SANJI?!
?!
THAT'S RIGHT! THE THING ABOUT SANJI IS...HE'S VERY KINDHEARTED.
ZSH...!!
WOBBLE
SO I KNEW THAT HE WOULD NOT RETURN TO US.
NO MATTER WHAT TRAP IT IS YOU'VE SET UP FOR HIM!!
HIS KINDNESS KNOWS NO BOUNDS!!
ONCE HE'S MADE UP HIS MIND TO SACRIFICE HIMSELF FOR SOMEONE, HE WILL NOT CHANGE HIS WAYS!!!
AND OUR CAPTAIN, MEANWHILE, IS A MAN WHO ALWAYS TRUSTS IN HIS OWN BELIEFS WHEN HE ACTS!!!
OM..!!
WE WILL HAVE TAKEN YOUR ROAD PONEGLIFF!!!

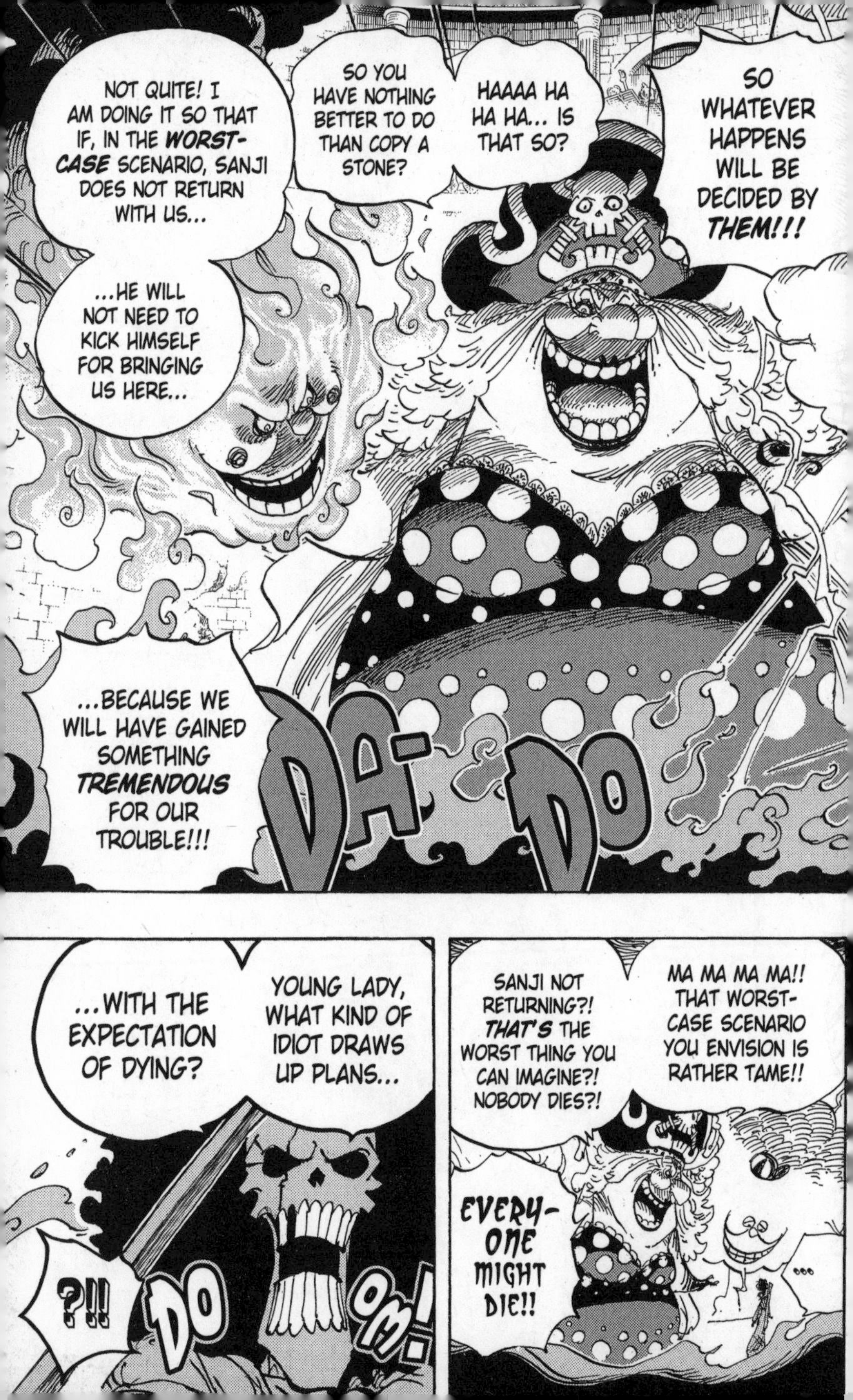
SO WHATEVER HAPPENS WILL BE DECIDED BY *THEM!!!*
HAAAA HA HA HA... IS THAT SO?
SO YOU HAVE NOTHING BETTER TO DO THAN COPY A STONE?
NOT QUITE! I AM DOING IT SO THAT IF, IN THE *WORST-CASE* SCENARIO, SANJI DOES NOT RETURN WITH US...
...HE WILL NOT NEED TO KICK HIMSELF FOR BRINGING US HERE...
...BECAUSE WE WILL HAVE GAINED SOMETHING *TREMENDOUS* FOR OUR TROUBLE!!!
DA-DO
MA MA MA MA!! THAT WORST-CASE SCENARIO YOU ENVISION IS RATHER TAME!!
SANJI NOT RETURNING?! *THAT'S* THE WORST THING YOU CAN IMAGINE?! NOBODY DIES?!
EVERYONE MIGHT DIE!!
...
YOUNG LADY, WHAT KIND OF IDIOT DRAWS UP PLANS...
...WITH THE EXPECTATION OF DYING?
?!!
DOOM!

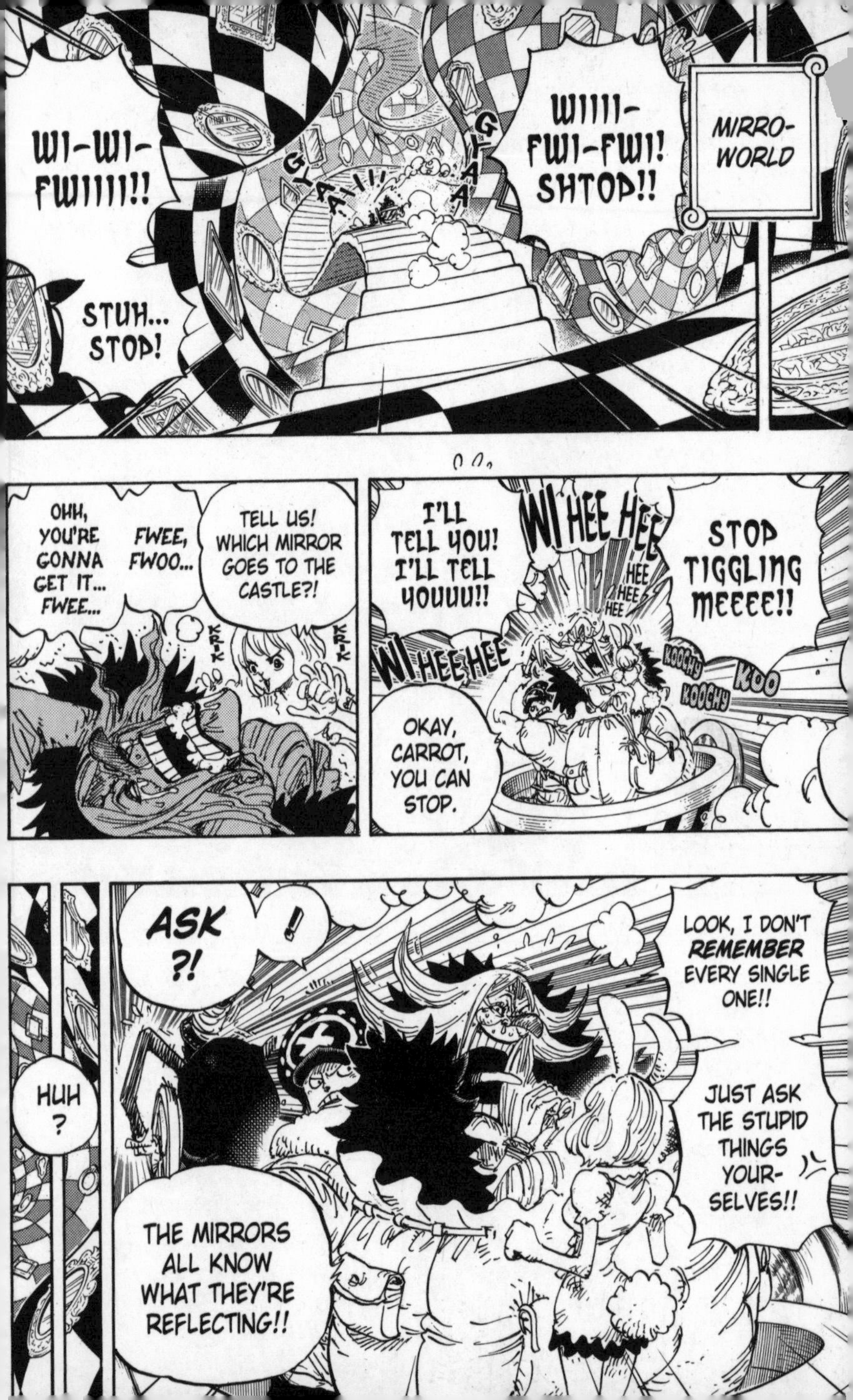
MIRRO-WORLD
WIIIII-FWI-FWI! SHTOP!!
GYAA
GYAA!!!
WI-WI-FWIIIII!!
STUH... STOP!
STOP TIGGLING MEEEE!!
WI HEE HEE
HEE HEE HEE
I'LL TELL YOU! I'LL TELL YOUUU!!
KOOCHY KOOCHY KOO
WI HEE HEE
OKAY, CARROT, YOU CAN STOP.
TELL US! WHICH MIRROR GOES TO THE CASTLE?!
FWEE, FWOO...
OHH, YOU'RE GONNA GET IT... FWEE...
KRIK
KRIK
LOOK, I DON'T REMEMBER EVERY SINGLE ONE!!
JUST ASK THE STUPID THINGS YOURSELVES!!
!
ASK?!
THE MIRRORS ALL KNOW WHAT THEY'RE REFLECTING!!
HUH?

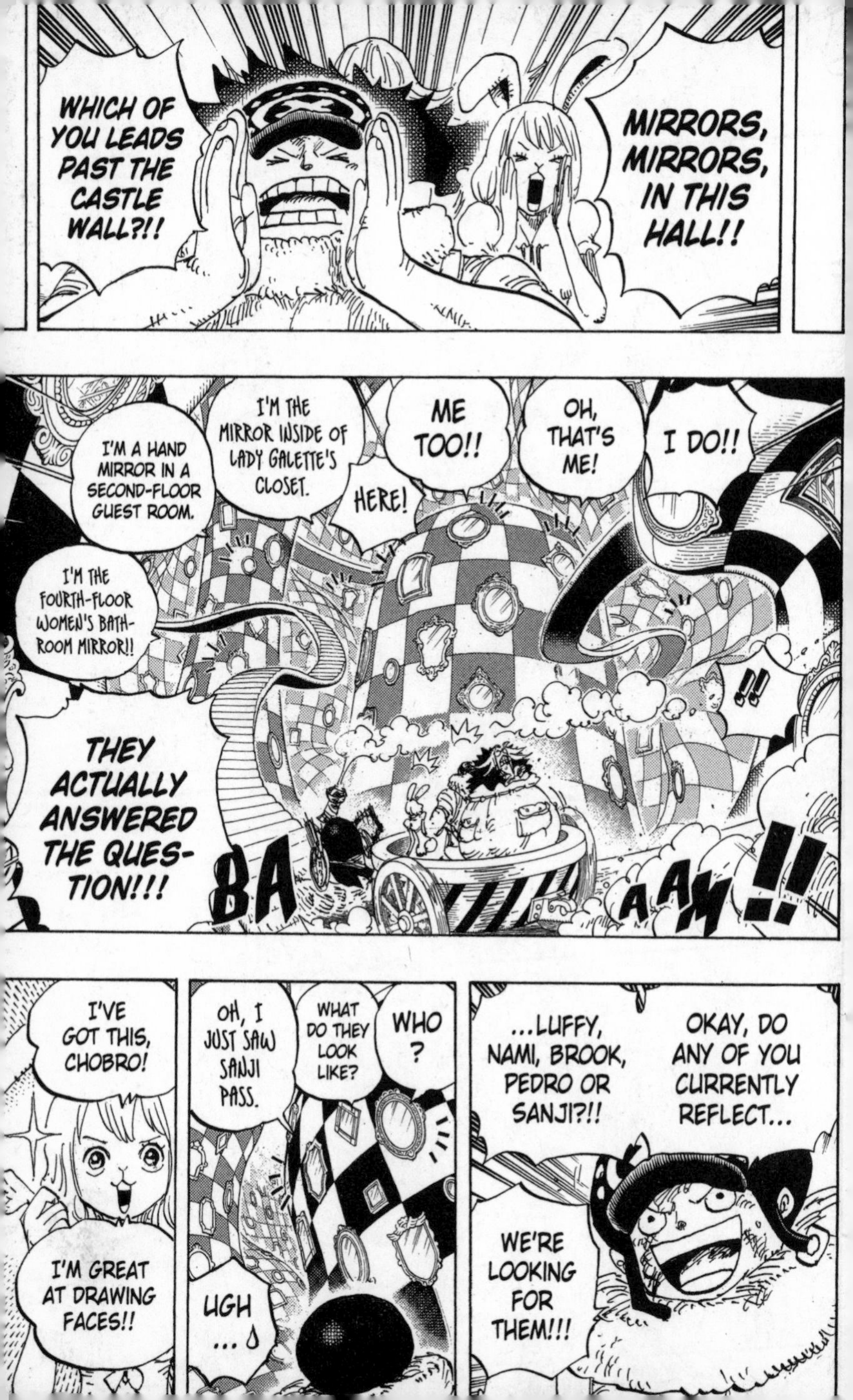
MIRRORS, MIRRORS, IN THIS HALL!!
WHICH OF YOU LEADS PAST THE CASTLE WALL?!!
I DO!!
OH, THAT'S ME!
ME TOO!!
HERE!
I'M THE MIRROR INSIDE OF LADY GALETTE'S CLOSET.
I'M A HAND MIRROR IN A SECOND-FLOOR GUEST ROOM.
I'M THE FOURTH-FLOOR WOMEN'S BATH-ROOM MIRROR!!
!!
BA
AAM!!
THEY ACTUALLY ANSWERED THE QUES-TION!!!
OKAY, DO ANY OF YOU CURRENTLY REFLECT...
...LUFFY, NAMI, BROOK, PEDRO OR SANJI?!!
WE'RE LOOKING FOR THEM!!!
WHO?
WHAT DO THEY LOOK LIKE?
OH, I JUST SAW SANJI PASS.
UGH...
I'VE GOT THIS, CHOBRO!
I'M GREAT AT DRAWING FACES!!

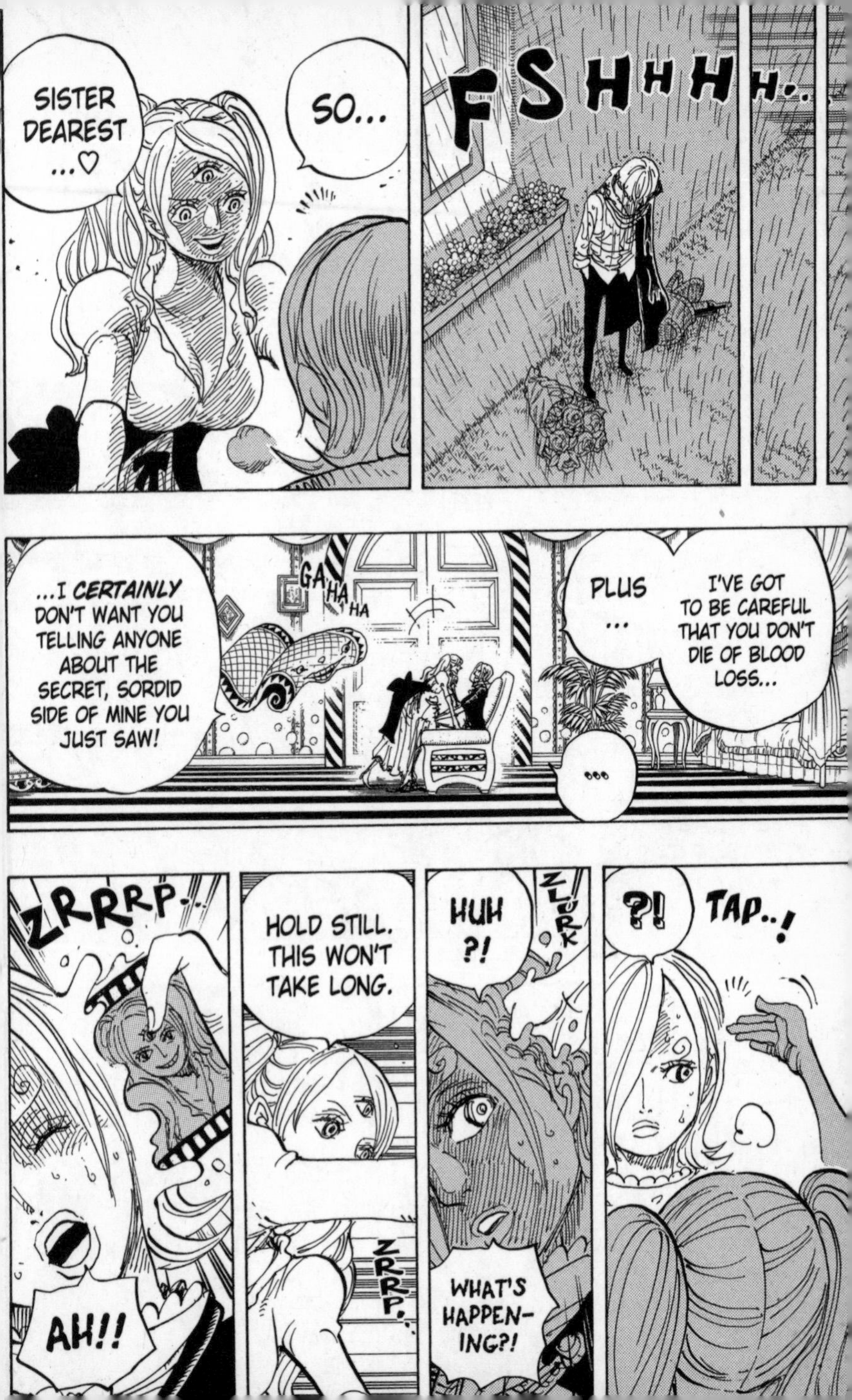
FSHHHHH..
SO...
SISTER DEAREST ...♡
I'VE GOT TO BE CAREFUL THAT YOU DON'T DIE OF BLOOD LOSS...
PLUS ...
...
GA HA HA
...I *CERTAINLY* DON'T WANT YOU TELLING ANYONE ABOUT THE SECRET, SORDID SIDE OF MINE YOU JUST SAW!
TAP..!
?!
ZLURK
HUH ?!
WHAT'S HAPPEN-ING?!
HOLD STILL. THIS WON'T TAKE LONG.
ZRRRP.
ZRRRP..
AH!!

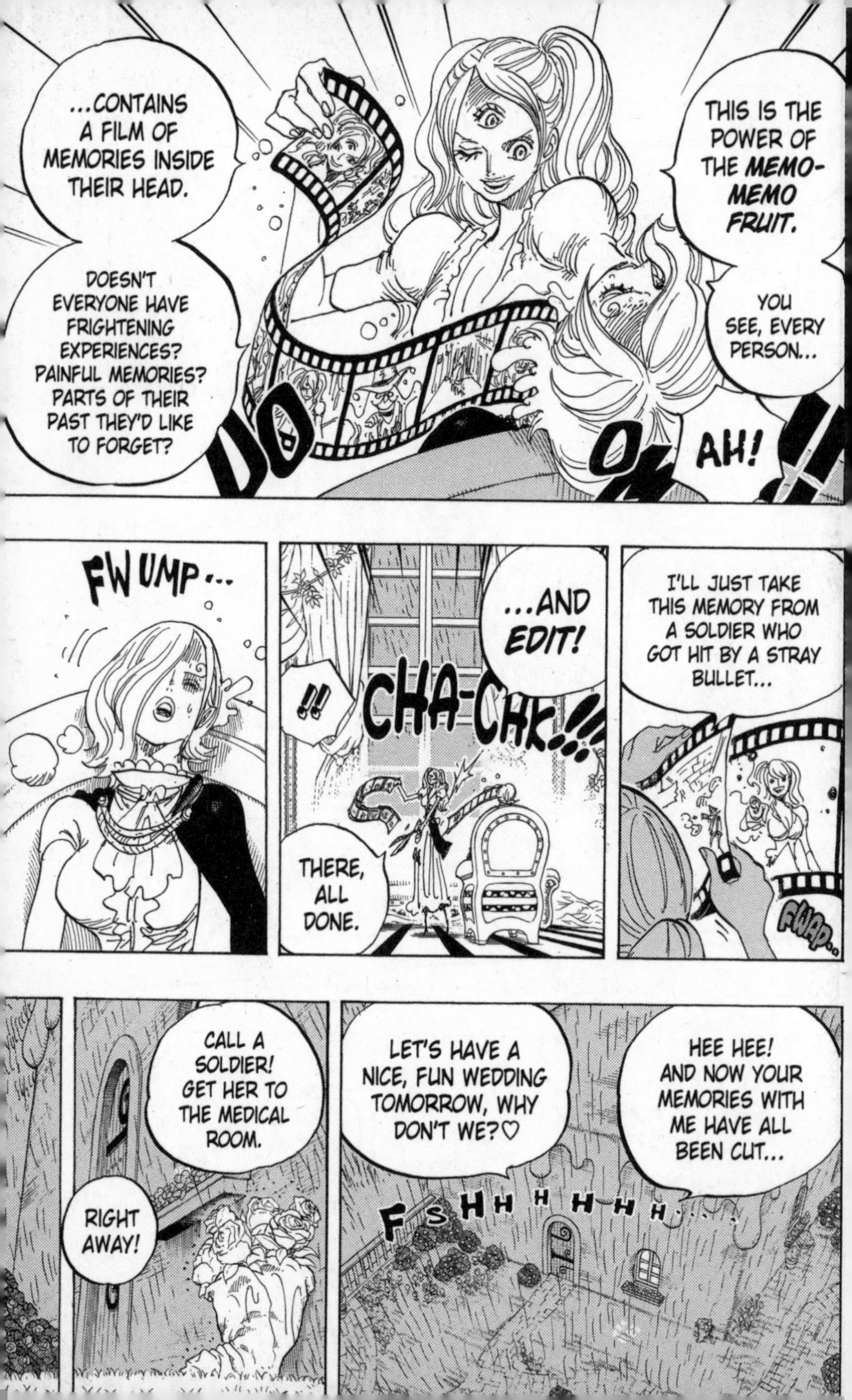
THIS IS THE POWER OF THE MEMO-MEMO FRUIT.
YOU SEE, EVERY PERSON...
...CONTAINS A FILM OF MEMORIES INSIDE THEIR HEAD.
DOESN'T EVERYONE HAVE FRIGHTENING EXPERIENCES? PAINFUL MEMORIES? PARTS OF THEIR PAST THEY'D LIKE TO FORGET?
AH!
DOON
I'LL JUST TAKE THIS MEMORY FROM A SOLDIER WHO GOT HIT BY A STRAY BULLET...
FWAP..
...AND EDIT!
!!
CHA-CHK!!!
THERE, ALL DONE.
FWUMP...
HEE HEE! AND NOW YOUR MEMORIES WITH ME HAVE ALL BEEN CUT...
LET'S HAVE A NICE, FUN WEDDING TOMORROW, WHY DON'T WE?♡
FSHHHHHH...
CALL A SOLDIER! GET HER TO THE MEDICAL ROOM.
RIGHT AWAY!

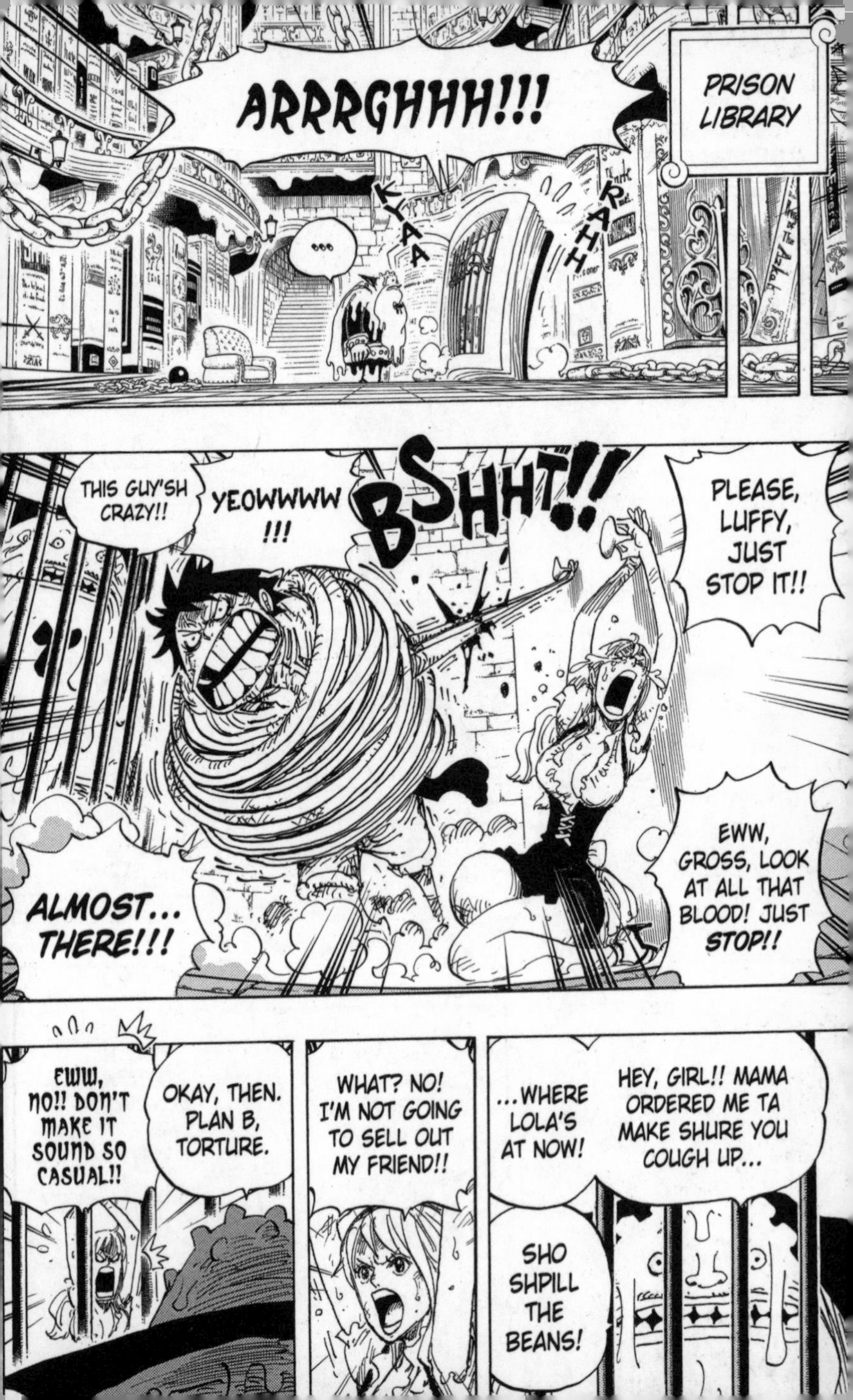
PRISON LIBRARY
ARRRGHHH!!!
RAHHH
KYAA
...
PLEASE, LUFFY, JUST STOP IT!!
BSHHT!!
YEOWWWW !!!
THIS GUY'SH CRAZY!!
EWW, GROSS, LOOK AT ALL THAT BLOOD! JUST STOP!!
ALMOST... THERE!!!
HEY, GIRL!! MAMA ORDERED ME TA MAKE SHURE YOU COUGH UP...
...WHERE LOLA'S AT NOW!
SHO SHPILL THE BEANS!
WHAT? NO! I'M NOT GOING TO SELL OUT MY FRIEND!!
OKAY, THEN. PLAN B, TORTURE.
EWW, NO!! DON'T MAKE IT SOUND SO CASUAL!!

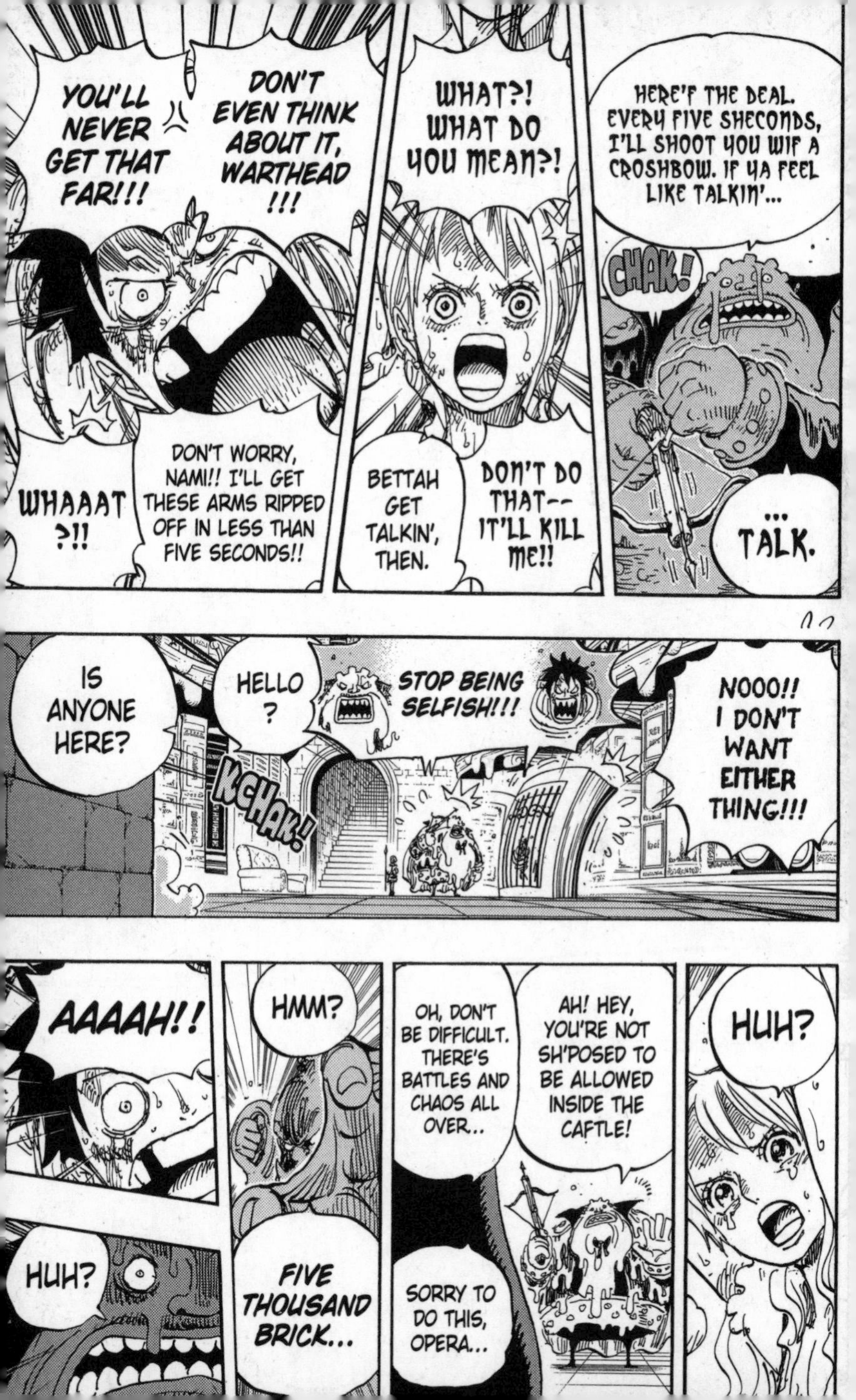
HERE'F THE DEAL. EVERY FIVE SHECONDS, I'LL SHOOT YOU WIF A CROSHBOW. IF YA FEEL LIKE TALKIN'...
CHAK!
... TALK.
WHAT?! WHAT DO YOU MEAN?!
DON'T DO THAT-- IT'LL KILL ME!!
BETTAH GET TALKIN', THEN.
DON'T EVEN THINK ABOUT IT, WARTHEAD!!!
YOU'LL NEVER GET THAT FAR!!!
DON'T WORRY, NAMI!! I'LL GET THESE ARMS RIPPED OFF IN LESS THAN FIVE SECONDS!!
WHAAAT?!!
NOOO!! I DON'T WANT EITHER THING!!!
STOP BEING SELFISH!!!
HELLO?
IS ANYONE HERE?
KCHAK!
HUH?
AH! HEY, YOU'RE NOT SH'POSED TO BE ALLOWED INSIDE THE CAFTLE!
OH, DON'T BE DIFFICULT. THERE'S BATTLES AND CHAOS ALL OVER...
SORRY TO DO THIS, OPERA...
HMM?
FIVE THOUSAND BRICK...
AAAAH!!
HUH?

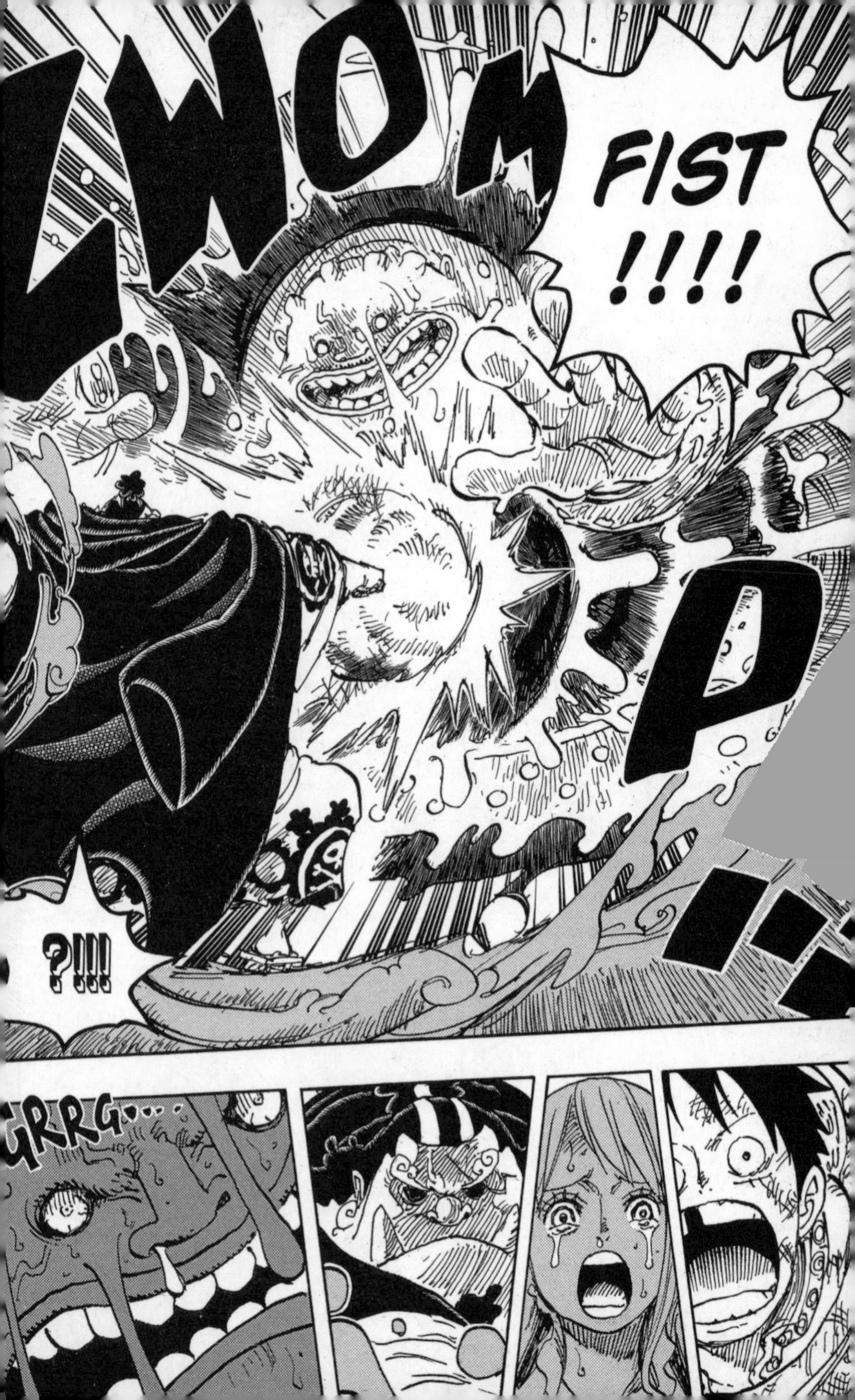
FIST !!!!
WHOMP
?!!!
GRRG...

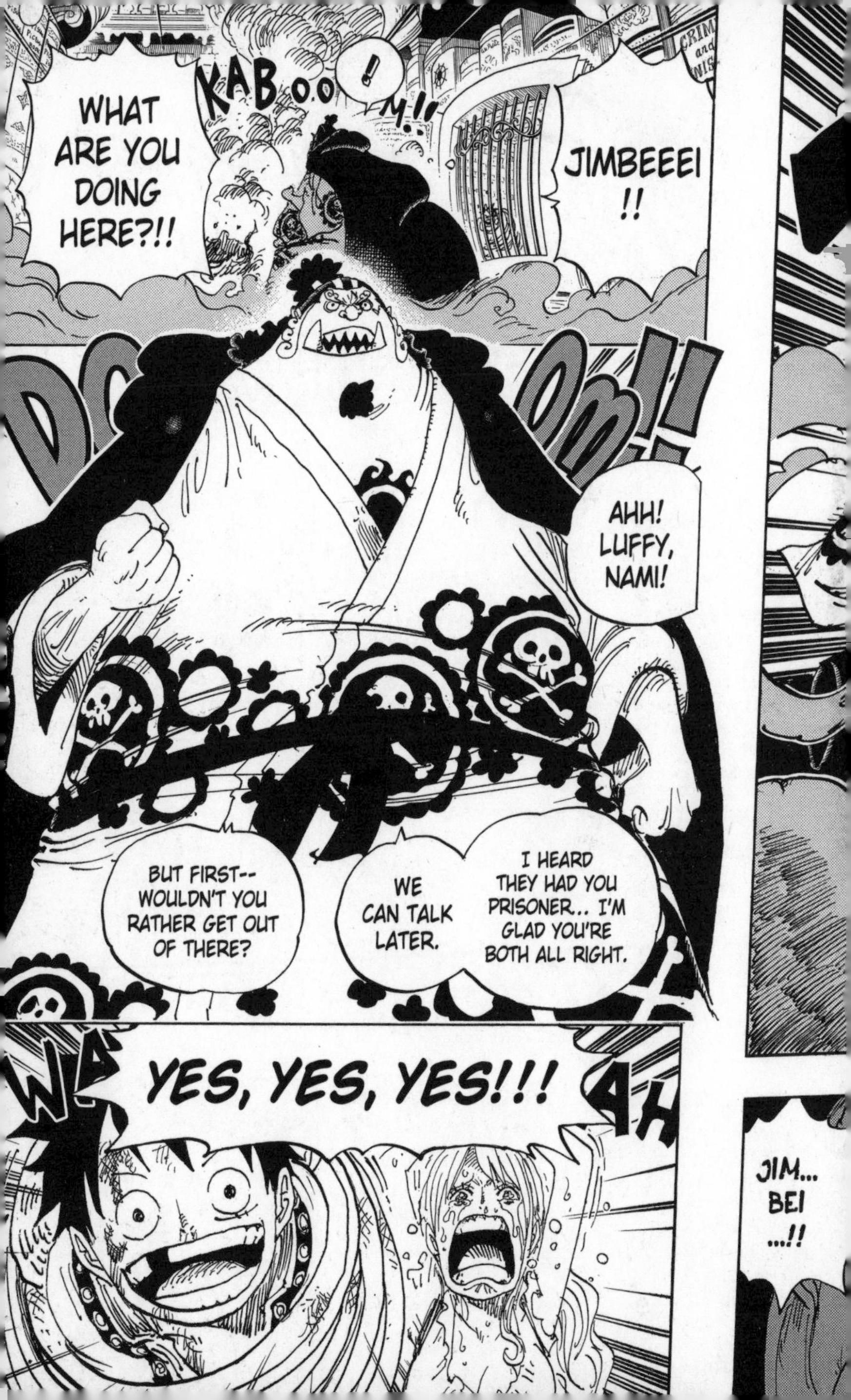
JIM... BEI ...!!
KABOOM!!
!
JIMBEEEI !!
WHAT ARE YOU DOING HERE?!!
AHH! LUFFY, NAMI!
I HEARD THEY HAD YOU PRISONER... I'M GLAD YOU'RE BOTH ALL RIGHT.
WE CAN TALK LATER.
BUT FIRST-- WOULDN'T YOU RATHER GET OUT OF THERE?
YES, YES, YES!!!

SBS Question Corner

(420 Land, Hong Kong)

Q: Heso, Oda Sensei!! The minks are animals, and yet in the food they gave Luffy in volume 82, there was meat. Are they cannibals? I'm so obsessed with this idea, I get five hours of sleep a night.

--Guru-Mayuki

A: That's right. In volume 81 there was a scene where he was chowing down, and the answer was revealed. In chapter 807, Carrot said the meat was "hippo, lizard, alligator and frog." The minks are essentially people who were born with the characteristics of furred animals, so they don't eat other furred animals, but they do eat the meat of birds, reptiles and amphibians.

Q: I bought this figure of Nami. Where should I put it?

--Captain Nobuo

A: I don't know, man!! ₹

Q: Odacchi… Let's start the SBS.
…Oh, actually, it started a while ago.
                    --Kakkun Shogo

A: What the heck, man?! ₹

©Eiichiro Oda/Shueisha -
Fuji TV - Toei Animation

Q: Odachiiii!!!!! In chapter 850, Pudding has a third eye on her forehead!! Does that mean the three-eyed girl in chapter 651 was Pudding? Clear this up for us!

--Resident of New Kama Land

A: That's right! You can see Nitro there too.

Chapter 852:
GERMA'S FAILURE

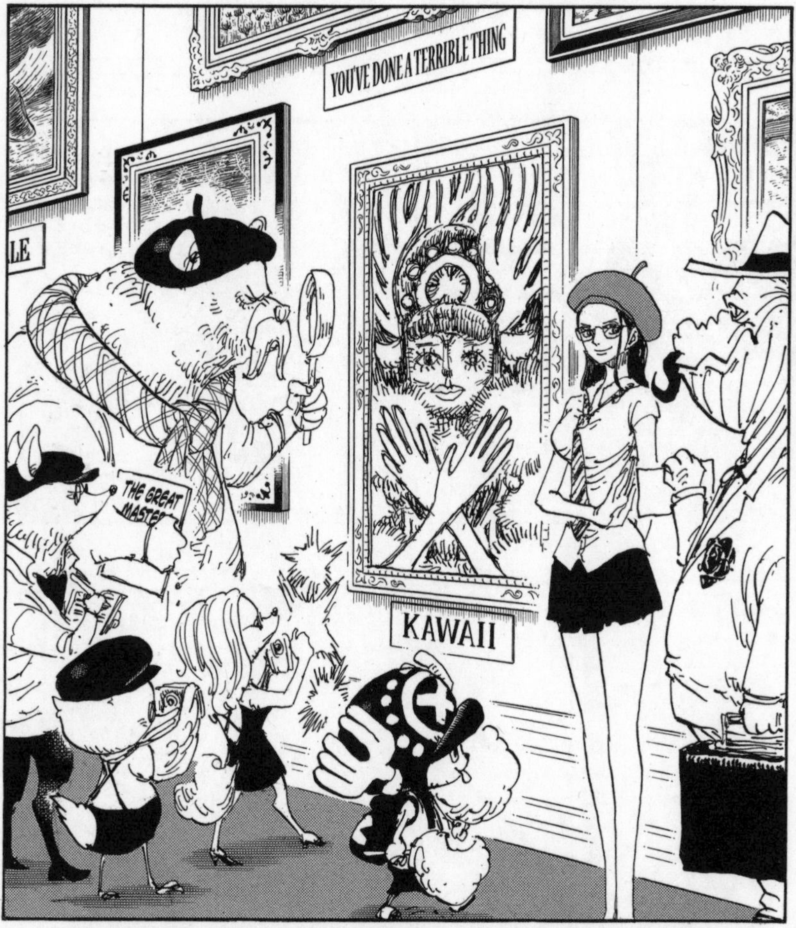
YOU'VE DONE A TERRIBLE THING
LE
THE GREAT MASTER
KAWAII

REQUEST: "AN ART CRITIC BEAR APPROVINGLY APPRAISES ROBIN'S GALLERY EXHIBITION" BY HIYU MORI FROM HYOGO

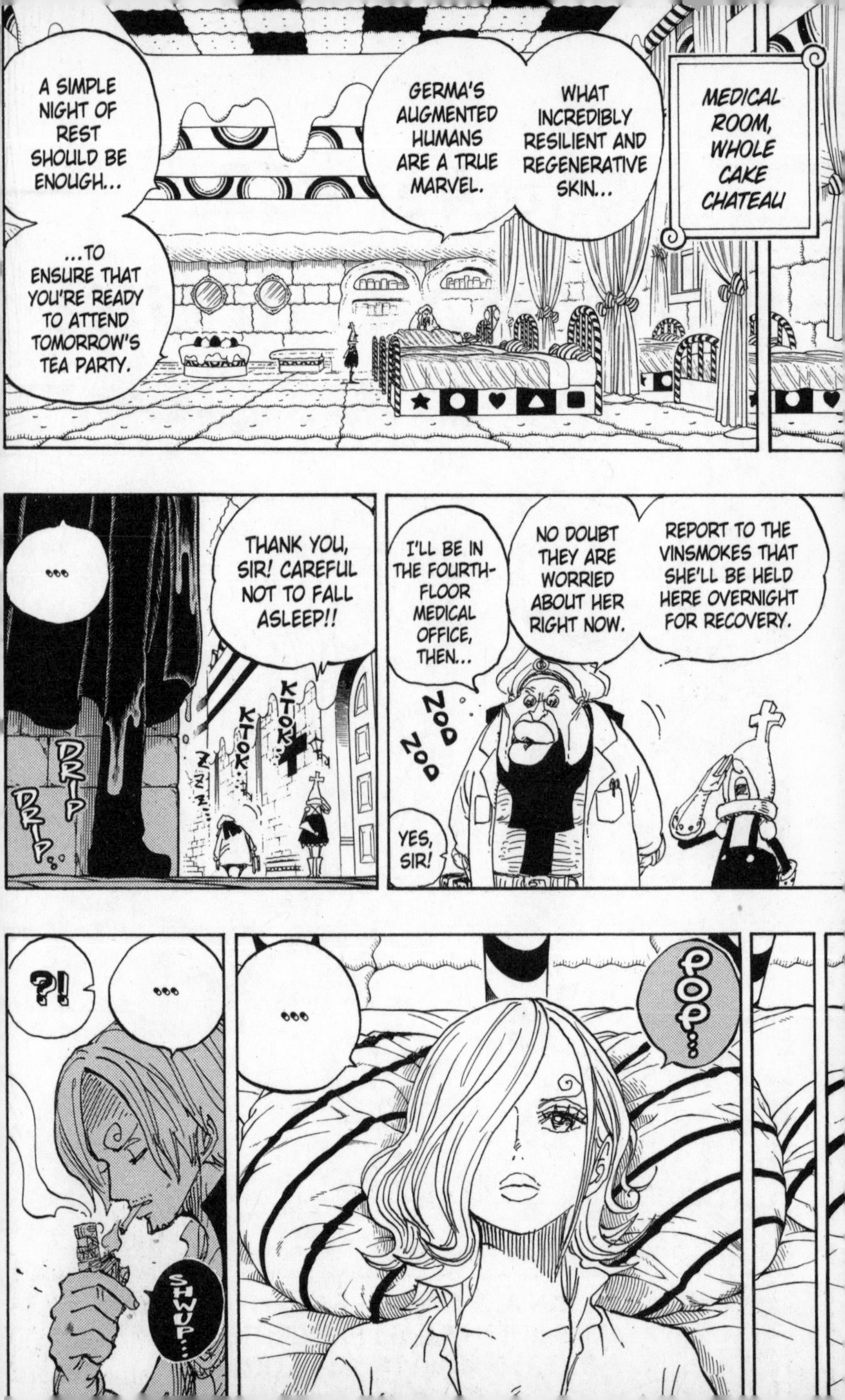
MEDICAL ROOM, WHOLE CAKE CHATEAU
WHAT INCREDIBLY RESILIENT AND REGENERATIVE SKIN...
GERMA'S AUGMENTED HUMANS ARE A TRUE MARVEL.
A SIMPLE NIGHT OF REST SHOULD BE ENOUGH...
...TO ENSURE THAT YOU'RE READY TO ATTEND TOMORROW'S TEA PARTY.
REPORT TO THE VINSMOKES THAT SHE'LL BE HELD HERE OVERNIGHT FOR RECOVERY.
NO DOUBT THEY ARE WORRIED ABOUT HER RIGHT NOW.
I'LL BE IN THE FOURTH-FLOOR MEDICAL OFFICE, THEN...
NOD NOD
YES, SIR!
THANK YOU, SIR! CAREFUL NOT TO FALL ASLEEP!!
KTOK
KTOK
ZZZ
...
DRIP
DRIP
POP...
...
...
?!
SHWUP...

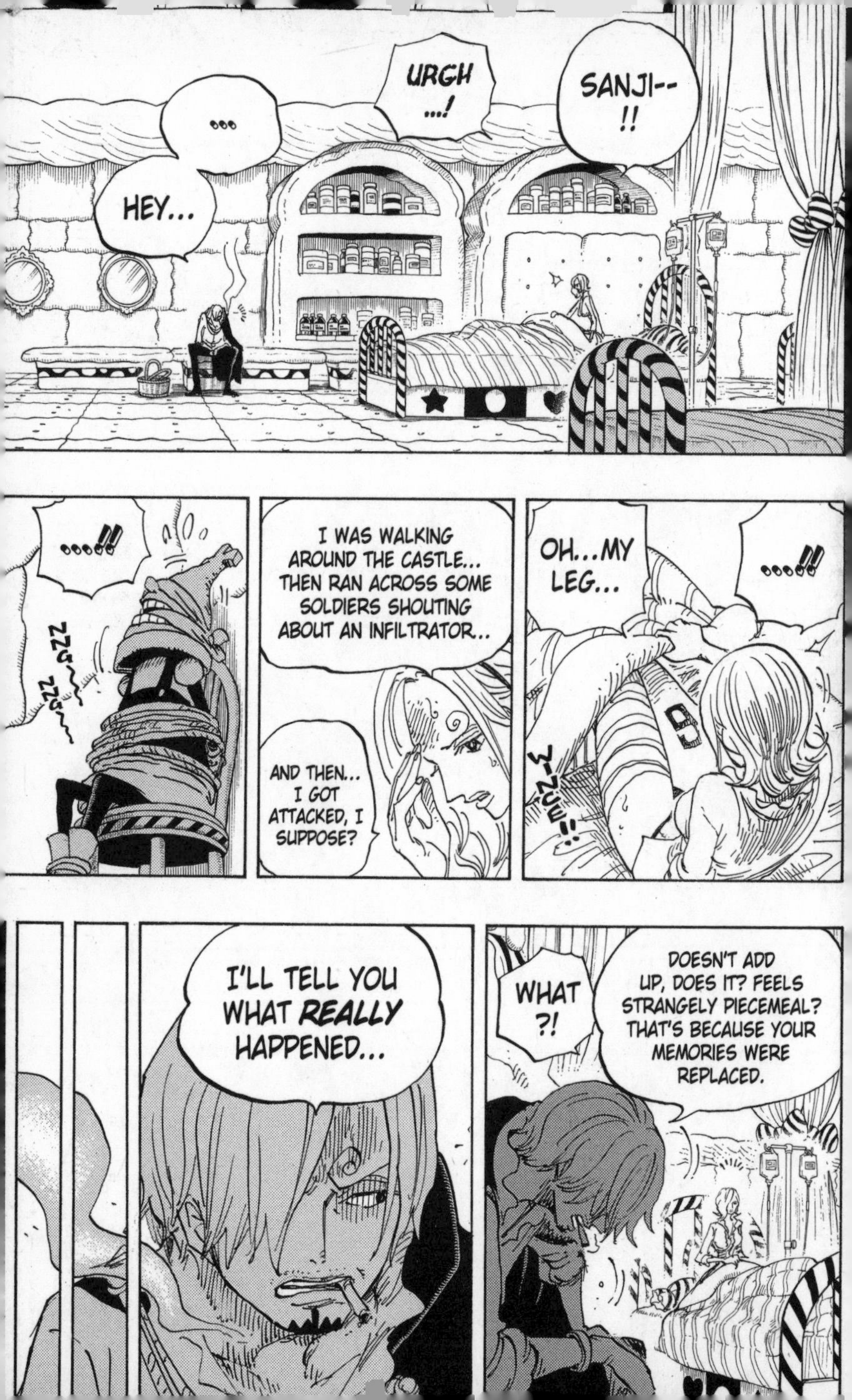
SANJI-- !!
URGH ...!
...
HEY...
...!!
OH...MY LEG...
W-ZUE!!
I WAS WALKING AROUND THE CASTLE... THEN RAN ACROSS SOME SOLDIERS SHOUTING ABOUT AN INFILTRATOR...
AND THEN... I GOT ATTACKED, I SUPPOSE?
...!!
ZZG~ ZZG~
DOESN'T ADD UP, DOES IT? FEELS STRANGELY PIECEMEAL? THAT'S BECAUSE YOUR MEMORIES WERE REPLACED.
WHAT ?!
I'LL TELL YOU WHAT *REALLY* HAPPENED...

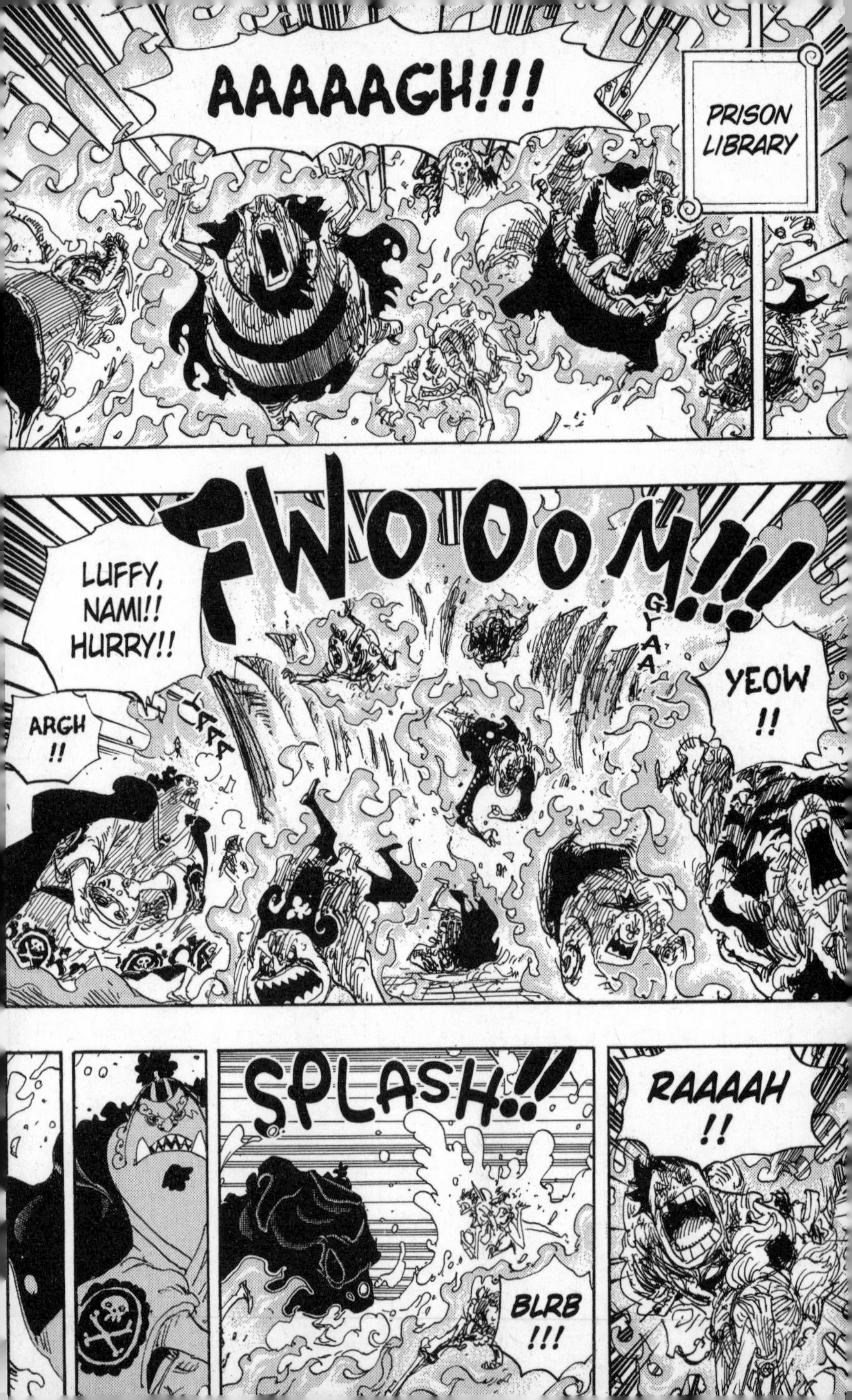
PRISON LIBRARY
AAAAAGH!!!
FWOOOM!!!
GYAA
LUFFY, NAMI!! HURRY!!
YEOW!!
YAAA
ARGH!!
RAAAAH!!
SPLASH!!
BLRB!!!

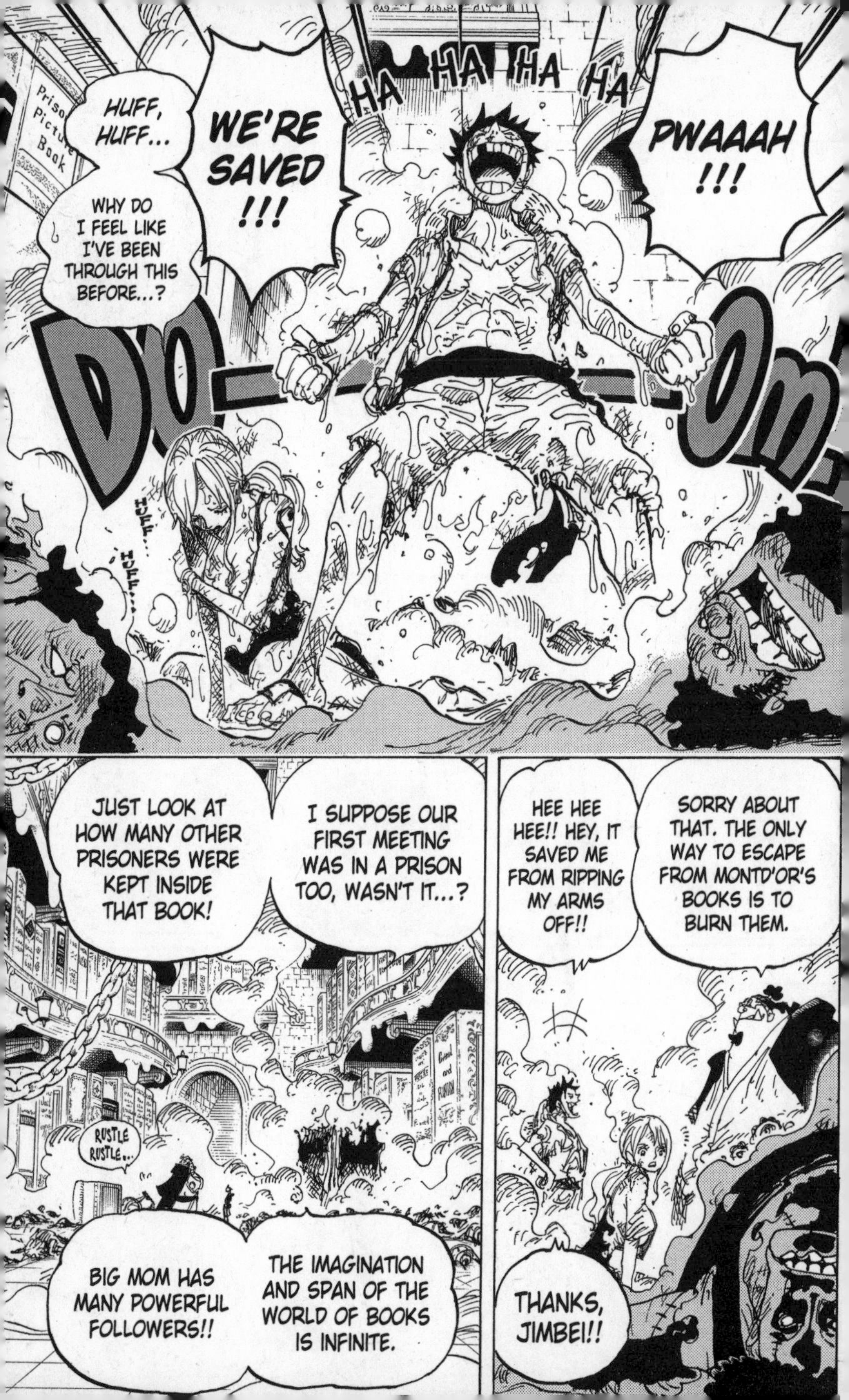
PWAAAH !!!
HA HA HA HA
WE'RE SAVED !!!
HUFF, HUFF...
WHY DO I FEEL LIKE I'VE BEEN THROUGH THIS BEFORE...?
DO—OM
HUFF... HUFF...
SORRY ABOUT THAT. THE ONLY WAY TO ESCAPE FROM MONTD'OR'S BOOKS IS TO BURN THEM.
HEE HEE HEE!! HEY, IT SAVED ME FROM RIPPING MY ARMS OFF!!
THANKS, JIMBEI!!
I SUPPOSE OUR FIRST MEETING WAS IN A PRISON TOO, WASN'T IT...?
JUST LOOK AT HOW MANY OTHER PRISONERS WERE KEPT INSIDE THAT BOOK!
RUSTLE RUSTLE...
THE IMAGINATION AND SPAN OF THE WORLD OF BOOKS IS INFINITE.
BIG MOM HAS MANY POWERFUL FOLLOWERS!!

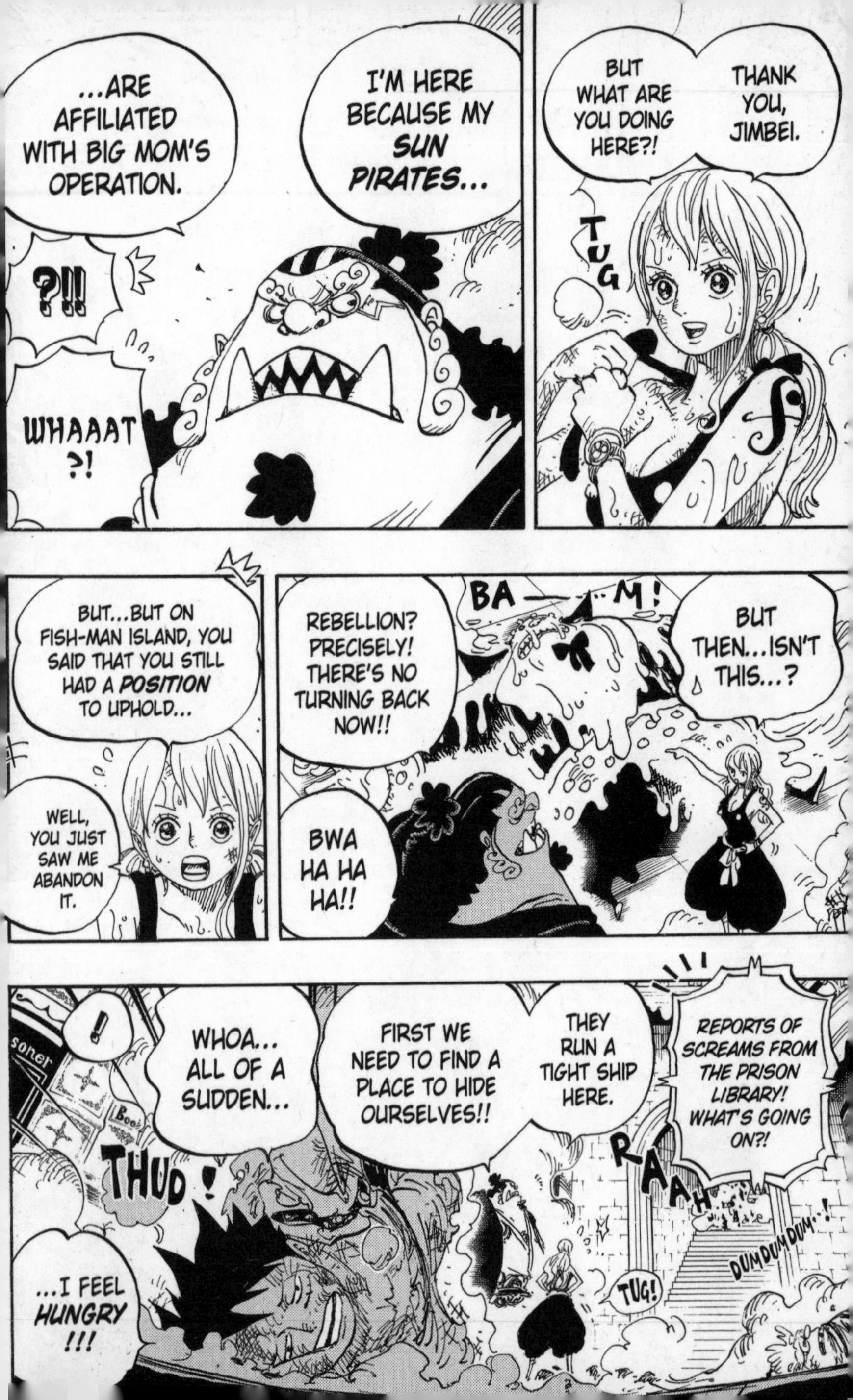
THANK YOU, JIMBEI.
BUT WHAT ARE YOU DOING HERE?!
TUG
I'M HERE BECAUSE MY SUN PIRATES...
...ARE AFFILIATED WITH BIG MOM'S OPERATION.
?!!
WHAAAT ?!
BUT THEN...ISN'T THIS...?
BA—M!
REBELLION? PRECISELY! THERE'S NO TURNING BACK NOW!!
BWA HA HA HA!!
BUT...BUT ON FISH-MAN ISLAND, YOU SAID THAT YOU STILL HAD A POSITION TO UPHOLD...
WELL, YOU JUST SAW ME ABANDON IT.
REPORTS OF SCREAMS FROM THE PRISON LIBRARY! WHAT'S GOING ON?!
THEY RUN A TIGHT SHIP HERE.
RAAAH
DUM DUM DUM
FIRST WE NEED TO FIND A PLACE TO HIDE OURSELVES!!
TUG!
WHOA... ALL OF A SUDDEN...
!
THUD!
...I FEEL HUNGRY!!!

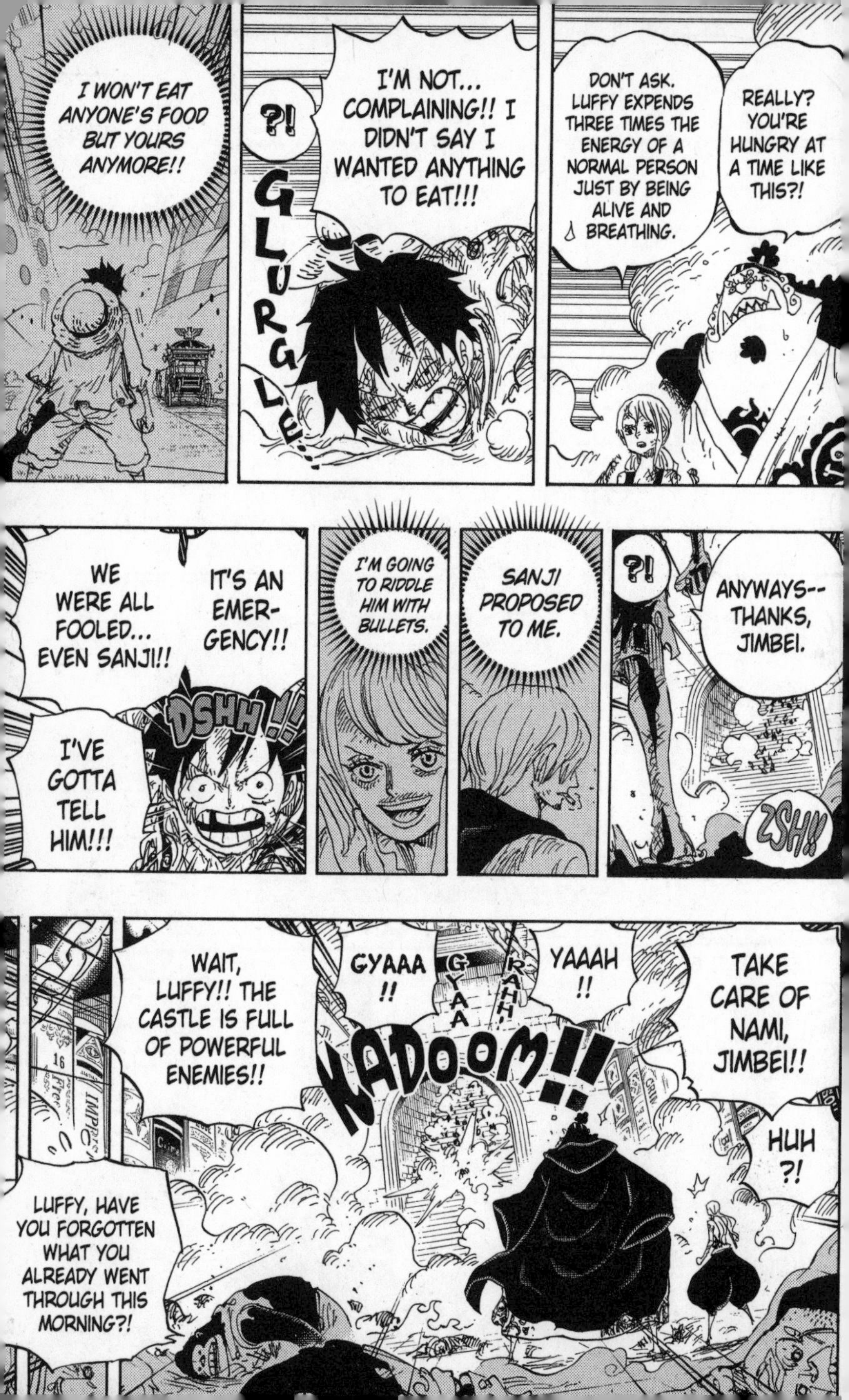
REALLY? YOU'RE HUNGRY AT A TIME LIKE THIS?!
DON'T ASK. LUFFY EXPENDS THREE TIMES THE ENERGY OF A NORMAL PERSON JUST BY BEING ALIVE AND BREATHING.
I'M NOT... COMPLAINING!! I DIDN'T SAY I WANTED ANYTHING TO EAT!!!
?!
GLURGLE...
I WON'T EAT ANYONE'S FOOD BUT YOURS ANYMORE!!
ANYWAYS--THANKS, JIMBEI.
?!
ZSH!!
SANJI PROPOSED TO ME.
I'M GOING TO RIDDLE HIM WITH BULLETS.
IT'S AN EMERGENCY!!
WE WERE ALL FOOLED... EVEN SANJI!!
DSHH!!
I'VE GOTTA TELL HIM!!!
TAKE CARE OF NAMI, JIMBEI!!
YAAAH!!
RAHH!
GYAAA!!
GYAA
WAIT, LUFFY!! THE CASTLE IS FULL OF POWERFUL ENEMIES!!
KADOOM!!
HUH?!
LUFFY, HAVE YOU FORGOTTEN WHAT YOU ALREADY WENT THROUGH THIS MORNING?!

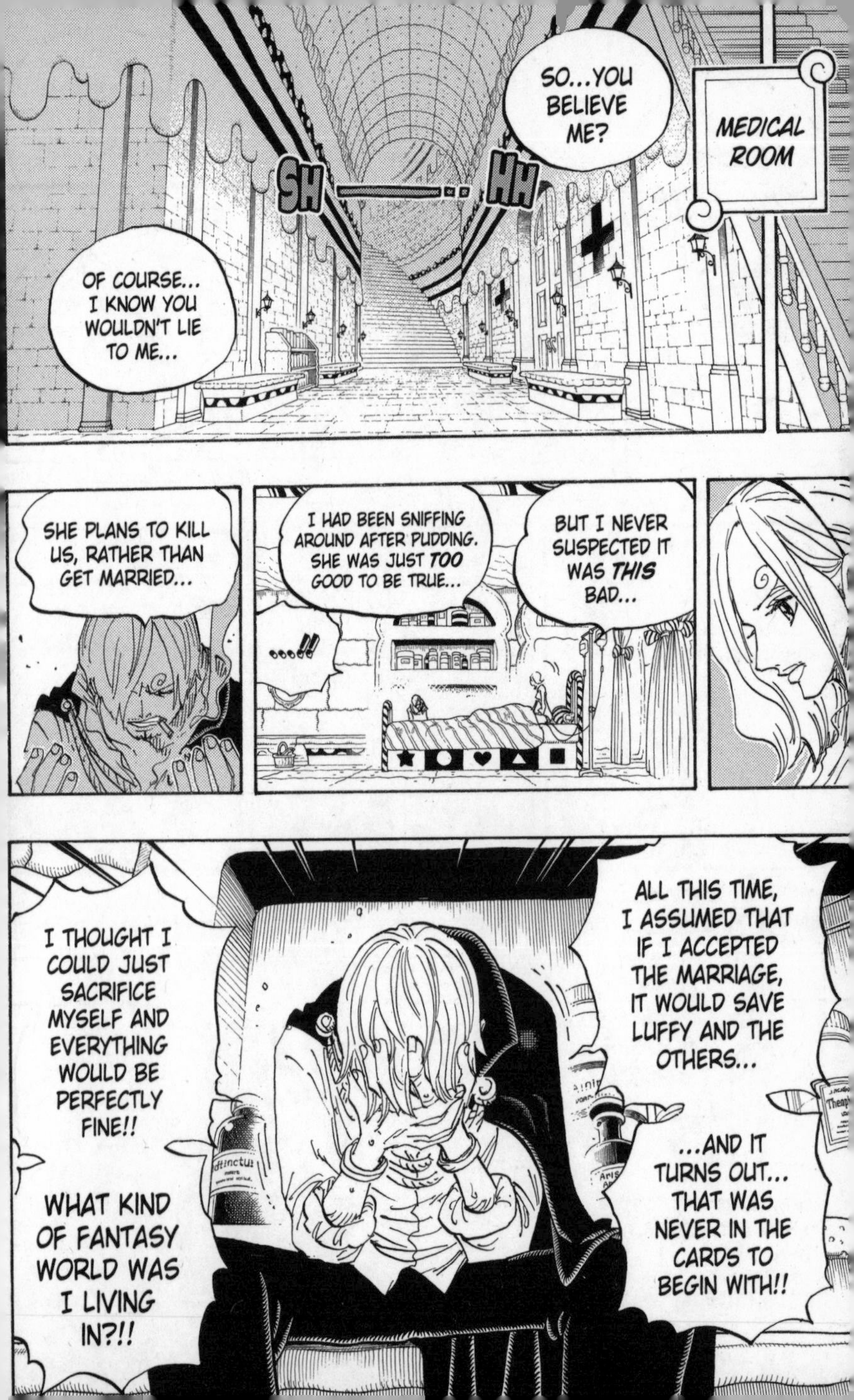
MEDICAL ROOM
SO...YOU BELIEVE ME?
SH——..HH
OF COURSE... I KNOW YOU WOULDN'T LIE TO ME...
BUT I NEVER SUSPECTED IT WAS *THIS* BAD...
I HAD BEEN SNIFFING AROUND AFTER PUDDING. SHE WAS JUST *TOO* GOOD TO BE TRUE...
....!!
SHE PLANS TO KILL US, RATHER THAN GET MARRIED...
ALL THIS TIME, I ASSUMED THAT IF I ACCEPTED THE MARRIAGE, IT WOULD SAVE LUFFY AND THE OTHERS...
I THOUGHT I COULD JUST SACRIFICE MYSELF AND EVERYTHING WOULD BE PERFECTLY FINE!!
...AND IT TURNS OUT... THAT WAS NEVER IN THE CARDS TO BEGIN WITH!!
WHAT KIND OF FANTASY WORLD WAS I LIVING IN?!!

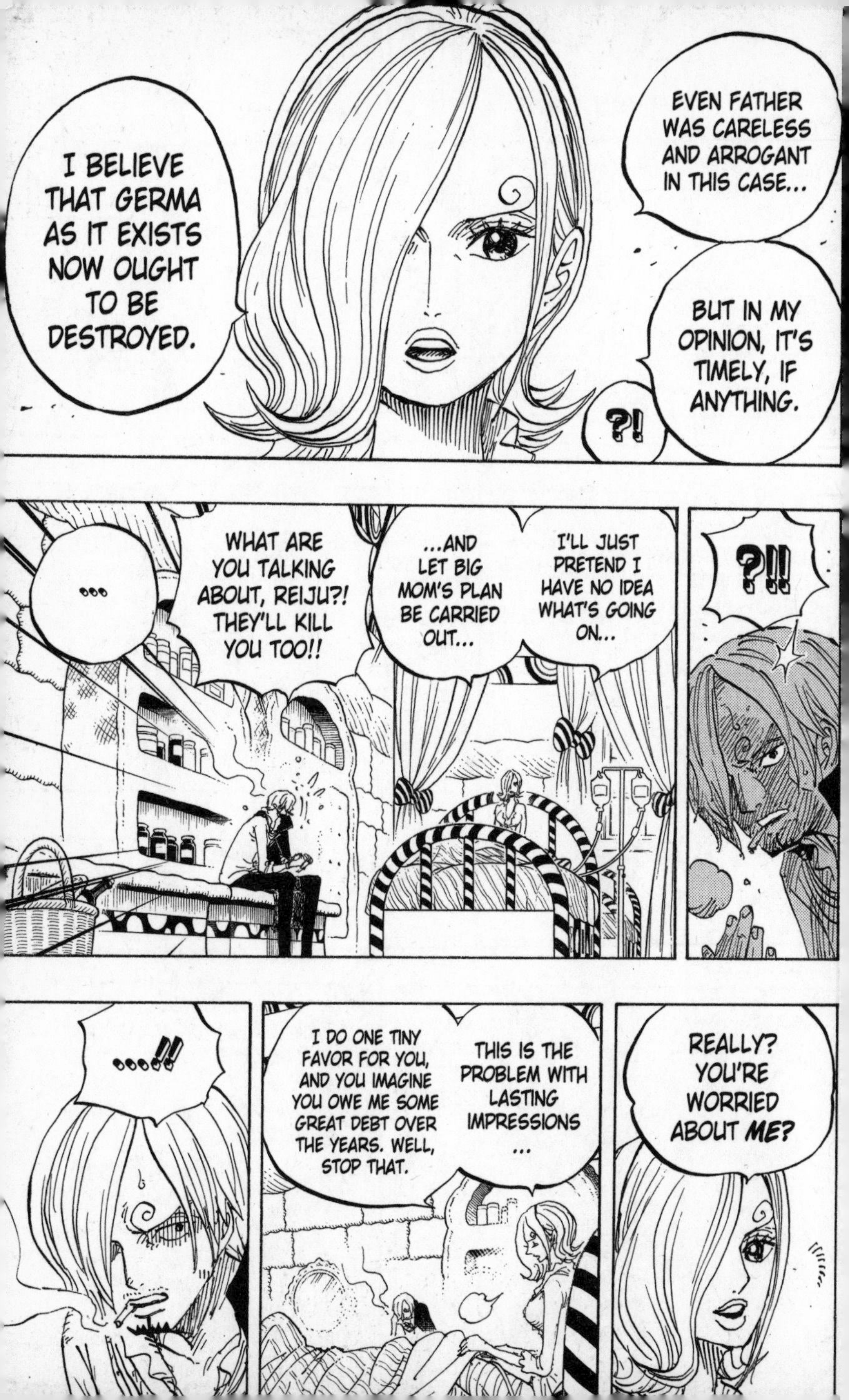
EVEN FATHER WAS CARELESS AND ARROGANT IN THIS CASE...
BUT IN MY OPINION, IT'S TIMELY, IF ANYTHING.
?!
I BELIEVE THAT GERMA AS IT EXISTS NOW OUGHT TO BE DESTROYED.
?!!
I'LL JUST PRETEND I HAVE NO IDEA WHAT'S GOING ON...
...AND LET BIG MOM'S PLAN BE CARRIED OUT...
WHAT ARE YOU TALKING ABOUT, REIJU?! THEY'LL KILL YOU TOO!!
...
REALLY? YOU'RE WORRIED ABOUT *ME*?
THIS IS THE PROBLEM WITH LASTING IMPRESSIONS...
I DO ONE TINY FAVOR FOR YOU, AND YOU IMAGINE YOU OWE ME SOME GREAT DEBT OVER THE YEARS. WELL, STOP THAT.
...!!

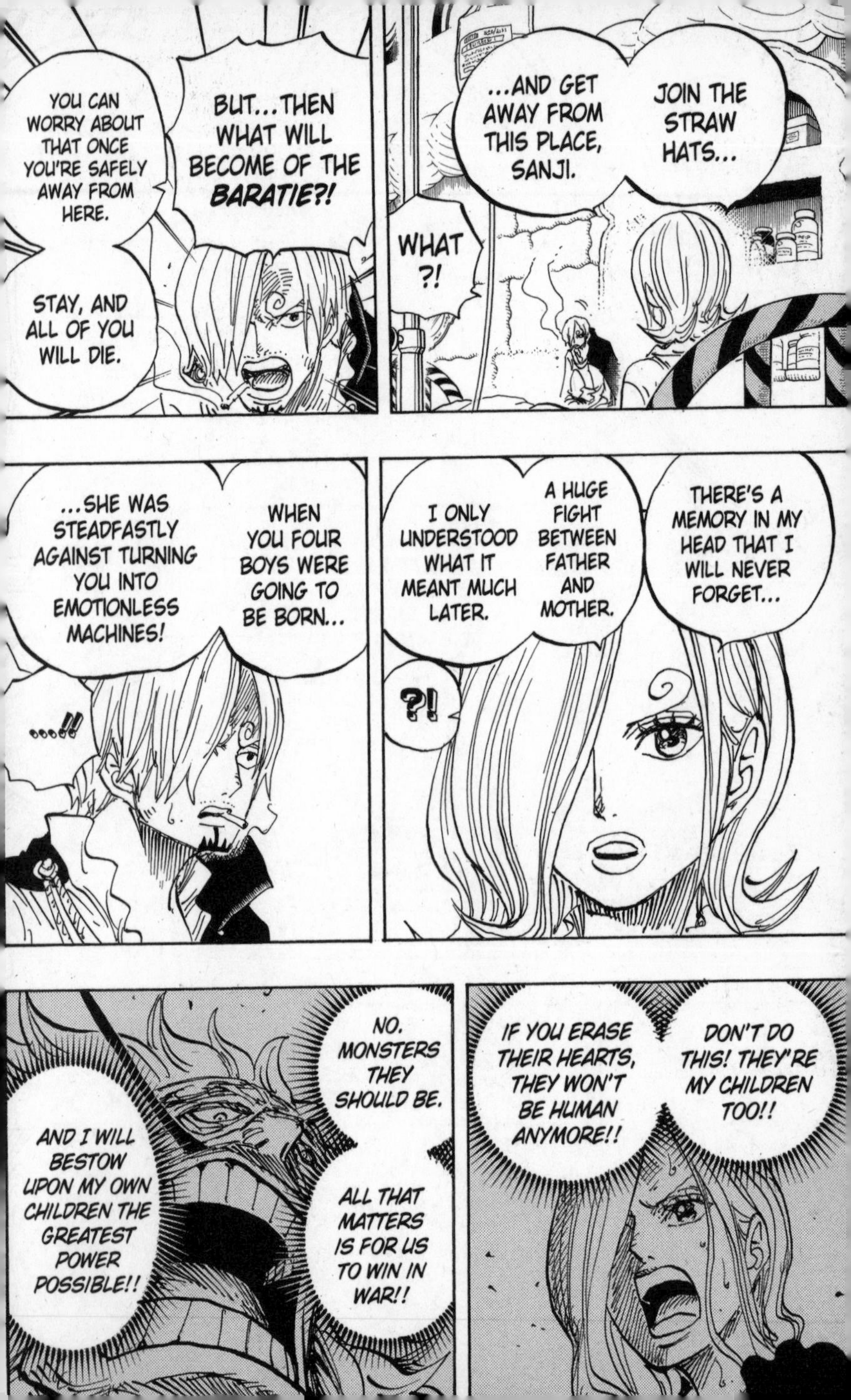
JOIN THE STRAW HATS...
...AND GET AWAY FROM THIS PLACE, SANJI.
WHAT ?!
BUT...THEN WHAT WILL BECOME OF THE BARATIE?!
YOU CAN WORRY ABOUT THAT ONCE YOU'RE SAFELY AWAY FROM HERE.
STAY, AND ALL OF YOU WILL DIE.
THERE'S A MEMORY IN MY HEAD THAT I WILL NEVER FORGET...
A HUGE FIGHT BETWEEN FATHER AND MOTHER.
I ONLY UNDERSTOOD WHAT IT MEANT MUCH LATER.
?!
WHEN YOU FOUR BOYS WERE GOING TO BE BORN...
...SHE WAS STEADFASTLY AGAINST TURNING YOU INTO EMOTIONLESS MACHINES!
...!!
DON'T DO THIS! THEY'RE MY CHILDREN TOO!!
IF YOU ERASE THEIR HEARTS, THEY WON'T BE HUMAN ANYMORE!!
NO. MONSTERS THEY SHOULD BE.
ALL THAT MATTERS IS FOR US TO WIN IN WAR!!
AND I WILL BESTOW UPON MY OWN CHILDREN THE GREATEST POWER POSSIBLE!!

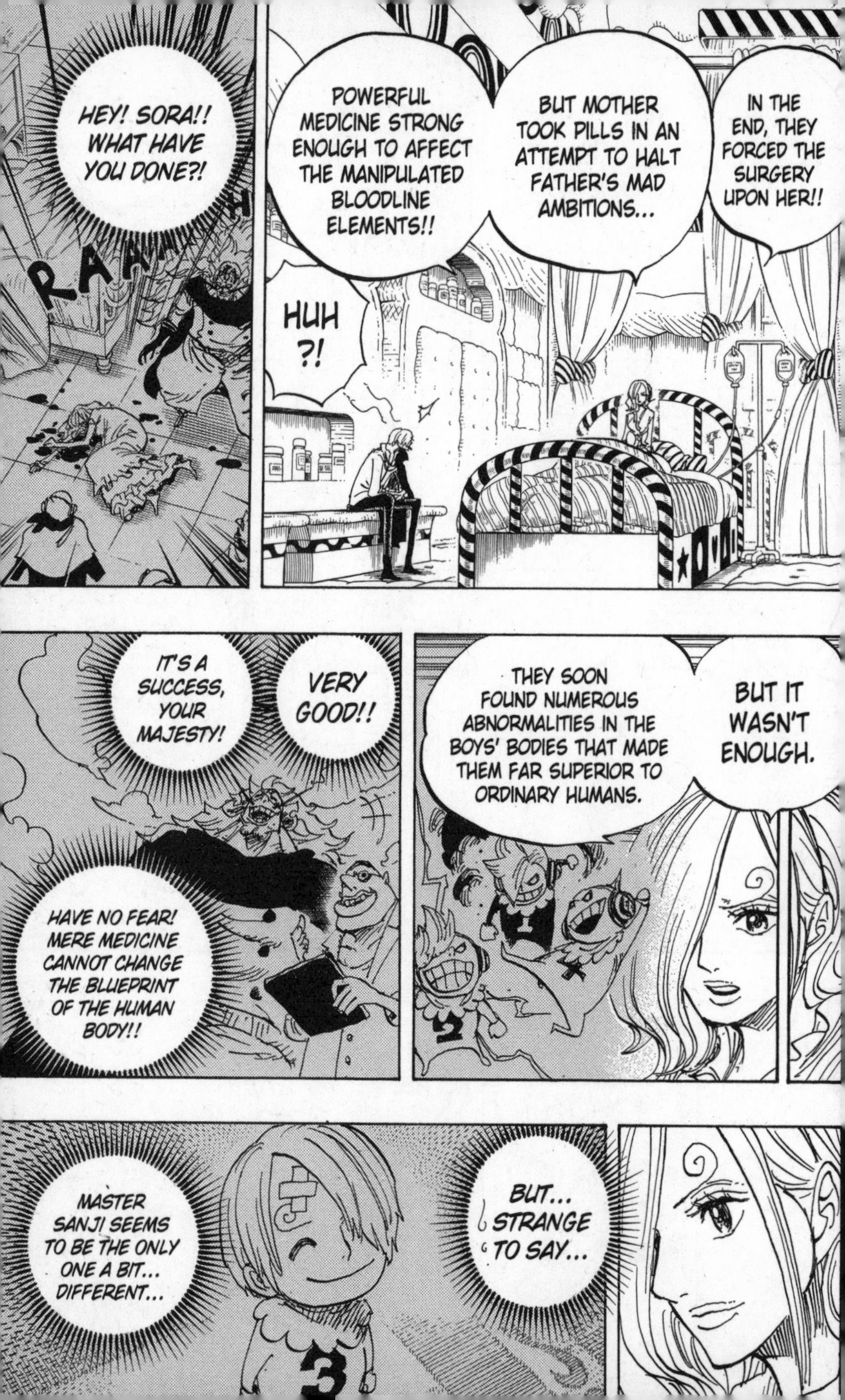
IN THE END, THEY FORCED THE SURGERY UPON HER!!
BUT MOTHER TOOK PILLS IN AN ATTEMPT TO HALT FATHER'S MAD AMBITIONS...
POWERFUL MEDICINE STRONG ENOUGH TO AFFECT THE MANIPULATED BLOODLINE ELEMENTS!!
HUH ?!
HEY! SORA!! WHAT HAVE YOU DONE?!
THEY SOON FOUND NUMEROUS ABNORMALITIES IN THE BOYS' BODIES THAT MADE THEM FAR SUPERIOR TO ORDINARY HUMANS.
BUT IT WASN'T ENOUGH.
IT'S A SUCCESS, YOUR MAJESTY!
VERY GOOD!!
HAVE NO FEAR! MERE MEDICINE CANNOT CHANGE THE BLUEPRINT OF THE HUMAN BODY!!
BUT... STRANGE TO SAY...
MASTER SANJI SEEMS TO BE THE ONLY ONE A BIT... DIFFERENT...

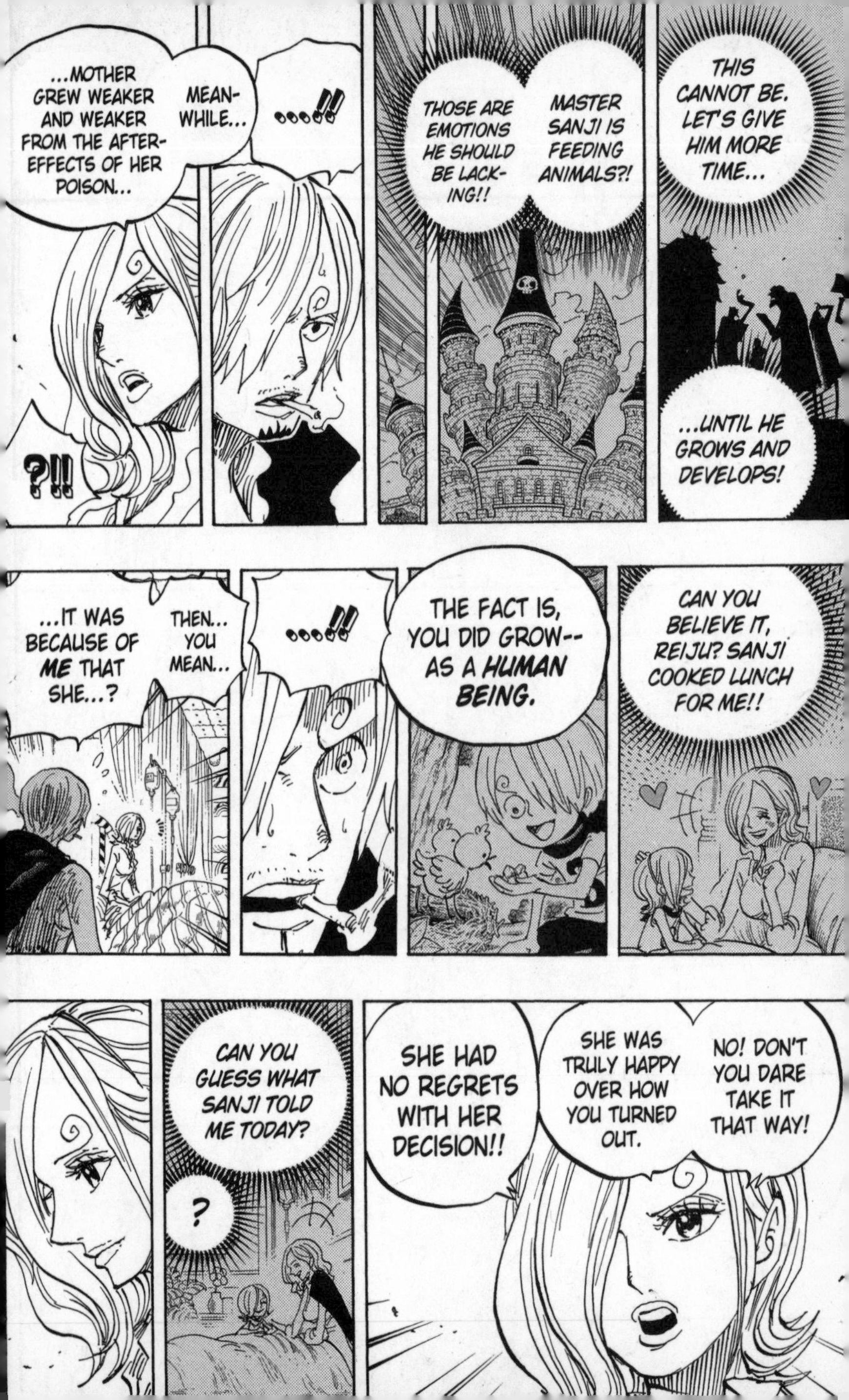
THIS CANNOT BE. LET'S GIVE HIM MORE TIME...
...UNTIL HE GROWS AND DEVELOPS!
MASTER SANJI IS FEEDING ANIMALS?!
THOSE ARE EMOTIONS HE SHOULD BE LACKING!!
...!!
MEAN-WHILE...
...MOTHER GREW WEAKER AND WEAKER FROM THE AFTER-EFFECTS OF HER POISON...
?!!
CAN YOU BELIEVE IT, REIJU? SANJI COOKED LUNCH FOR ME!!
THE FACT IS, YOU DID GROW-- AS A HUMAN BEING.
...!!
THEN... YOU MEAN...
...IT WAS BECAUSE OF ME THAT SHE...?
NO! DON'T YOU DARE TAKE IT THAT WAY!
SHE WAS TRULY HAPPY OVER HOW YOU TURNED OUT.
SHE HAD NO REGRETS WITH HER DECISION!!
CAN YOU GUESS WHAT SANJI TOLD ME TODAY?
?

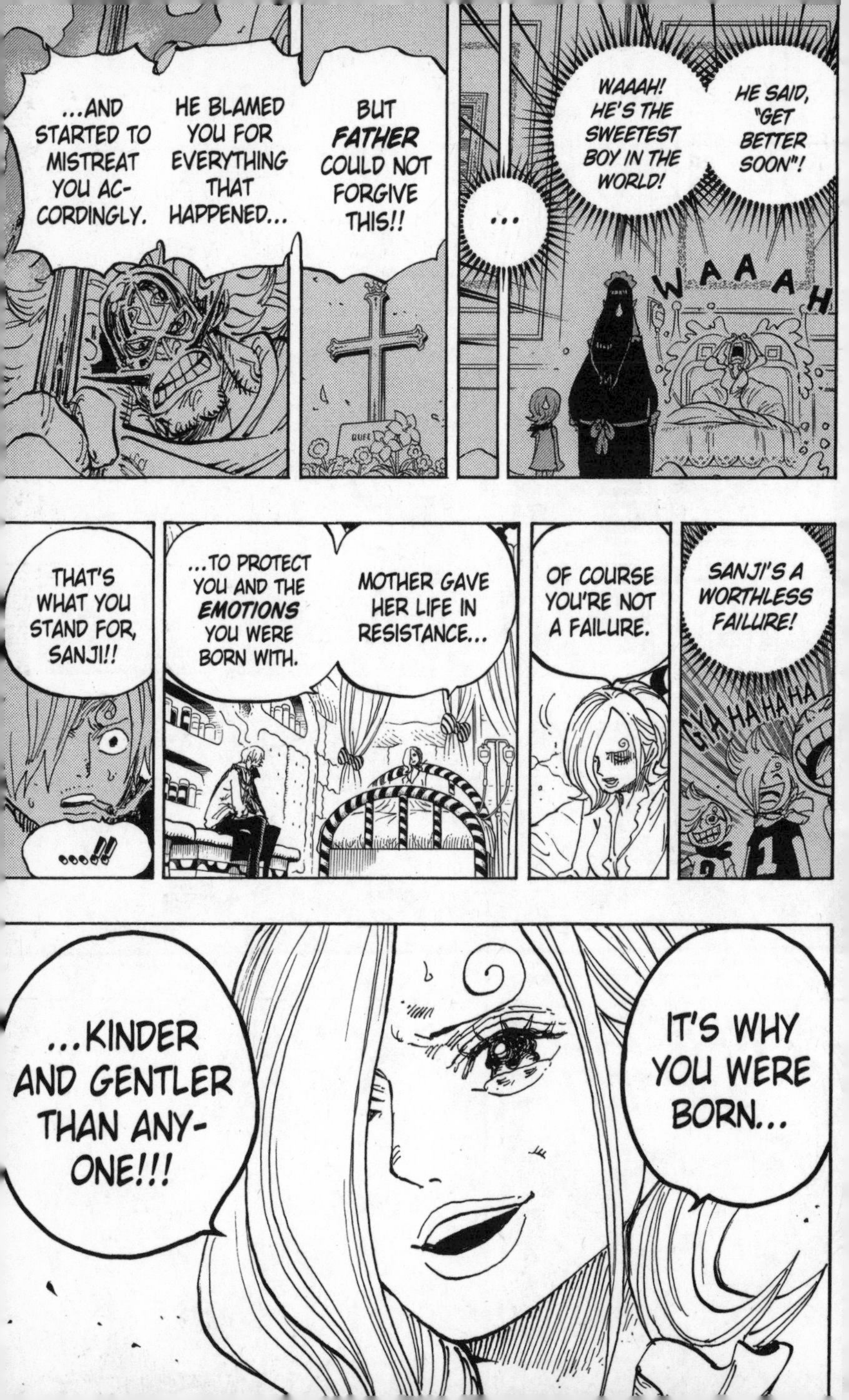

HE SAID, "GET BETTER SOON"!
WAAAH! HE'S THE SWEETEST BOY IN THE WORLD!
...
WAAAH
BUT *FATHER* COULD NOT FORGIVE THIS!!
HE BLAMED YOU FOR EVERYTHING THAT HAPPENED...
...AND STARTED TO MISTREAT YOU AC-CORDINGLY.
SANJI'S A WORTHLESS FAILURE!
GYAHAHAHA
OF COURSE YOU'RE NOT A FAILURE.
MOTHER GAVE HER LIFE IN RESISTANCE...
...TO PROTECT YOU AND THE *EMOTIONS* YOU WERE BORN WITH.
THAT'S WHAT YOU STAND FOR, SANJI!!
....!!
IT'S WHY YOU WERE BORN...
...KINDER AND GENTLER THAN ANY-ONE!!!

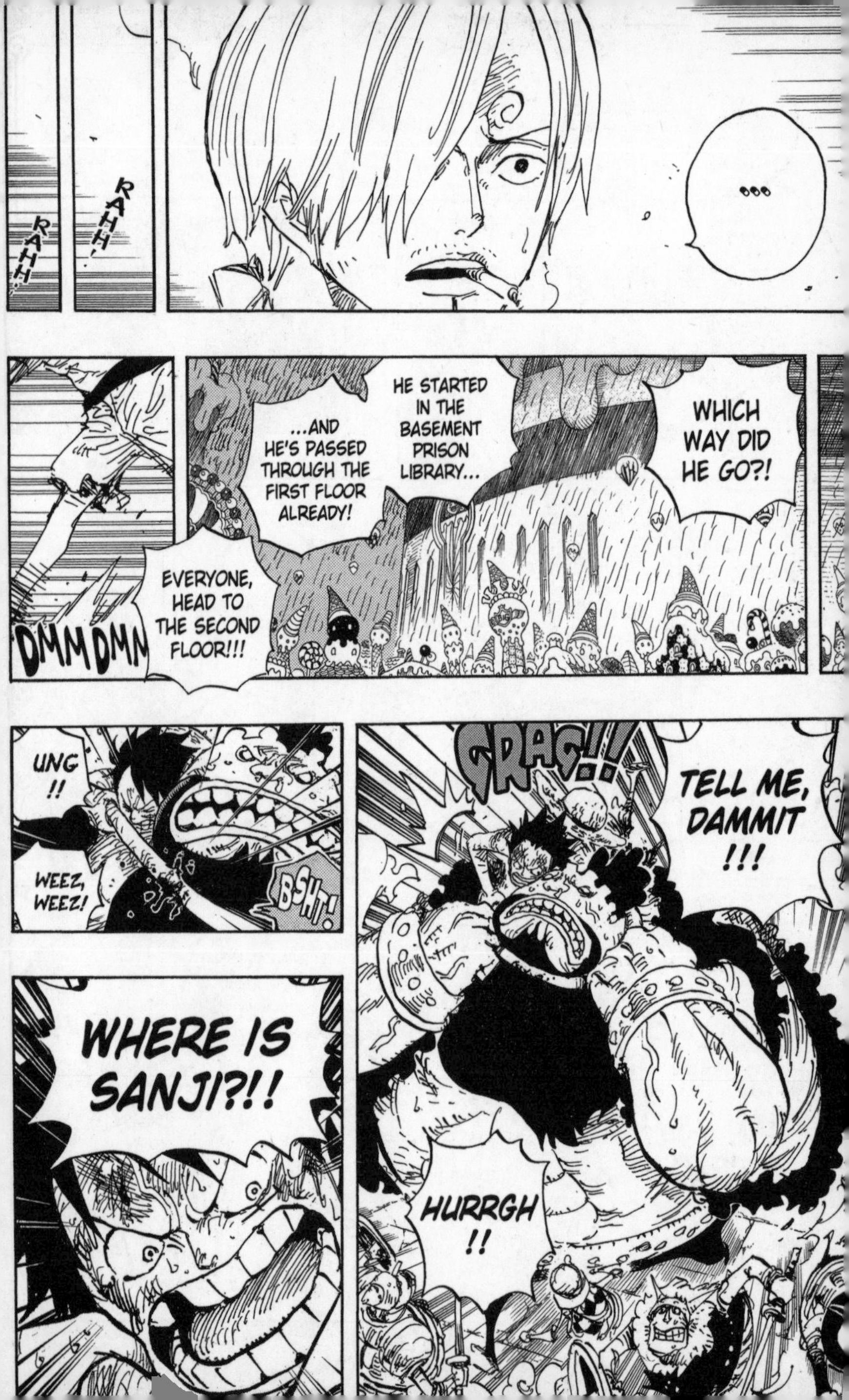
...
RAHHH!
RAHHH!
WHICH WAY DID HE GO?!
HE STARTED IN THE BASEMENT PRISON LIBRARY...
...AND HE'S PASSED THROUGH THE FIRST FLOOR ALREADY!
EVERYONE, HEAD TO THE SECOND FLOOR!!!
DMM DMN
GRAG!!!
TELL ME, DAMMIT!!!
HURRGH!!
UNG!!
BSHT!
WEEZ, WEEZ!
WHERE IS SANJI?!!

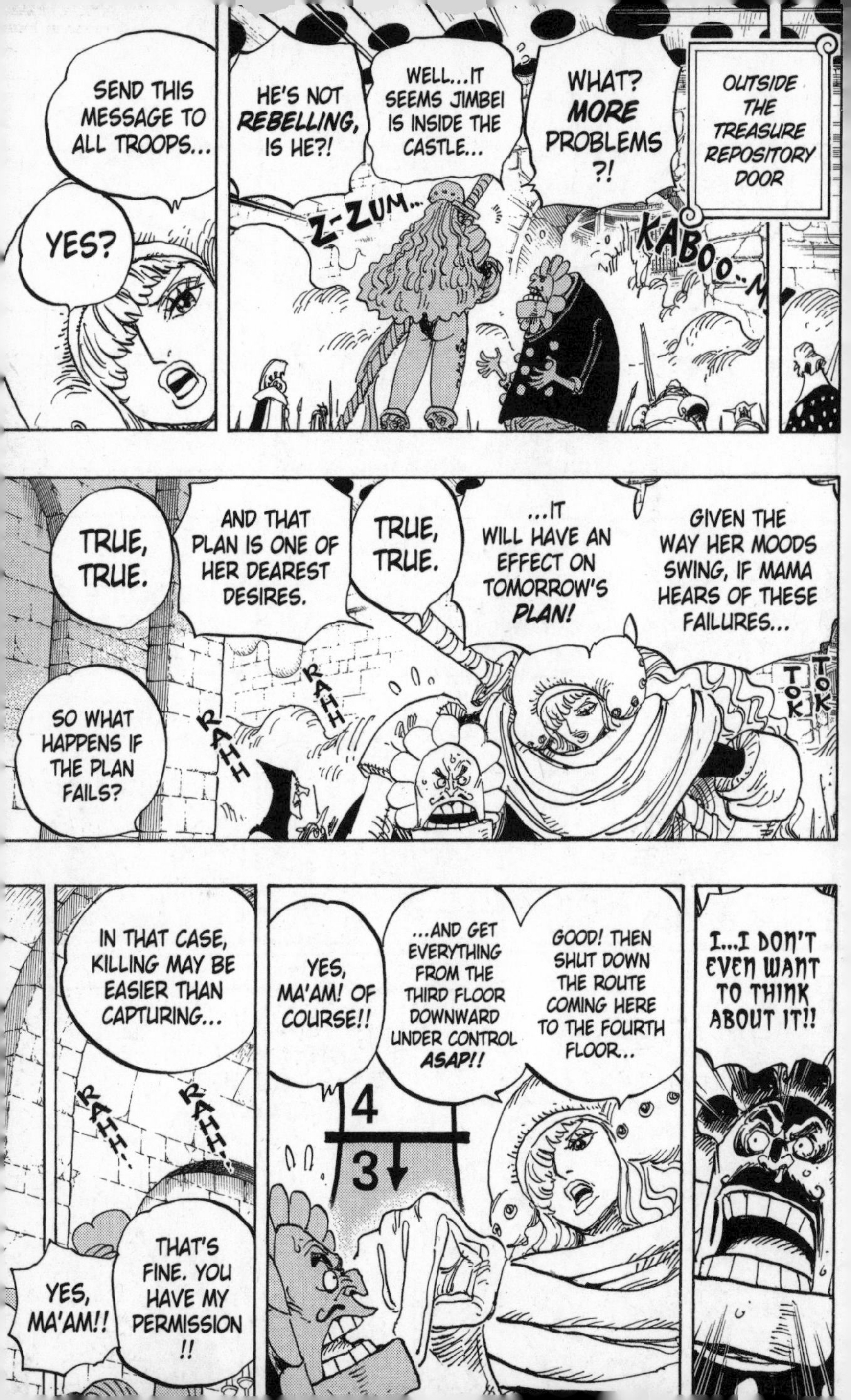
OUTSIDE THE TREASURE REPOSITORY DOOR
KABOO..M
WHAT? MORE PROBLEMS ?!
WELL...IT SEEMS JIMBEI IS INSIDE THE CASTLE...
HE'S NOT REBELLING, IS HE?!
Z-ZUM...
SEND THIS MESSAGE TO ALL TROOPS...
YES?
GIVEN THE WAY HER MOODS SWING, IF MAMA HEARS OF THESE FAILURES...
...IT WILL HAVE AN EFFECT ON TOMORROW'S PLAN!
TRUE, TRUE.
AND THAT PLAN IS ONE OF HER DEAREST DESIRES.
TRUE, TRUE.
TOK TOK
RAHH
RAHH
SO WHAT HAPPENS IF THE PLAN FAILS?
I...I DON'T EVEN WANT TO THINK ABOUT IT!!
GOOD! THEN SHUT DOWN THE ROUTE COMING HERE TO THE FOURTH FLOOR...
...AND GET EVERYTHING FROM THE THIRD FLOOR DOWNWARD UNDER CONTROL ASAP!!
YES, MA'AM! OF COURSE!!
4
3
IN THAT CASE, KILLING MAY BE EASIER THAN CAPTURING...
RAHH..
RAHH..
THAT'S FINE. YOU HAVE MY PERMISSION !!
YES, MA'AM!!

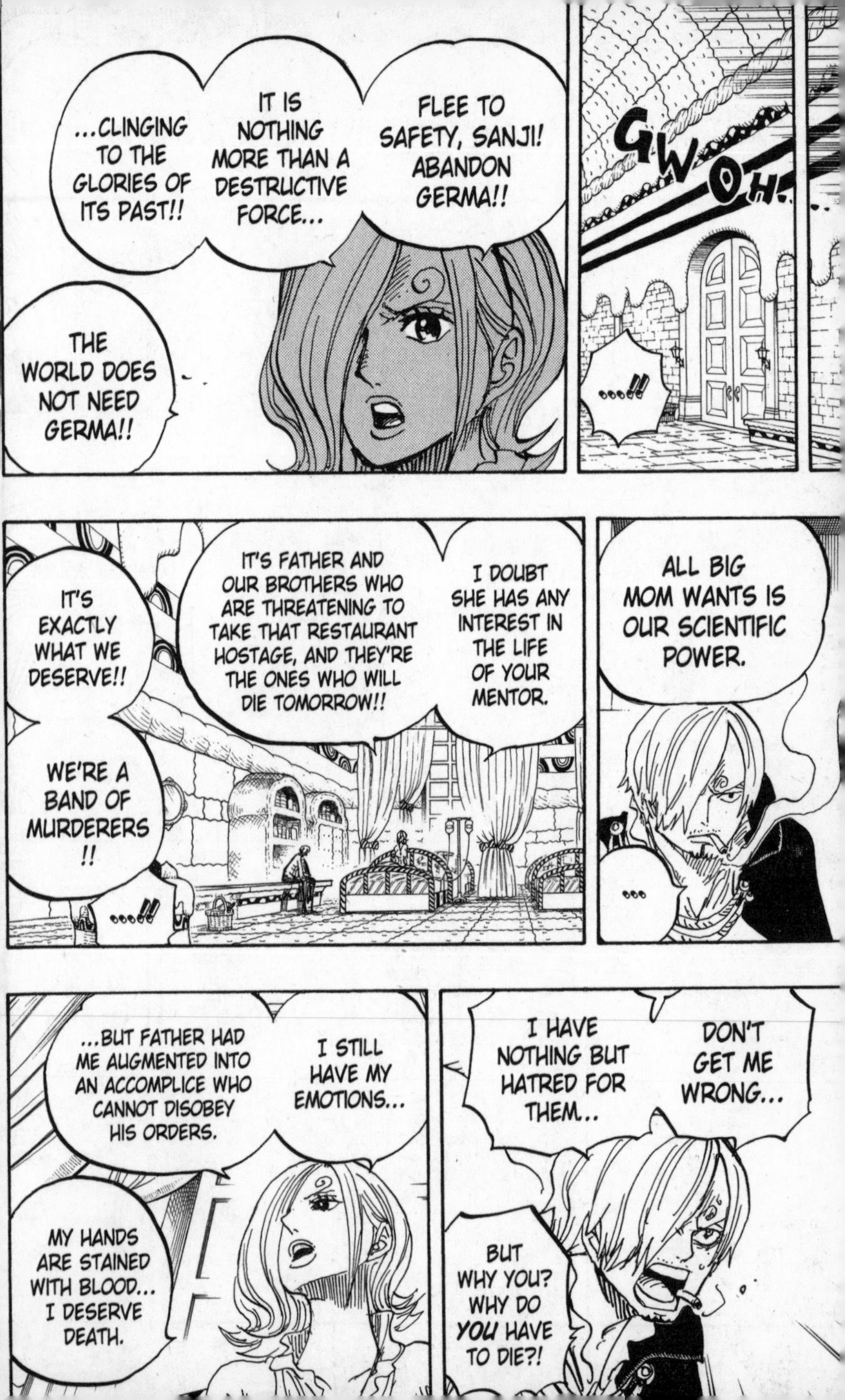
GWOH!...
....!!
FLEE TO SAFETY, SANJI! ABANDON GERMA!!
IT IS NOTHING MORE THAN A DESTRUCTIVE FORCE...
...CLINGING TO THE GLORIES OF ITS PAST!!
THE WORLD DOES NOT NEED GERMA!!
ALL BIG MOM WANTS IS OUR SCIENTIFIC POWER.
...
I DOUBT SHE HAS ANY INTEREST IN THE LIFE OF YOUR MENTOR.
IT'S FATHER AND OUR BROTHERS WHO ARE THREATENING TO TAKE THAT RESTAURANT HOSTAGE, AND THEY'RE THE ONES WHO WILL DIE TOMORROW!!
IT'S EXACTLY WHAT WE DESERVE!!
WE'RE A BAND OF MURDERERS !!
....!!
DON'T GET ME WRONG...
I HAVE NOTHING BUT HATRED FOR THEM...
BUT WHY YOU? WHY DO *YOU* HAVE TO DIE?!
I STILL HAVE MY EMOTIONS...
...BUT FATHER HAD ME AUGMENTED INTO AN ACCOMPLICE WHO CANNOT DISOBEY HIS ORDERS.
MY HANDS ARE STAINED WITH BLOOD... I DESERVE DEATH.

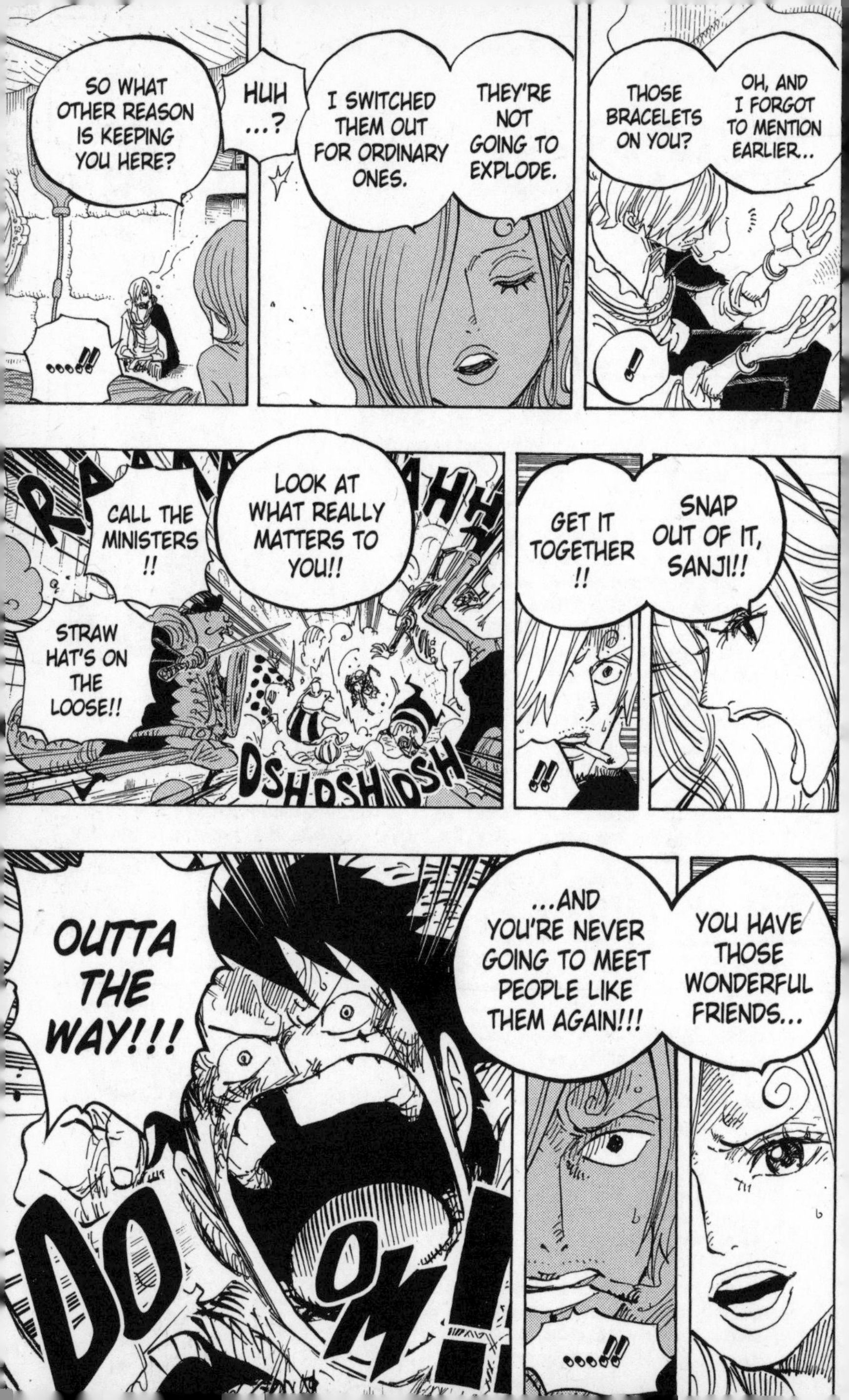
OH, AND I FORGOT TO MENTION EARLIER...
THOSE BRACELETS ON YOU?
!
THEY'RE NOT GOING TO EXPLODE.
I SWITCHED THEM OUT FOR ORDINARY ONES.
HUH ...?
SO WHAT OTHER REASON IS KEEPING YOU HERE?
...!!
SNAP OUT OF IT, SANJI!!
GET IT TOGETHER !!
!!
LOOK AT WHAT REALLY MATTERS TO YOU!!
CALL THE MINISTERS !!
STRAW HAT'S ON THE LOOSE!!
DSHDSHDSH
YOU HAVE THOSE WONDERFUL FRIENDS...
...AND YOU'RE NEVER GOING TO MEET PEOPLE LIKE THEM AGAIN!!!
...!!
OUTTA THE WAY!!!

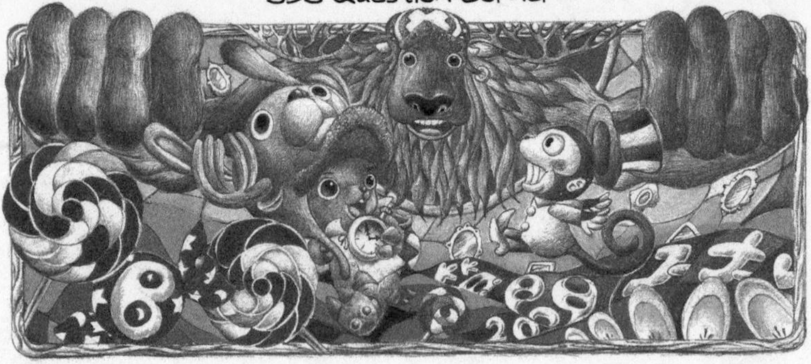

(Takahisa Fujimoto, Nara)

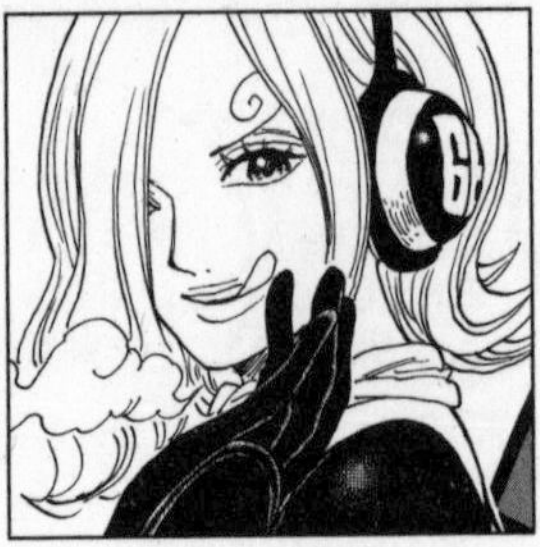

Q: Why doesn't Sanji get heart-eyes with Reiju? Could he maintain his reason even if he saw her naked?

--Match & Takeshi

A: Isn't that how siblings go? (laughs) I have an older sister, and all we ever did was scream and fight, so maybe my experience has me biased. I know this is Sanji we're talking about, but wouldn't it be creepy if he was perving out about his own sister?

Q: Mr. Oda! Here's a question I've been wondering about for ages. If the Straw Hat Crew ran a 50-meter dash, who would come in first?

--Nagatanigawa

A: Ooh, tough question! After all, the weak-willed members are pretty quick to escape. And Franky's Coup de Boo doesn't count.

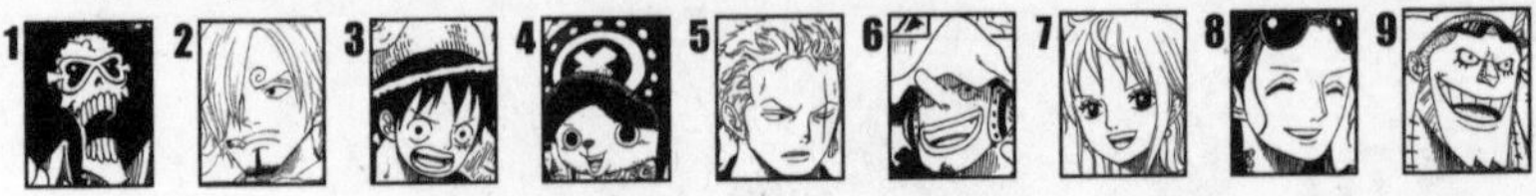
1
2
3
4
5
6
7
8
9

Brook is so light! And Chopper can go faster thanks to Walk Point. Zolo has the power burst necessary to speed over short distances, but at 50 meters, I'd be concerned with him straying off the course. Franky would probably be last because he's so heavy.

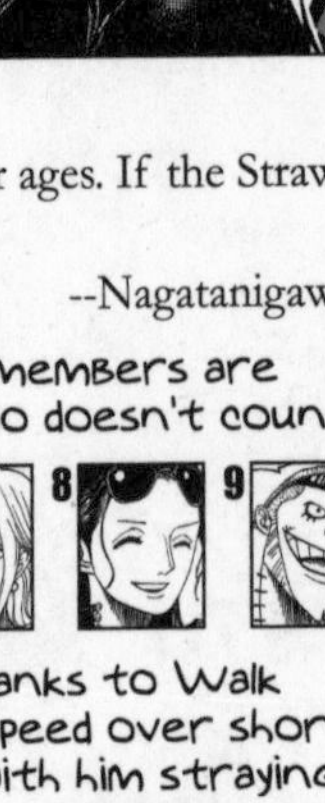

Q: Big Mom is a woman, but in Japanese, she uses a masculine pronoun. Why is this?

--Youth Age 12

A: Even today, there are regions of the country where women still use the pronoun "ore" when referring to themselves. In the past, it was once used equally by both men and women, so I didn't really think it was that unusual of an idea. But if that's weird to you, I'm surprised that I didn't get more questions about the pronoun that I completely invented for Ivankov.

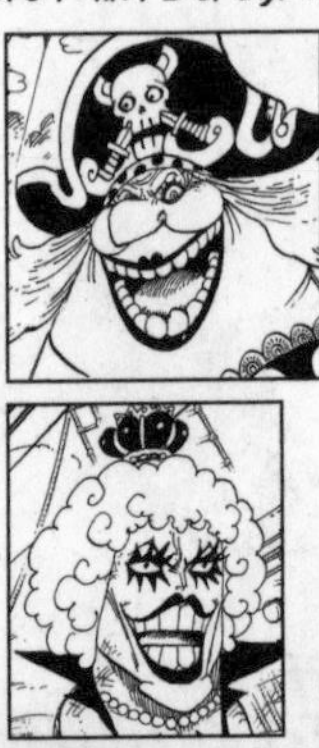

Chapter 853:
NOT HERE

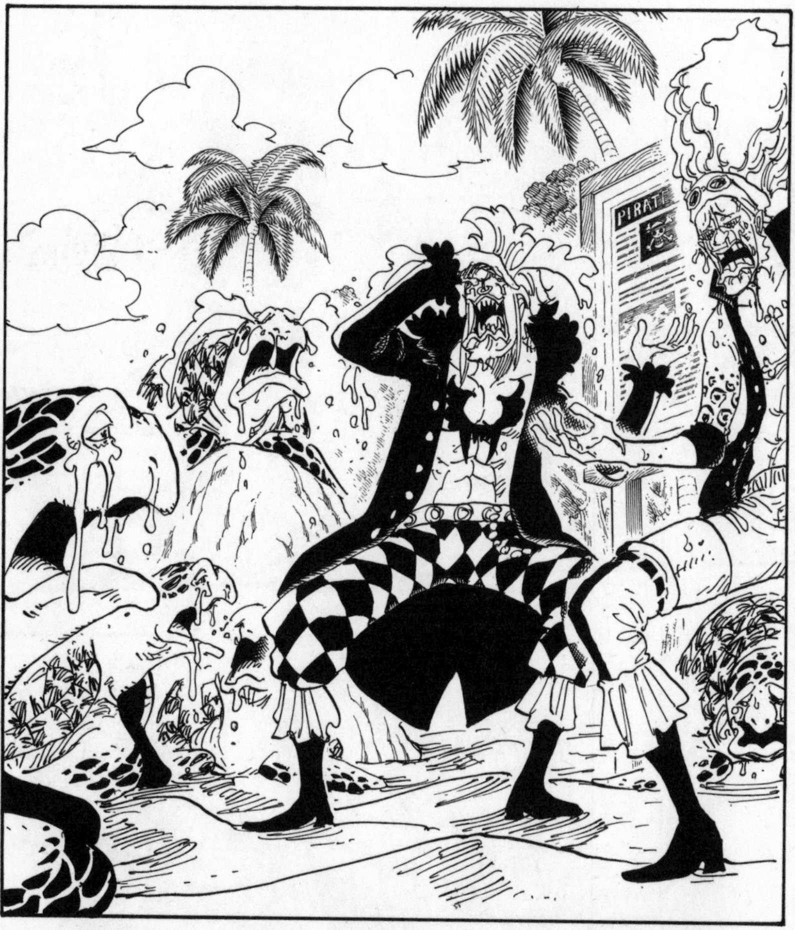
PIRAT

REQUEST: "BARTOLOMEO AND GAMBIA TEARFULLY PREACHING THE GREATNESS OF THE STRAW HAT CREW TO OVERWHELMED SEA TURTLES" BY HIYU MORI FROM HYOGO

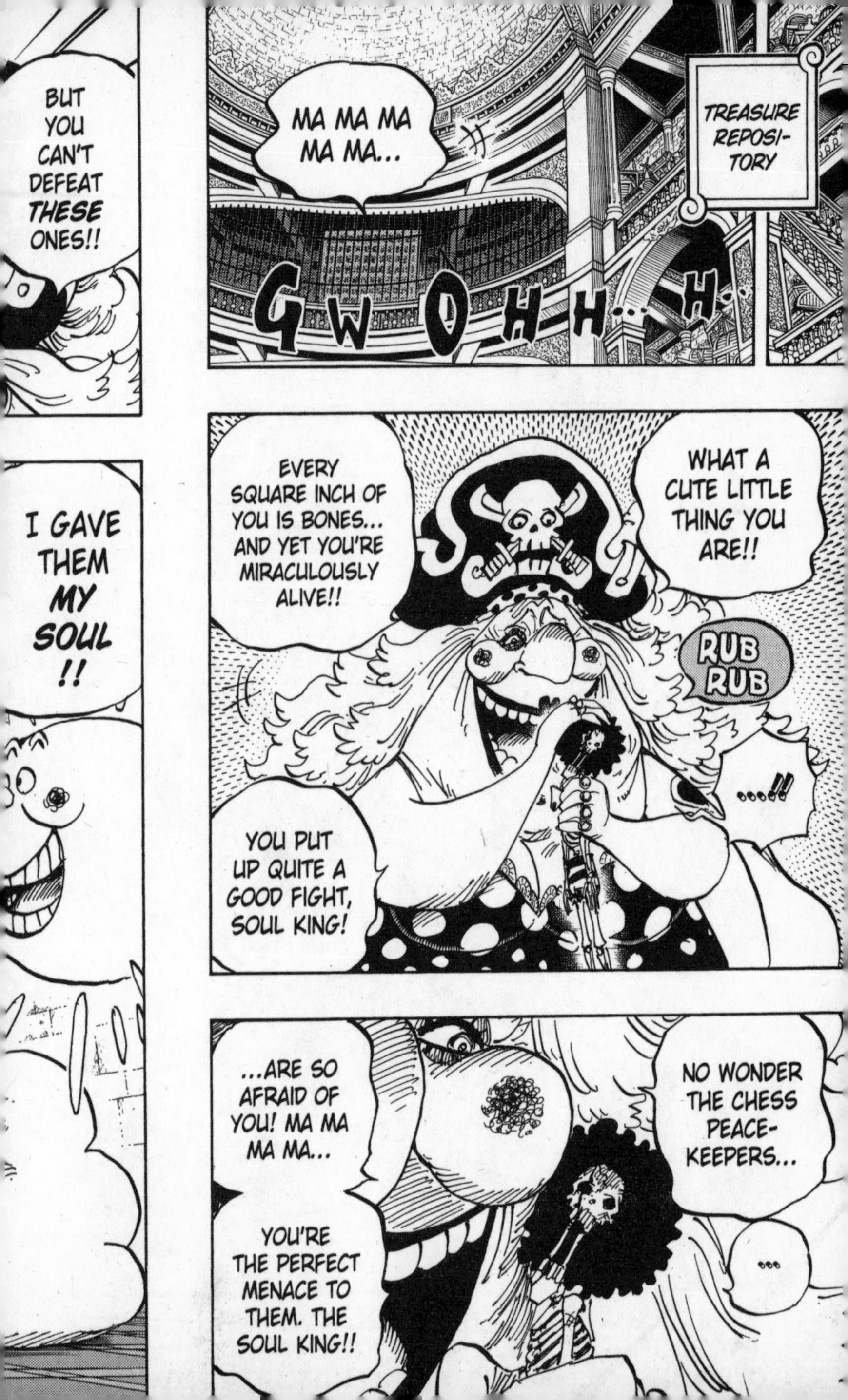
TREASURE REPOSITORY
MA MA MA MA MA...
GWOHH...H...
WHAT A CUTE LITTLE THING YOU ARE!!
EVERY SQUARE INCH OF YOU IS BONES... AND YET YOU'RE MIRACULOUSLY ALIVE!!
RUB RUB
...!!
YOU PUT UP QUITE A GOOD FIGHT, SOUL KING!
NO WONDER THE CHESS PEACEKEEPERS...
...ARE SO AFRAID OF YOU! MA MA MA MA...
...
YOU'RE THE PERFECT MENACE TO THEM. THE SOUL KING!!
BUT YOU CAN'T DEFEAT THESE ONES!!
I GAVE THEM MY SOUL!!

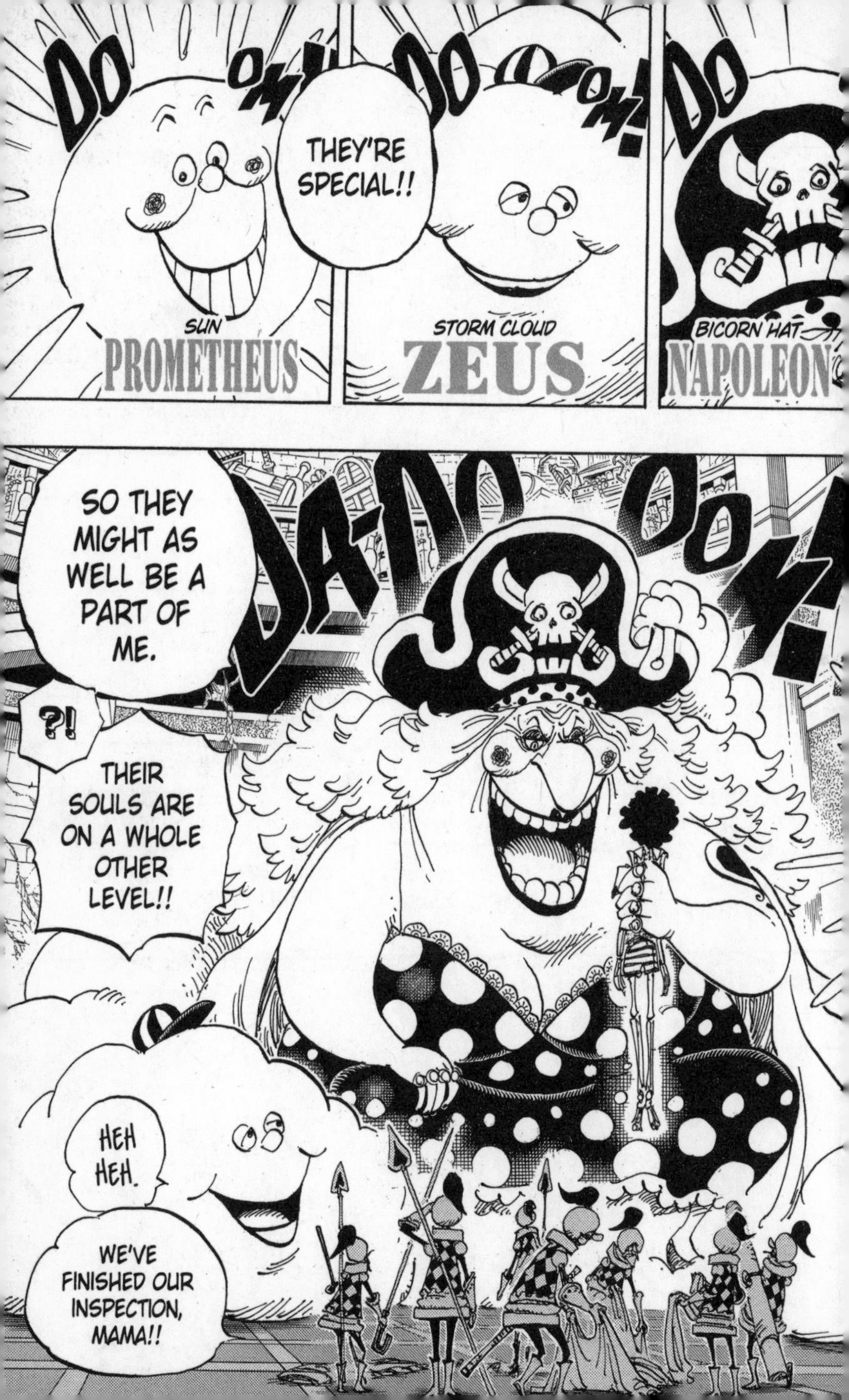
DO
BICORN HAT
NAPOLEON
DO
OM!
THEY'RE SPECIAL!!
STORM CLOUD
ZEUS
DO
OM!
SUN
PROMETHEUS
JA-DOOOM!!
SO THEY MIGHT AS WELL BE A PART OF ME.
?!
THEIR SOULS ARE ON A WHOLE OTHER LEVEL!!
HEH HEH.
WE'VE FINISHED OUR INSPECTION, MAMA!!

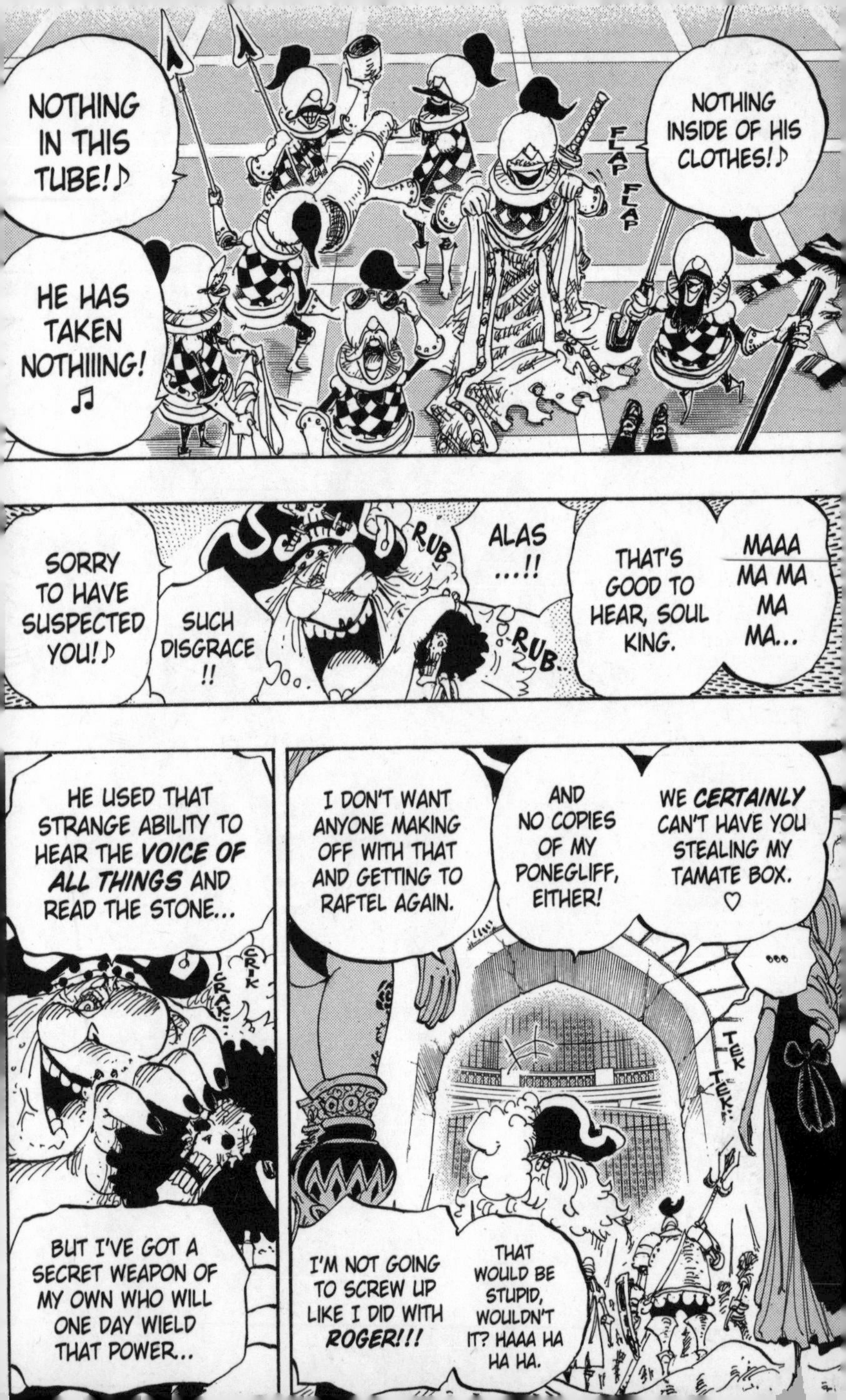
NOTHING INSIDE OF HIS CLOTHES!♪
FLAP FLAP
NOTHING IN THIS TUBE!♪
HE HAS TAKEN NOTHIIING! ♫
MAAA MA MA MA MA...
THAT'S GOOD TO HEAR, SOUL KING.
ALAS...!!
RUB RUB
SUCH DISGRACE!!
SORRY TO HAVE SUSPECTED YOU!♪
WE CERTAINLY CAN'T HAVE YOU STEALING MY TAMATE BOX. ♡
AND NO COPIES OF MY PONEGLIFF, EITHER!
I DON'T WANT ANYONE MAKING OFF WITH THAT AND GETTING TO RAFTEL AGAIN.
...
TEK TEK
THAT WOULD BE STUPID, WOULDN'T IT? HAAA HA HA HA.
I'M NOT GOING TO SCREW UP LIKE I DID WITH ROGER!!!
HE USED THAT STRANGE ABILITY TO HEAR THE VOICE OF ALL THINGS AND READ THE STONE...
CRIK CRAK
BUT I'VE GOT A SECRET WEAPON OF MY OWN WHO WILL ONE DAY WIELD THAT POWER...

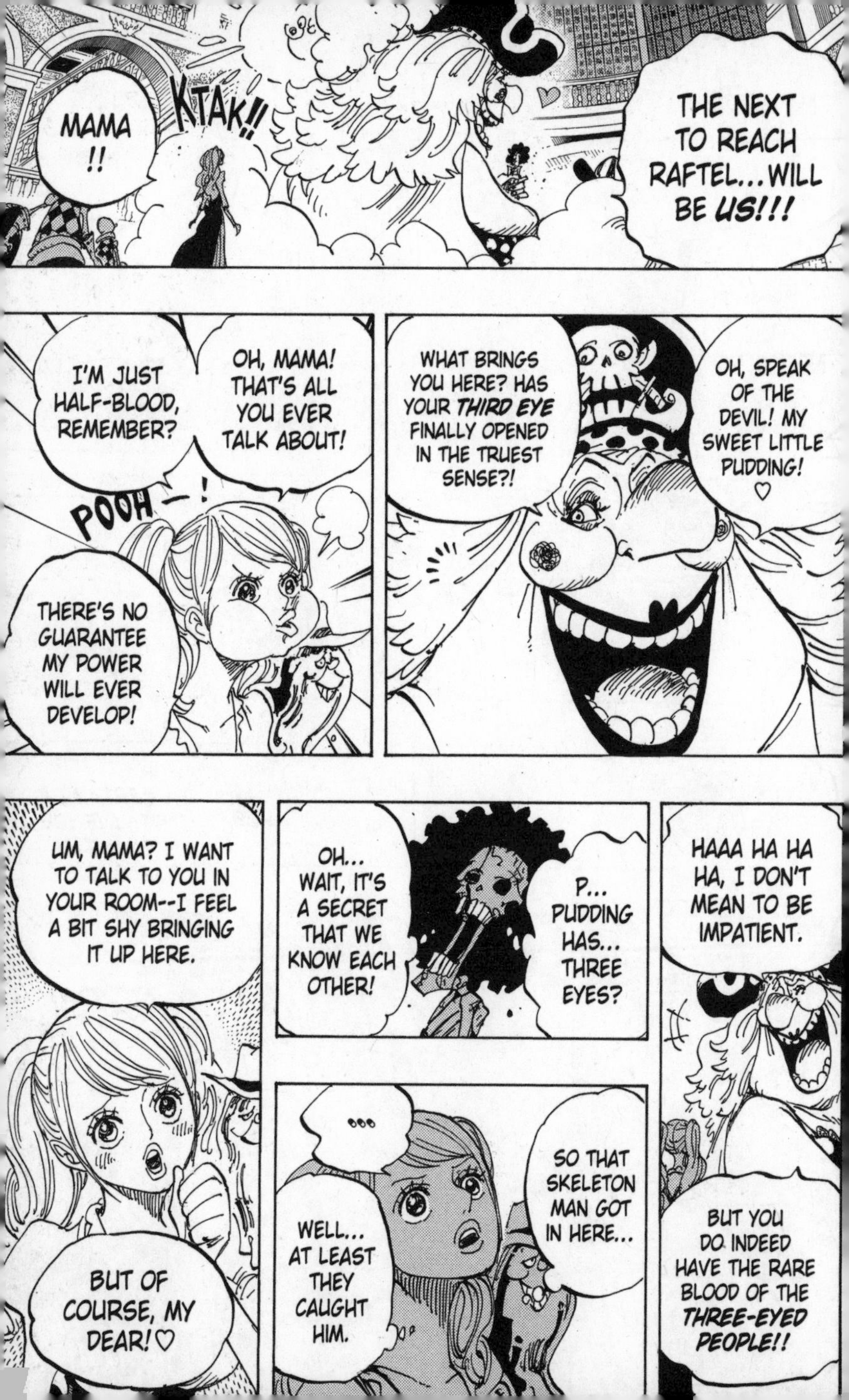
THE NEXT TO REACH RAFTEL... WILL BE US!!!
KTAK!!
MAMA !!
OH, SPEAK OF THE DEVIL! MY SWEET LITTLE PUDDING! ♡
WHAT BRINGS YOU HERE? HAS YOUR THIRD EYE FINALLY OPENED IN THE TRUEST SENSE?!
OH, MAMA! THAT'S ALL YOU EVER TALK ABOUT!
I'M JUST HALF-BLOOD, REMEMBER?
POOH—!
THERE'S NO GUARANTEE MY POWER WILL EVER DEVELOP!
HAAA HA HA HA, I DON'T MEAN TO BE IMPATIENT.
BUT YOU DO INDEED HAVE THE RARE BLOOD OF THE THREE-EYED PEOPLE!!
P... PUDDING HAS... THREE EYES?
OH... WAIT, IT'S A SECRET THAT WE KNOW EACH OTHER!
SO THAT SKELETON MAN GOT IN HERE...
...
WELL... AT LEAST THEY CAUGHT HIM.
UM, MAMA? I WANT TO TALK TO YOU IN YOUR ROOM--I FEEL A BIT SHY BRINGING IT UP HERE.
BUT OF COURSE, MY DEAR! ♡

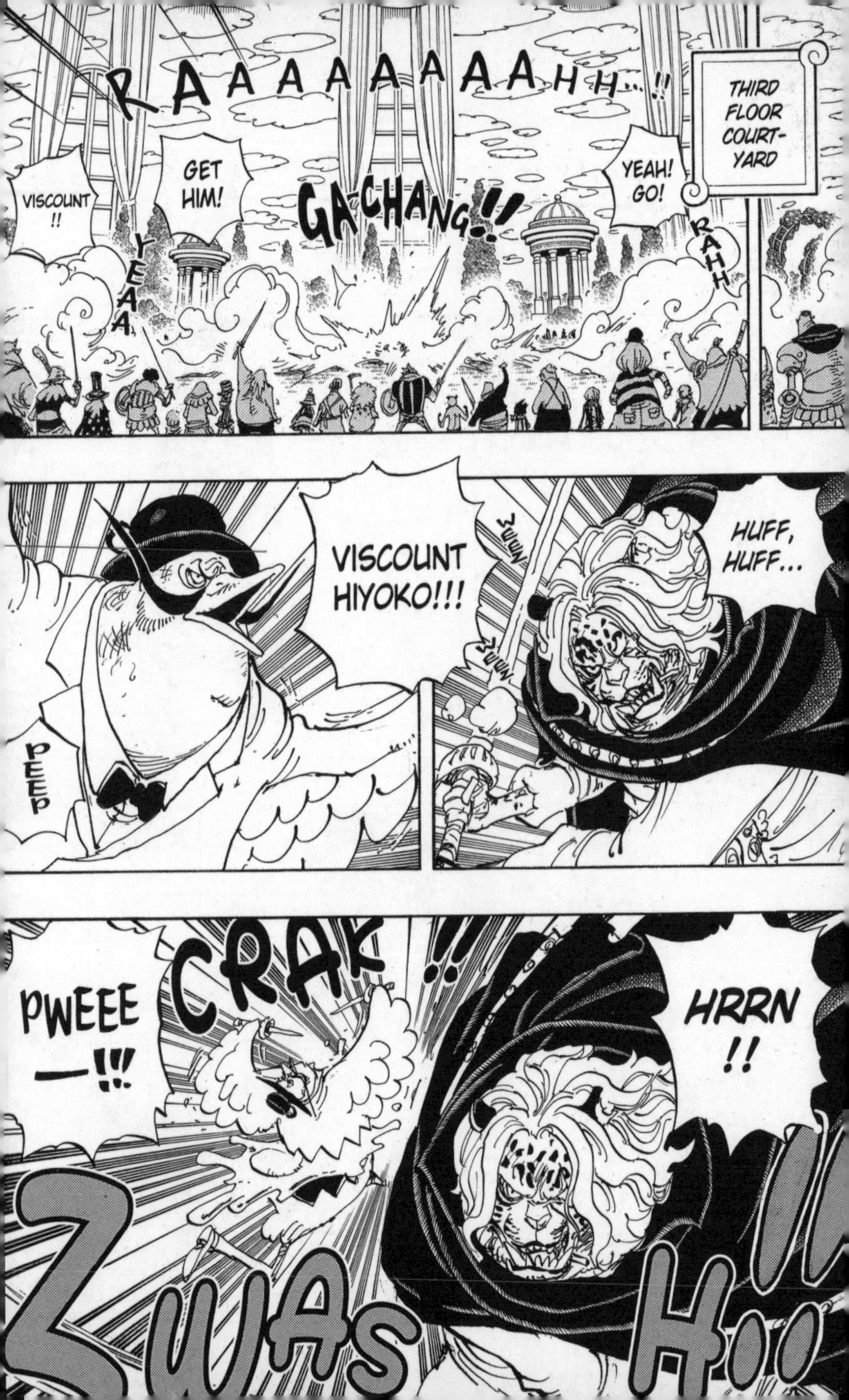
THIRD FLOOR COURT-YARD
RAAAAAAAAHH...!!
YEAH! GO!
RAHH
GA-CHANG!!
GET HIM!
VISCOUNT!!
YEAA
HUFF, HUFF...
VISCOUNT HIYOKO!!!
PEEP
HRRN!!
CRAK!!
PWEEE—!!!
ZUASH!!

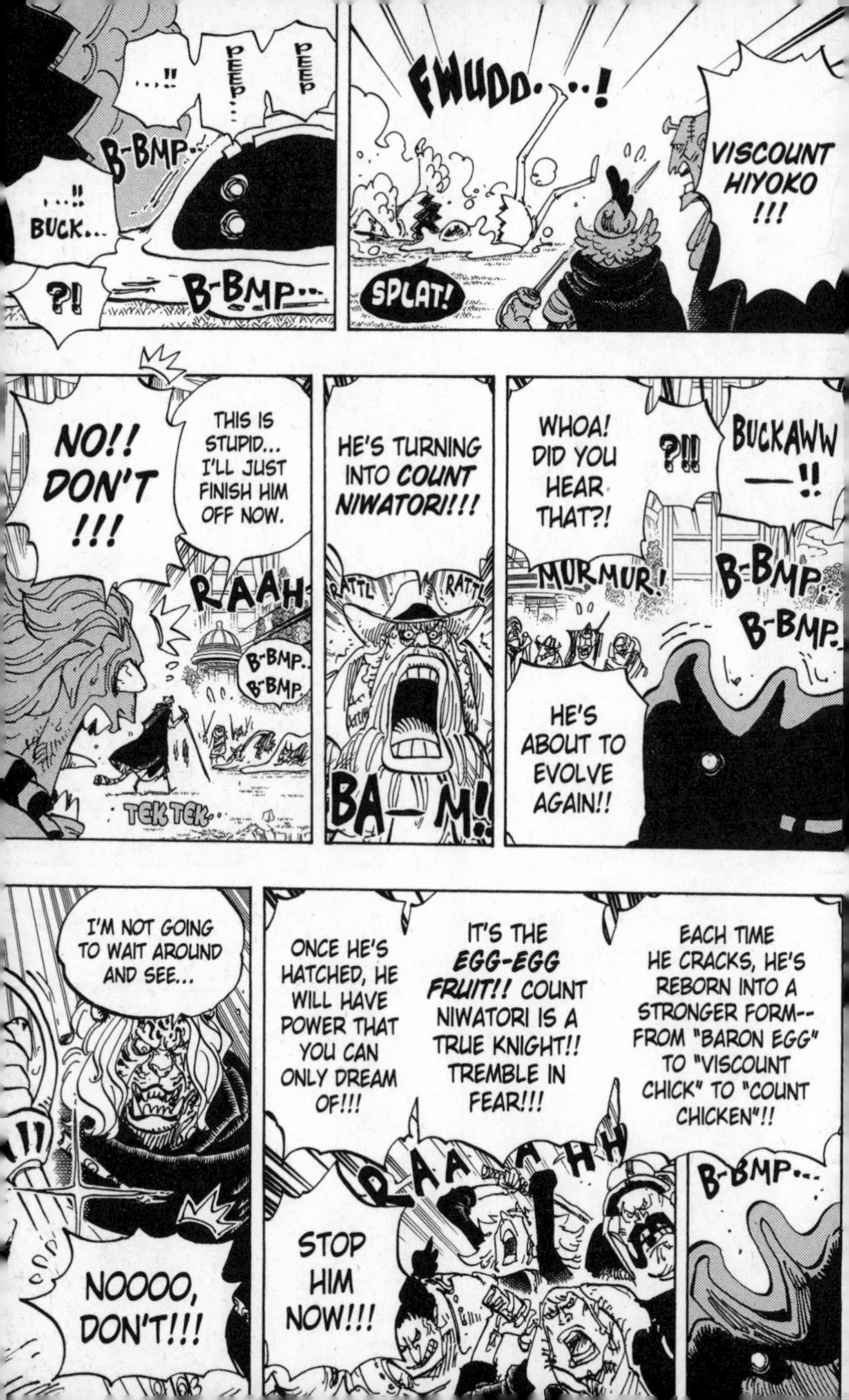
VISCOUNT HIYOKO!!!
FWUDD...!
SPLAT!
PEEP
PEEP...
...!!
B-BMP...
...!!
BUCK...
?!
B-BMP...
BUCKAWW—!!
?!!
WHOA! DID YOU HEAR THAT?!
B-BMP
MURMUR!
B-BMP...
HE'S ABOUT TO EVOLVE AGAIN!!
HE'S TURNING INTO COUNT NIWATORI!!!
RATTL
RATTL
BA—M!
THIS IS STUPID... I'LL JUST FINISH HIM OFF NOW.
NO!! DON'T!!!
RAAH
B-BMP.. B-BMP
TEK TEK
EACH TIME HE CRACKS, HE'S REBORN INTO A STRONGER FORM-- FROM "BARON EGG" TO "VISCOUNT CHICK" TO "COUNT CHICKEN"!!
IT'S THE EGG-EGG FRUIT!! COUNT NIWATORI IS A TRUE KNIGHT!! TREMBLE IN FEAR!!!
ONCE HE'S HATCHED, HE WILL HAVE POWER THAT YOU CAN ONLY DREAM OF!!!
B-BMP...
RAAAHH
STOP HIM NOW!!!
I'M NOT GOING TO WAIT AROUND AND SEE...
!!!
NOOOO, DON'T!!!

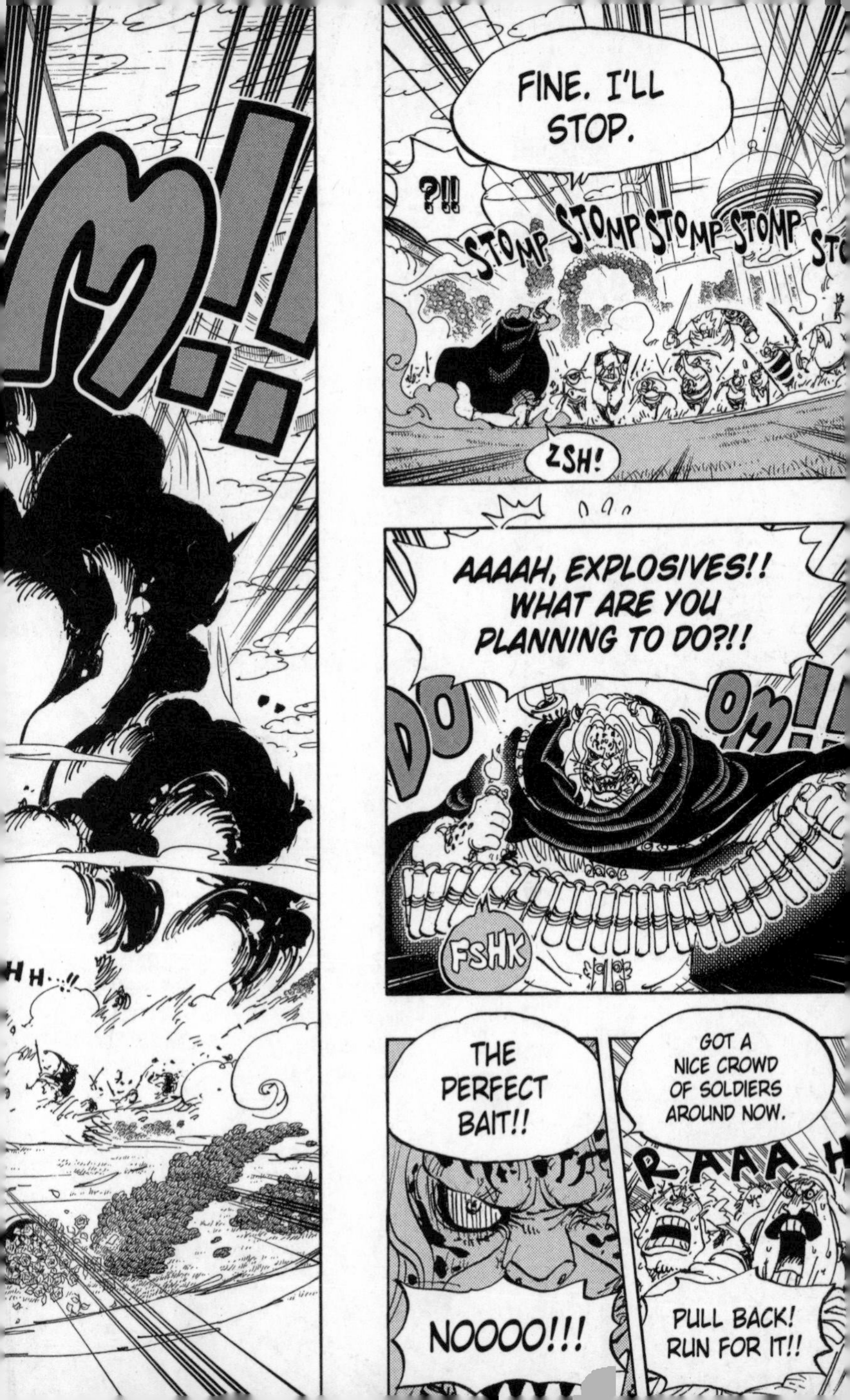
FINE. I'LL STOP.
?!!
STOMP STOMP STOMP STOMP STO
ZSH!
AAAAH, EXPLOSIVES!! WHAT ARE YOU PLANNING TO DO?!!
DOOM!!
FSHK
GOT A NICE CROWD OF SOLDIERS AROUND NOW.
RAAAH
PULL BACK! RUN FOR IT!!
THE PERFECT BAIT!!
NOOOO!!!
M!!
HH...!!

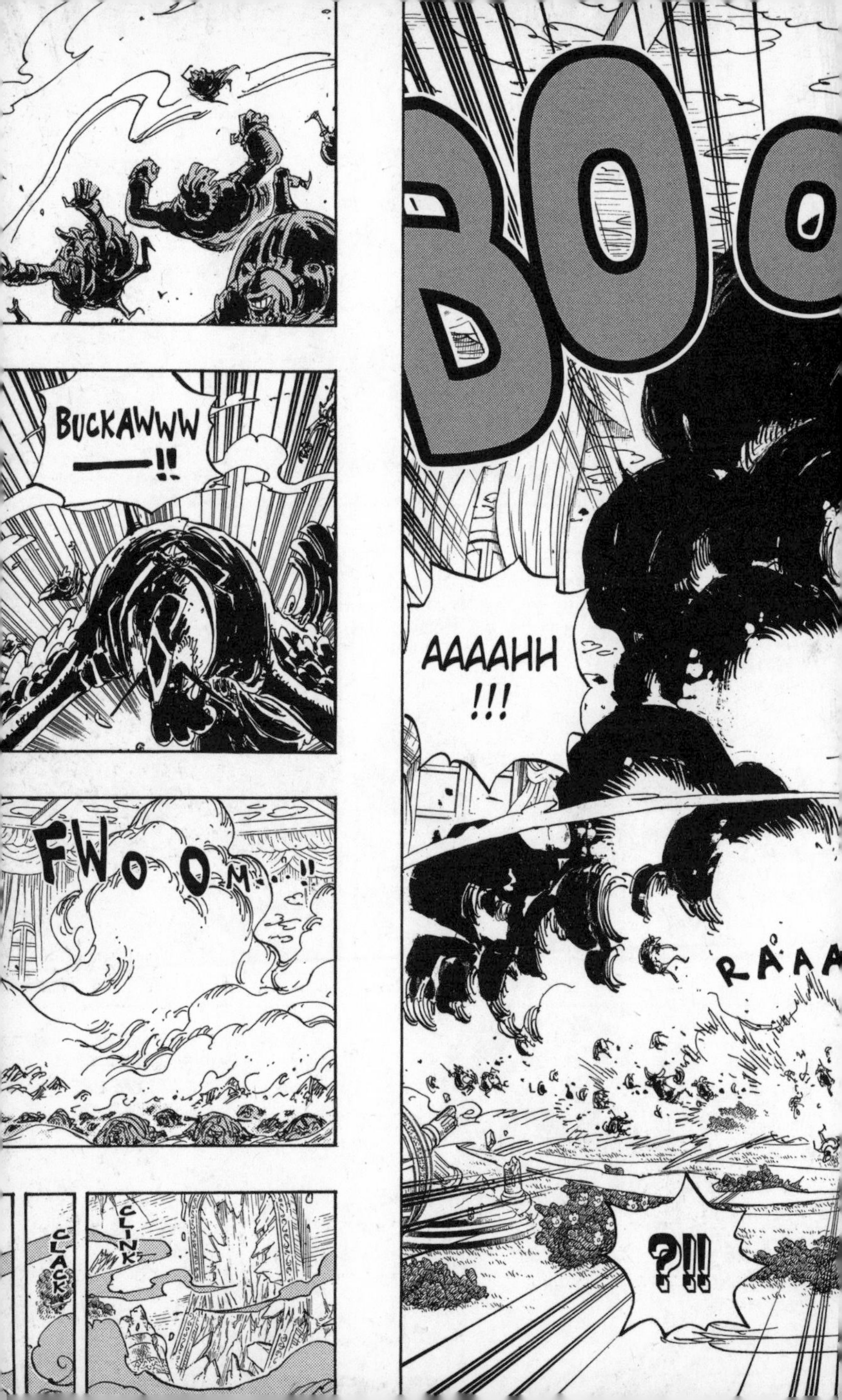
BOO
AAAAHH !!!
RAAA
?!!
BUCKAWWW ——!!
FWOOOM..!!
CLINK
CLACK

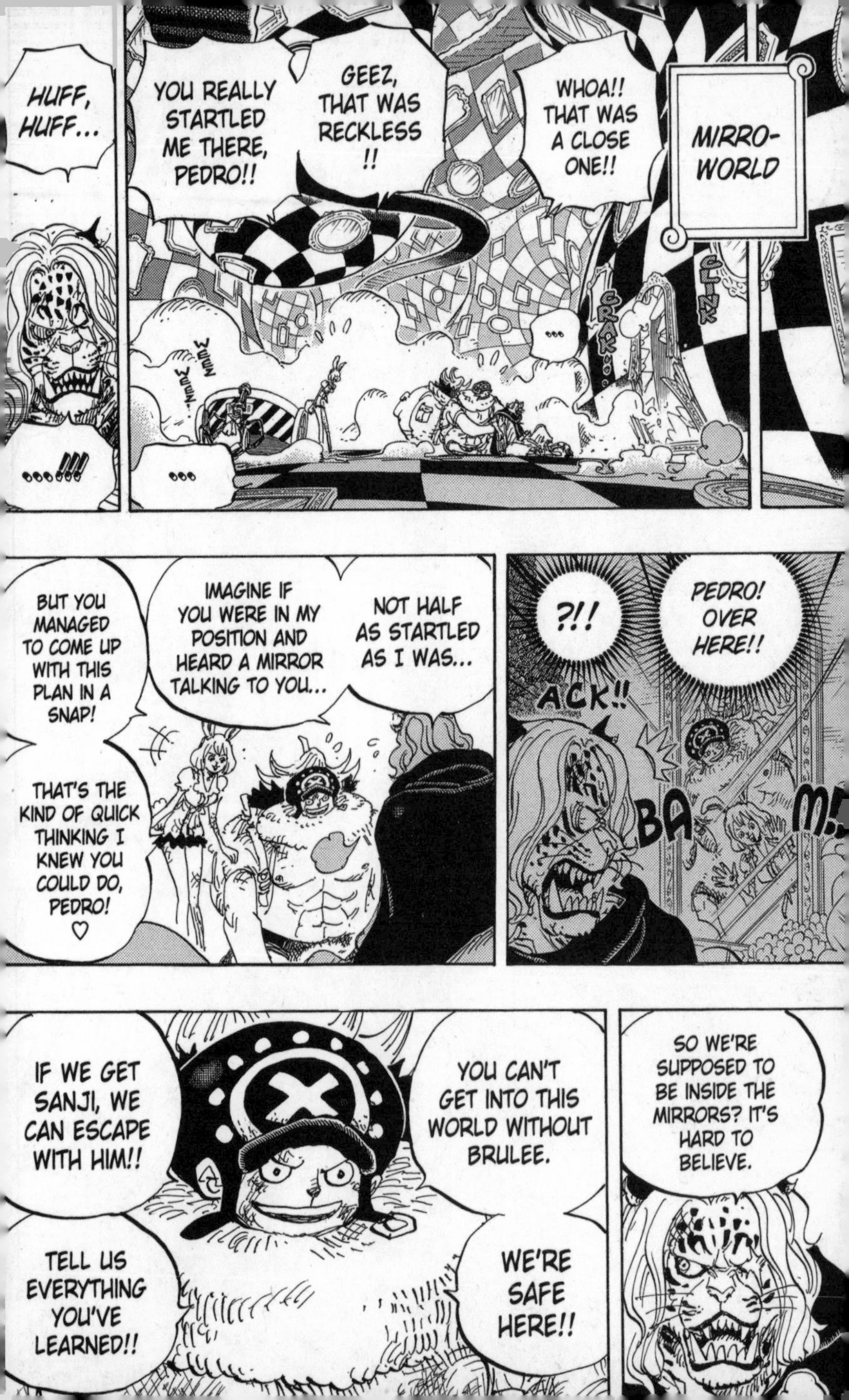
MIRRO-WORLD
WHOA!! THAT WAS A CLOSE ONE!!
GEEZ, THAT WAS RECKLESS !!
YOU REALLY STARTLED ME THERE, PEDRO!!
CLINK
SRAK
...
WEEN WEEN
...
HUFF, HUFF...
...!!!
PEDRO! OVER HERE!!
?!!
ACK!!
BAM!!
NOT HALF AS STARTLED AS I WAS...
IMAGINE IF YOU WERE IN MY POSITION AND HEARD A MIRROR TALKING TO YOU...
BUT YOU MANAGED TO COME UP WITH THIS PLAN IN A SNAP!
THAT'S THE KIND OF QUICK THINKING I KNEW YOU COULD DO, PEDRO! ♡
SO WE'RE SUPPOSED TO BE INSIDE THE MIRRORS? IT'S HARD TO BELIEVE.
YOU CAN'T GET INTO THIS WORLD WITHOUT BRULEE.
IF WE GET SANJI, WE CAN ESCAPE WITH HIM!!
WE'RE SAFE HERE!!
TELL US EVERYTHING YOU'VE LEARNED!!

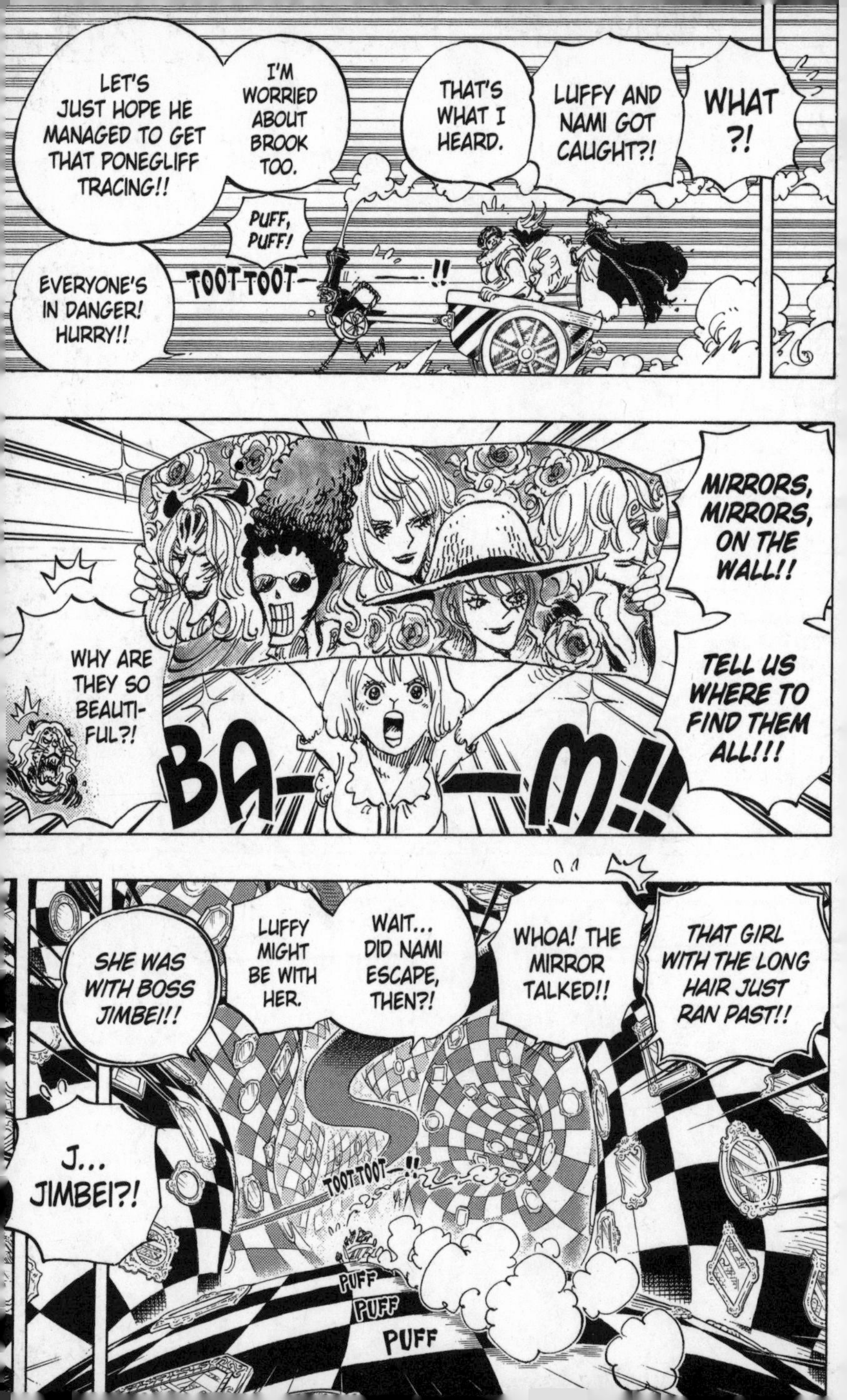
WHAT?!
LUFFY AND NAMI GOT CAUGHT?!
THAT'S WHAT I HEARD.
I'M WORRIED ABOUT BROOK TOO.
LET'S JUST HOPE HE MANAGED TO GET THAT PONEGLIFF TRACING!!
PUFF, PUFF!
!!
TOOT TOOT
EVERYONE'S IN DANGER! HURRY!!
MIRRORS, MIRRORS, ON THE WALL!!
TELL US WHERE TO FIND THEM ALL!!!
BA-—M!!
WHY ARE THEY SO BEAUTI-FUL?!
THAT GIRL WITH THE LONG HAIR JUST RAN PAST!!
WHOA! THE MIRROR TALKED!!
WAIT... DID NAMI ESCAPE, THEN?!
LUFFY MIGHT BE WITH HER.
SHE WAS WITH BOSS JIMBEI!!
J... JIMBEI?!
TOOT TOOT—!!
PUFF
PUFF
PUFF

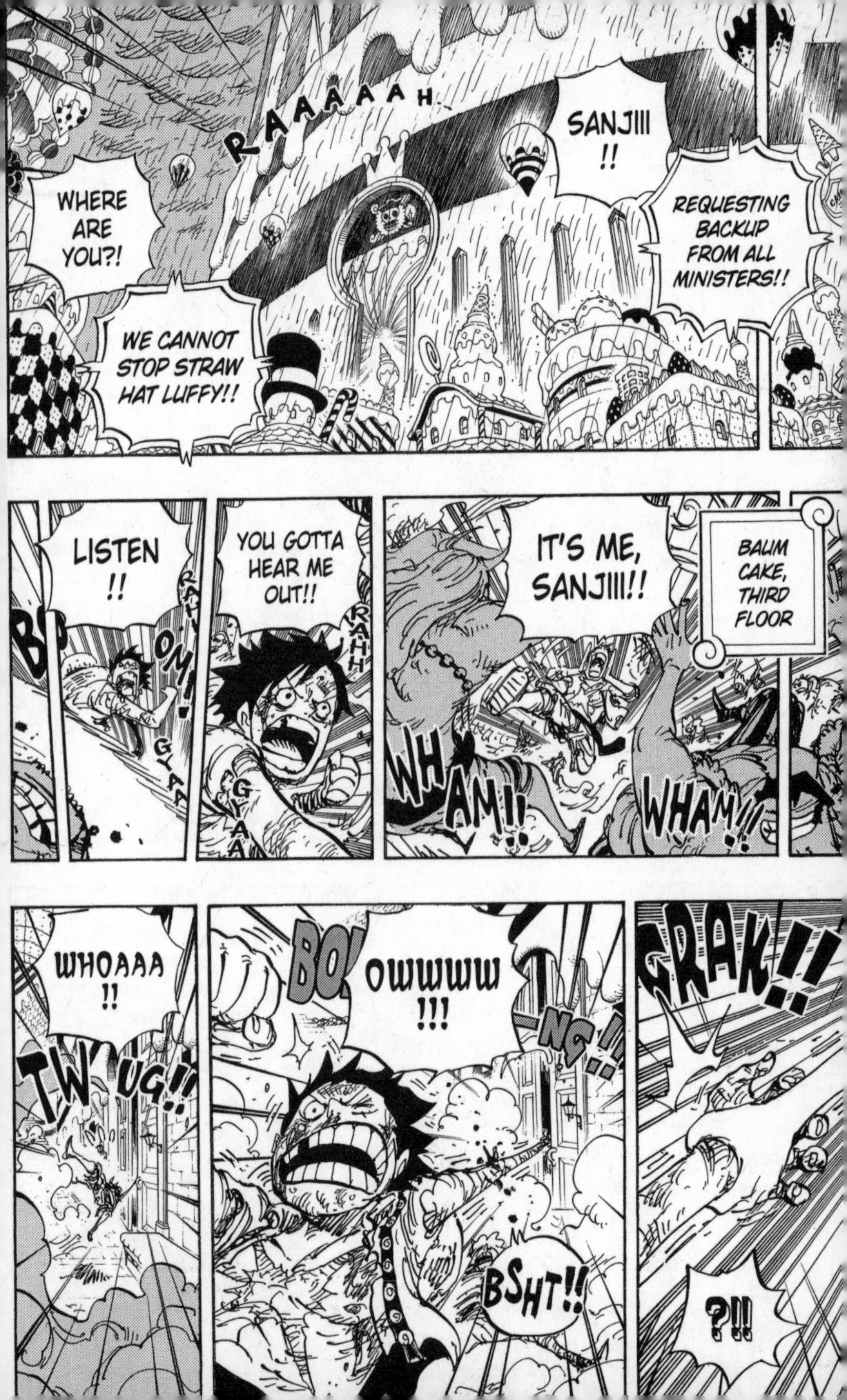
REQUESTING BACKUP FROM ALL MINISTERS!!
SANJIII !!
RAAAAAAH
WHERE ARE YOU?!
WE CANNOT STOP STRAW HAT LUFFY!!
BAUM CAKE, THIRD FLOOR
IT'S ME, SANJIII!!
WHAM!!
WHAM!!
YOU GOTTA HEAR ME OUT!!
RAHH
GYAA
LISTEN !!
GYAA
CRAK!!
?!!
OWWWW !!!
-NG!!
BSHT!!
WHOAAA !!
TW UG!!

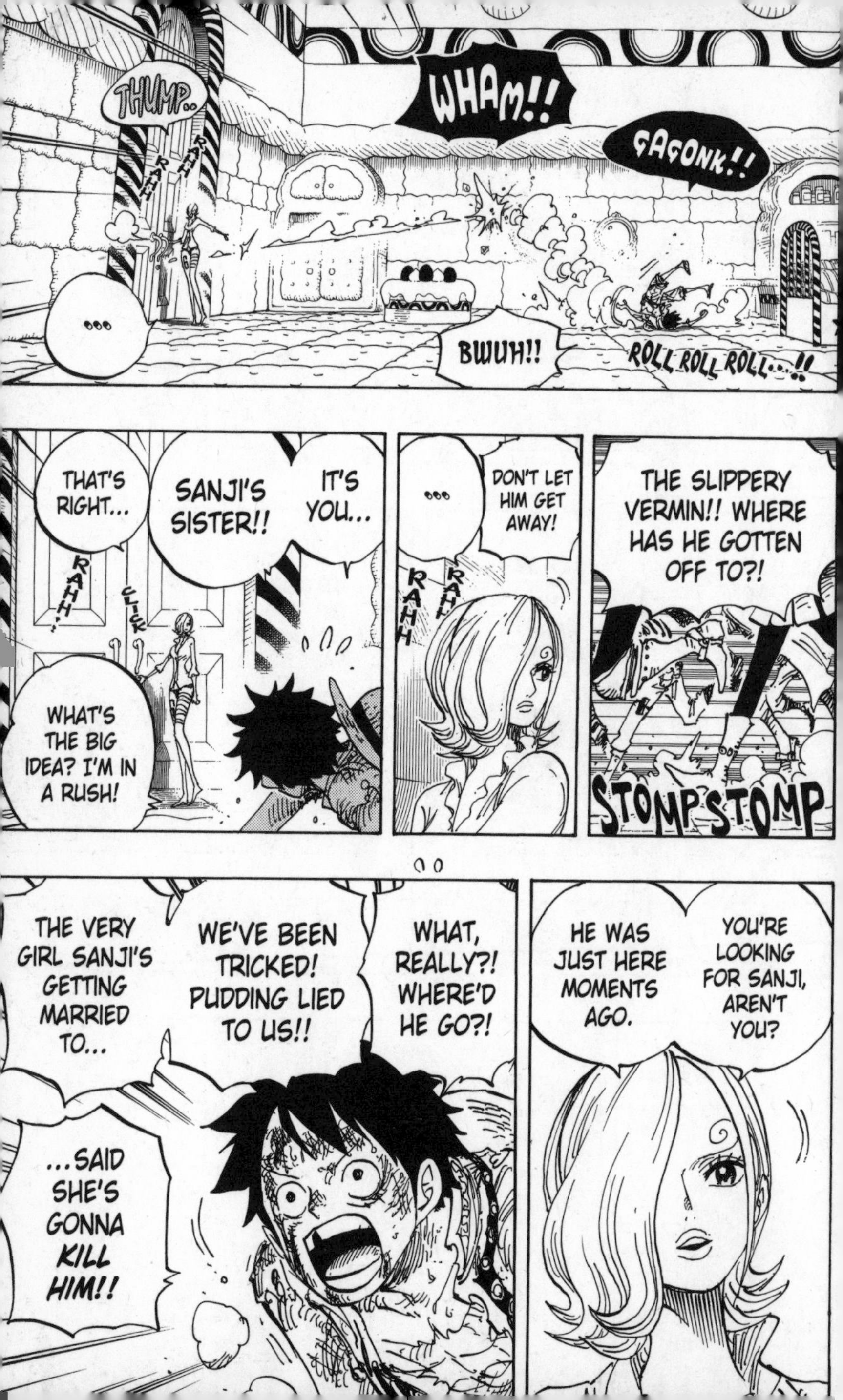
GAGONK!!
WHAM!!
THUMP..
RAHH
RAHH
ROLL ROLL ROLL...!!
BWUH!!
...
THE SLIPPERY VERMIN!! WHERE HAS HE GOTTEN OFF TO?!
STOMP STOMP
DON'T LET HIM GET AWAY!
...
RAHH
RAHH
IT'S YOU...
SANJI'S SISTER!!
THAT'S RIGHT...
RAHH!
CLICK
WHAT'S THE BIG IDEA? I'M IN A RUSH!
YOU'RE LOOKING FOR SANJI, AREN'T YOU?
HE WAS JUST HERE MOMENTS AGO.
WHAT, REALLY?! WHERE'D HE GO?!
WE'VE BEEN TRICKED! PUDDING LIED TO US!!
THE VERY GIRL SANJI'S GETTING MARRIED TO...
...SAID SHE'S GONNA KILL HIM!!

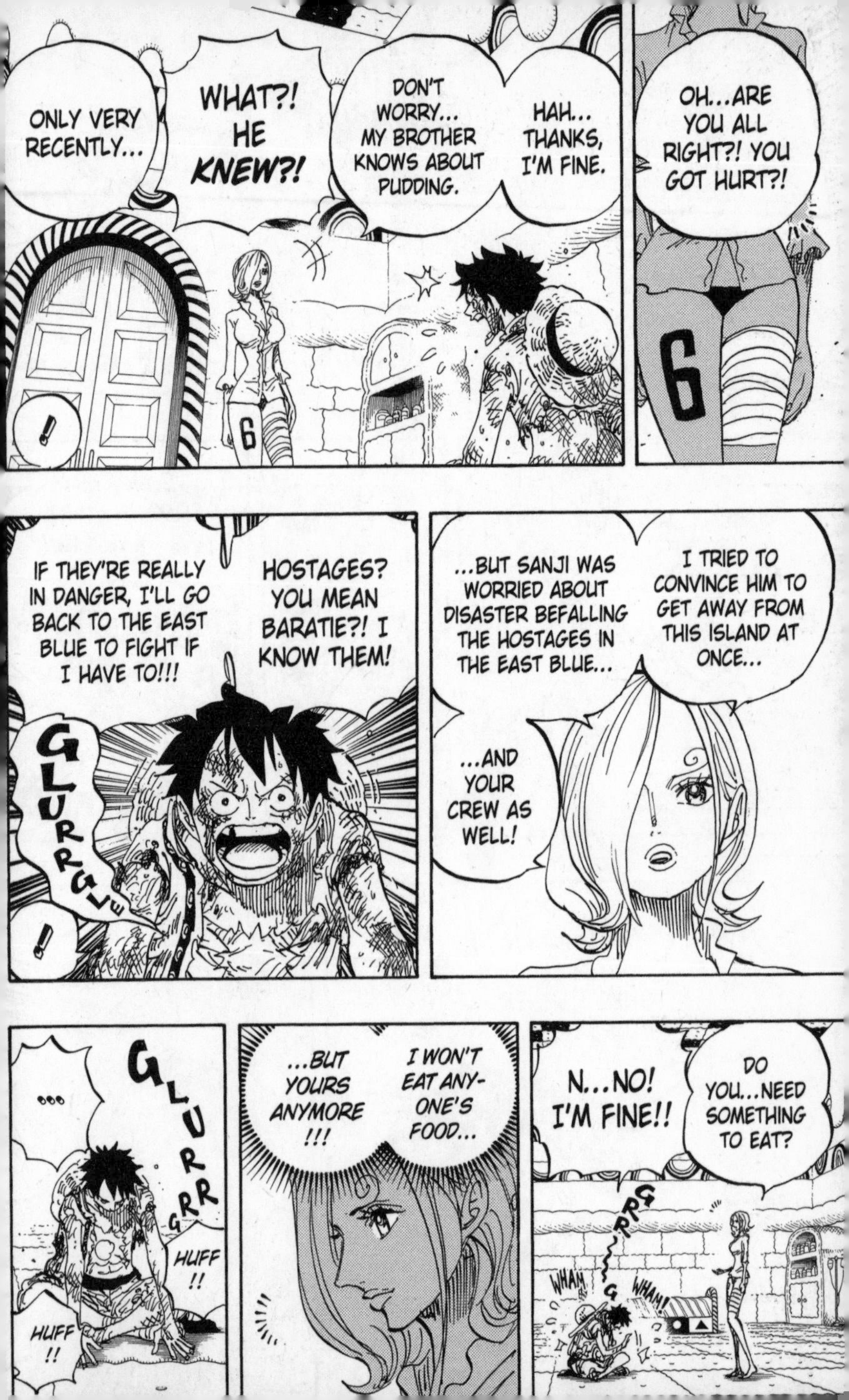
OH...ARE YOU ALL RIGHT?! YOU GOT HURT?!
HAH... THANKS, I'M FINE.
DON'T WORRY... MY BROTHER KNOWS ABOUT PUDDING.
WHAT?! HE KNEW?!
ONLY VERY RECENTLY...
!
I TRIED TO CONVINCE HIM TO GET AWAY FROM THIS ISLAND AT ONCE...
...BUT SANJI WAS WORRIED ABOUT DISASTER BEFALLING THE HOSTAGES IN THE EAST BLUE...
...AND YOUR CREW AS WELL!
HOSTAGES? YOU MEAN BARATIE?! I KNOW THEM!
IF THEY'RE REALLY IN DANGER, I'LL GO BACK TO THE EAST BLUE TO FIGHT IF I HAVE TO!!!
GLURRGLE
!
DO YOU...NEED SOMETHING TO EAT?
N...NO! I'M FINE!!
GRRR~~G
WHAM
WHAM!
I WON'T EAT ANY-ONE'S FOOD...
...BUT YOURS ANYMORE!!!
...
GLURR
GRR
HUFF!!
HUFF!!

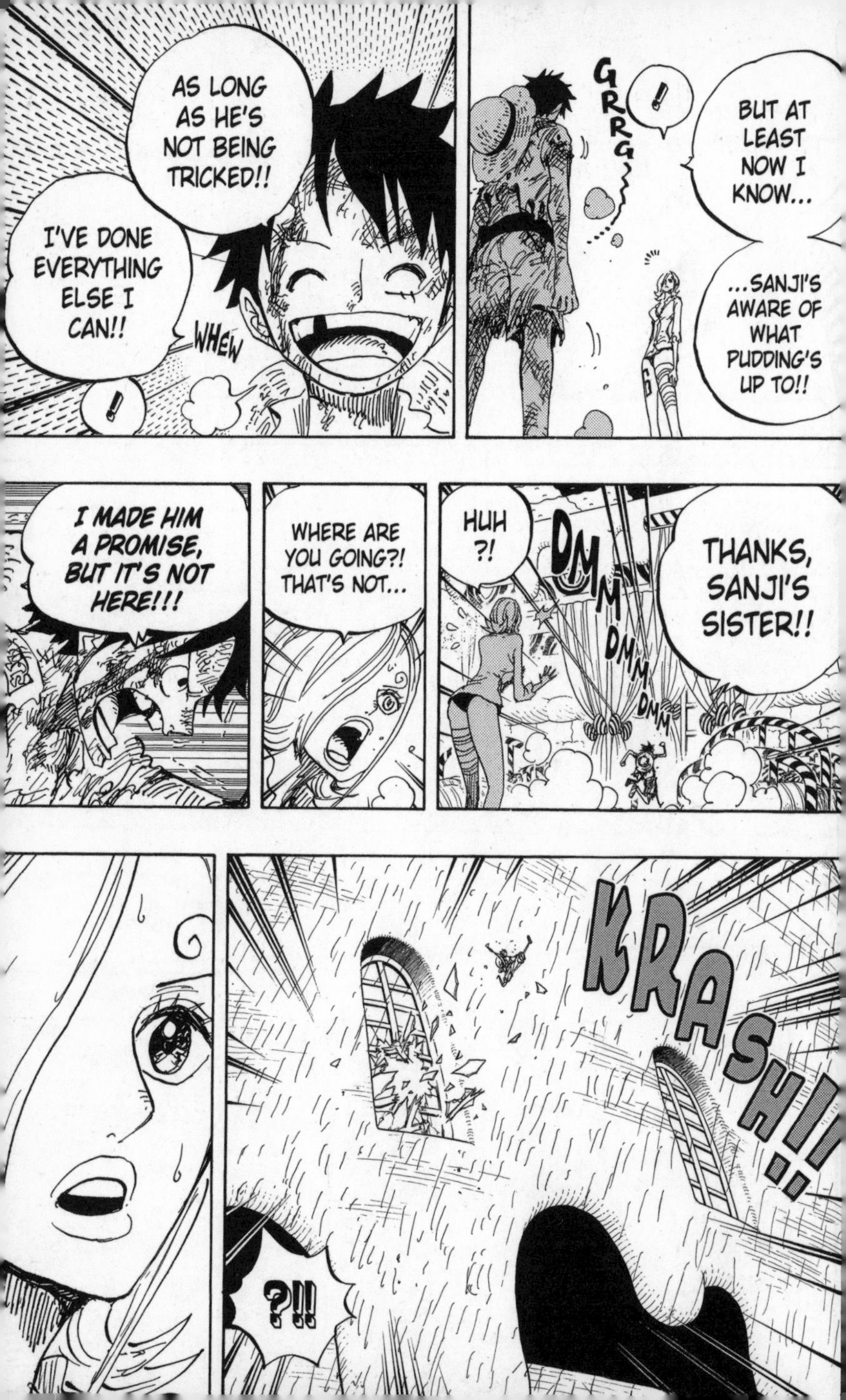
BUT AT LEAST NOW I KNOW...
...SANJI'S AWARE OF WHAT PUDDING'S UP TO!!
!
GRRRG
AS LONG AS HE'S NOT BEING TRICKED!!
I'VE DONE EVERYTHING ELSE I CAN!!
WHEW
!
THANKS, SANJI'S SISTER!!
DMM
DMM
DMM
HUH ?!
WHERE ARE YOU GOING?! THAT'S NOT...
I MADE HIM A PROMISE, BUT IT'S NOT HERE!!!
KRASH!!!
?!!

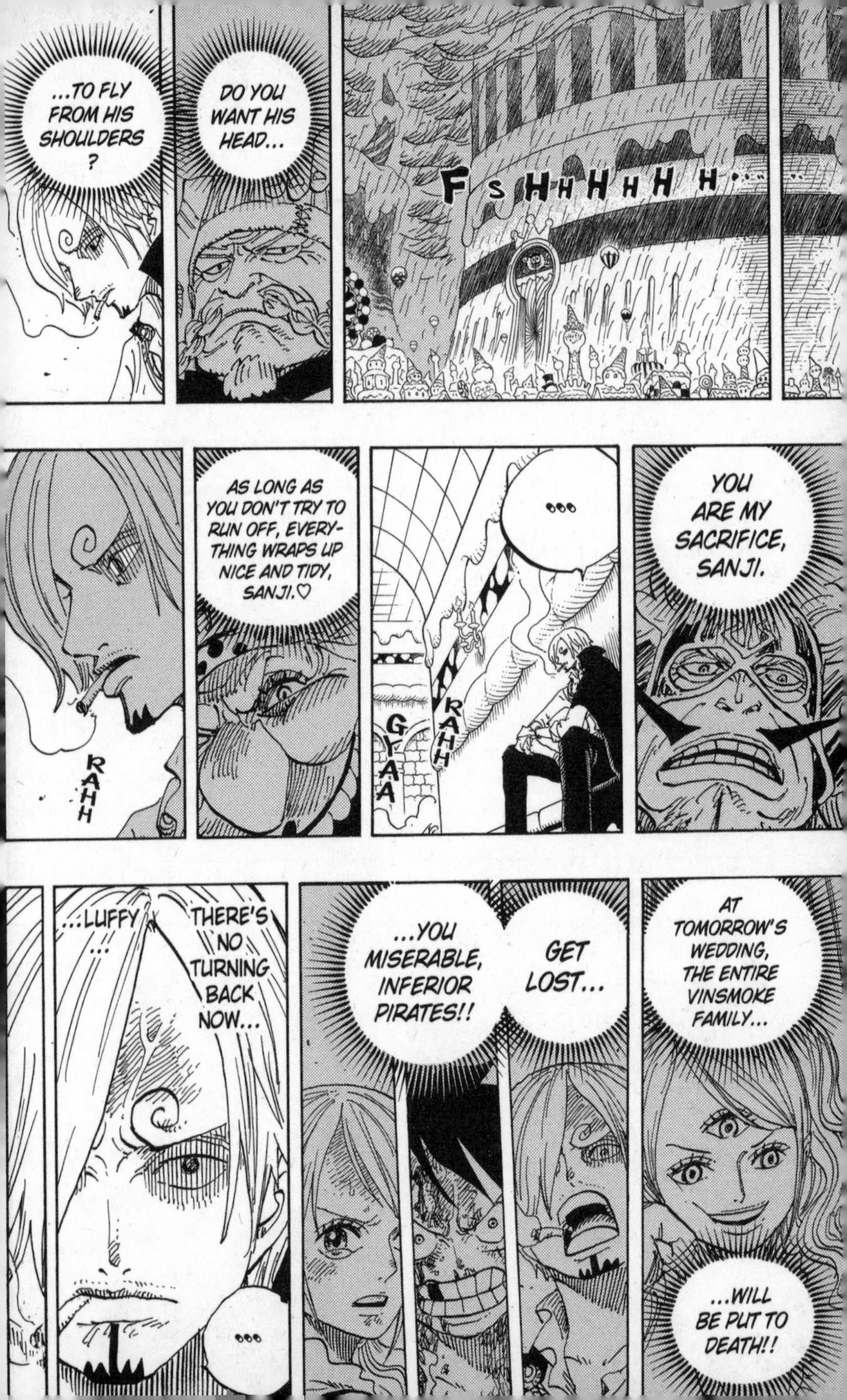
FSHHHHHH
DO YOU WANT HIS HEAD...
...TO FLY FROM HIS SHOULDERS ?
YOU ARE MY SACRIFICE, SANJI.
...
RAHH
GYAA
AS LONG AS YOU DON'T TRY TO RUN OFF, EVERY-THING WRAPS UP NICE AND TIDY, SANJI.♡
RAHH
AT TOMORROW'S WEDDING, THE ENTIRE VINSMOKE FAMILY...
...WILL BE PUT TO DEATH!!
GET LOST...
...YOU MISERABLE, INFERIOR PIRATES!!
THERE'S NO TURNING BACK NOW...
...LUFFY ...
...

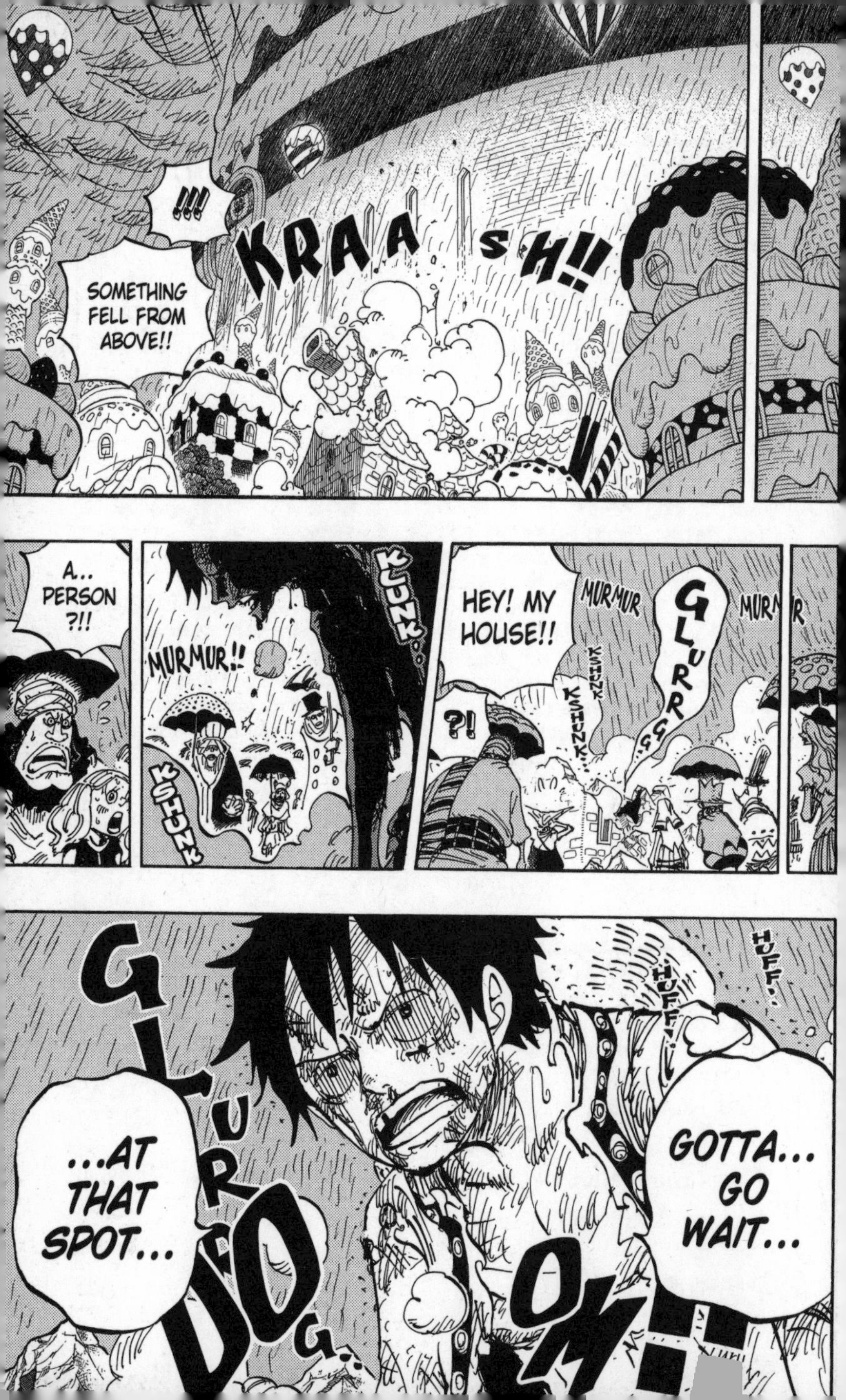
KRAA SH!!
!!!
SOMETHING FELL FROM ABOVE!!
MURMUR
HEY! MY HOUSE!!
MURMUR
GLURRRGG
KSHUNK
KSHUNK...
?!
KLUNK..
MURMUR!!
KSHUNK
A... PERSON ?!!
HUFF..
HUFF...
GOTTA... GO WAIT...
...AT THAT SPOT...

SBS Question Corner

GUM-GUM ?!
OH YEAH !!
WHAT ARE YOU DOING, LUFFY?

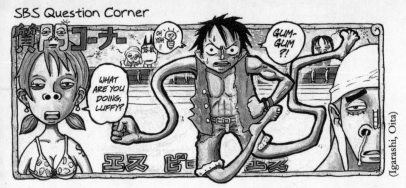

(Igarashi, Oita)

Q: I have a question. How does someone get to be an editor at *Shonen Jump?* Do the editors all graduate from elite colleges?

--Koichiro

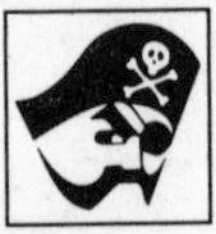

A: I can feel your sincerity about this, Koichiro. You really want to be an editor, don't you? As a matter of fact, many editors do have higher education degrees. But they're all freaks and weirdos. The only requirement for hiring at Shueisha, the publisher of Jump, is a degree from a four-year college. You don't need to have graduated from a very famous university to take the company test. And everyone turns into a weirdo as a result of all the studying. Keep your head straight, work hard, and you can be my editor someday, Koichiro.

Q: Can I lick the syrup off of Nami's body?

--Chamoro Shimizu

...TO BE CAPABLE OF SUCH TREMENDOUS LIGHTNING!
UGH...
AAAH
DRRM

A: It's you again, you pervert!! You keep ruining the morals of this manga!! But hang on!! I feel like the handwriting on this postcard is different!! Did you always have such nice handwriting?! You better not be an imposter!! If this isn't the real Chamoro...you can go.
No, you can't!!! Don't send me these postcards, whoever you are!!

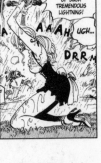

Q: I was the leader of the Whitebeard Pirates 2nd Division before Ace was.

--Capt. Nobuo

A: **Liar!!!** Huff...huff...

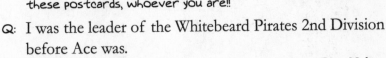

Chapter 854:
WHAT ARE YOU DOING?

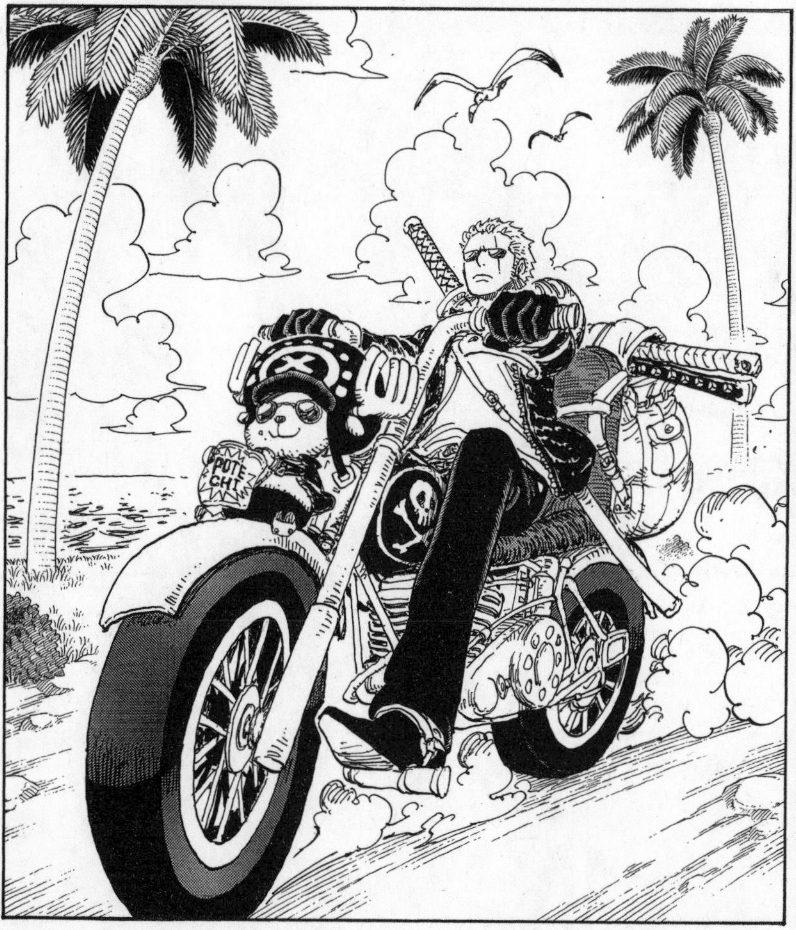
POTE CHI

REQUEST: "PLEASE DRAW ZOLO WEARING SHADES AND RIDING A HARLEY LOOK-ALIKE" BY RORONOA NATSUKI

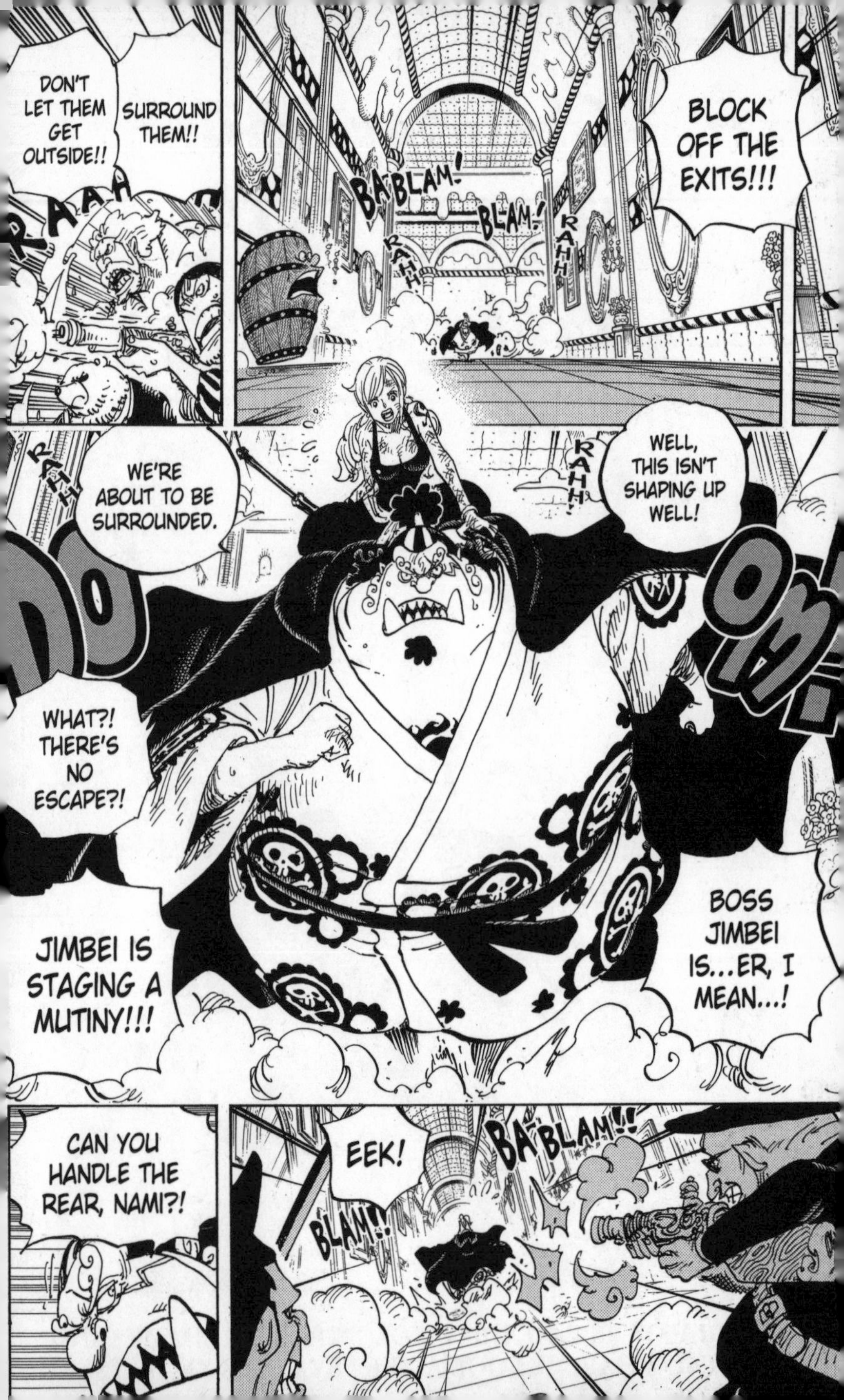
BLOCK OFF THE EXITS!!!
BA-BLAM!
BLAM!
RAHH
RAHH
SURROUND THEM!!
DON'T LET THEM GET OUTSIDE!!
RAAAH
WELL, THIS ISN'T SHAPING UP WELL!
RAHH!
WE'RE ABOUT TO BE SURROUNDED.
RAHH
OM!
DO
BOSS JIMBEI IS...ER, I MEAN...!
WHAT?! THERE'S NO ESCAPE?!
JIMBEI IS STAGING A MUTINY!!!
BA-BLAM!!
EEK!
BLAM!!
CAN YOU HANDLE THE REAR, NAMI?!

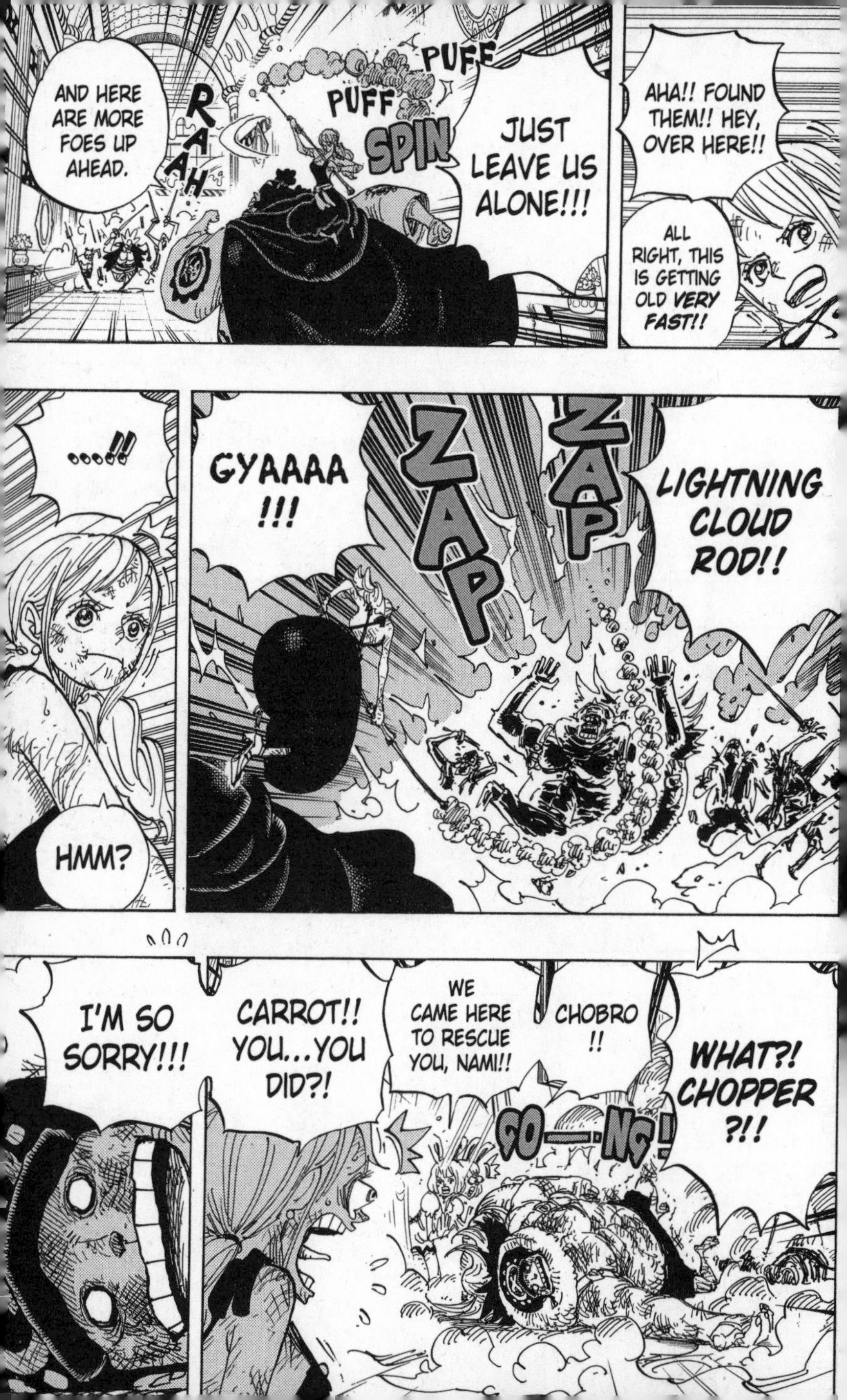
AHA!! FOUND THEM!! HEY, OVER HERE!!
ALL RIGHT, THIS IS GETTING OLD *VERY FAST*!!
JUST LEAVE US ALONE!!!
PUFF
PUFF
SPIN
AND HERE ARE MORE FOES UP AHEAD.
RAAH
LIGHTNING CLOUD ROD!!
ZAP
ZAP
GYAAAA!!!
...!!
HMM?
WHAT?! CHOPPER?!!
CHOBRO!!
GO—NG!
WE CAME HERE TO RESCUE YOU, NAMI!!
CARROT!! YOU...YOU DID?!
I'M SO SORRY!!!

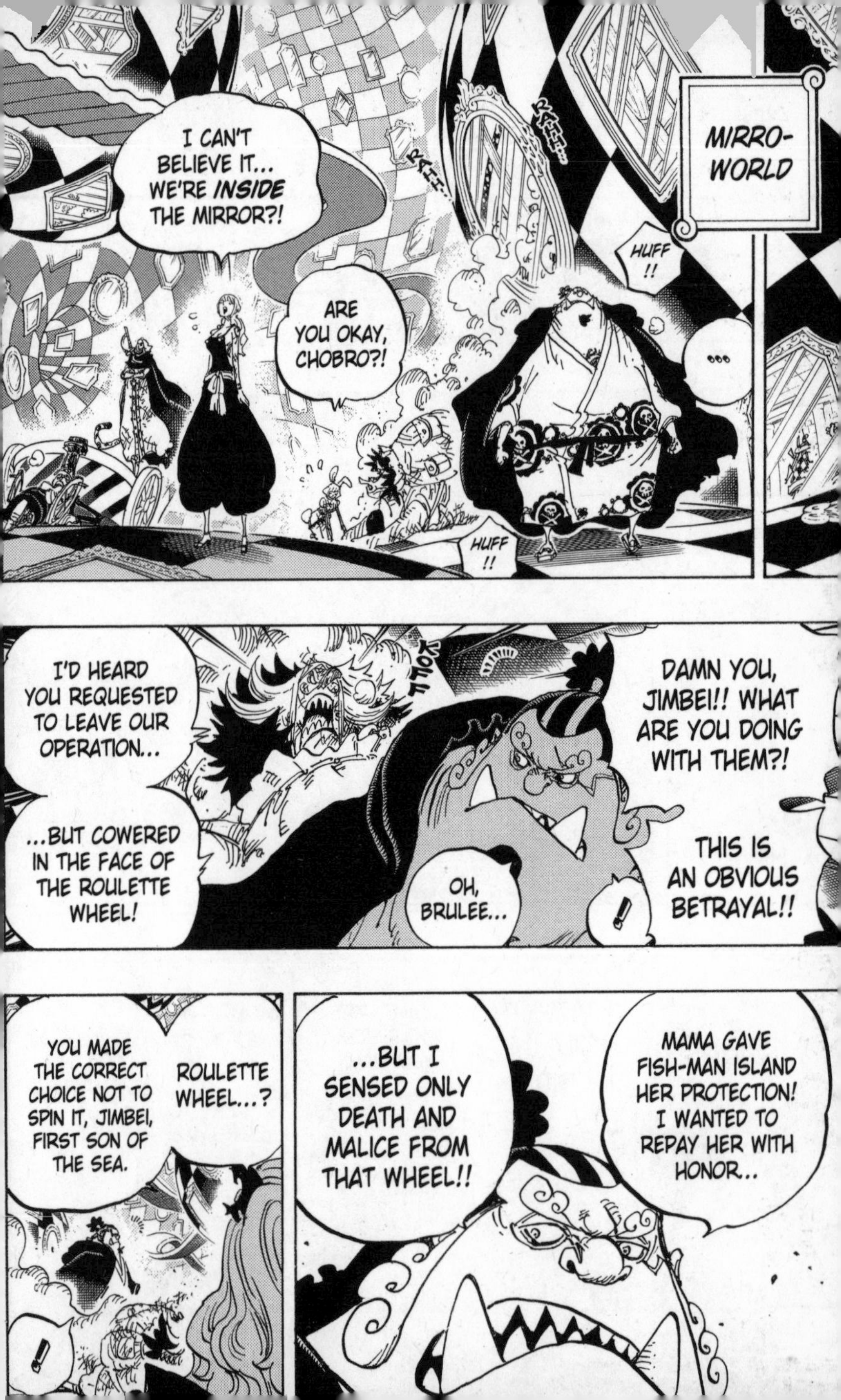
MIRRO-WORLD
...
HUFF !!
ARE YOU OKAY, CHOBRO?!
I CAN'T BELIEVE IT... WE'RE *INSIDE* THE MIRROR?!
HUFF !!
DAMN YOU, JIMBEI!! WHAT ARE YOU DOING WITH THEM?!
THIS IS AN OBVIOUS BETRAYAL!!
!
OH, BRULEE...
KOFF
I'D HEARD YOU REQUESTED TO LEAVE OUR OPERATION...
...BUT COWERED IN THE FACE OF THE ROULETTE WHEEL!
MAMA GAVE FISH-MAN ISLAND HER PROTECTION! I WANTED TO REPAY HER WITH HONOR...
...BUT I SENSED ONLY DEATH AND MALICE FROM THAT WHEEL!!
ROULETTE WHEEL...?
YOU MADE THE CORRECT CHOICE NOT TO SPIN IT, JIMBEI, FIRST SON OF THE SEA.
!

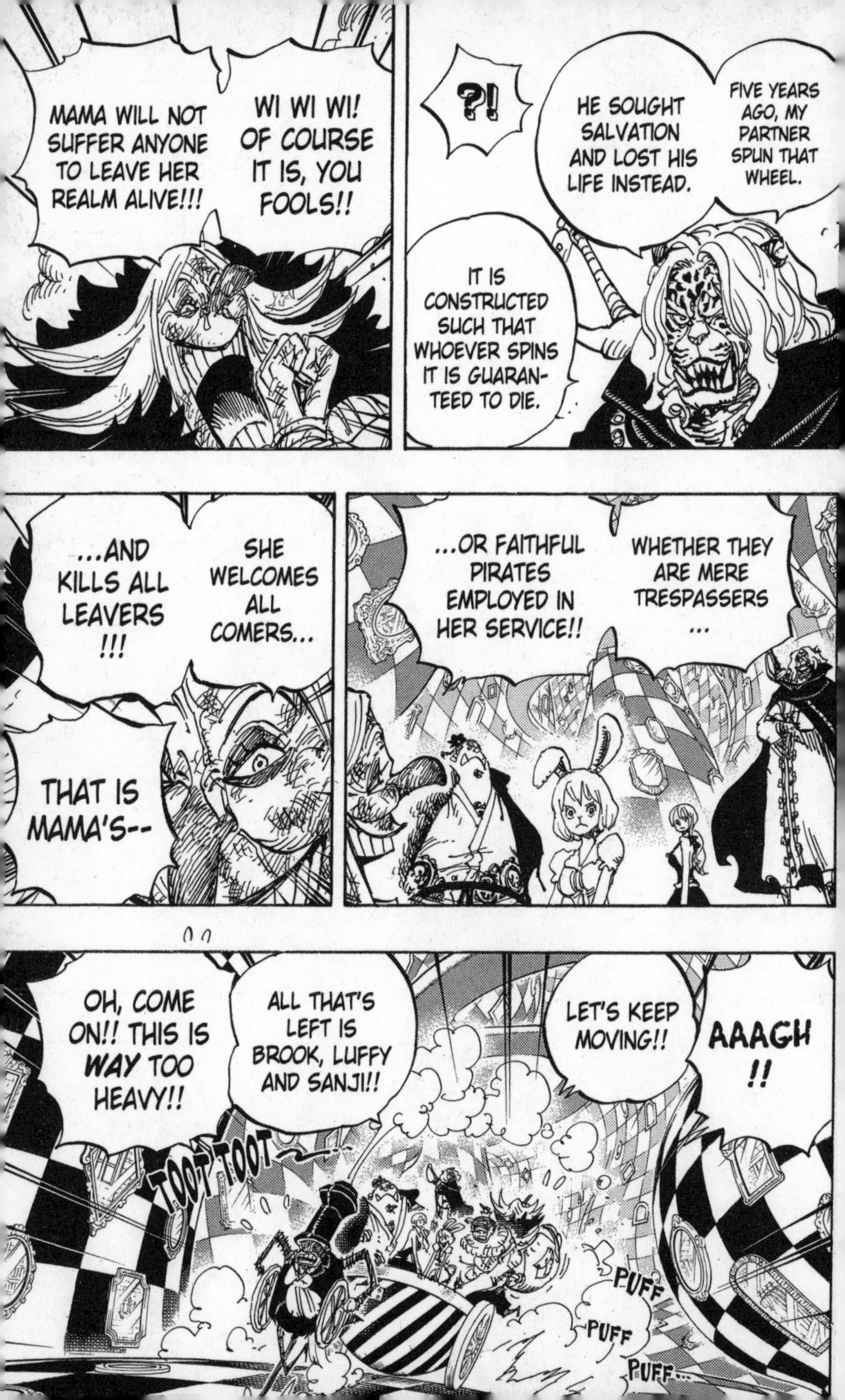
FIVE YEARS AGO, MY PARTNER SPUN THAT WHEEL.
HE SOUGHT SALVATION AND LOST HIS LIFE INSTEAD.
?!
IT IS CONSTRUCTED SUCH THAT WHOEVER SPINS IT IS GUARAN-TEED TO DIE.
WI WI WI! OF COURSE IT IS, YOU FOOLS!!
MAMA WILL NOT SUFFER ANYONE TO LEAVE HER REALM ALIVE!!!
WHETHER THEY ARE MERE TRESPASSERS ...
...OR FAITHFUL PIRATES EMPLOYED IN HER SERVICE!!
SHE WELCOMES ALL COMERS...
...AND KILLS ALL LEAVERS !!!
THAT IS MAMA'S--
AAAGH !!
LET'S KEEP MOVING!!
ALL THAT'S LEFT IS BROOK, LUFFY AND SANJI!!
OH, COME ON!! THIS IS *WAY* TOO HEAVY!!
TOOT TOOT
PUFF
PUFF
PUFF...

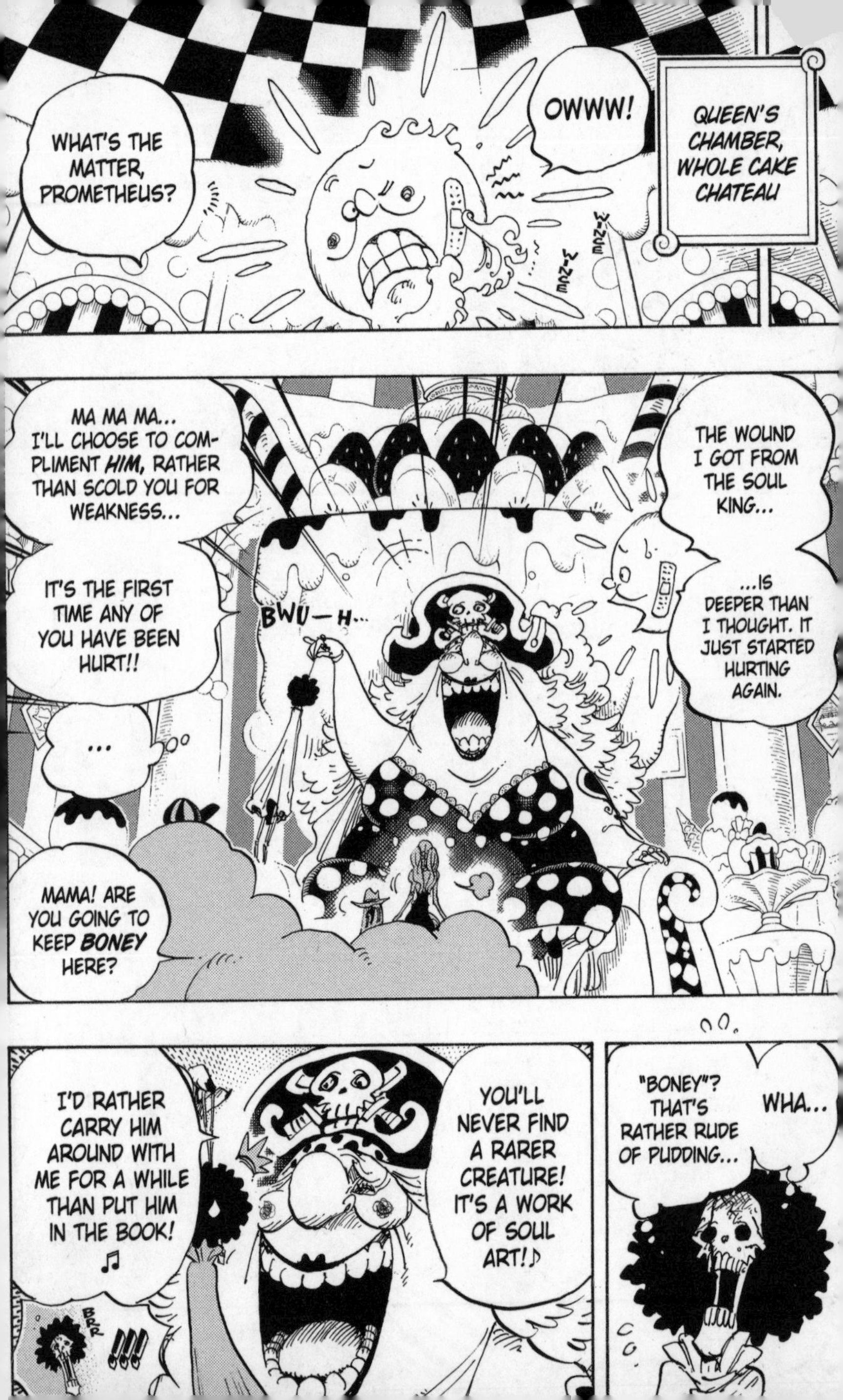
QUEEN'S CHAMBER, WHOLE CAKE CHATEAU
OWWW!
WINCE
WINCE
WHAT'S THE MATTER, PROMETHEUS?
THE WOUND I GOT FROM THE SOUL KING...
...IS DEEPER THAN I THOUGHT. IT JUST STARTED HURTING AGAIN.
BWU—H...
MA MA MA... I'LL CHOOSE TO COMPLIMENT *HIM*, RATHER THAN SCOLD YOU FOR WEAKNESS...
IT'S THE FIRST TIME ANY OF YOU HAVE BEEN HURT!!
...
MAMA! ARE YOU GOING TO KEEP *BONEY* HERE?
WHA...
"BONEY"? THAT'S RATHER RUDE OF PUDDING...
YOU'LL NEVER FIND A RARER CREATURE! IT'S A WORK OF SOUL ART!♪
I'D RATHER CARRY HIM AROUND WITH ME FOR A WHILE THAN PUT HIM IN THE BOOK! ♫
BRR
!!!

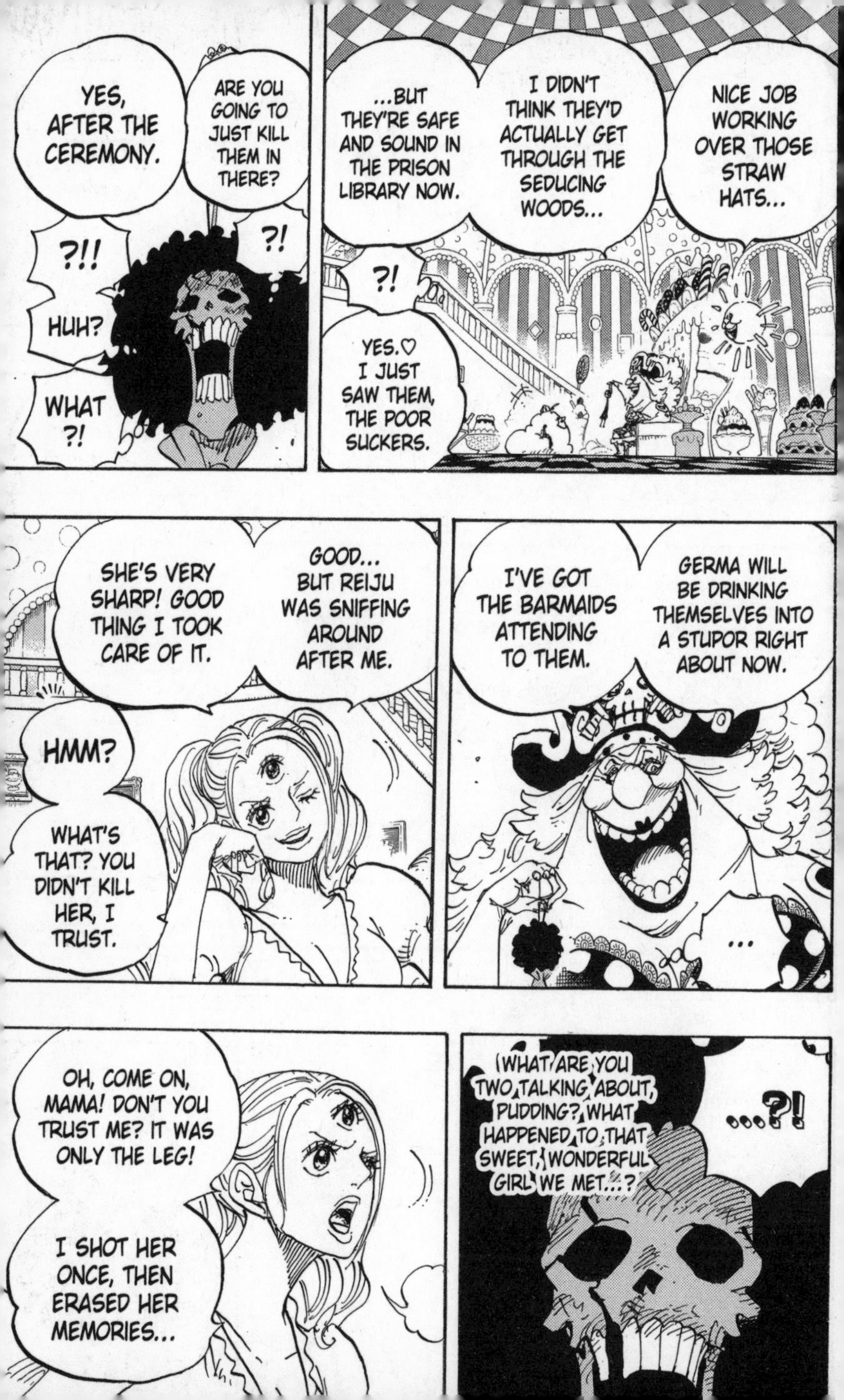
NICE JOB WORKING OVER THOSE STRAW HATS...
I DIDN'T THINK THEY'D ACTUALLY GET THROUGH THE SEDUCING WOODS...
...BUT THEY'RE SAFE AND SOUND IN THE PRISON LIBRARY NOW.
?!
YES.♡ I JUST SAW THEM, THE POOR SUCKERS.
ARE YOU GOING TO JUST KILL THEM IN THERE?
YES, AFTER THE CEREMONY.
?!
?!!
HUH?
WHAT?!
GERMA WILL BE DRINKING THEMSELVES INTO A STUPOR RIGHT ABOUT NOW.
I'VE GOT THE BARMAIDS ATTENDING TO THEM.
...
GOOD... BUT REIJU WAS SNIFFING AROUND AFTER ME.
SHE'S VERY SHARP! GOOD THING I TOOK CARE OF IT.
HMM?
WHAT'S THAT? YOU DIDN'T KILL HER, I TRUST.
...?!
WHAT ARE YOU TWO TALKING ABOUT, PUDDING? WHAT HAPPENED TO THAT SWEET, WONDERFUL GIRL WE MET...?
OH, COME ON, MAMA! DON'T YOU TRUST ME? IT WAS ONLY THE LEG!
I SHOT HER ONCE, THEN ERASED HER MEMORIES...

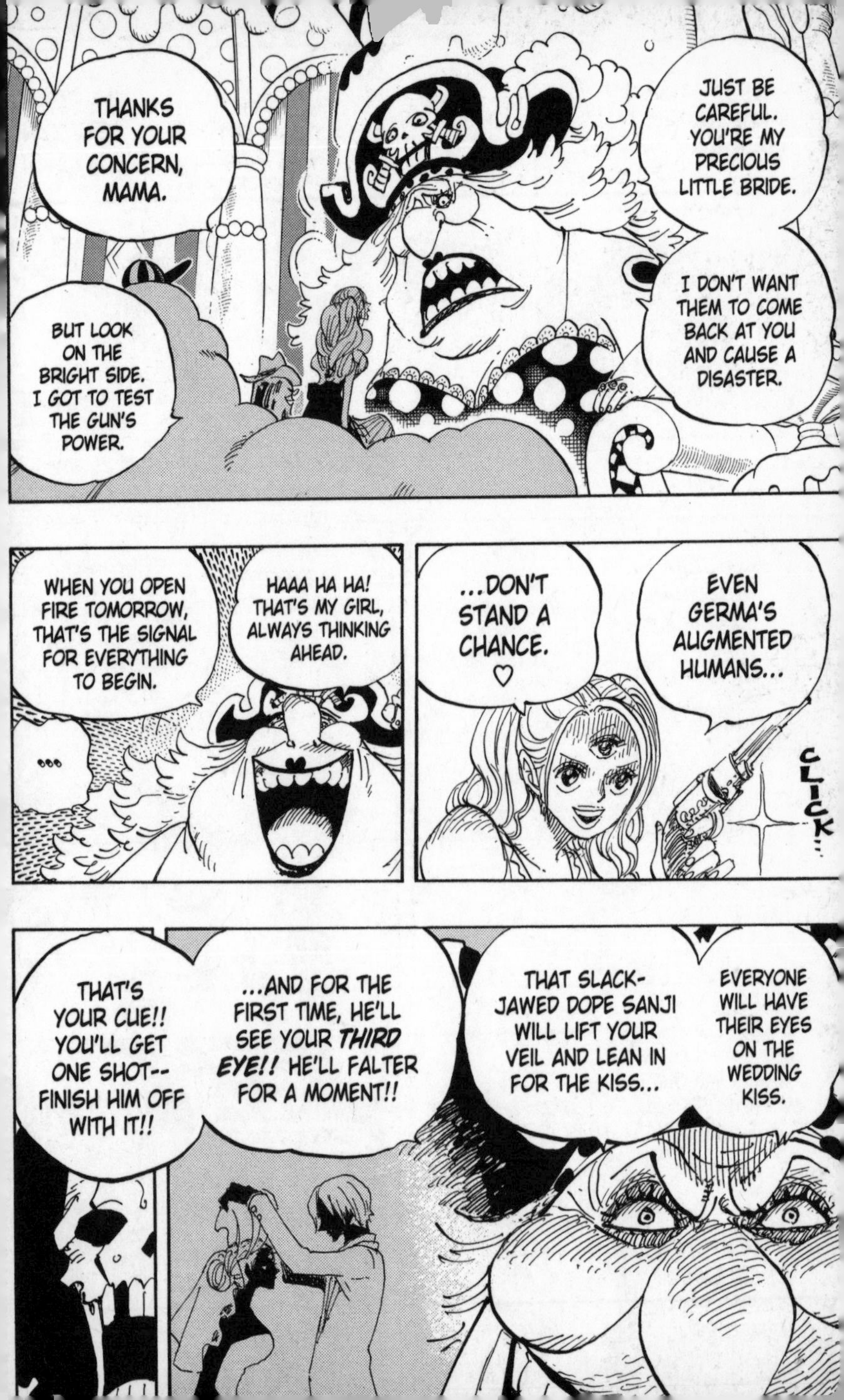
JUST BE CAREFUL. YOU'RE MY PRECIOUS LITTLE BRIDE.
I DON'T WANT THEM TO COME BACK AT YOU AND CAUSE A DISASTER.
THANKS FOR YOUR CONCERN, MAMA.
BUT LOOK ON THE BRIGHT SIDE. I GOT TO TEST THE GUN'S POWER.
EVEN GERMA'S AUGMENTED HUMANS...
...DON'T STAND A CHANCE. ♡
CLICK
HAAA HA HA! THAT'S MY GIRL, ALWAYS THINKING AHEAD.
WHEN YOU OPEN FIRE TOMORROW, THAT'S THE SIGNAL FOR EVERYTHING TO BEGIN.
...
EVERYONE WILL HAVE THEIR EYES ON THE WEDDING KISS.
THAT SLACK-JAWED DOPE SANJI WILL LIFT YOUR VEIL AND LEAN IN FOR THE KISS...
...AND FOR THE FIRST TIME, HE'LL SEE YOUR *THIRD EYE!!* HE'LL FALTER FOR A MOMENT!!
THAT'S YOUR CUE!! YOU'LL GET ONE SHOT--FINISH HIM OFF WITH IT!!

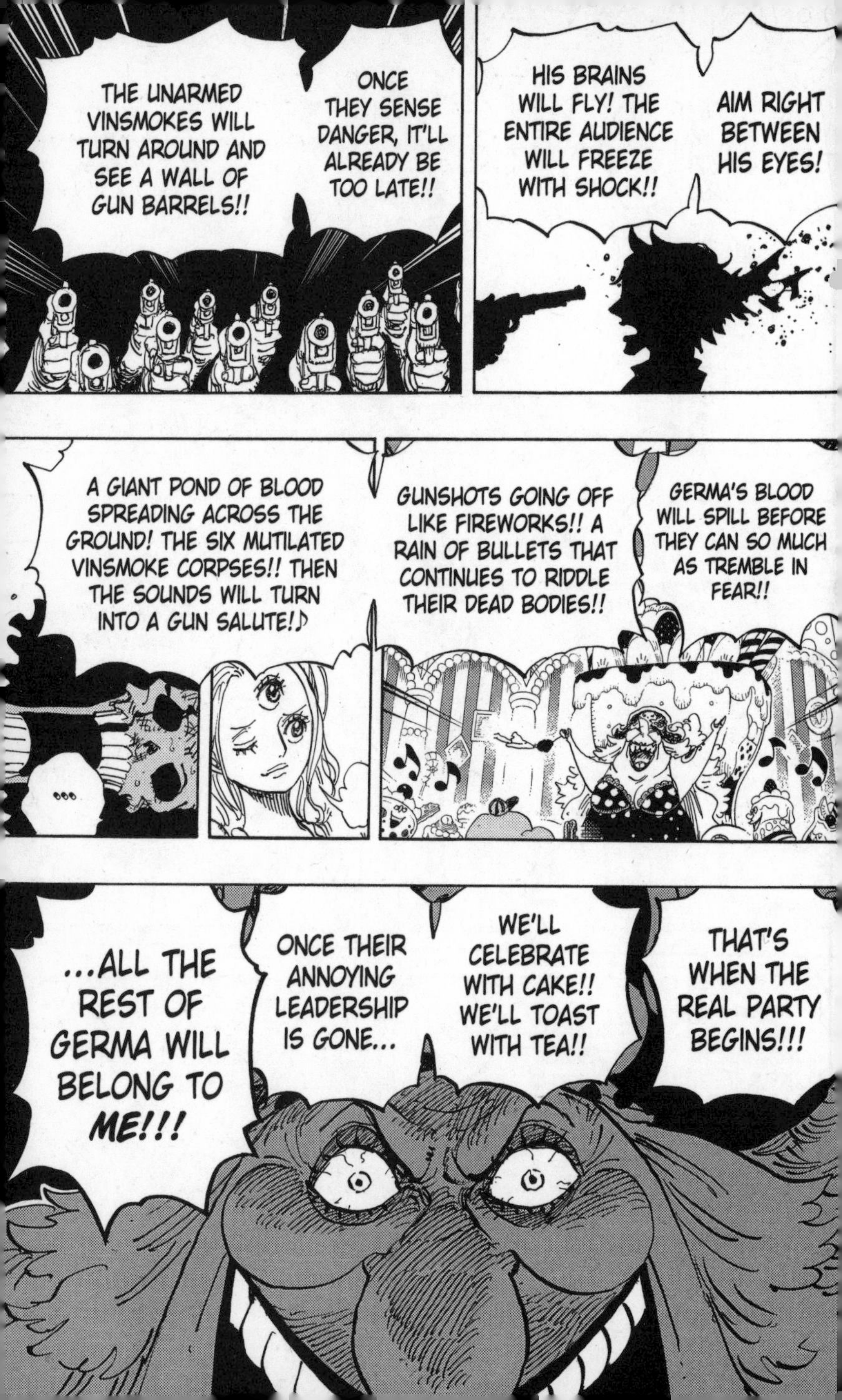
AIM RIGHT BETWEEN HIS EYES!
HIS BRAINS WILL FLY! THE ENTIRE AUDIENCE WILL FREEZE WITH SHOCK!!
ONCE THEY SENSE DANGER, IT'LL ALREADY BE TOO LATE!!
THE UNARMED VINSMOKES WILL TURN AROUND AND SEE A WALL OF GUN BARRELS!!
GERMA'S BLOOD WILL SPILL BEFORE THEY CAN SO MUCH AS TREMBLE IN FEAR!!
GUNSHOTS GOING OFF LIKE FIREWORKS!! A RAIN OF BULLETS THAT CONTINUES TO RIDDLE THEIR DEAD BODIES!!
A GIANT POND OF BLOOD SPREADING ACROSS THE GROUND! THE SIX MUTILATED VINSMOKE CORPSES!! THEN THE SOUNDS WILL TURN INTO A GUN SALUTE!♪
...
THAT'S WHEN THE REAL PARTY BEGINS!!!
WE'LL CELEBRATE WITH CAKE!! WE'LL TOAST WITH TEA!!
ONCE THEIR ANNOYING LEADERSHIP IS GONE...
...ALL THE REST OF GERMA WILL BELONG TO ME!!!

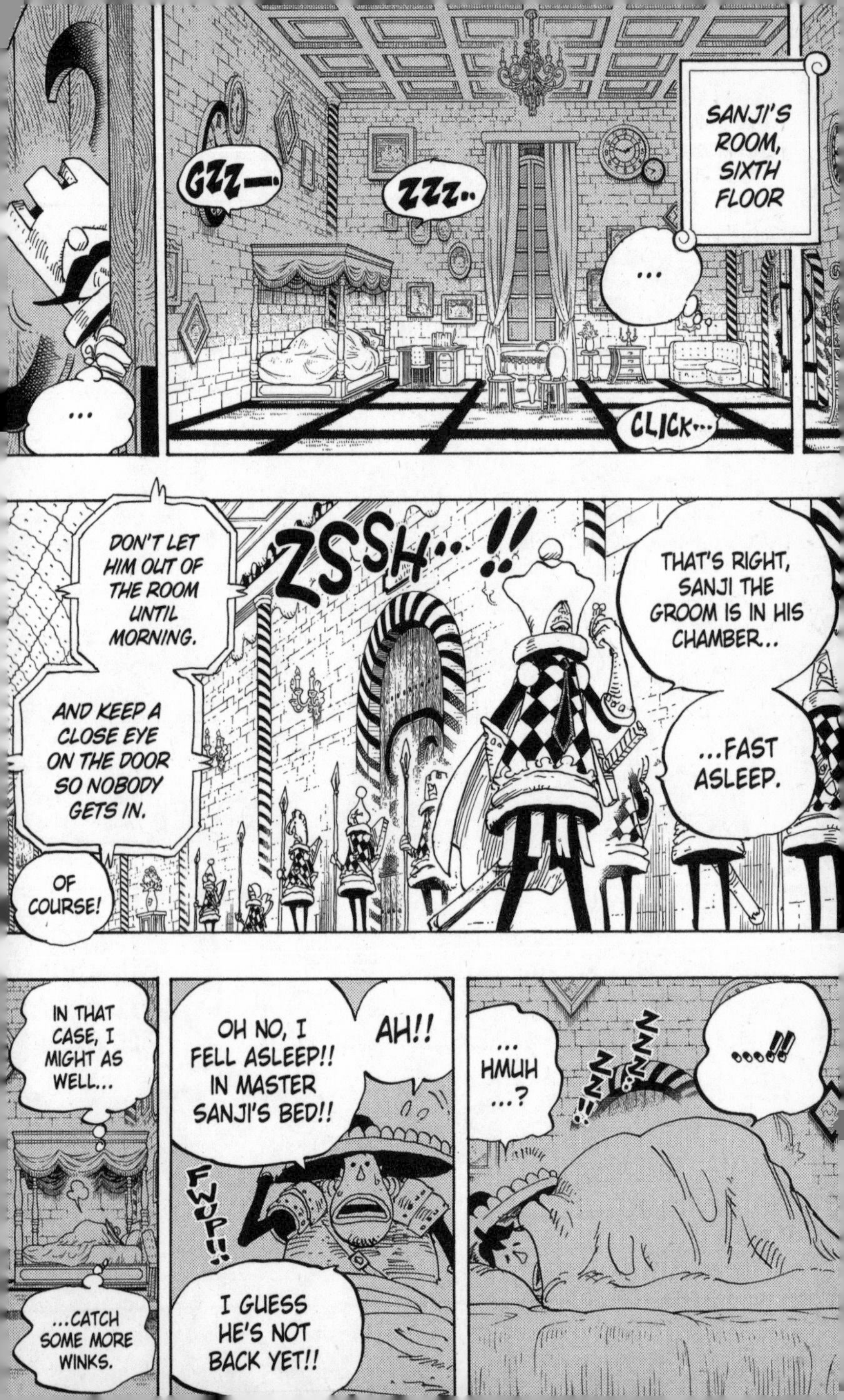
SANJI'S ROOM, SIXTH FLOOR
...
ZZZ..
GZZ—.
CLICK...
...
THAT'S RIGHT, SANJI THE GROOM IS IN HIS CHAMBER...
...FAST ASLEEP.
ZSSH...!!
DON'T LET HIM OUT OF THE ROOM UNTIL MORNING.
AND KEEP A CLOSE EYE ON THE DOOR SO NOBODY GETS IN.
OF COURSE!
...!!
... HMUH ...?
AH!!
OH NO, I FELL ASLEEP!! IN MASTER SANJI'S BED!!
FWUP!!
I GUESS HE'S NOT BACK YET!!
IN THAT CASE, I MIGHT AS WELL...
...CATCH SOME MORE WINKS.

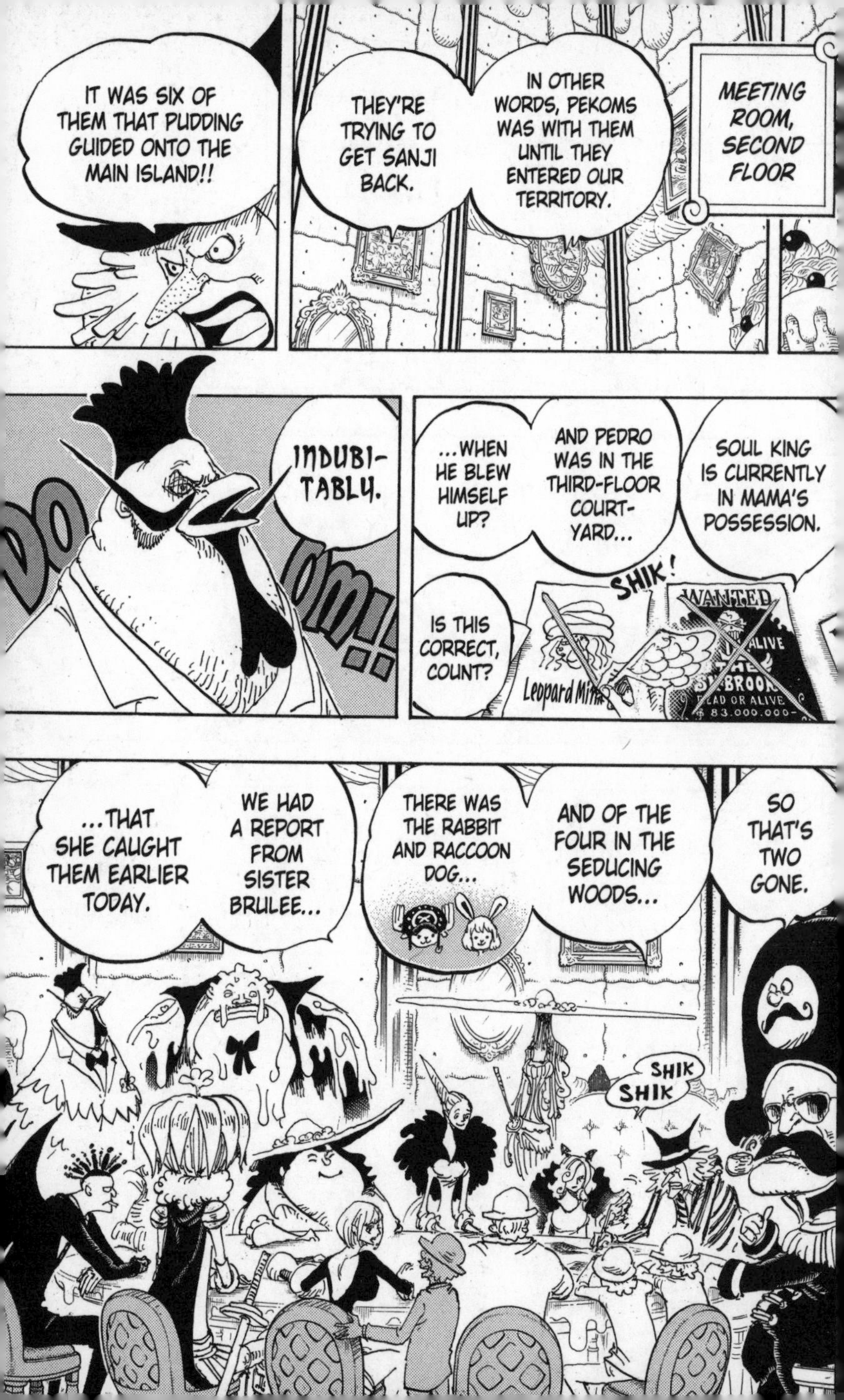
MEETING ROOM, SECOND FLOOR
IN OTHER WORDS, PEKOMS WAS WITH THEM UNTIL THEY ENTERED OUR TERRITORY.
THEY'RE TRYING TO GET SANJI BACK.
IT WAS SIX OF THEM THAT PUDDING GUIDED ONTO THE MAIN ISLAND!!
SOUL KING IS CURRENTLY IN MAMA'S POSSESSION.
AND PEDRO WAS IN THE THIRD-FLOOR COURT-YARD...
...WHEN HE BLEW HIMSELF UP?
SHIK!
WANTED
ALIVE
DEAD OR ALIVE
$ 83.000.000-
IS THIS CORRECT, COUNT?
INDUBI-TABLY.
DOOM!!
SO THAT'S TWO GONE.
AND OF THE FOUR IN THE SEDUCING WOODS...
THERE WAS THE RABBIT AND RACCOON DOG...
WE HAD A REPORT FROM SISTER BRULEE...
...THAT SHE CAUGHT THEM EARLIER TODAY.
SHIK SHIK

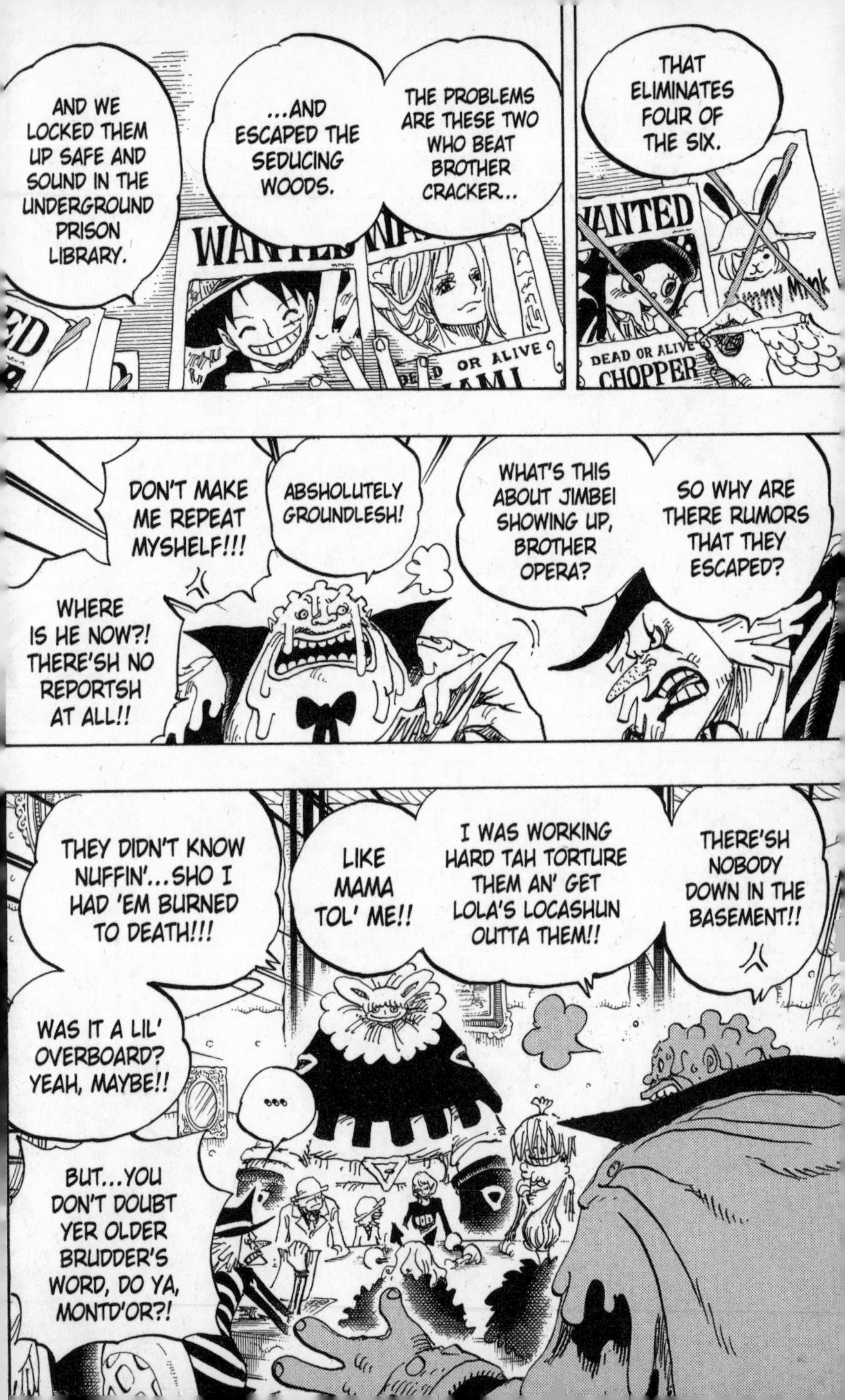
THAT ELIMINATES FOUR OF THE SIX.
WANTED
DEAD OR ALIVE
CHOPPER
THE PROBLEMS ARE THESE TWO WHO BEAT BROTHER CRACKER...
...AND ESCAPED THE SEDUCING WOODS.
DEAD OR ALIVE
AND WE LOCKED THEM UP SAFE AND SOUND IN THE UNDERGROUND PRISON LIBRARY.
SO WHY ARE THERE RUMORS THAT THEY ESCAPED?
WHAT'S THIS ABOUT JIMBEI SHOWING UP, BROTHER OPERA?
ABSHOLUTELY GROUNDLESH!
DON'T MAKE ME REPEAT MYSHELF!!!
WHERE IS HE NOW?! THERE'SH NO REPORTSH AT ALL!!
THERE'SH NOBODY DOWN IN THE BASEMENT!!
I WAS WORKING HARD TAH TORTURE THEM AN' GET LOLA'S LOCASHUN OUTTA THEM!!
LIKE MAMA TOL' ME!!
THEY DIDN'T KNOW NUFFIN'...SHO I HAD 'EM BURNED TO DEATH!!!
WAS IT A LIL' OVERBOARD? YEAH, MAYBE!!
...
BUT...YOU DON'T DOUBT YER OLDER BRUDDER'S WORD, DO YA, MONTD'OR?!

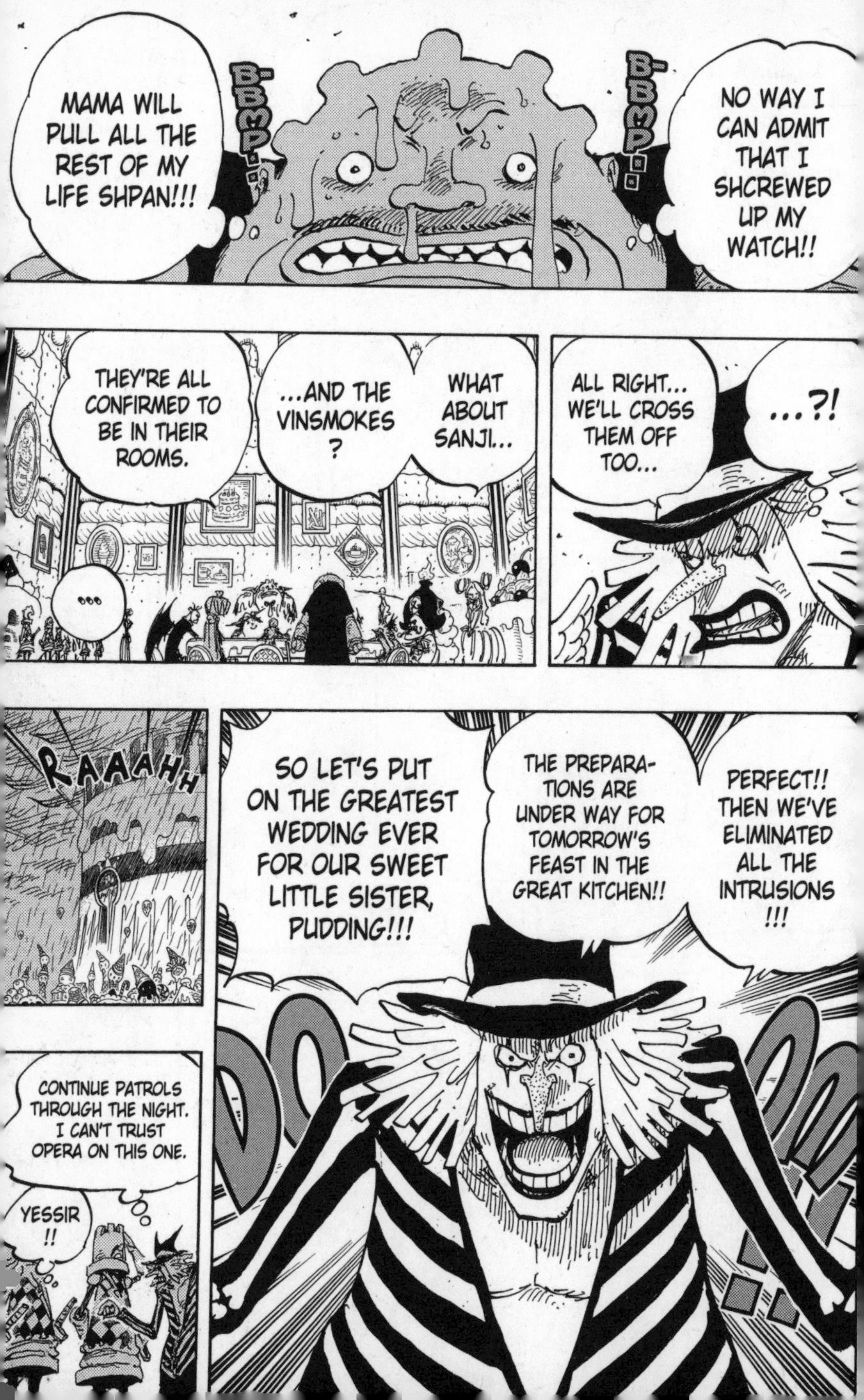
B-BMP
NO WAY I CAN ADMIT THAT I SHCREWED UP MY WATCH!!
B-BMP
MAMA WILL PULL ALL THE REST OF MY LIFE SHPAN!!!
...?!
ALL RIGHT... WE'LL CROSS THEM OFF TOO...
WHAT ABOUT SANJI...
...AND THE VINSMOKES ?
THEY'RE ALL CONFIRMED TO BE IN THEIR ROOMS.
...
PERFECT!! THEN WE'VE ELIMINATED ALL THE INTRUSIONS !!!
THE PREPARATIONS ARE UNDER WAY FOR TOMORROW'S FEAST IN THE GREAT KITCHEN!!
SO LET'S PUT ON THE GREATEST WEDDING EVER FOR OUR SWEET LITTLE SISTER, PUDDING!!!
RAAAHH
CONTINUE PATROLS THROUGH THE NIGHT. I CAN'T TRUST OPERA ON THIS ONE.
YESSIR !!

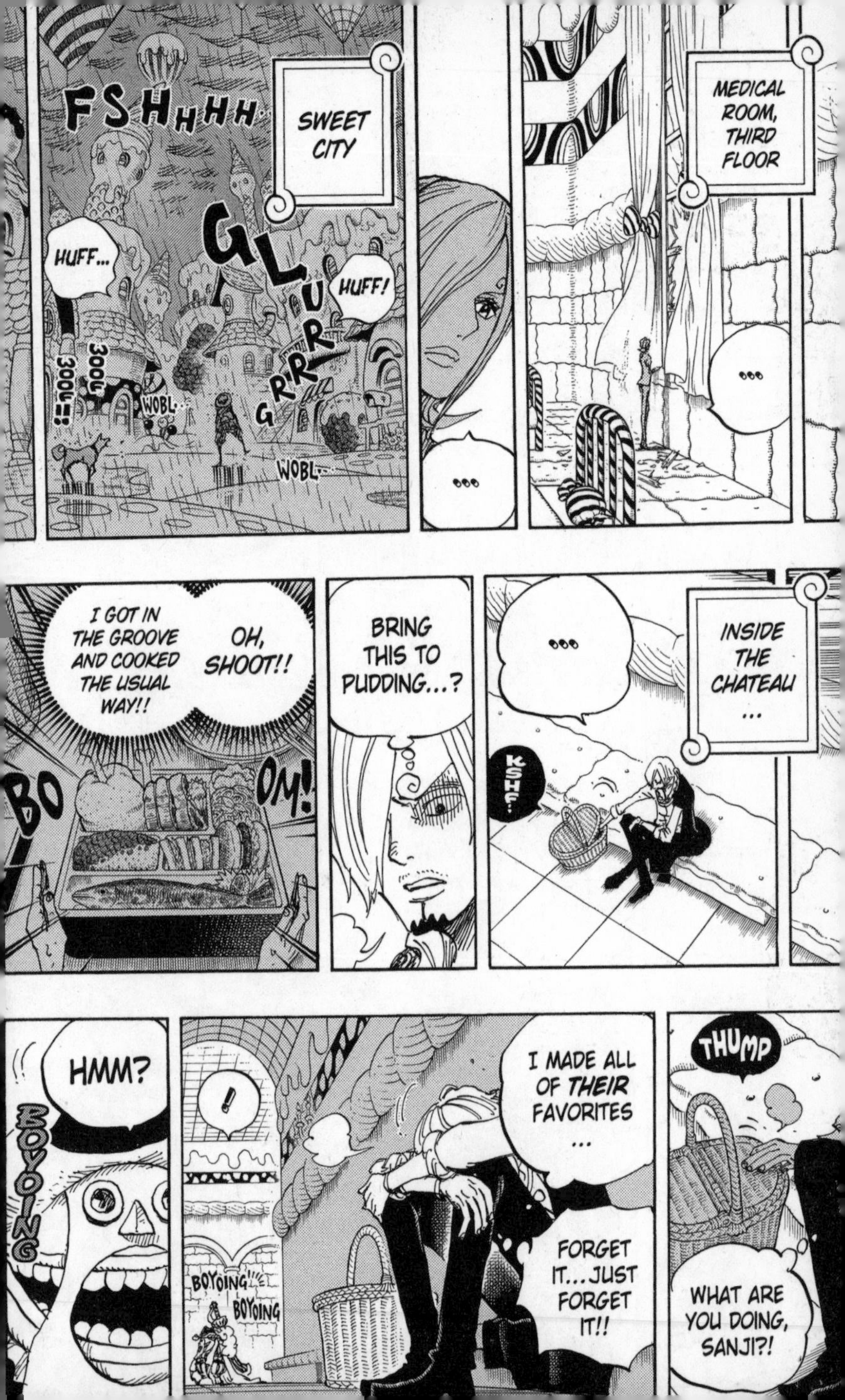
MEDICAL ROOM, THIRD FLOOR
...
...
SWEET CITY
FSHHHH..
HUFF!
HUFF...
WOBL..
WOBL..
INSIDE THE CHATEAU ...
...
KSHF..
BRING THIS TO PUDDING...?
OH, SHOOT!!
I GOT IN THE GROOVE AND COOKED THE USUAL WAY!!
BOOM!
THUMP
WHAT ARE YOU DOING, SANJI?!
I MADE ALL OF THEIR FAVORITES ...
FORGET IT... JUST FORGET IT!!
!
BOYOING
BOYOING
HMM?
BOYOING

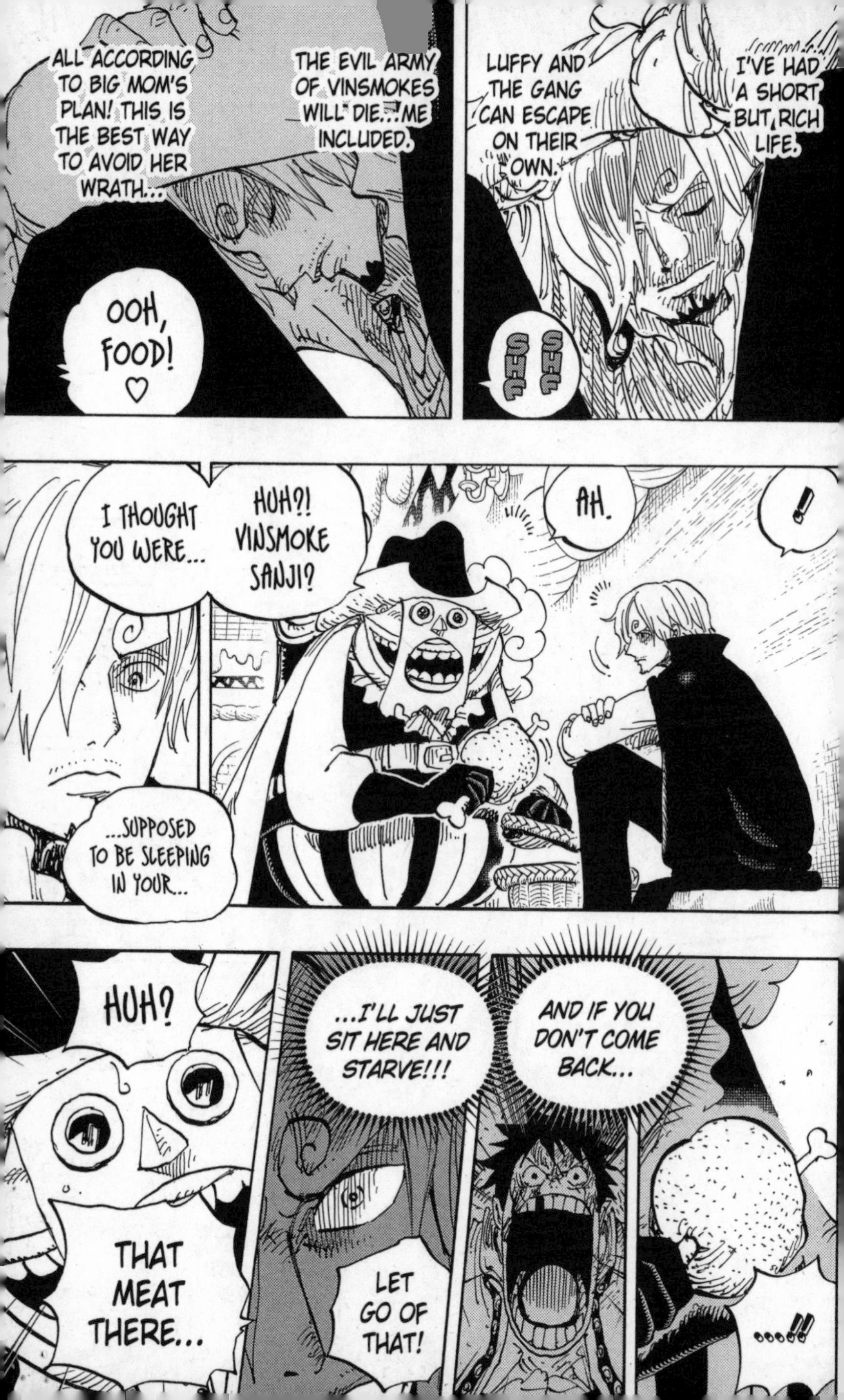
I'VE HAD A SHORT BUT RICH LIFE.
LUFFY AND THE GANG CAN ESCAPE ON THEIR OWN.
SHF SHF
THE EVIL ARMY OF VINSMOKES WILL DIE... ME INCLUDED.
ALL ACCORDING TO BIG MOM'S PLAN! THIS IS THE BEST WAY TO AVOID HER WRATH...
OOH, FOOD! ♡
!
AH.
HUH?! VINSMOKE SANJI?
I THOUGHT YOU WERE...
...SUPPOSED TO BE SLEEPING IN YOUR...
...!!
AND IF YOU DON'T COME BACK...
...I'LL JUST SIT HERE AND STARVE!!!
LET GO OF THAT!
HUH?
THAT MEAT THERE...

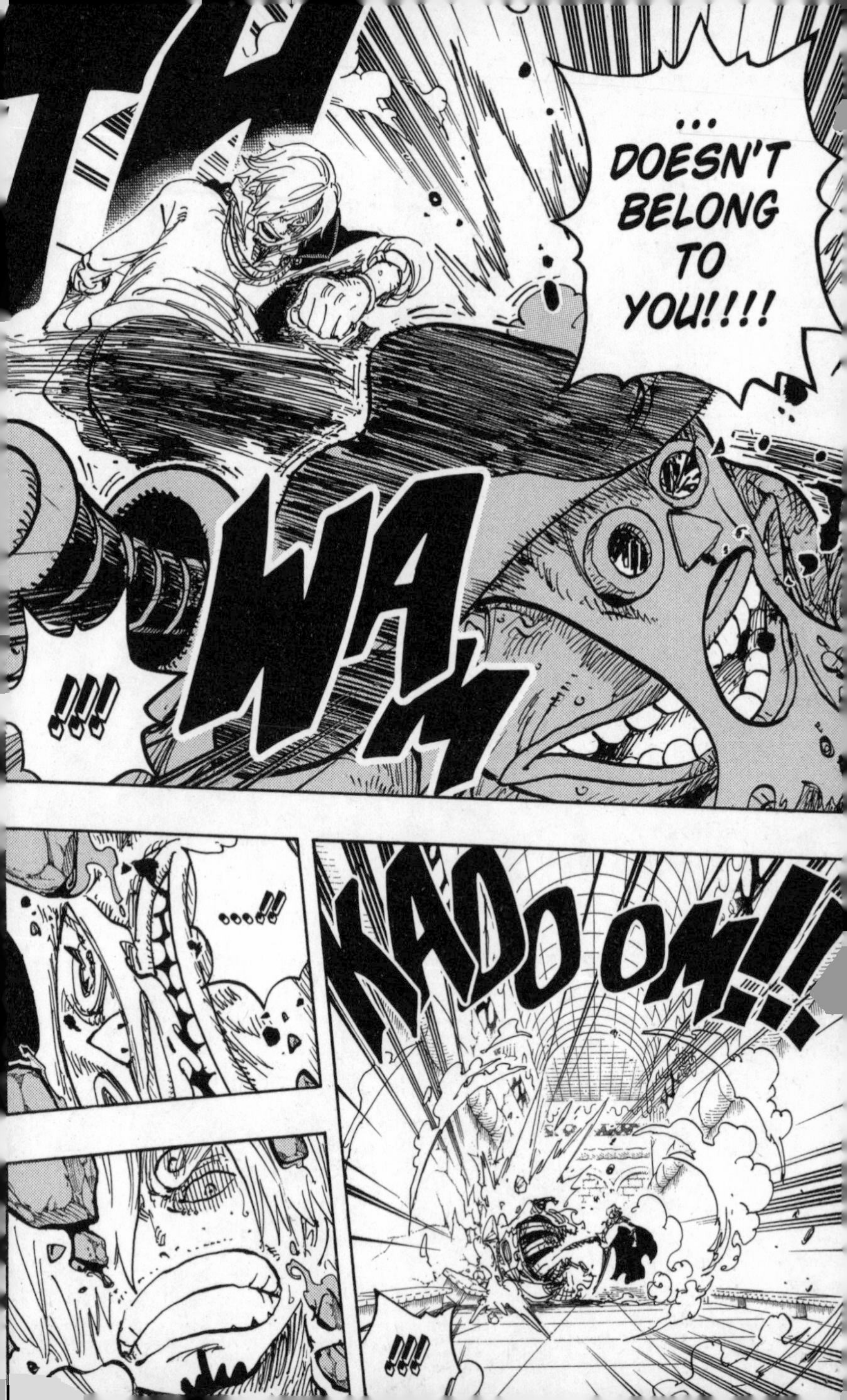
...DOESN'T BELONG TO YOU!!!!
WHAM
!!!
KADOOM!!
!!!
...!!

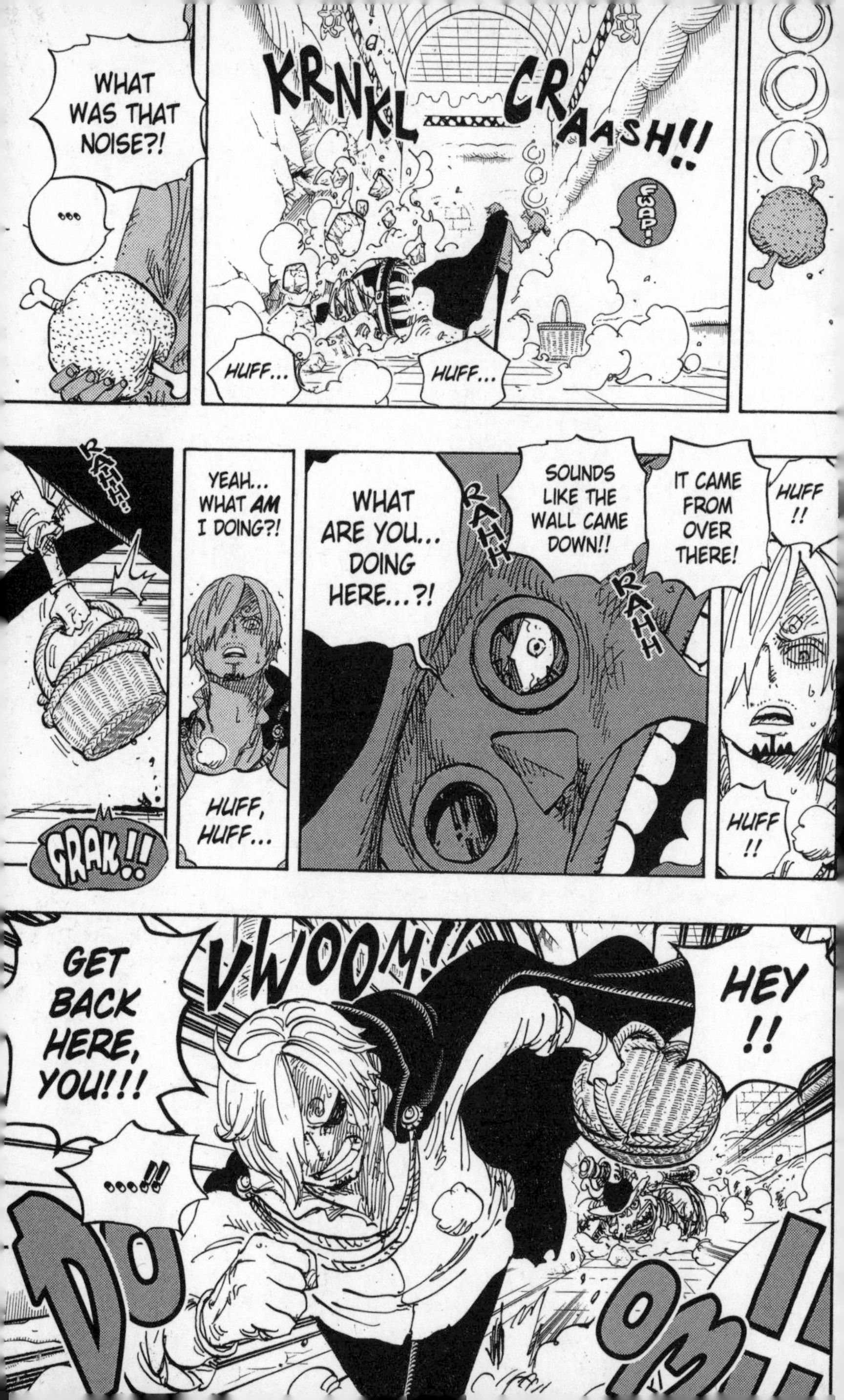
CRAASH!!
KRNKL
FWAP!
HUFF...
HUFF...
WHAT WAS THAT NOISE?!
...
HUFF!!
IT CAME FROM OVER THERE!
HUFF!!
SOUNDS LIKE THE WALL CAME DOWN!!
RAHH
RAHH
WHAT ARE YOU... DOING HERE...?!
YEAH... WHAT AM I DOING?!
HUFF, HUFF...
RAHH!
GRAK!!
HEY!!
VWOOM!!
GET BACK HERE, YOU!!!
...!!
DOOM!!

SBS Question Corner

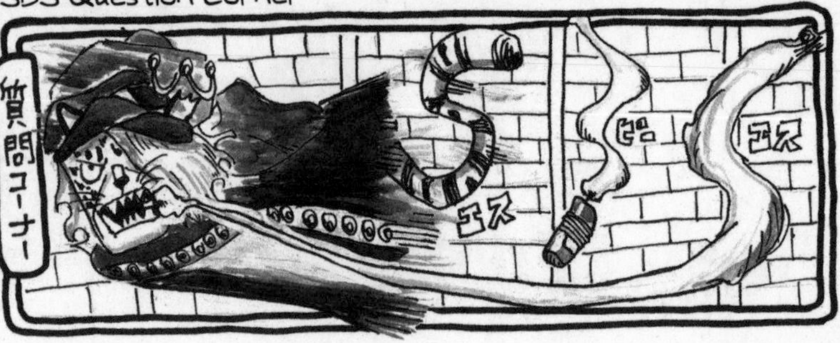

質問コーナー
エス
ビー
エス

(Hayato Asami, Kanagawa)

Q: In the "sons' cups" scene in chapter 800 (volume 80), there's a panel where everyone holds out their cups. On the sound effect bubble, there are eight } marks! But there are seven of them! So who was the last one?! Tell us!

--Mutsu 2

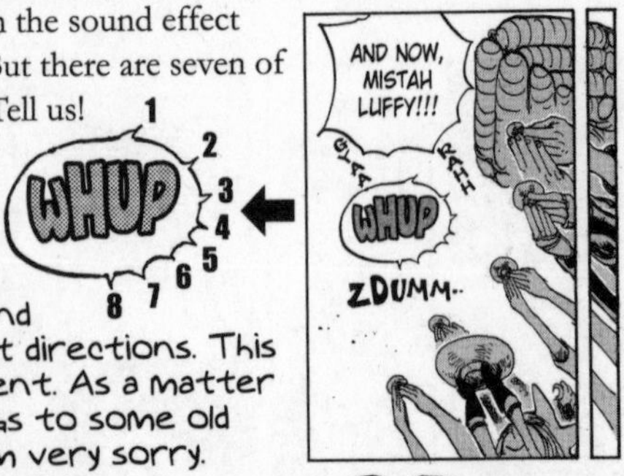

AND NOW, MISTAH LUFFY!!!
GYAA
RAHH
WHUP
ZDUMM..
WHUP
1
2
3
4
5
6
7
8

A: Whoa...! You noticed that?! Who does that?! It does seem weird that there are seven cups, and yet the sound effect is coming from eight directions. This is kind of like a live-TV incident. As a matter of fact, the last one belongs to some old lady who just wandered by. I'm very sorry. She's very sorry too, so I hope you can let this one slide.

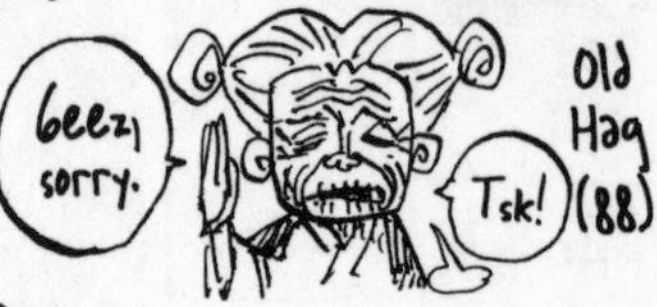

Tsk!
beezy sorry.
Old Hag (88)

Q: What is a heart full of belief?!

--Rukia, Age 12

A: It could be, for example, the strength of mind not to be led astray by the deceptive lies of adults who cannot admit their own mistakes. You have to be strong enough to say, "No old lady's just gonna be 'passing by' on a boat! That makes no sense!!"

Q: What does Doflamingo look like when he takes off his sunglasses?

--Saki & Shun

A: Oh! Good timing! Look, Doflamingo's about to remove his glasses right now!!

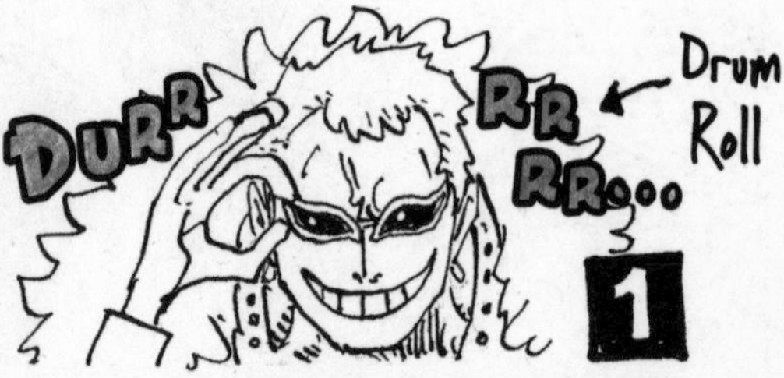

Drum Roll
DURR
RR
RRooo
1

Argh, hurry up!! He's gonna carry this over to pg. 132!! Take those shades off!!

Chapter 855: GLURRGLE!!!

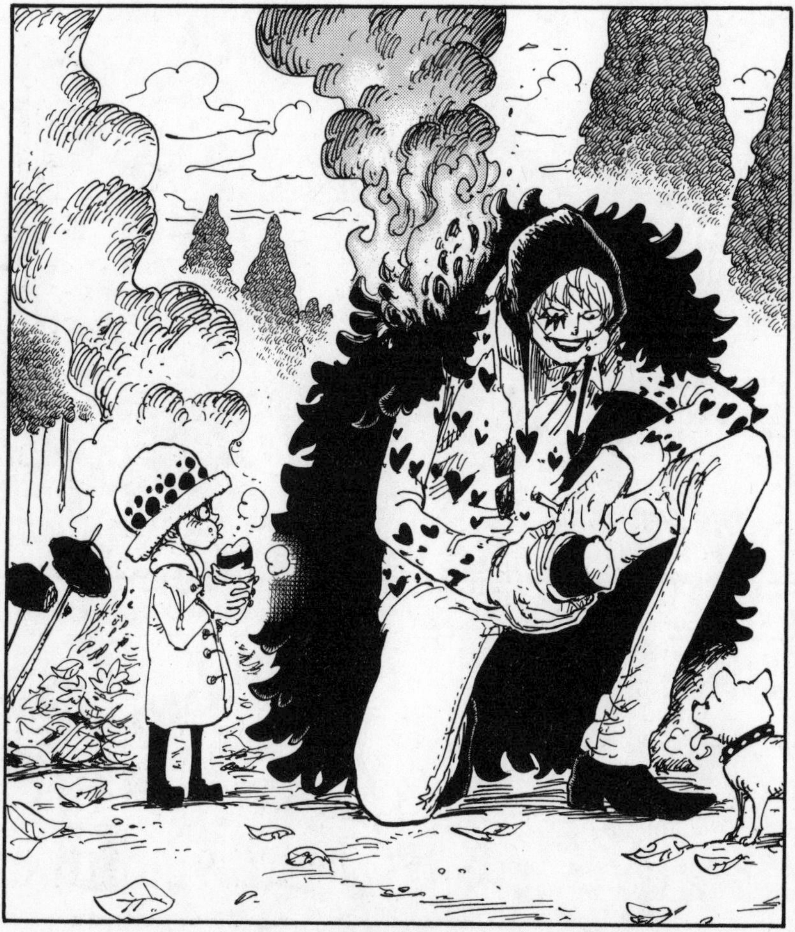

REQUEST: "LAW NOTICING CORA IS ON FIRE AS THEY ROAST YAMS OVER A PILE OF LEAVES" BY NAOMIN SHIRAKI FROM TOKYO

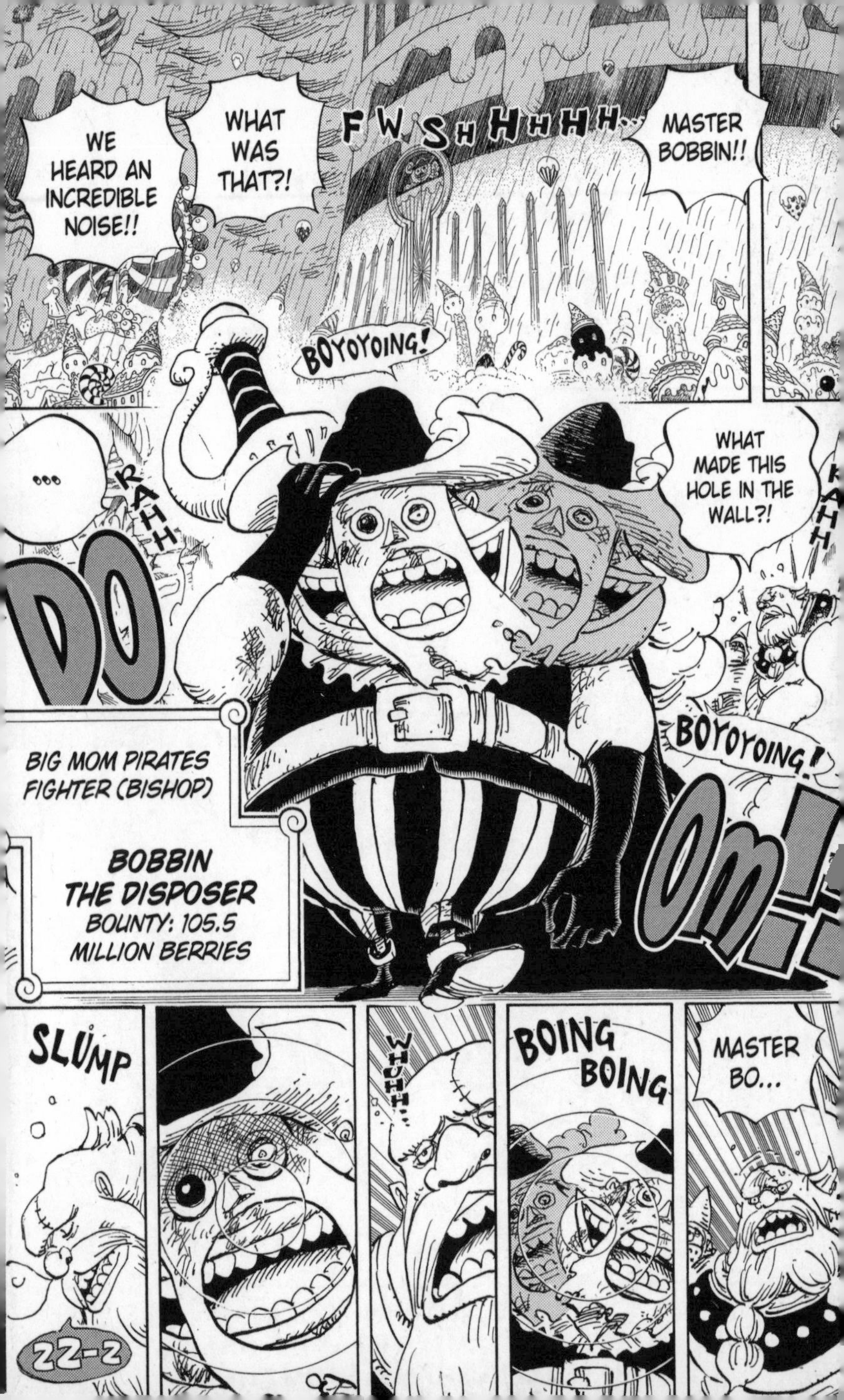
MASTER BOBBIN!!
FWSHHHHH...
WHAT WAS THAT?!
WE HEARD AN INCREDIBLE NOISE!!
BOYOYOING!
RAHHH
WHAT MADE THIS HOLE IN THE WALL?!
BOYOYOING!
OM!!
DO
RAHHH
...
BIG MOM PIRATES FIGHTER (BISHOP)
BOBBIN THE DISPOSER
BOUNTY: 105.5 MILLION BERRIES
MASTER BO...
BOING BOING
WHUHH...
SLUMP
22-2

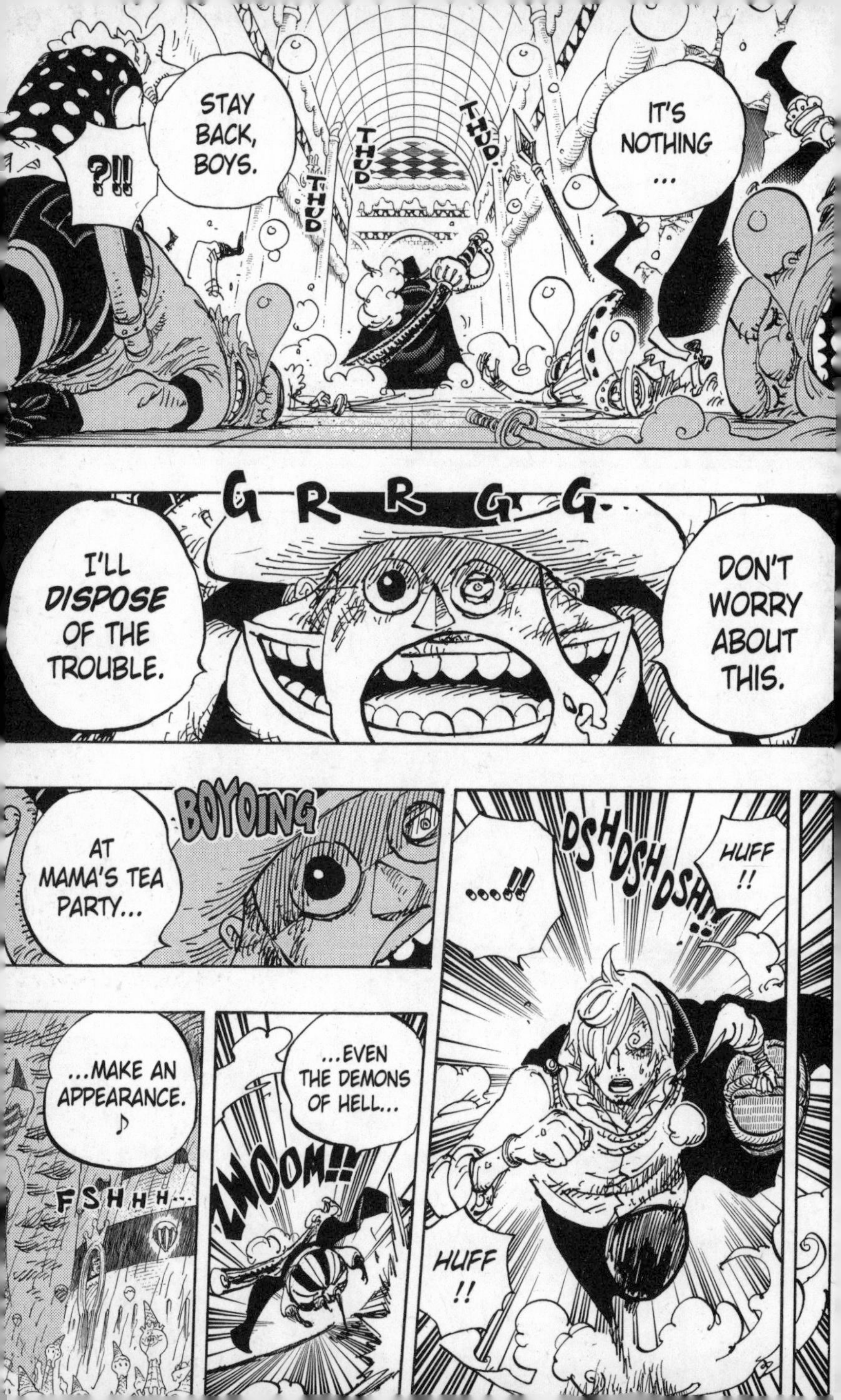

IT'S NOTHING ...
THUD
THUD
THUD
STAY BACK, BOYS.
?!!
GRRGG
DON'T WORRY ABOUT THIS.
I'LL *DISPOSE* OF THE TROUBLE.
HUFF !!
DSHDSHDSHDSH!!
...!!
HUFF !!
AT MAMA'S TEA PARTY...
BOYOING
...EVEN THE DEMONS OF HELL...
ZWOOM!!
...MAKE AN APPEARANCE. ♪
FSHHH...

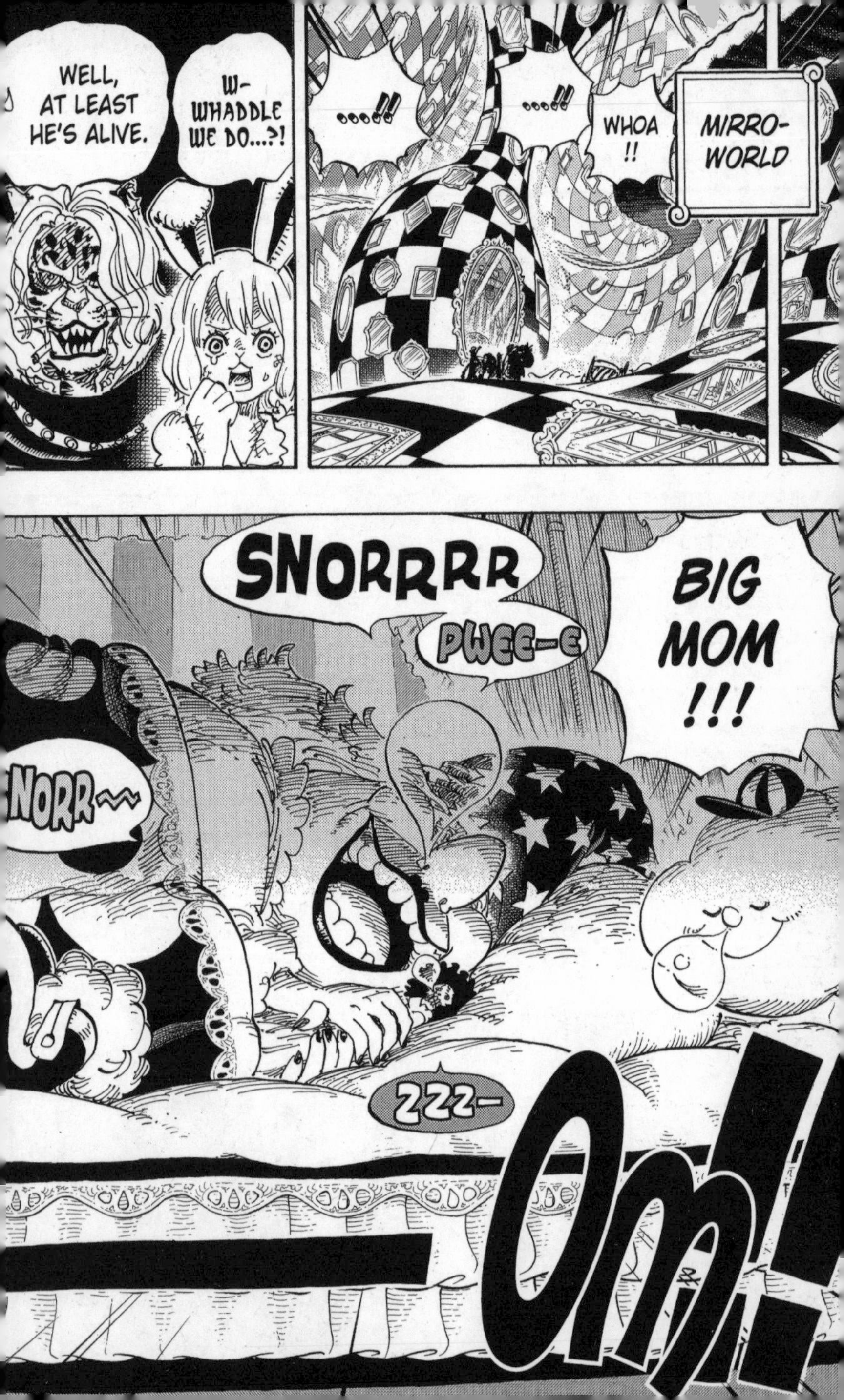

MIRRO-WORLD
WHOA !!
....!!
....!!
W-WHADDLE WE DO...?!
WELL, AT LEAST HE'S ALIVE.
BIG MOM !!!
SNORRRR
PWEE-E
NORR~
ZZZ-
OM!

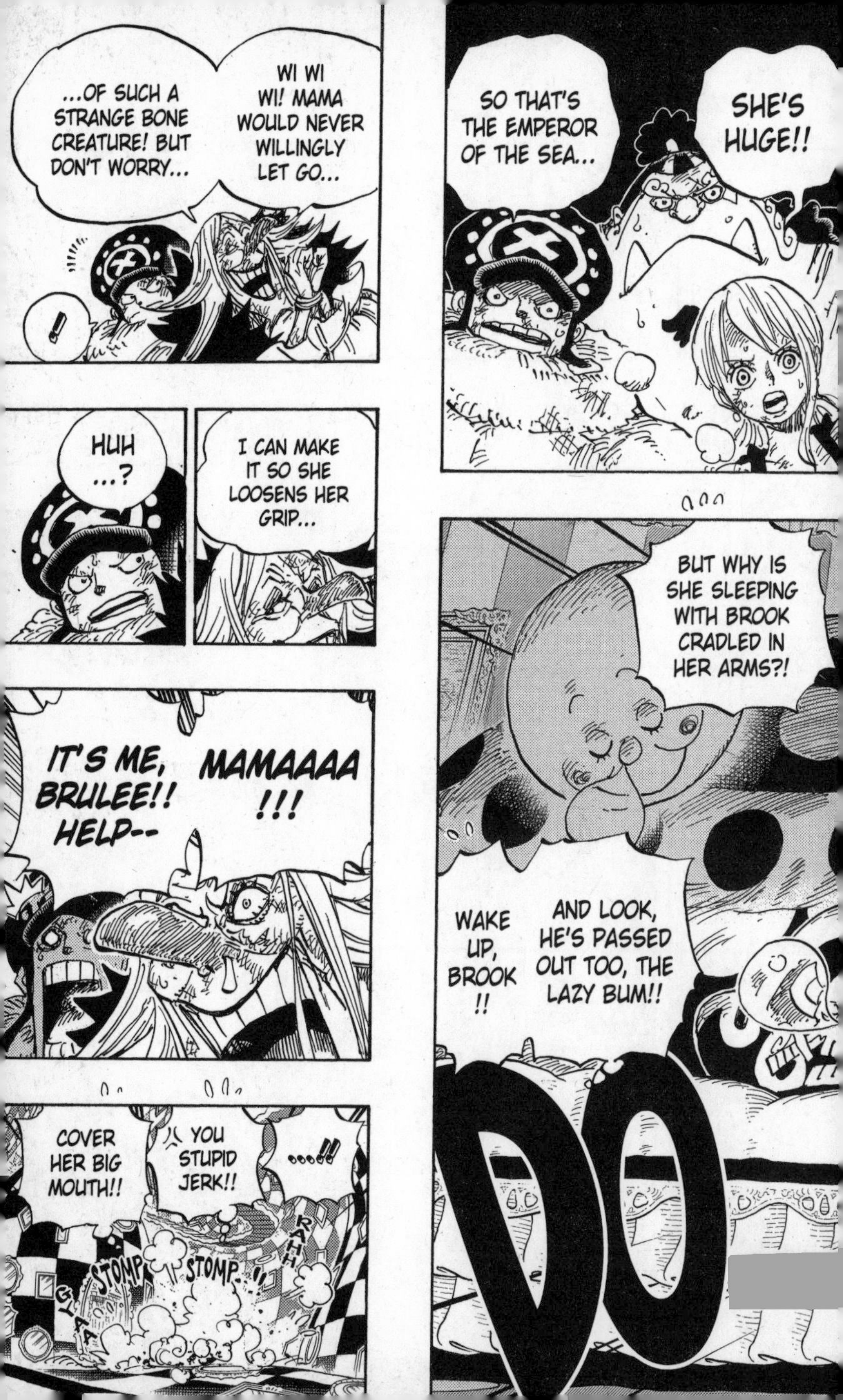

SHE'S HUGE!!
SO THAT'S THE EMPEROR OF THE SEA...
BUT WHY IS SHE SLEEPING WITH BROOK CRADLED IN HER ARMS?!
AND LOOK, HE'S PASSED OUT TOO, THE LAZY BUM!!
WAKE UP, BROOK!!
WI WI WI! MAMA WOULD NEVER WILLINGLY LET GO...
...OF SUCH A STRANGE BONE CREATURE! BUT DON'T WORRY...
!
I CAN MAKE IT SO SHE LOOSENS HER GRIP...
HUH ...?
MAMAAAA!!!
IT'S ME, BRULEE!! HELP--
...!!
YOU STUPID JERK!!
COVER HER BIG MOUTH!!
RAHH
STOMP
STOMP
GYAA

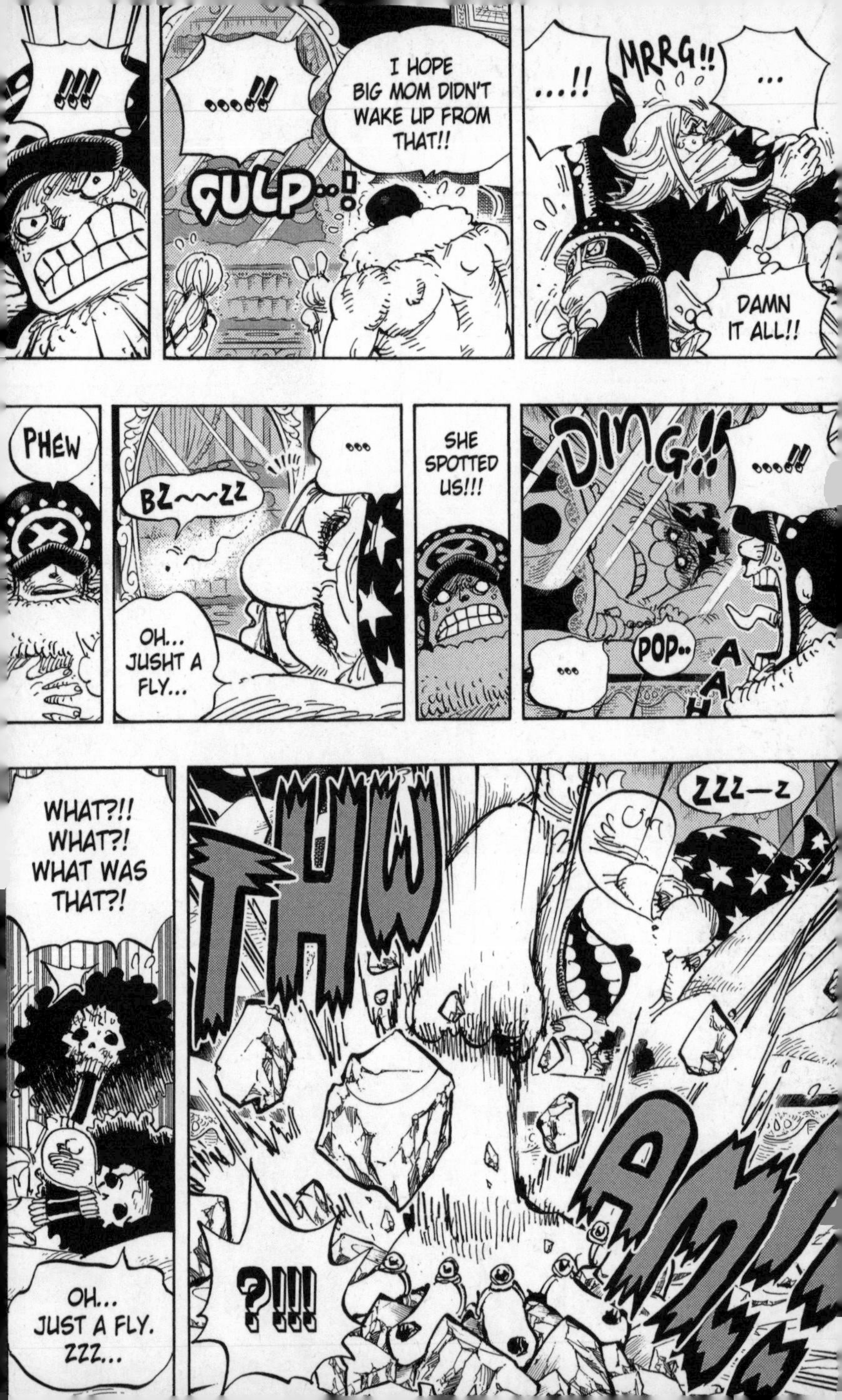
...
MRRG!!
...!!
DAMN IT ALL!!
I HOPE BIG MOM DIDN'T WAKE UP FROM THAT!!
...!!
GULP..!
!!!
...!!
DING!!
POP..
AAH
...
SHE SPOTTED US!!!
...
BZ~~ZZ
OH... JUSHT A FLY...
PHEW
ZZZ—Z
THW
AM
?!!!
WHAT?!! WHAT?! WHAT WAS THAT?!
OH... JUST A FLY. ZZZ...

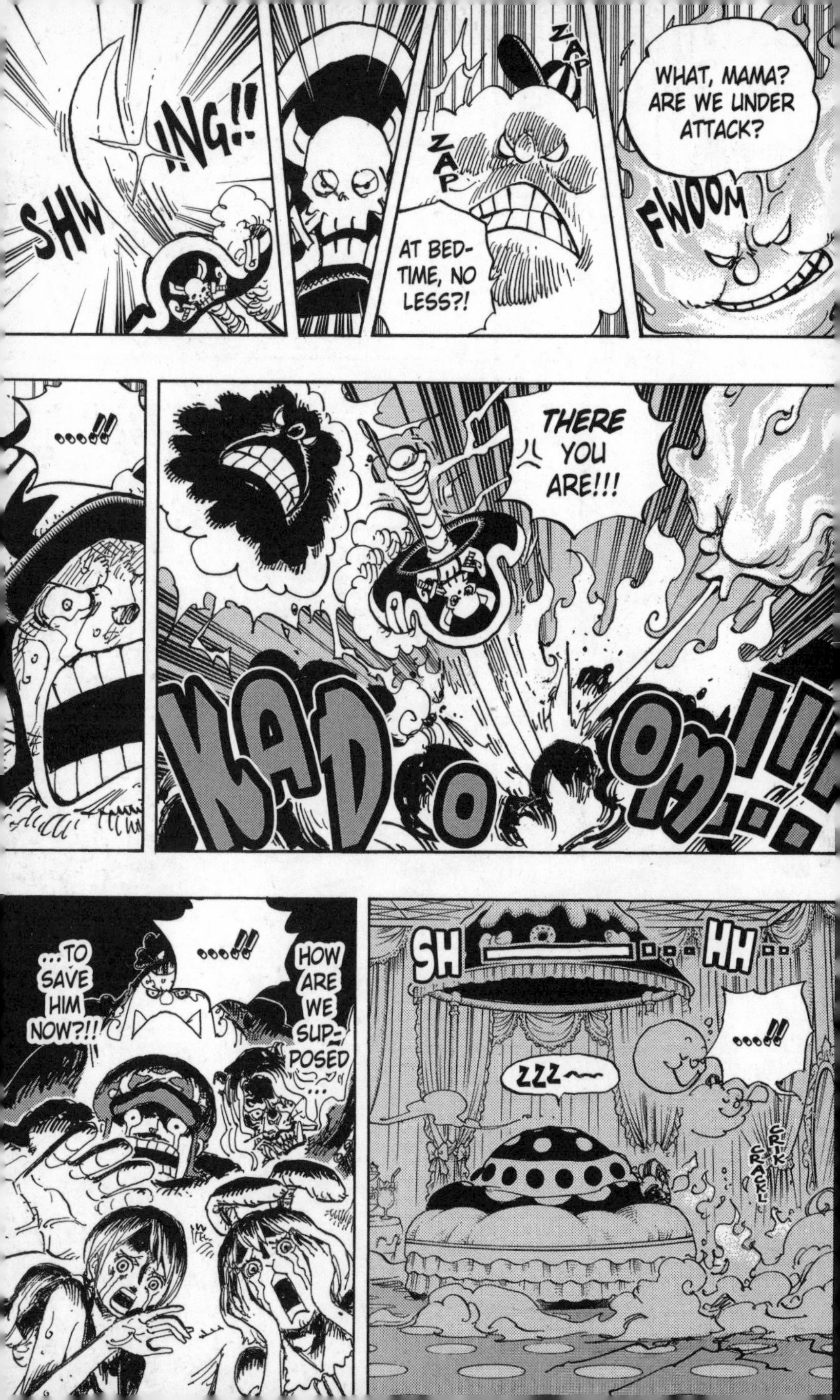
WHAT, MAMA? ARE WE UNDER ATTACK?
FWOOM
ZAP
ZAP
AT BED-TIME, NO LESS?!
SHWING!!
THERE YOU ARE!!!
KADOOOM!!!
...!!
SH...HH...
...!!
ZZZ~~
CRIK
CRACKL
...!!
HOW ARE WE SUPPOSED...
...TO SAVE HIM NOW?!!

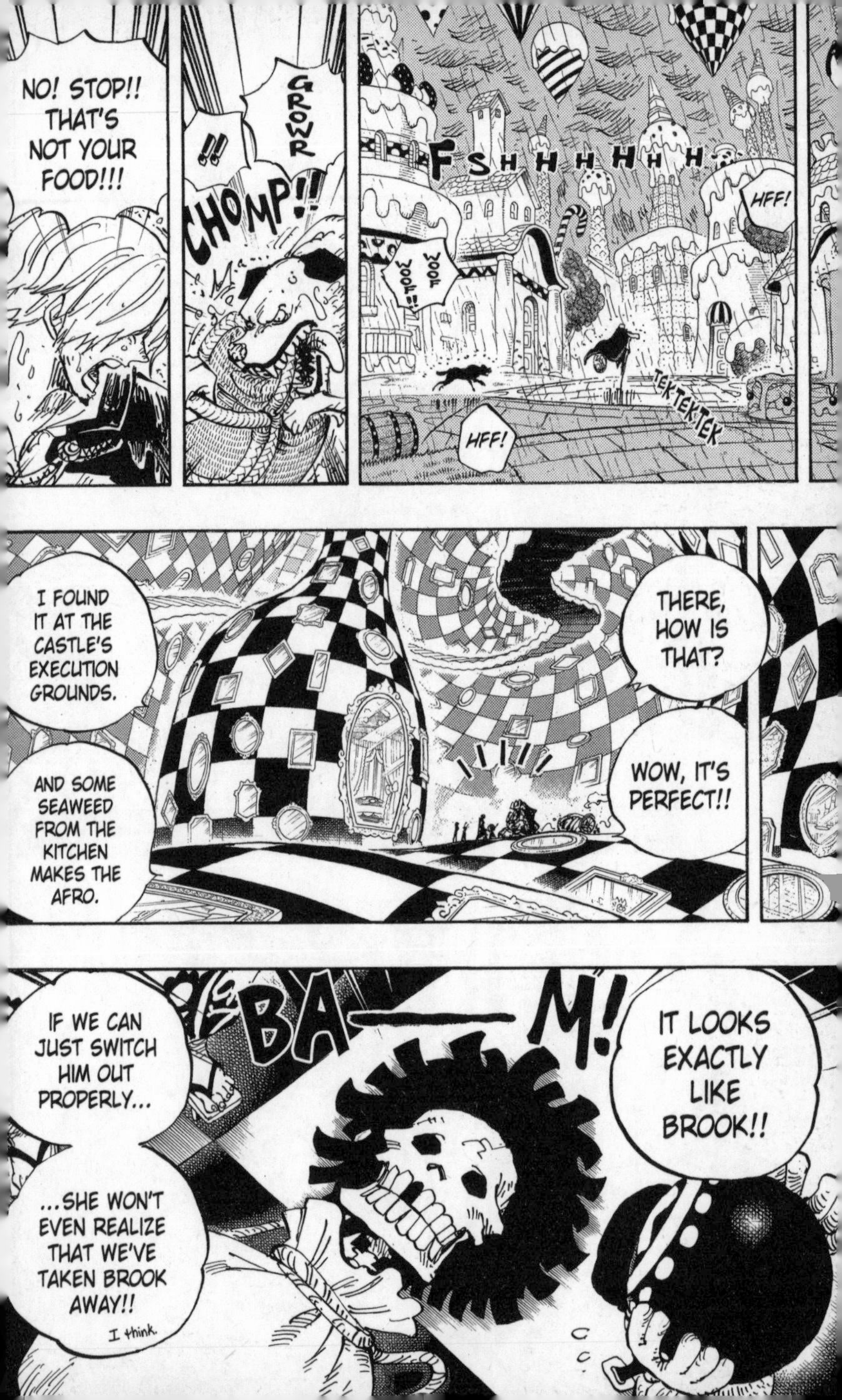

HFF!
FSHHHHHHH
WOOF WOOF!!
TEKTEKTEK
HFF!
GROWR
!!
CHOMP!!
NO! STOP!! THAT'S NOT YOUR FOOD!!!
THERE, HOW IS THAT?
WOW, IT'S PERFECT!!
I FOUND IT AT THE CASTLE'S EXECUTION GROUNDS.
AND SOME SEAWEED FROM THE KITCHEN MAKES THE AFRO.
BA—M!
IT LOOKS EXACTLY LIKE BROOK!!
IF WE CAN JUST SWITCH HIM OUT PROPERLY...
...SHE WON'T EVEN REALIZE THAT WE'VE TAKEN BROOK AWAY!!
I think.

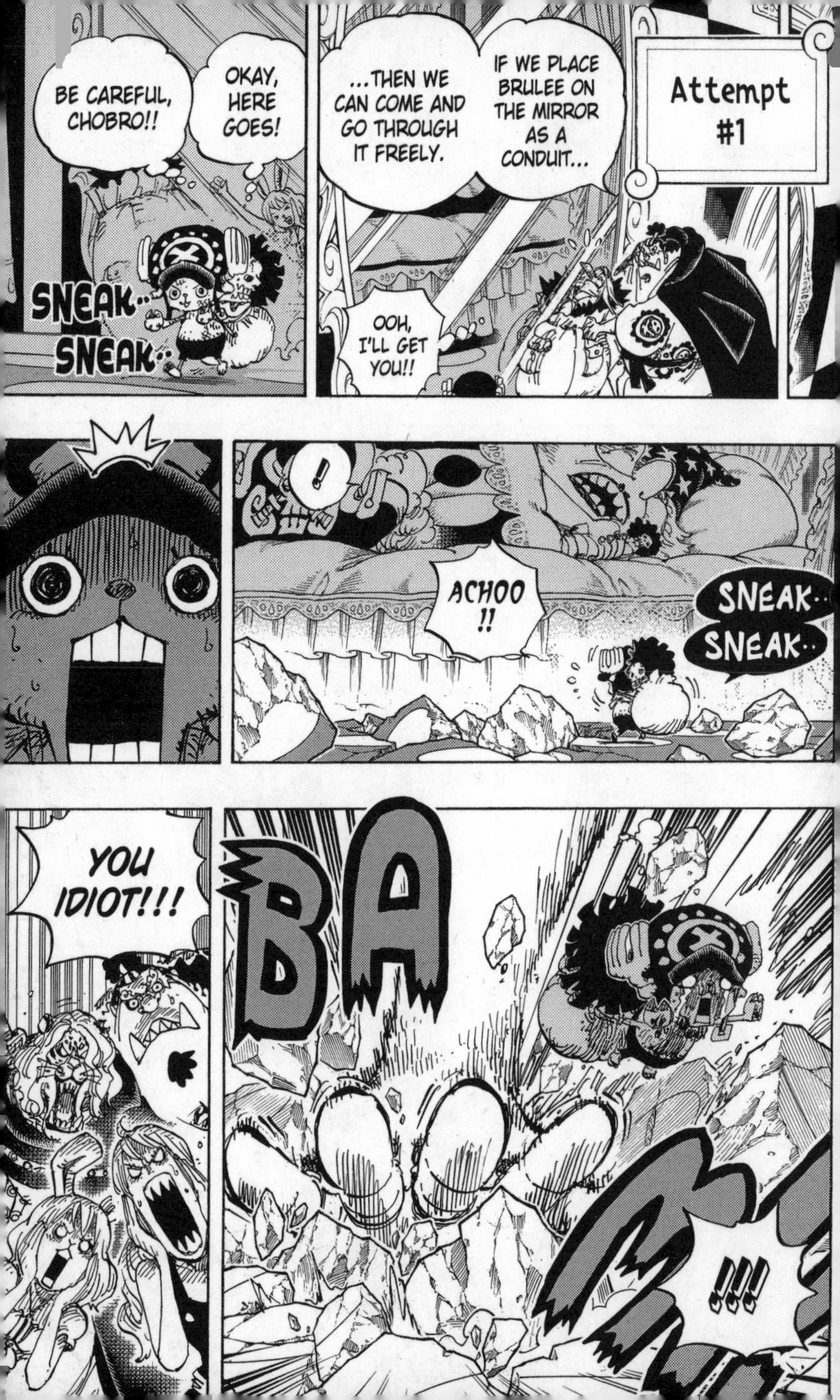

Attempt #1
IF WE PLACE BRULEE ON THE MIRROR AS A CONDUIT...
...THEN WE CAN COME AND GO THROUGH IT FREELY.
OOH, I'LL GET YOU!!
OKAY, HERE GOES!
BE CAREFUL, CHOBRO!!
SNEAK.. SNEAK..
SNEAK.. SNEAK..
ACHOO !!
!
BA
!!!
YOU IDIOT!!!

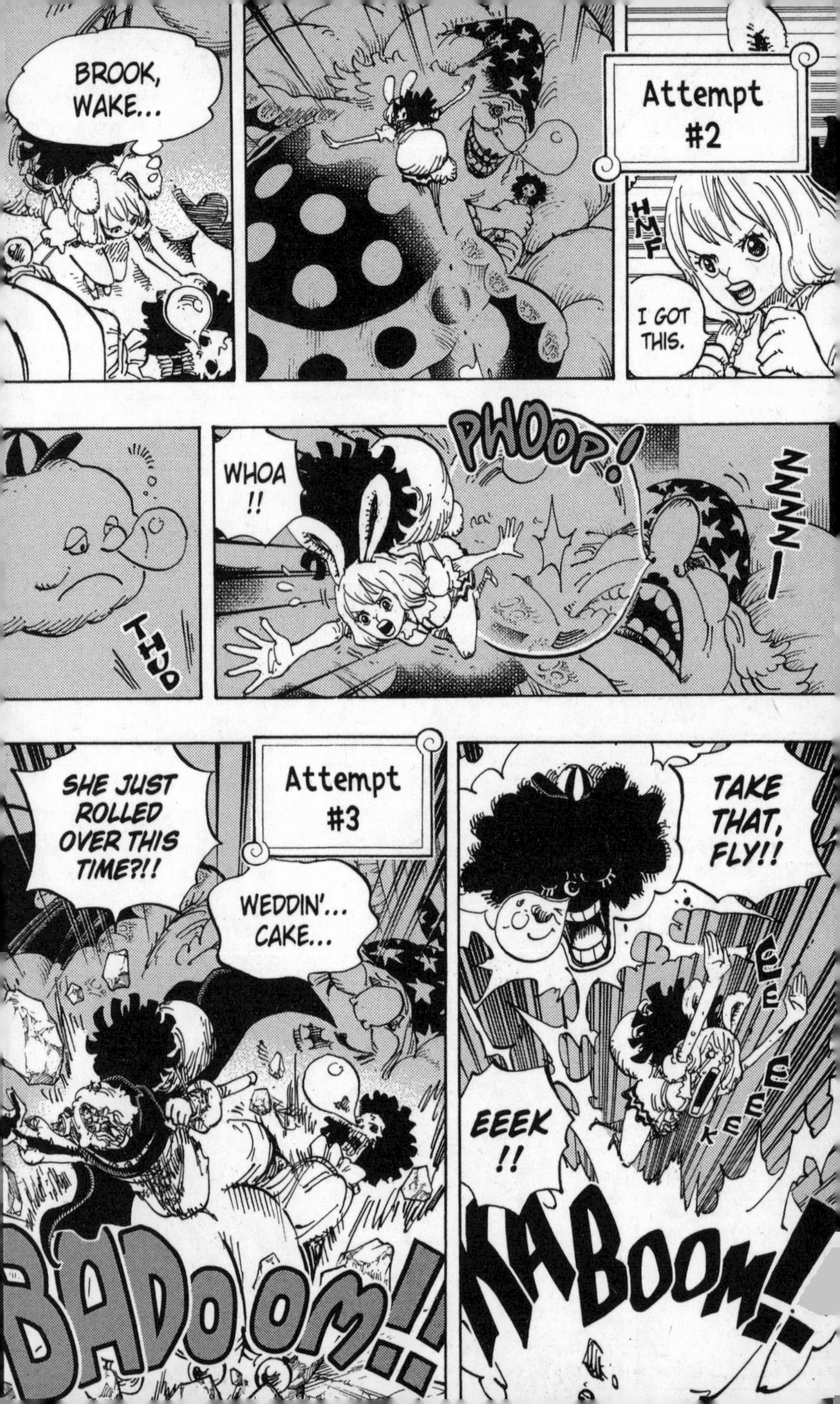
Attempt #2
HMF
I GOT THIS.
BROOK, WAKE...
PHOOP!
NNNN—
WHOA !!
THUD
TAKE THAT, FLY!!
EEEEK
EEEK !!
KABOOM!!
Attempt #3
SHE JUST ROLLED OVER THIS TIME?!!
WEDDIN'... CAKE...
BADOOM!!

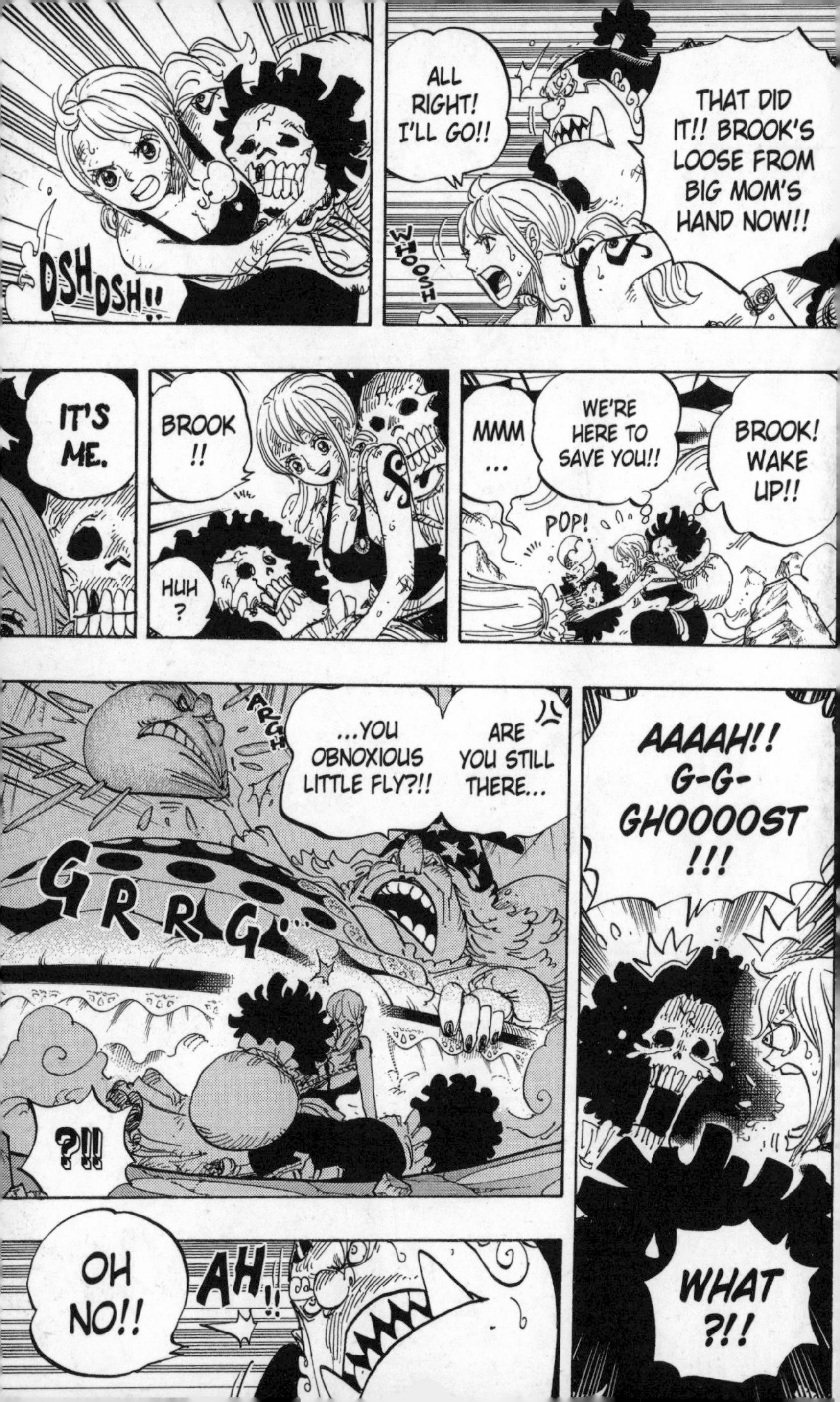
THAT DID IT!! BROOK'S LOOSE FROM BIG MOM'S HAND NOW!!
ALL RIGHT! I'LL GO!!
WHOOSH
DSH DSH!!
BROOK! WAKE UP!!
WE'RE HERE TO SAVE YOU!!
MMM ...
POP!
BROOK !!
HUH ?
IT'S ME.
AAAAH!! G-G-GHOOOOST !!!
WHAT ?!!
ARE YOU STILL THERE...
...YOU OBNOXIOUS LITTLE FLY?!!
ARGH
GRRRG...
?!!
AH!!
OH NO!!

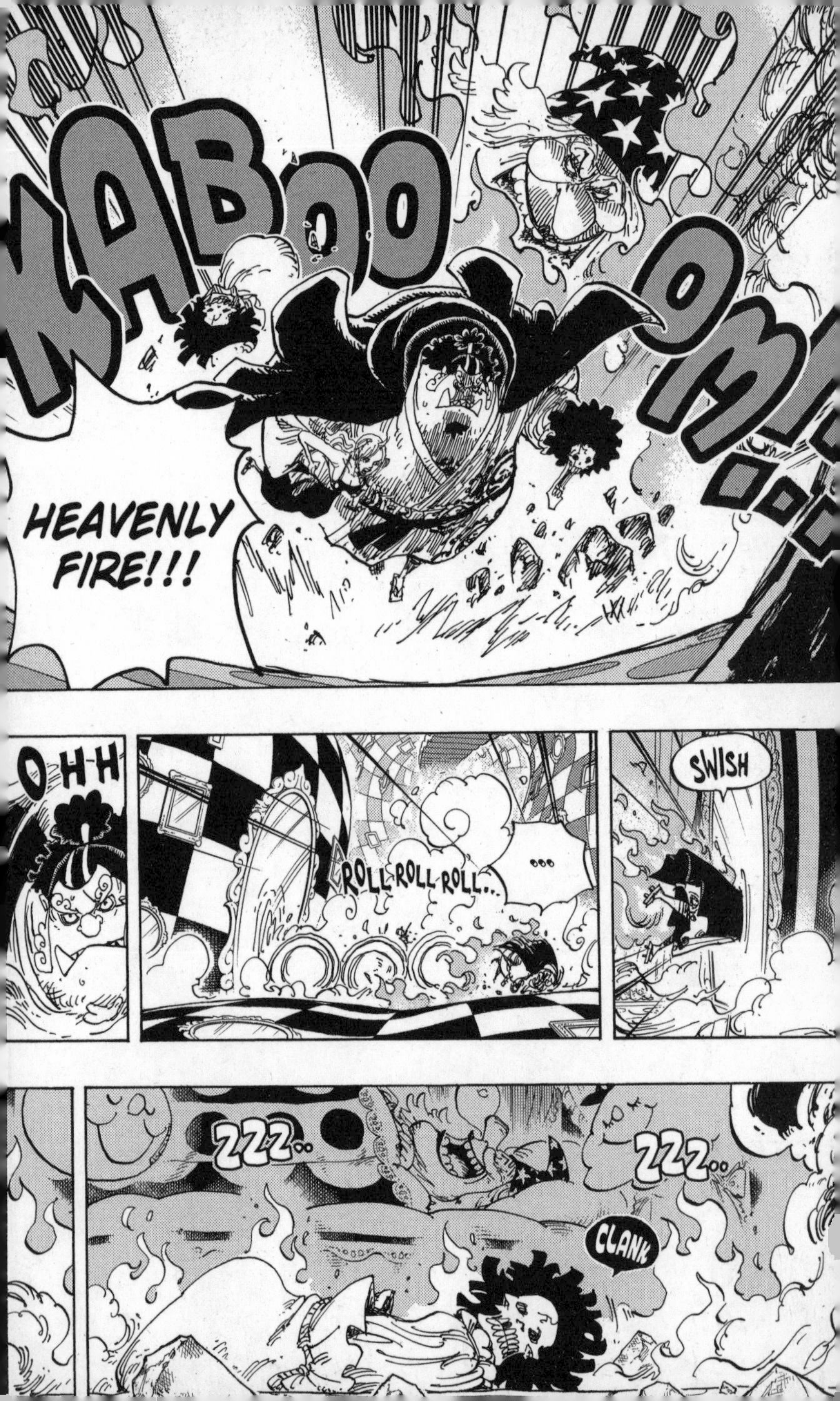
HEAVENLY FIRE!!!
SWISH
...
ROLL ROLL ROLL...
OHH
ZZZ..
ZZZ..
CLANK

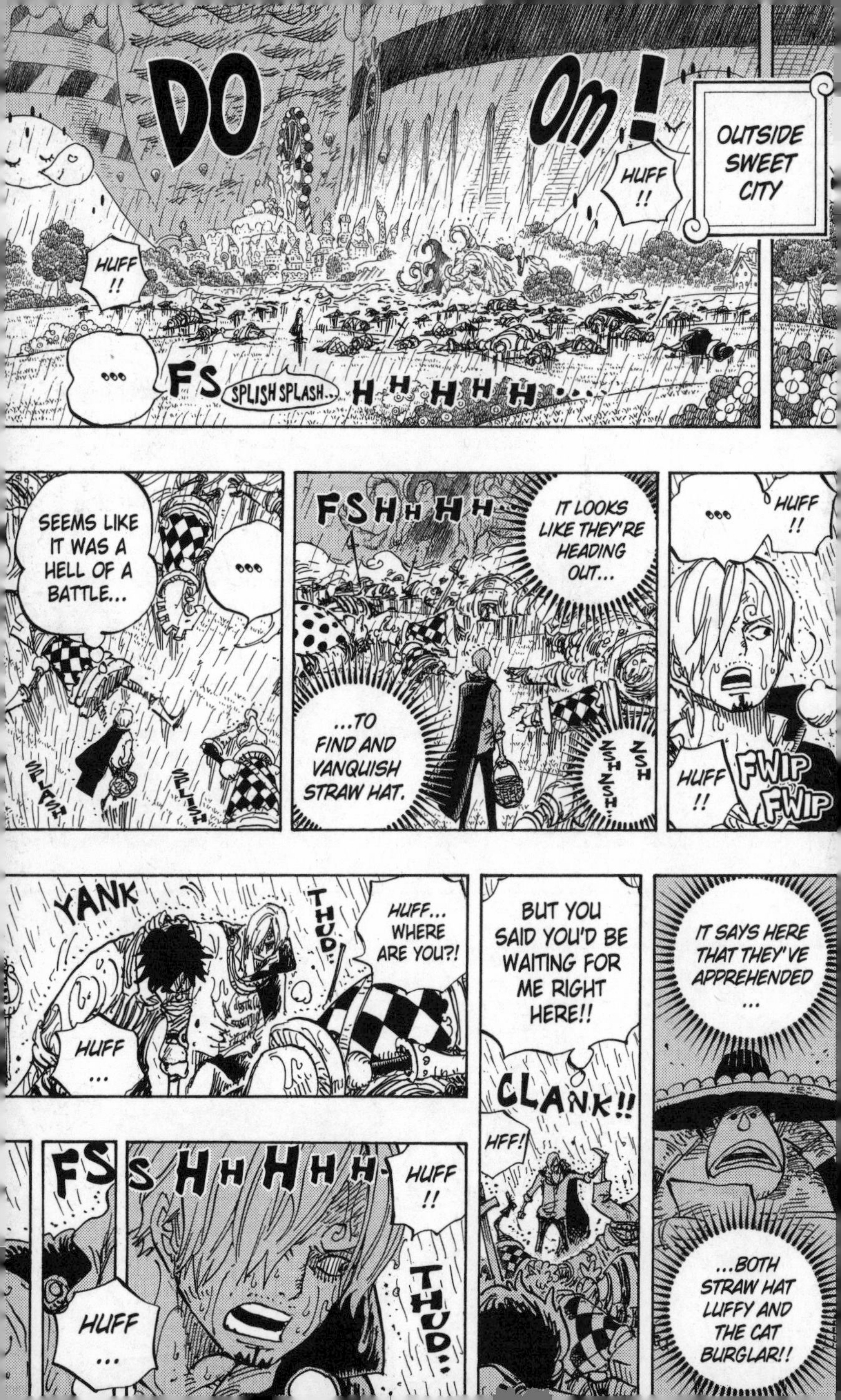

OUTSIDE SWEET CITY
HUFF!!
DOOM!
HUFF!!
...
FSHHHHH...
SPLISH SPLASH...
HUFF!!
...
HUFF!!
FWIP FWIP
IT LOOKS LIKE THEY'RE HEADING OUT...
FSHHHHH...
...TO FIND AND VANQUISH STRAW HAT.
ZSH ZSH ZSH
...
SEEMS LIKE IT WAS A HELL OF A BATTLE...
SPLISH
SPLASH
IT SAYS HERE THAT THEY'VE APPREHENDED...
...BOTH STRAW HAT LUFFY AND THE CAT BURGLAR!!
BUT YOU SAID YOU'D BE WAITING FOR ME RIGHT HERE!!
CLANK!!
HFF!
HUFF... WHERE ARE YOU?!
THUD
YANK
HUFF...
HUFF!!
FSSHHHHH-
THUD!!
HUFF...

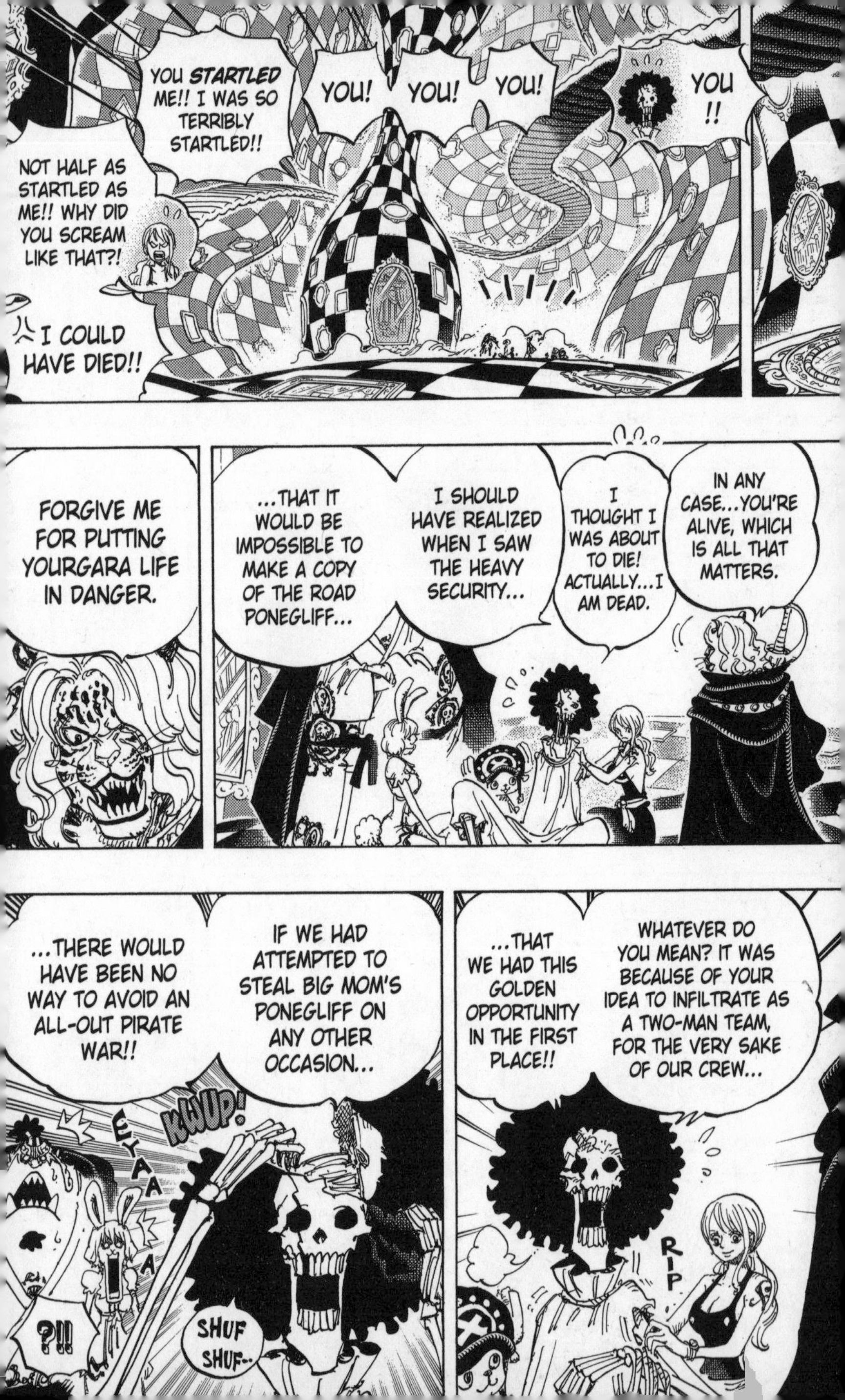
YOU !!
YOU! YOU! YOU!
YOU STARTLED ME!! I WAS SO TERRIBLY STARTLED!!
NOT HALF AS STARTLED AS ME!! WHY DID YOU SCREAM LIKE THAT?!
I COULD HAVE DIED!!
IN ANY CASE...YOU'RE ALIVE, WHICH IS ALL THAT MATTERS.
I THOUGHT I WAS ABOUT TO DIE! ACTUALLY...I AM DEAD.
I SHOULD HAVE REALIZED WHEN I SAW THE HEAVY SECURITY...
...THAT IT WOULD BE IMPOSSIBLE TO MAKE A COPY OF THE ROAD PONEGLIFF...
FORGIVE ME FOR PUTTING YOURGARA LIFE IN DANGER.
WHATEVER DO YOU MEAN? IT WAS BECAUSE OF YOUR IDEA TO INFILTRATE AS A TWO-MAN TEAM, FOR THE VERY SAKE OF OUR CREW...
...THAT WE HAD THIS GOLDEN OPPORTUNITY IN THE FIRST PLACE!!
RIP
IF WE HAD ATTEMPTED TO STEAL BIG MOM'S PONEGLIFF ON ANY OTHER OCCASION...
...THERE WOULD HAVE BEEN NO WAY TO AVOID AN ALL-OUT PIRATE WAR!!
KWUP!
EYAAA
SHUF SHUF..
?!!

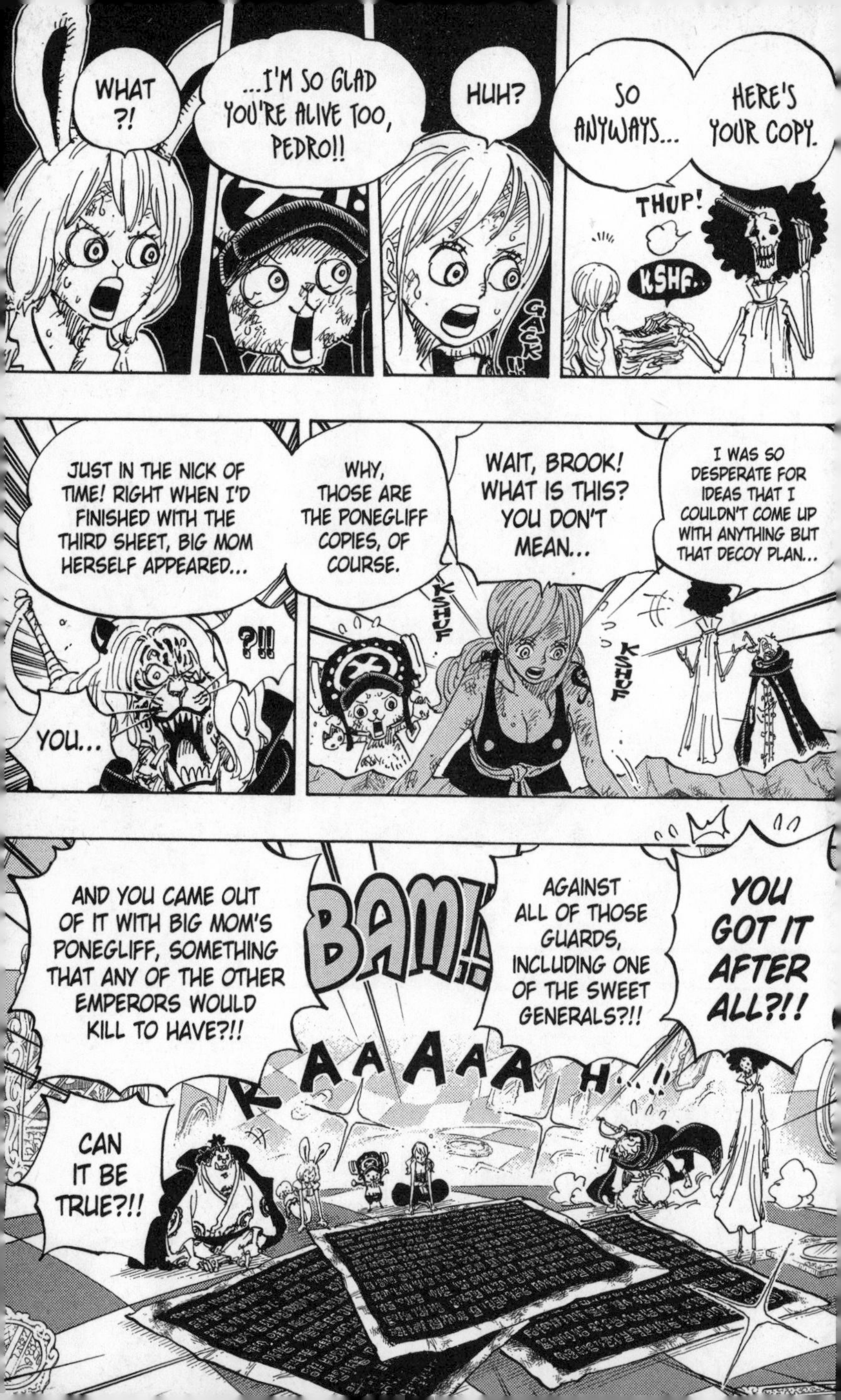
SO ANYWAYS...
HERE'S YOUR COPY.
THUP!
KSHF..
HUH?
GACK!!
...I'M SO GLAD YOU'RE ALIVE TOO, PEDRO!!
WHAT ?!
WAIT, BROOK! WHAT IS THIS? YOU DON'T MEAN...
KSHUF
KSHUF
WHY, THOSE ARE THE PONEGLIFF COPIES, OF COURSE.
I WAS SO DESPERATE FOR IDEAS THAT I COULDN'T COME UP WITH ANYTHING BUT THAT DECOY PLAN...
JUST IN THE NICK OF TIME! RIGHT WHEN I'D FINISHED WITH THE THIRD SHEET, BIG MOM HERSELF APPEARED...
?!!
YOU...
YOU GOT IT AFTER ALL?!!
AGAINST ALL OF THOSE GUARDS, INCLUDING ONE OF THE SWEET GENERALS?!!
BAM!!
AND YOU CAME OUT OF IT WITH BIG MOM'S PONEGLIFF, SOMETHING THAT ANY OF THE OTHER EMPERORS WOULD KILL TO HAVE?!!
KAAAAAH...!!
CAN IT BE TRUE?!!

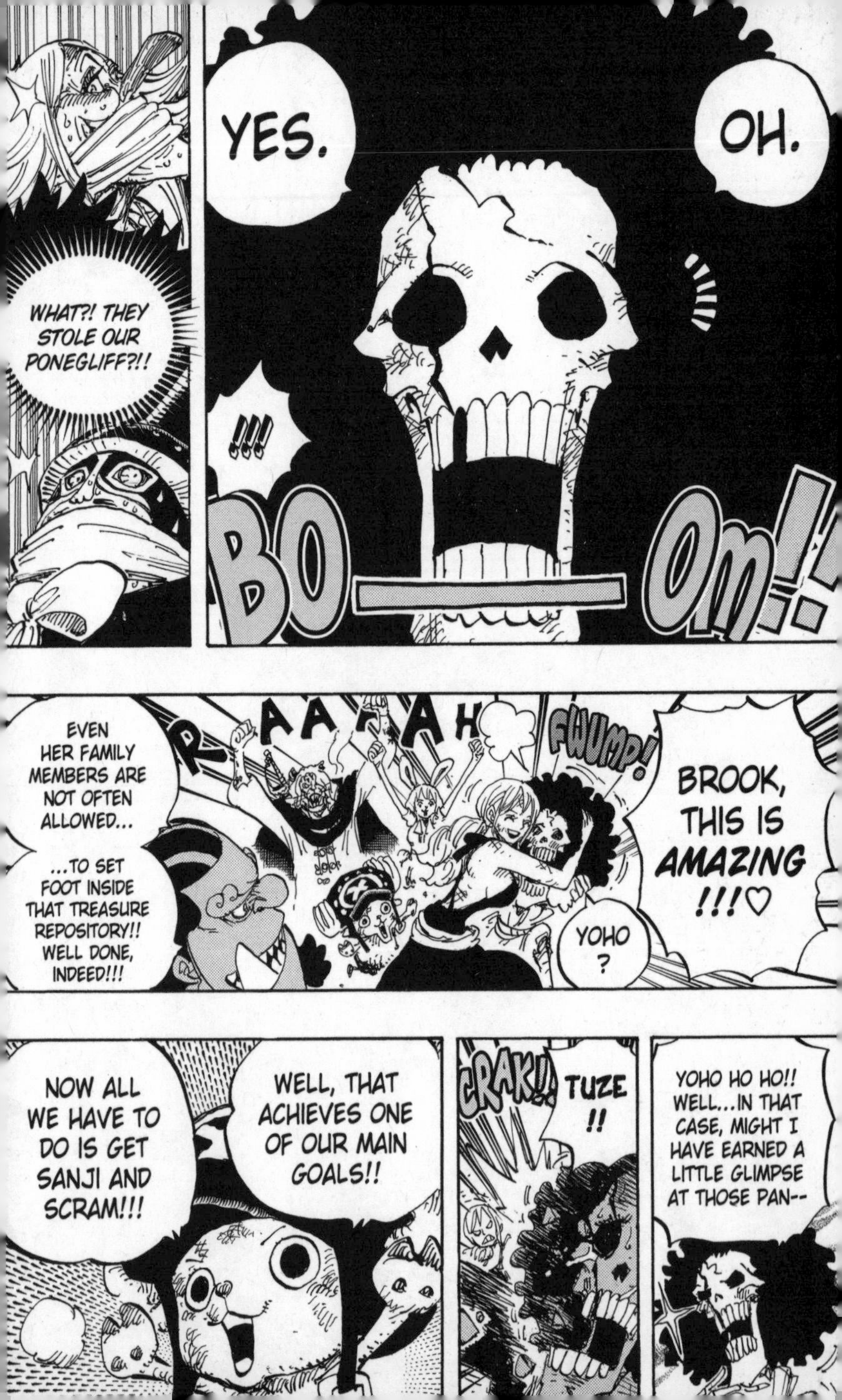
OH.
YES.
!!!
BO—OM!!
WHAT?! THEY STOLE OUR PONEGLIFF?!!
BROOK, THIS IS AMAZING !!!♡
FWUMP!
RAAAAH
YOHO ?
EVEN HER FAMILY MEMBERS ARE NOT OFTEN ALLOWED...
...TO SET FOOT INSIDE THAT TREASURE REPOSITORY!! WELL DONE, INDEED!!!
YOHO HO HO!! WELL...IN THAT CASE, MIGHT I HAVE EARNED A LITTLE GLIMPSE AT THOSE PAN--
TUZE !!
CRAK!!
WELL, THAT ACHIEVES ONE OF OUR MAIN GOALS!!
NOW ALL WE HAVE TO DO IS GET SANJI AND SCRAM!!!

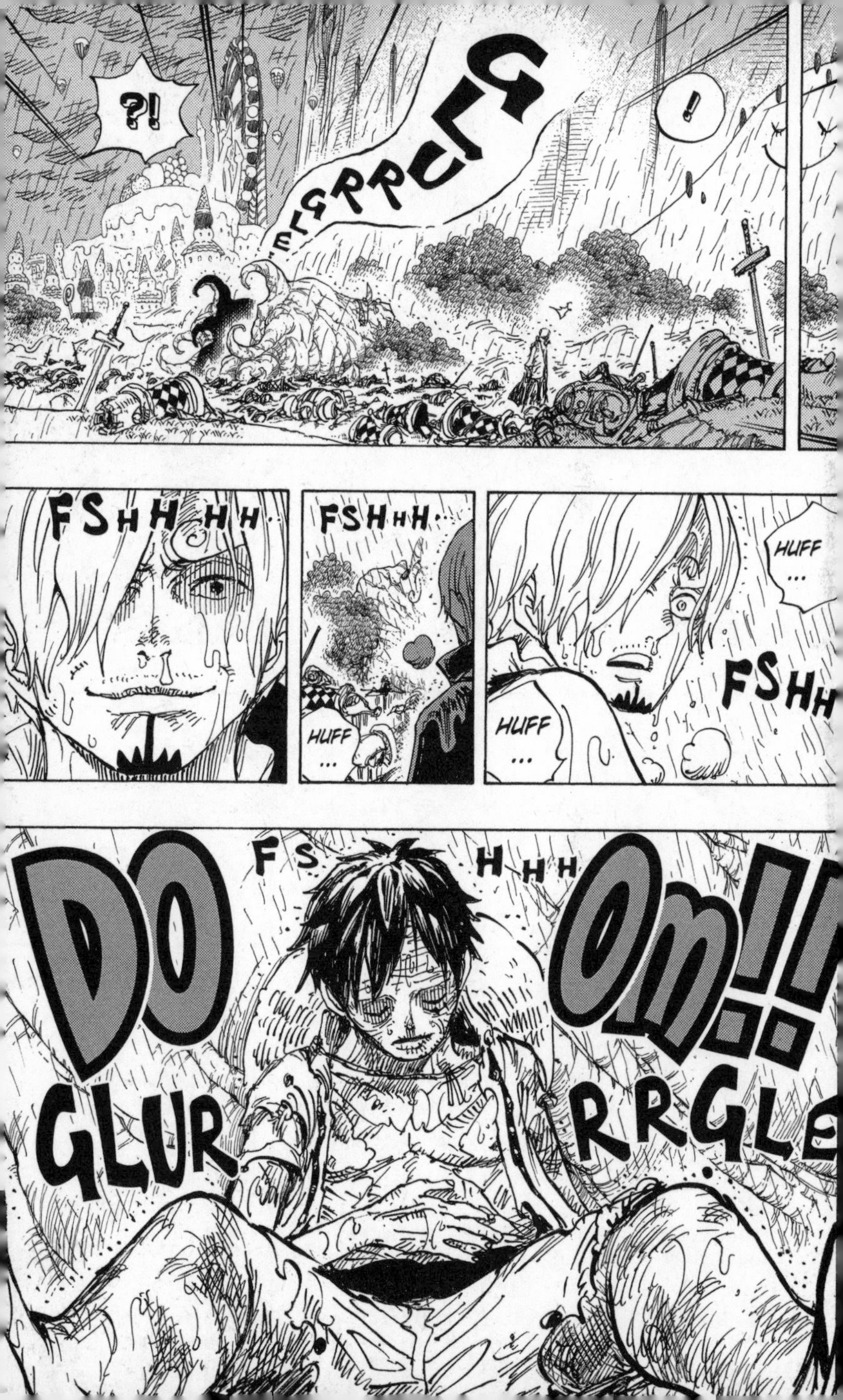
!
GURRRGLE
?!
HUFF ...
FSHH
HUFF ...
FSHHH...
HUFF ...
FSHH HHH...
FS HHH
DOOM!!
GLURRRGLE

SBS Question Corner

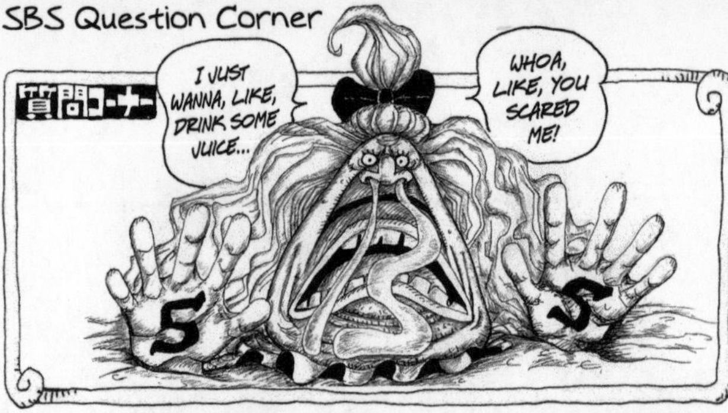
質問コーナー
I JUST WANNA, LIKE, DRINK SOME JUICE...
WHOA, LIKE, YOU SCARED ME!
5
5
(Sasaaki, Okinawa)

A:

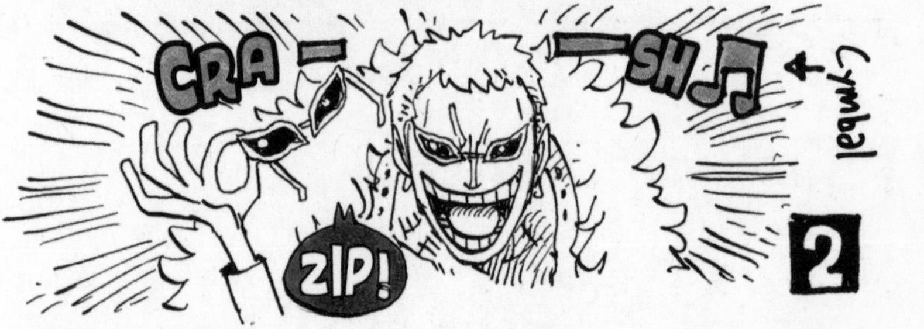
CRA — — SH♫
← Cymbal
ZIP!
2

Aaaaah!! Underneath his sunglasses was another pair of sunglasses!! So what's under that pair, then?! (Return to 1 on pg. 114)

Q: Hello, Oda Sensei! My birthday is October 11. There were no characters on my birthday so far, so I came up with an idea! 10/11 could be *ichi (1) ban oo (0) kii wan-wan (1 1),* meaning "the biggest doggy"! That could be the birthday for Duke Dogstorm, King of the Day of the Mokomo Dukedom!!

--Masaju

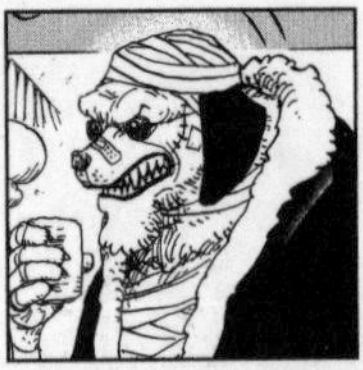

A: What?! You want to decide it just like that?! Okay.

Q: My birthday is July 9, but there aren't any characters that share it! So how about if Sanji's mother, Vinsmoke Sora, was born on 7/9? July for its beautiful clear "sky" (sora), and 9th for the ku sound in "Vinsmoke"!

--Space Planet Peace

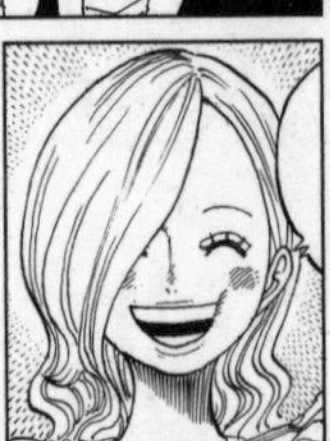

A: Oof, what a stretch! You know what? I'm not going...to turn that down!!

Q: Oda Sensei! I thought of a birthday. The most famous of all the hidden characters of *One Piece,* Pandaman, is born on February 29. (Because it's a special day that's usually hiding.)

--Kajusa

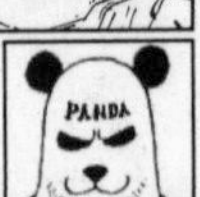
PANDA

A: Oh man, that's perfect! But I can't just rubber-stamp that...unless I do! Do you share a birthday with any characters? You can check the birthday calendar on the One-piece.com website.

Chapter 856:
LIAR

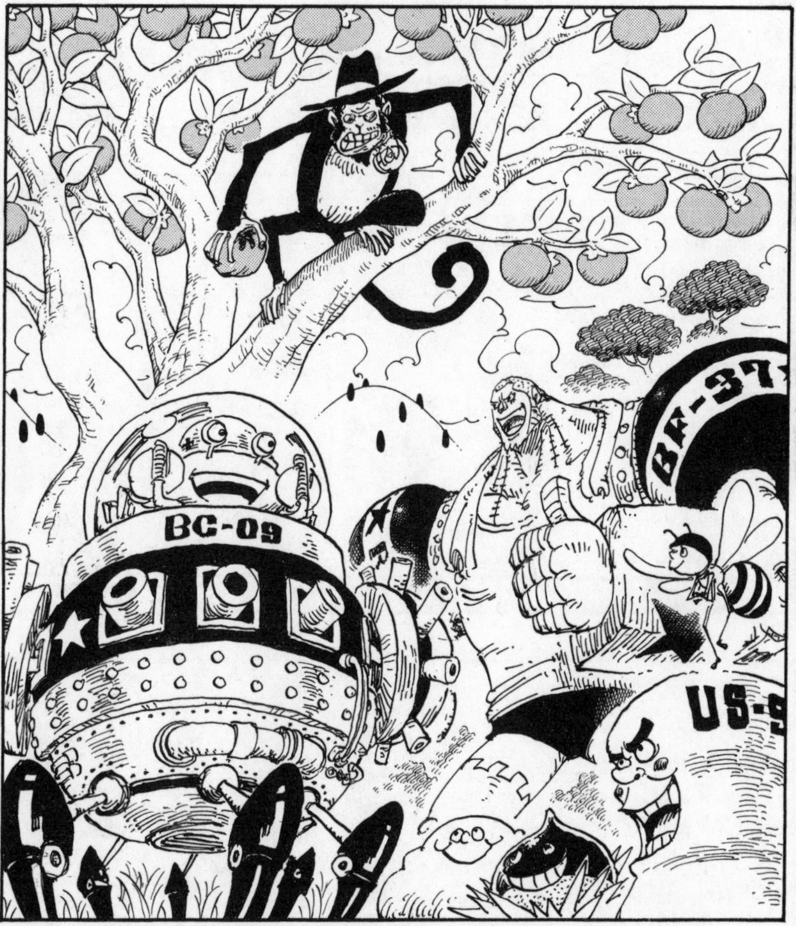

BC-09
BA-37
US-9

REQUEST: "FRANKY GIVING A CRAB A MECHA BODY TO PROTECT IT FROM A BULLYING MONKEY" BY NODA SKYWALKER FROM OSAKA

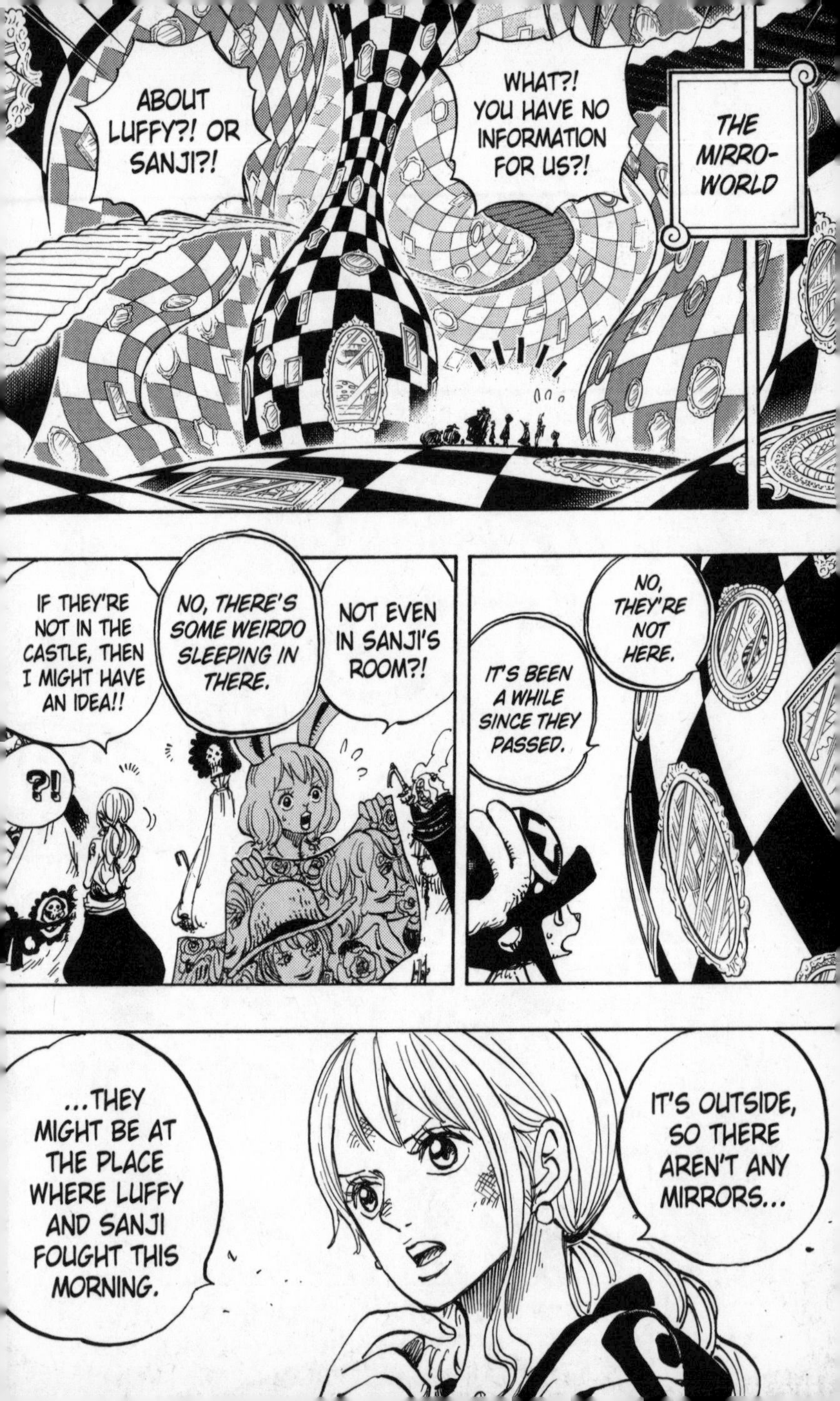
THE MIRRO-WORLD
WHAT?! YOU HAVE NO INFORMATION FOR US?!
ABOUT LUFFY?! OR SANJI?!
NO, THEY'RE NOT HERE.
IT'S BEEN A WHILE SINCE THEY PASSED.
NOT EVEN IN SANJI'S ROOM?!
NO, THERE'S SOME WEIRDO SLEEPING IN THERE.
IF THEY'RE NOT IN THE CASTLE, THEN I MIGHT HAVE AN IDEA!!
?!
IT'S OUTSIDE, SO THERE AREN'T ANY MIRRORS...
...THEY MIGHT BE AT THE PLACE WHERE LUFFY AND SANJI FOUGHT THIS MORNING.

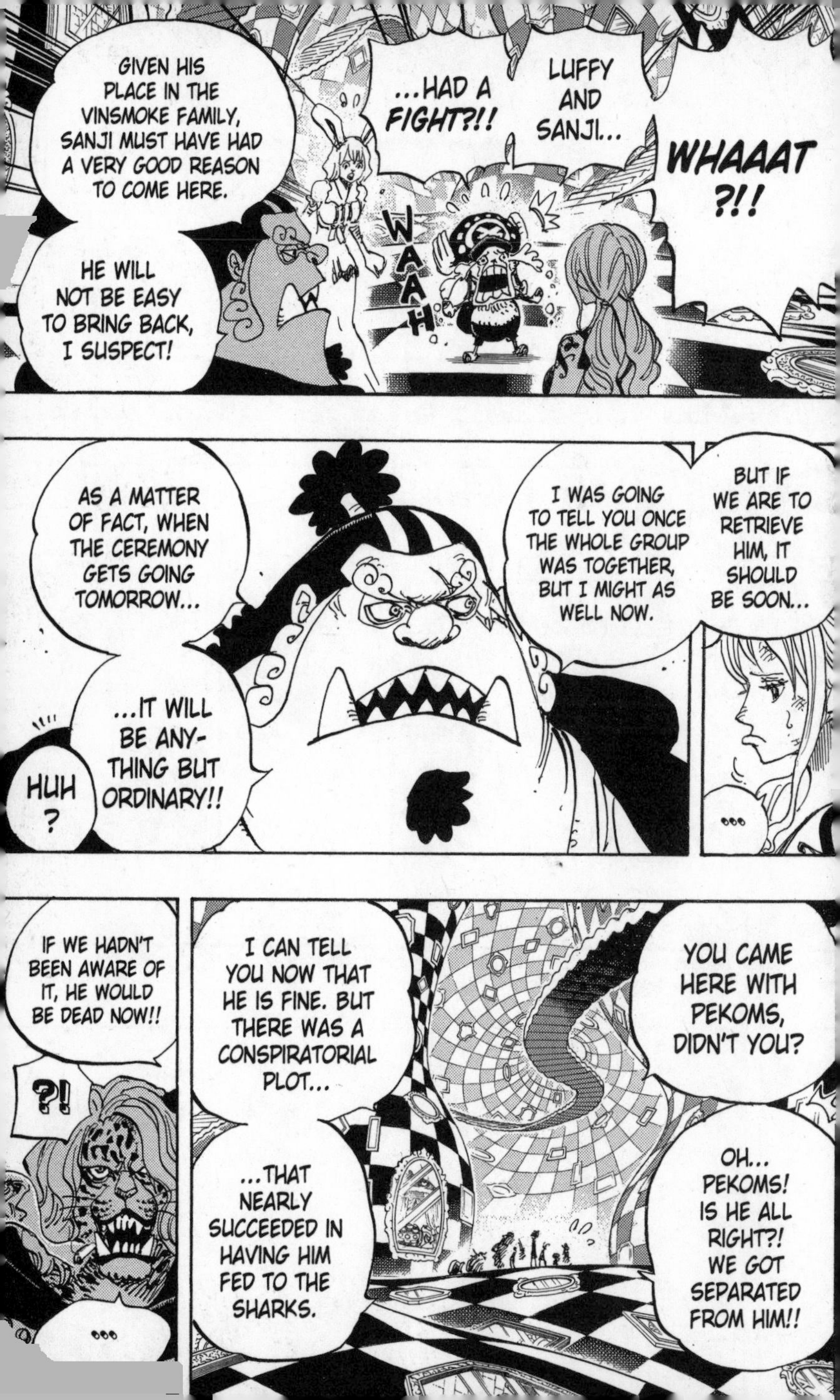
WHAAAT?!!
LUFFY AND SANJI...
...HAD A FIGHT?!!
WAAH
GIVEN HIS PLACE IN THE VINSMOKE FAMILY, SANJI MUST HAVE HAD A VERY GOOD REASON TO COME HERE.
HE WILL NOT BE EASY TO BRING BACK, I SUSPECT!
BUT IF WE ARE TO RETRIEVE HIM, IT SHOULD BE SOON...
...
I WAS GOING TO TELL YOU ONCE THE WHOLE GROUP WAS TOGETHER, BUT I MIGHT AS WELL NOW.
AS A MATTER OF FACT, WHEN THE CEREMONY GETS GOING TOMORROW...
...IT WILL BE ANY-THING BUT ORDINARY!!
HUH?
YOU CAME HERE WITH PEKOMS, DIDN'T YOU?
I CAN TELL YOU NOW THAT HE IS FINE. BUT THERE WAS A CONSPIRATORIAL PLOT...
OH... PEKOMS! IS HE ALL RIGHT?! WE GOT SEPARATED FROM HIM!!
...THAT NEARLY SUCCEEDED IN HAVING HIM FED TO THE SHARKS.
IF WE HADN'T BEEN AWARE OF IT, HE WOULD BE DEAD NOW!!
?!
...

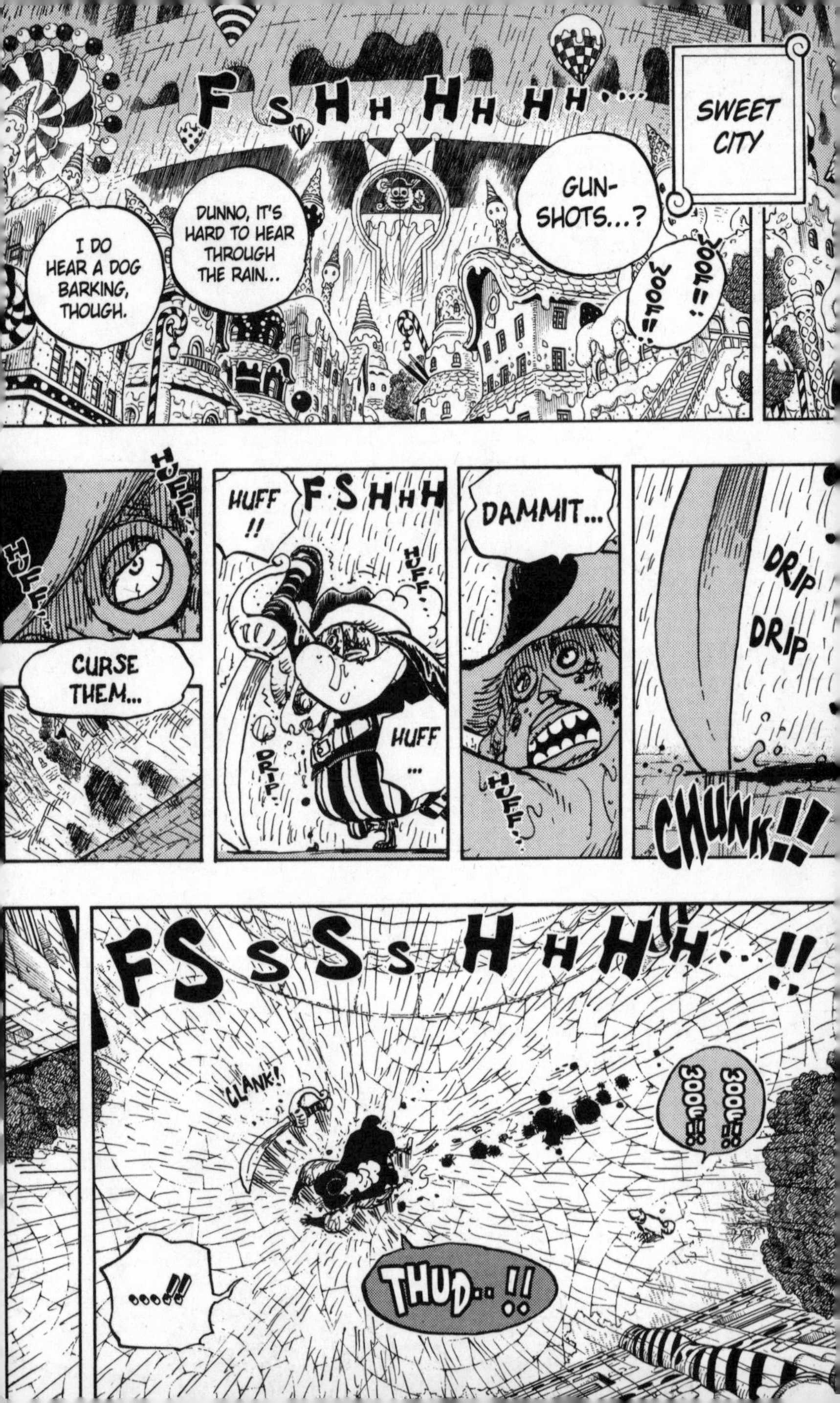
SWEET CITY
FSHHHHHH...
GUN-SHOTS...?
WOOF!!
WOOF!!
DUNNO, IT'S HARD TO HEAR THROUGH THE RAIN...
I DO HEAR A DOG BARKING, THOUGH.
DRIP DRIP
CHUNK!!
DAMMIT...
HUFF...
HUFF !!
FSHHH
HUFF...
HUFF ...
DRIP...
HUFF...
HUFF...
CURSE THEM...
FSSSSHHHHH...!!
WOOF!!
WOOF!!
CLANK!
THUD..!!
...!!

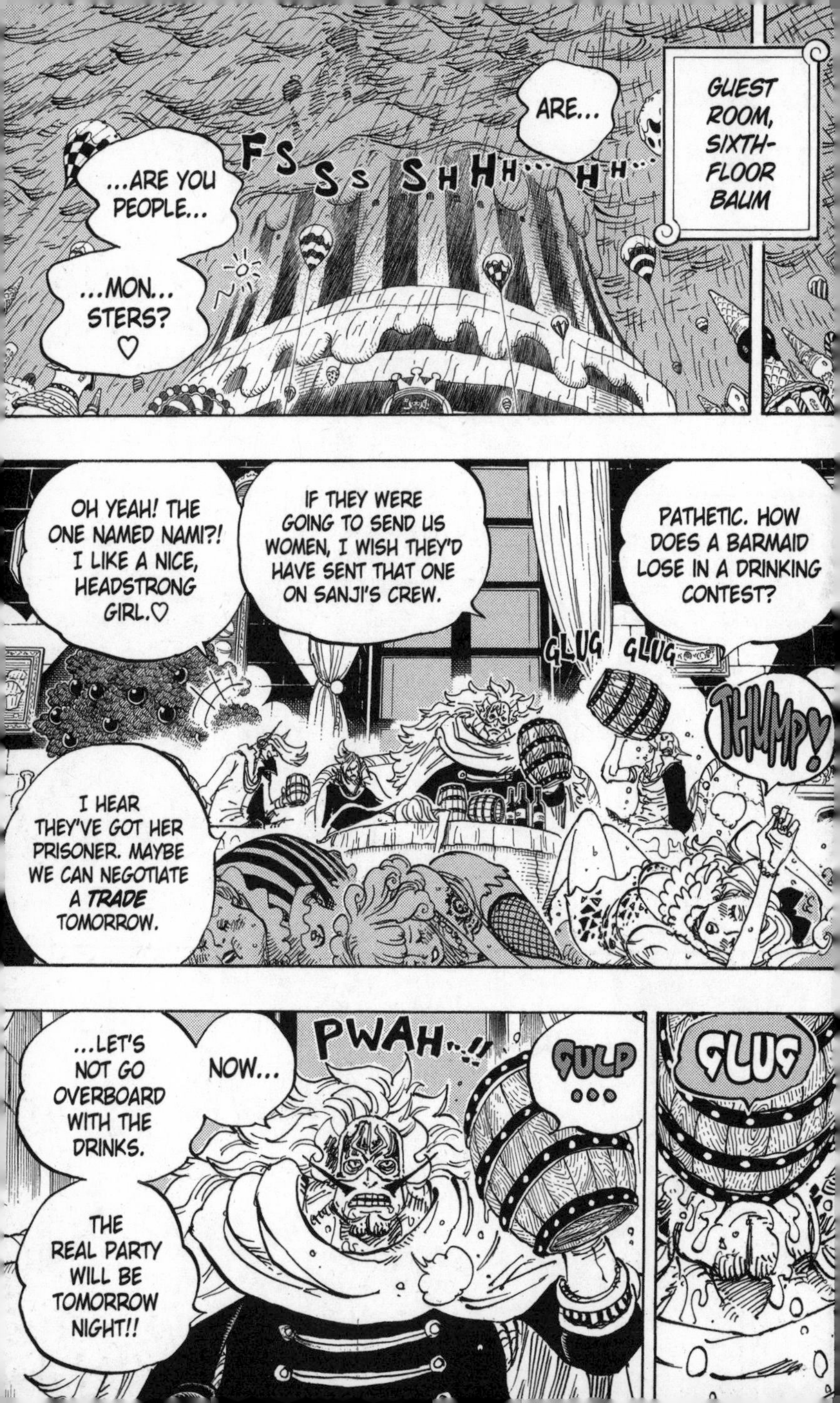
GUEST ROOM, SIXTH-FLOOR BAUM
ARE...
FSSSSHHH... HH...
...ARE YOU PEOPLE...
...MON... STERS? ♡
PATHETIC. HOW DOES A BARMAID LOSE IN A DRINKING CONTEST?
GLUG GLUG
THUMP!♥
IF THEY WERE GOING TO SEND US WOMEN, I WISH THEY'D HAVE SENT THAT ONE ON SANJI'S CREW.
OH YEAH! THE ONE NAMED NAMI?! I LIKE A NICE, HEADSTRONG GIRL.♡
I HEAR THEY'VE GOT HER PRISONER. MAYBE WE CAN NEGOTIATE A *TRADE* TOMORROW.
GLUG
GULP •••
PWAH..!!
NOW...
...LET'S NOT GO OVERBOARD WITH THE DRINKS.
THE REAL PARTY WILL BE TOMORROW NIGHT!!

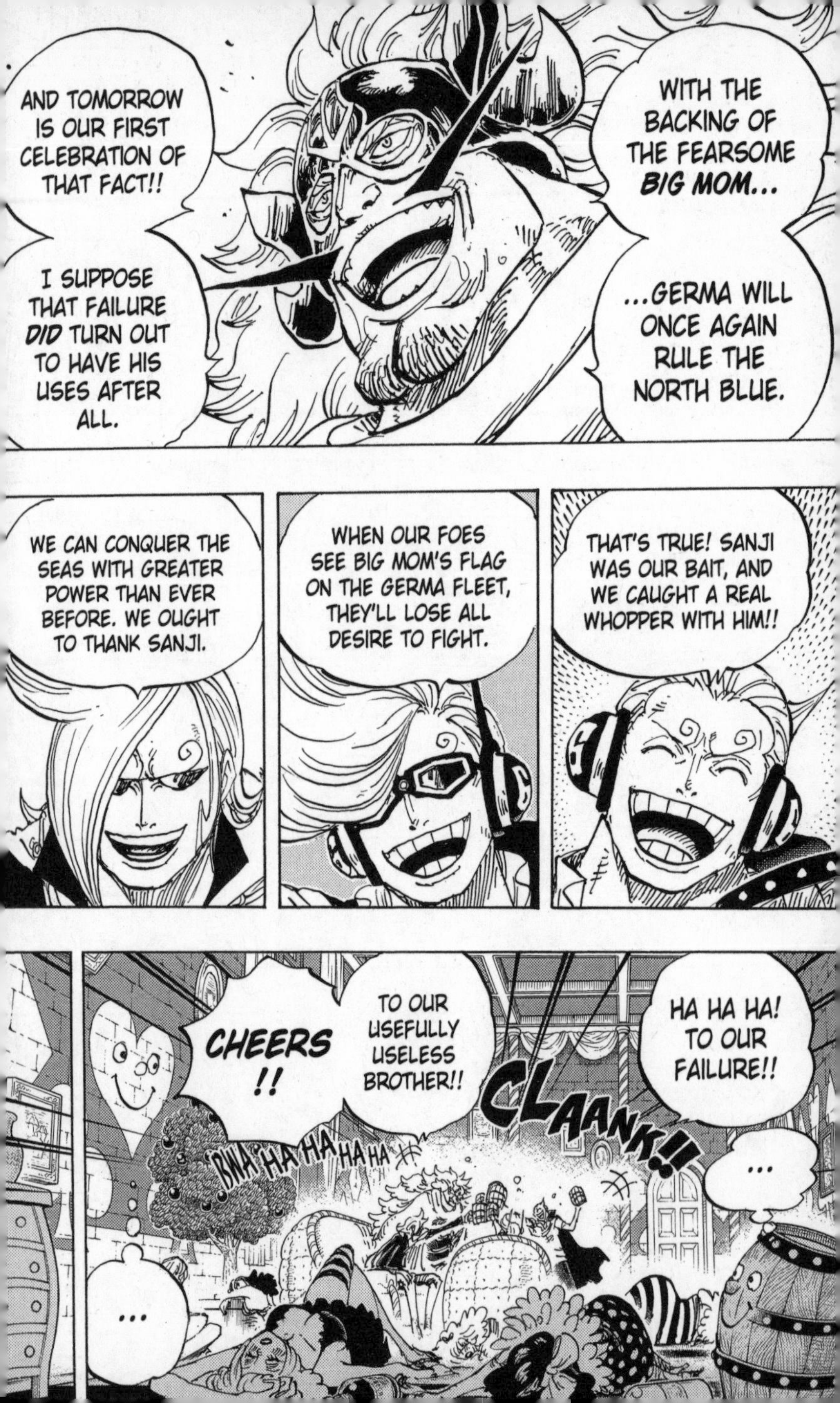
WITH THE BACKING OF THE FEARSOME *BIG MOM...*
...GERMA WILL ONCE AGAIN RULE THE NORTH BLUE.
AND TOMORROW IS OUR FIRST CELEBRATION OF THAT FACT!!
I SUPPOSE THAT FAILURE *DID* TURN OUT TO HAVE HIS USES AFTER ALL.
THAT'S TRUE! SANJI WAS OUR BAIT, AND WE CAUGHT A REAL WHOPPER WITH HIM!!
WHEN OUR FOES SEE BIG MOM'S FLAG ON THE GERMA FLEET, THEY'LL LOSE ALL DESIRE TO FIGHT.
WE CAN CONQUER THE SEAS WITH GREATER POWER THAN EVER BEFORE. WE OUGHT TO THANK SANJI.
HA HA HA! TO OUR FAILURE!!
...
CLAANK!!
TO OUR USEFULLY USELESS BROTHER!!
CHEERS !!
BWA HA HA HA HA
...

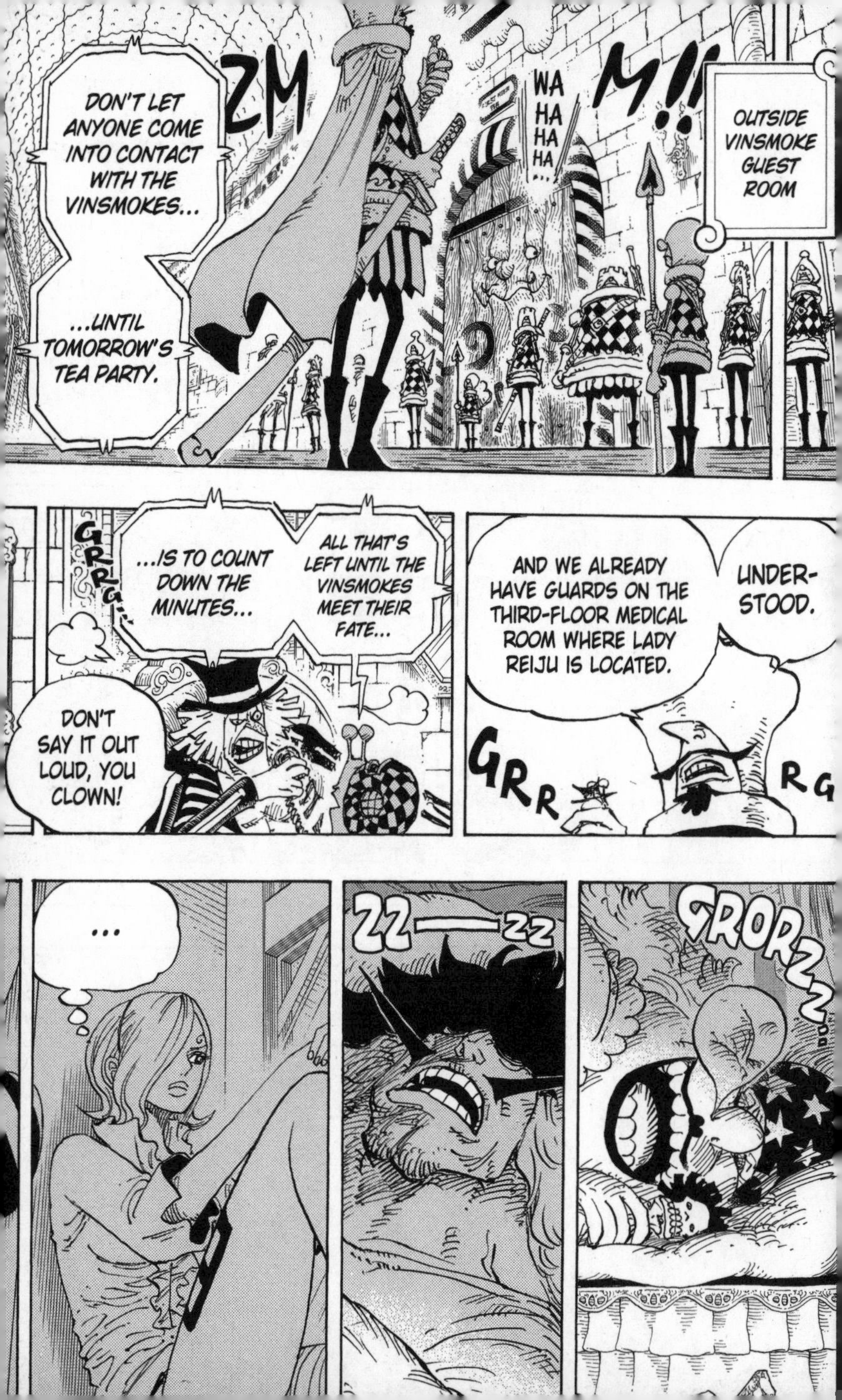

OUTSIDE VINSMOKE GUEST ROOM
ZM M!!
WA HA HA HA...
DON'T LET ANYONE COME INTO CONTACT WITH THE VINSMOKES...
...UNTIL TOMORROW'S TEA PARTY.
UNDER-STOOD.
AND WE ALREADY HAVE GUARDS ON THE THIRD-FLOOR MEDICAL ROOM WHERE LADY REIJU IS LOCATED.
GRRRG
ALL THAT'S LEFT UNTIL THE VINSMOKES MEET THEIR FATE...
...IS TO COUNT DOWN THE MINUTES...
GRRG...
DON'T SAY IT OUT LOUD, YOU CLOWN!
GRORZZZ...
ZZ——ZZ
...

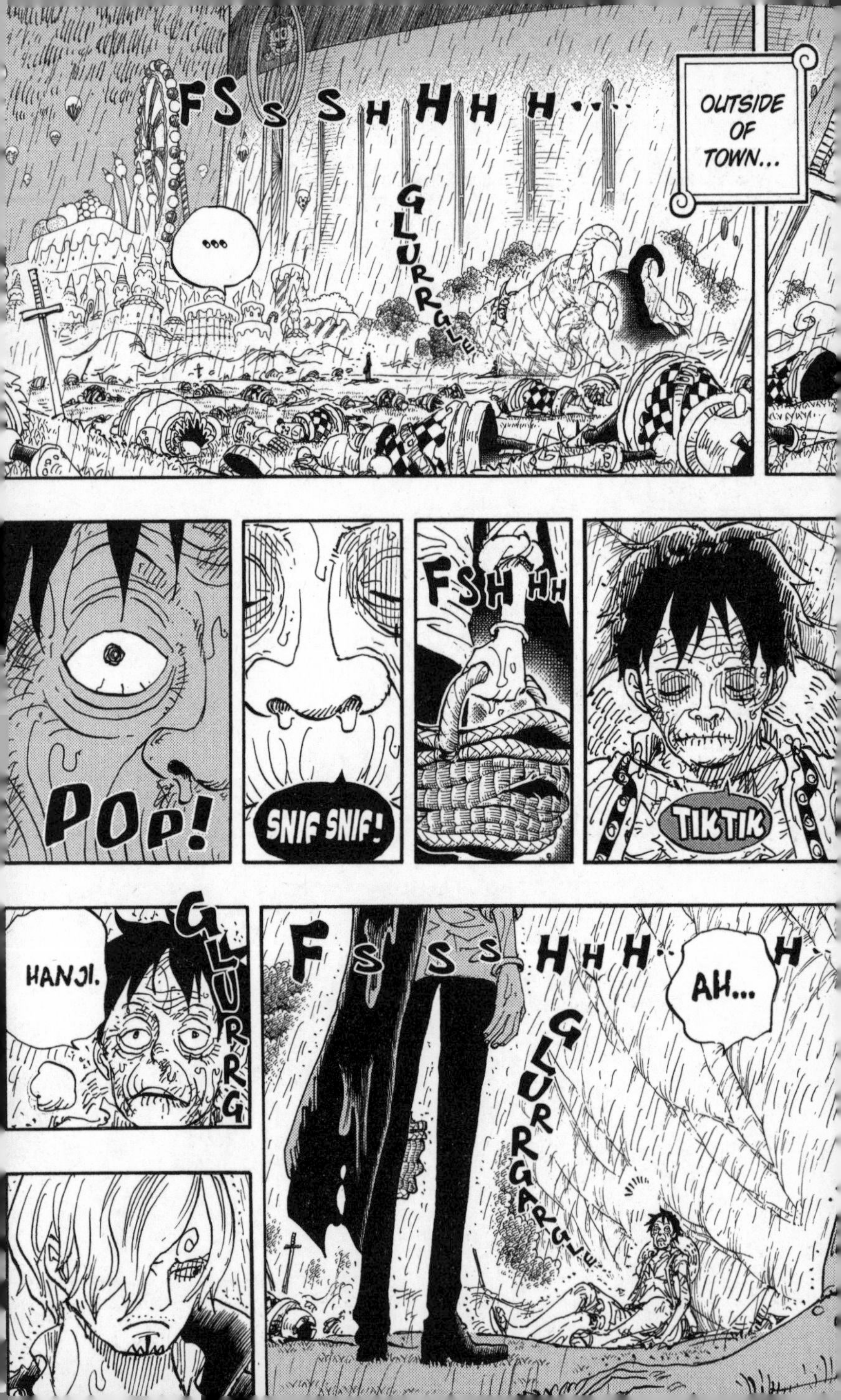

OUTSIDE OF TOWN...
FSSSHHHH...
...
GLURRGLE
TIKTIK
FSHHHH
SNIF SNIF!
POP!
FSSSHHH..H
AH...
GLURRGARGLE
HANJI.
GLURRG

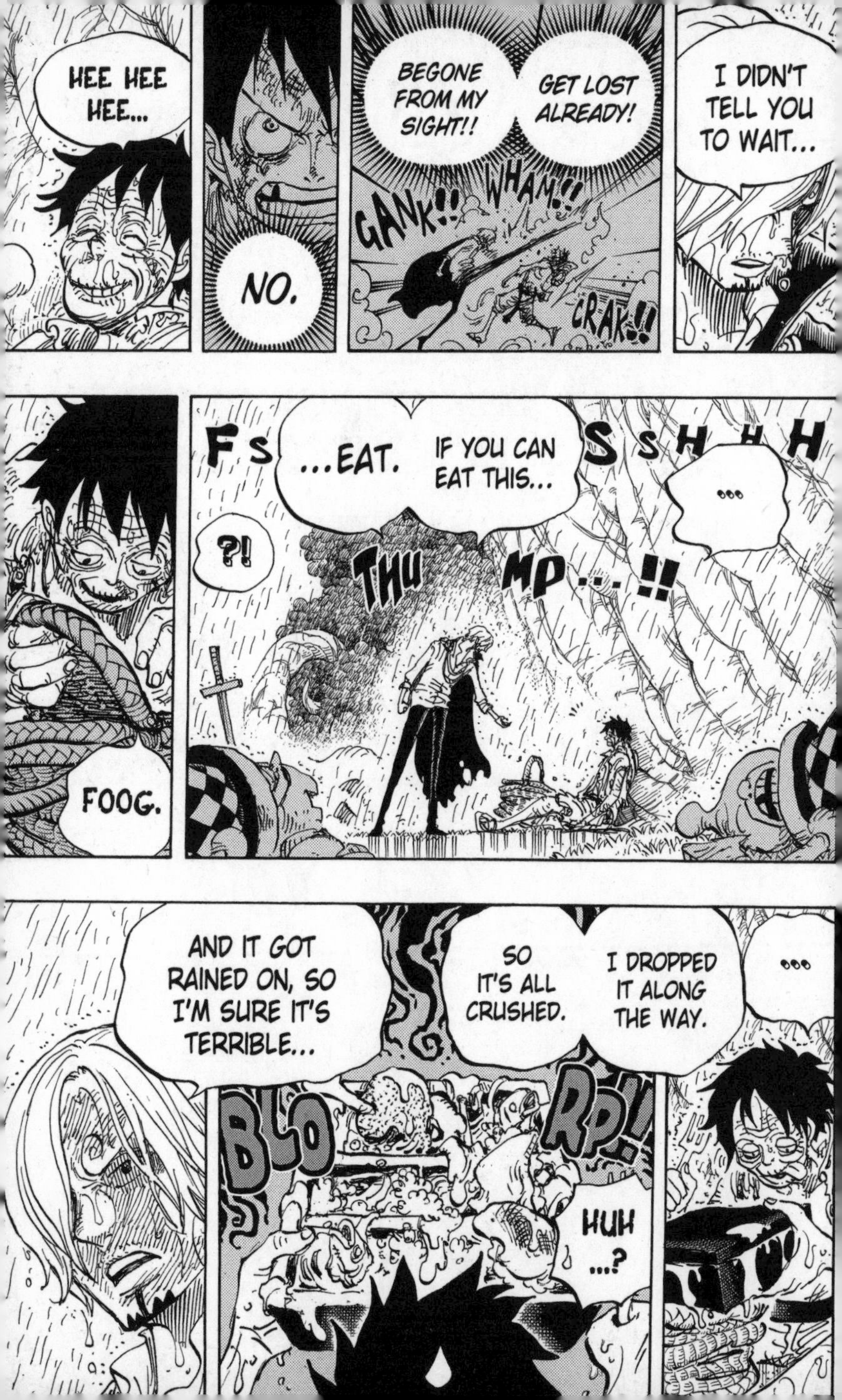

I DIDN'T TELL YOU TO WAIT...
GET LOST ALREADY!
BEGONE FROM MY SIGHT!!
WHAM!!
GANK!!
CRAK!!
NO.
HEE HEE HEE...
SSHHH
...
IF YOU CAN EAT THIS...
...EAT.
FS
?!
THUMP...!!
FOOG.
...
I DROPPED IT ALONG THE WAY.
SO IT'S ALL CRUSHED.
BLORP!!
HUH ...?
AND IT GOT RAINED ON, SO I'M SURE IT'S TERRIBLE...

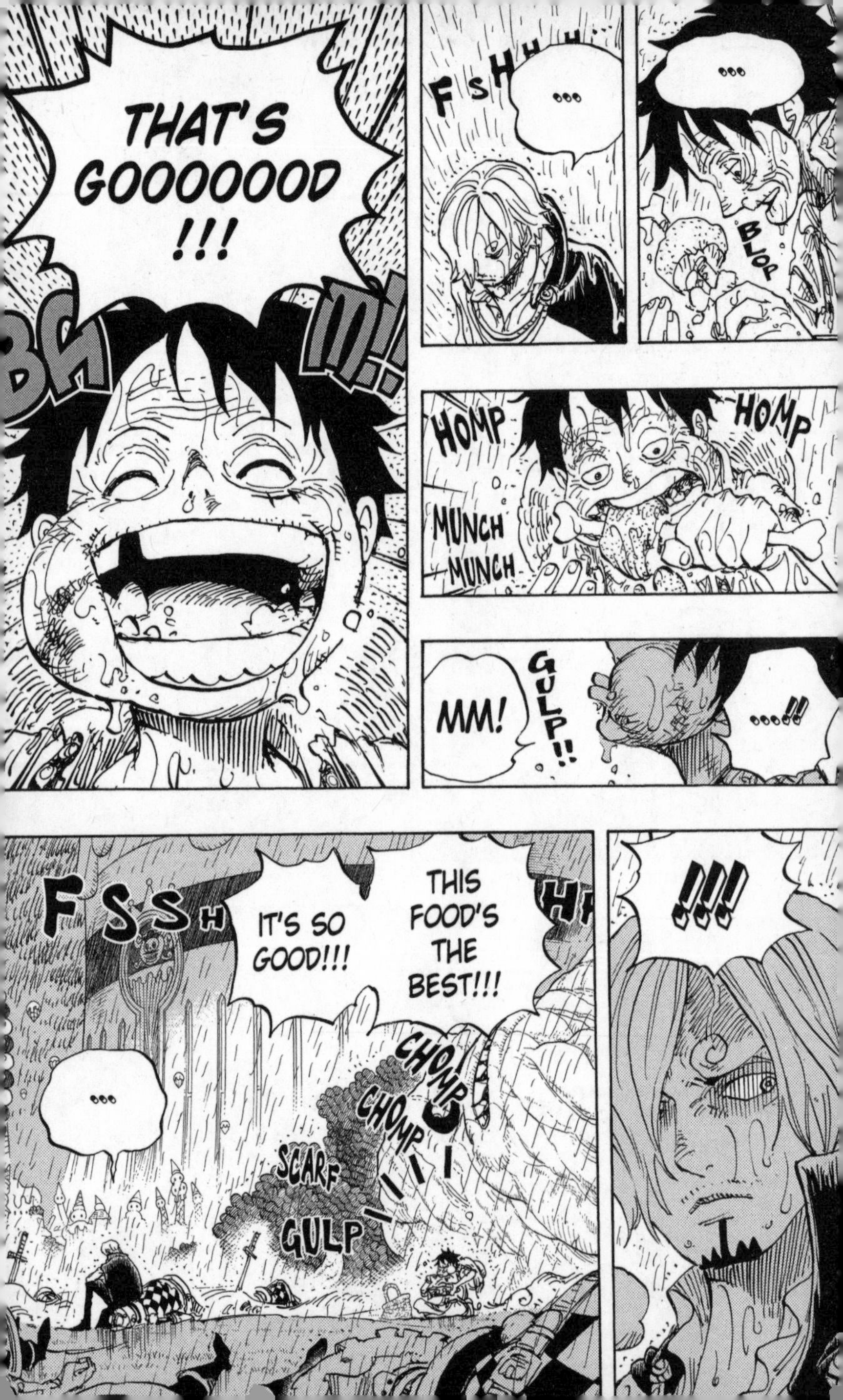
...
BLOP
FSHHH
...
HOMP
HOMP
MUNCH
MUNCH
...!!
GULP!!
MM!
THAT'S GOOOOOOD!!!
BAM!!
!!!
THIS FOOD'S THE BEST!!!
IT'S SO GOOD!!!
FSSH
HH
CHOMP
CHOMP
SCARF
GULP
...

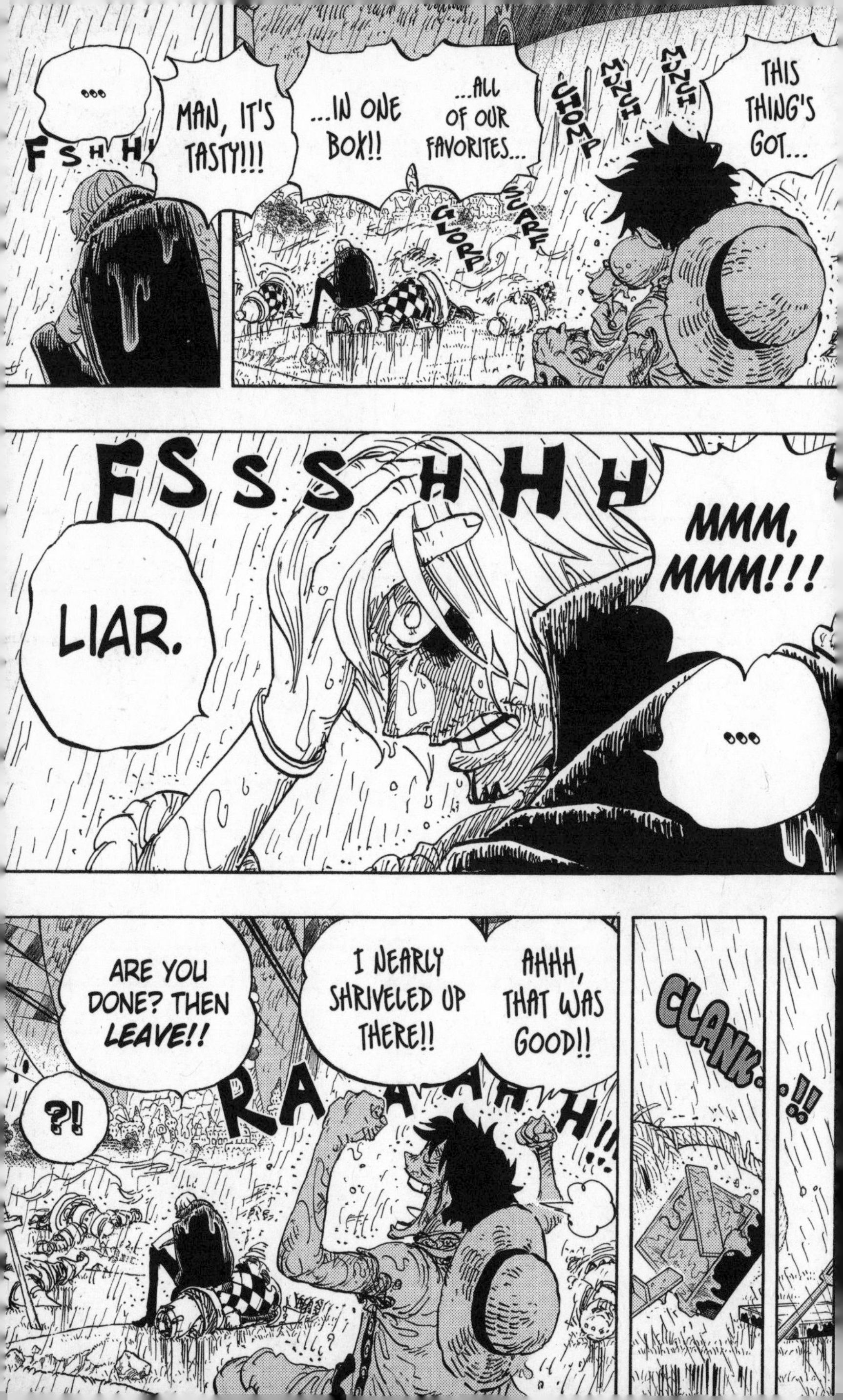
THIS THING'S GOT...
MUNCH
MUNCH
CHOMP
...ALL OF OUR FAVORITES...
...IN ONE BOX!!
MAN, IT'S TASTY!!!
SLURP
GLORP
...
FSHH
FSSSHHH
MMM, MMM!!!
...
LIAR.
CLANK...!!
AHHH, THAT WAS GOOD!!
I NEARLY SHRIVELED UP THERE!!
RAAAHH!!!
ARE YOU DONE? THEN LEAVE!!
?!

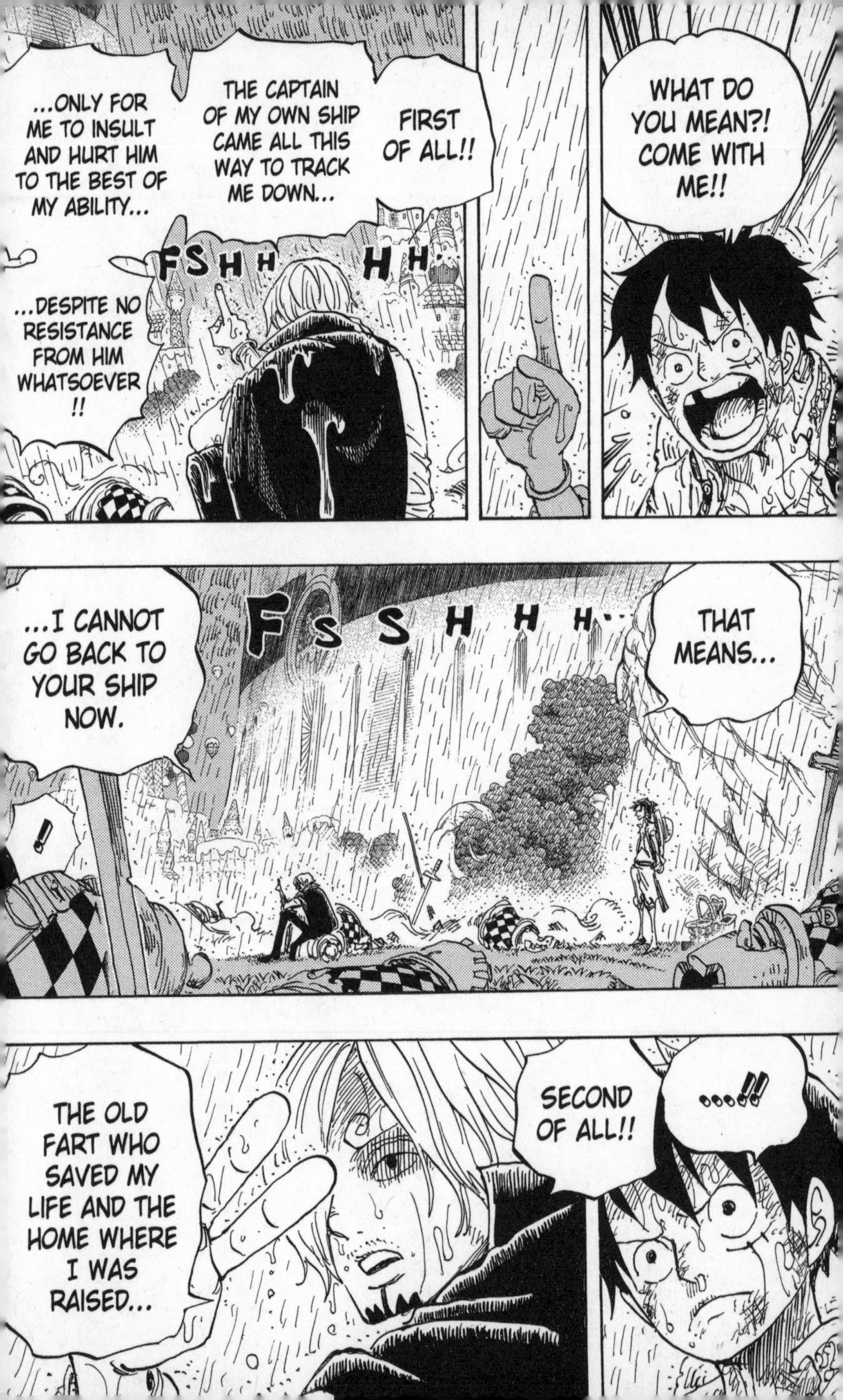
WHAT DO YOU MEAN?! COME WITH ME!!
FIRST OF ALL!!
THE CAPTAIN OF MY OWN SHIP CAME ALL THIS WAY TO TRACK ME DOWN...
...ONLY FOR ME TO INSULT AND HURT HIM TO THE BEST OF MY ABILITY...
FSHHHH
...DESPITE NO RESISTANCE FROM HIM WHATSOEVER!!
THAT MEANS...
FSSHHH...
...I CANNOT GO BACK TO YOUR SHIP NOW.
!
...!!
SECOND OF ALL!!
THE OLD FART WHO SAVED MY LIFE AND THE HOME WHERE I WAS RAISED...

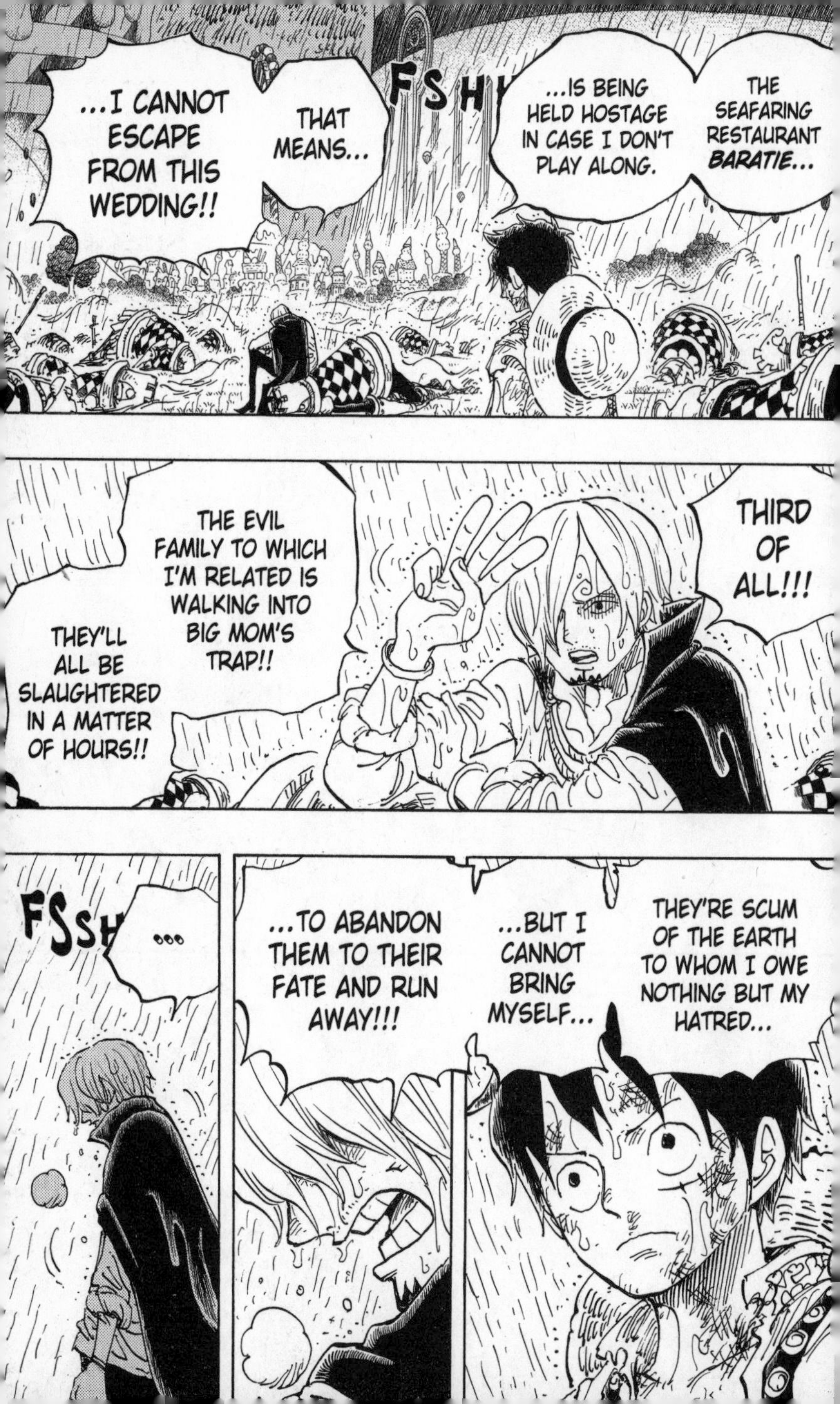
THE SEAFARING RESTAURANT *BARATIE...*
...IS BEING HELD HOSTAGE IN CASE I DON'T PLAY ALONG.
FSH
THAT MEANS...
...I CANNOT ESCAPE FROM THIS WEDDING!!
THIRD OF ALL!!!
THE EVIL FAMILY TO WHICH I'M RELATED IS WALKING INTO BIG MOM'S TRAP!!
THEY'LL ALL BE SLAUGHTERED IN A MATTER OF HOURS!!
THEY'RE SCUM OF THE EARTH TO WHOM I OWE NOTHING BUT MY HATRED...
...BUT I CANNOT BRING MYSELF...
...TO ABANDON THEM TO THEIR FATE AND RUN AWAY!!!
FSSH
...

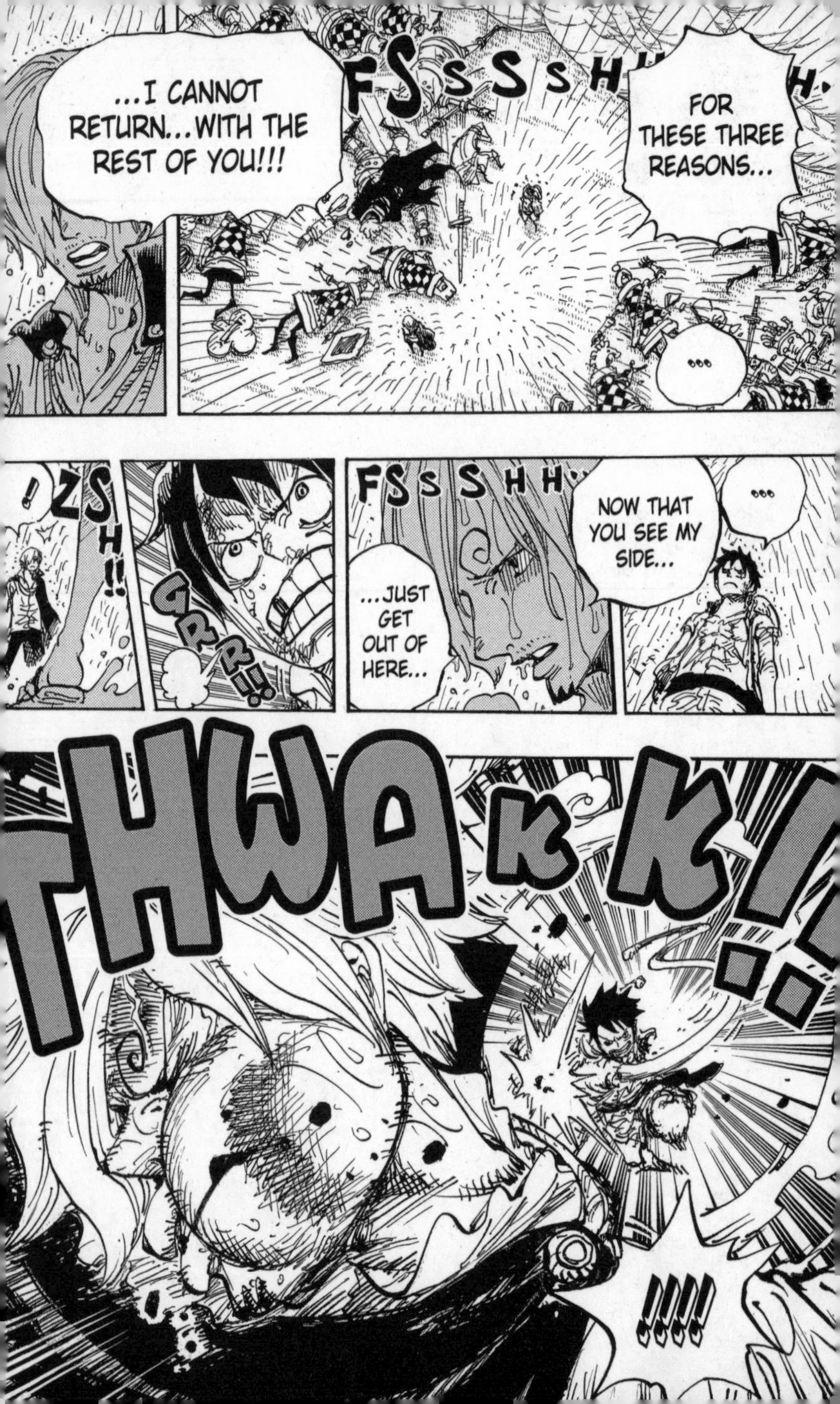
FSSSSH
FOR THESE THREE REASONS...
...
...I CANNOT RETURN...WITH THE REST OF YOU!!!
...
FSSSHH
NOW THAT YOU SEE MY SIDE...
...JUST GET OUT OF HERE...
GRR!!
ZSH!!
!
THWAKK!!
!!!!

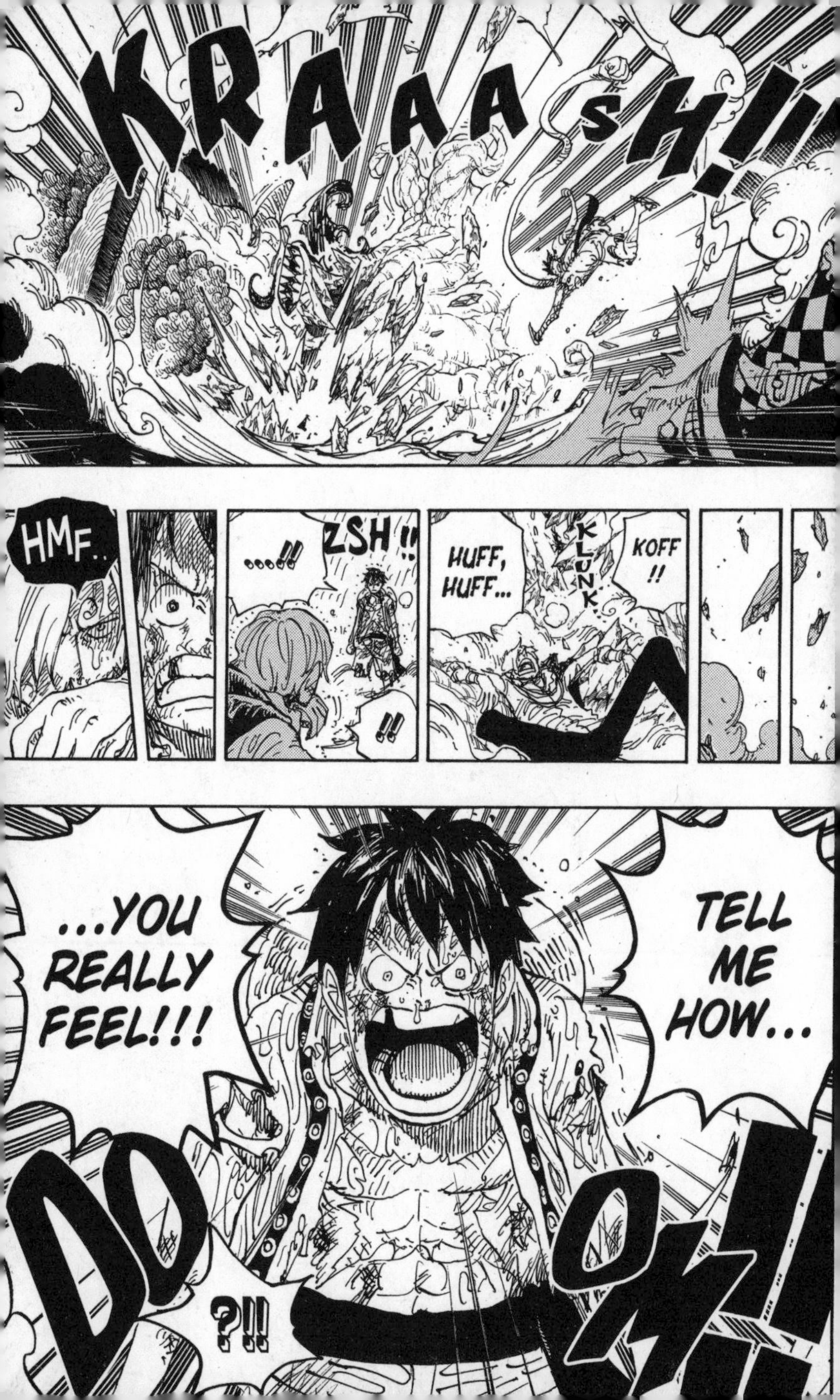
KRAAASH!!
KOFF !!
KLUNK
HUFF, HUFF...
ZSH !!
...!!
!!
HMF..
TELL ME HOW...
...YOU REALLY FEEL!!!
DOON!!
?!!

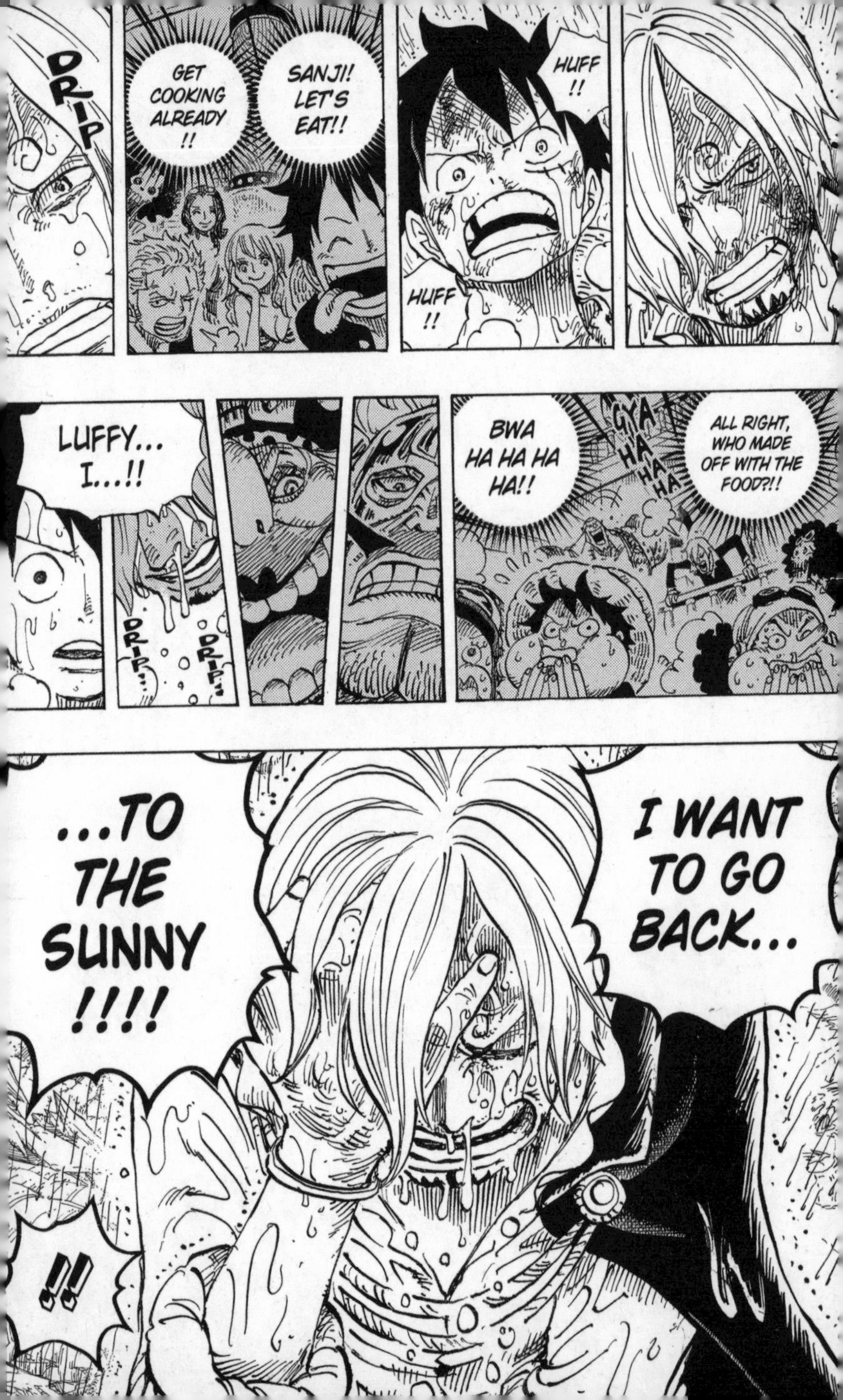
HUFF !!
HUFF !!
SANJI! LET'S EAT!!
GET COOKING ALREADY !!
DRIP
ALL RIGHT, WHO MADE OFF WITH THE FOOD?!!
GYA HA HA HA HA
BWA HA HA HA HA!!
DRIP...
DRIP...
LUFFY... I...!!
I WANT TO GO BACK...
...TO THE SUNNY !!!!
!!

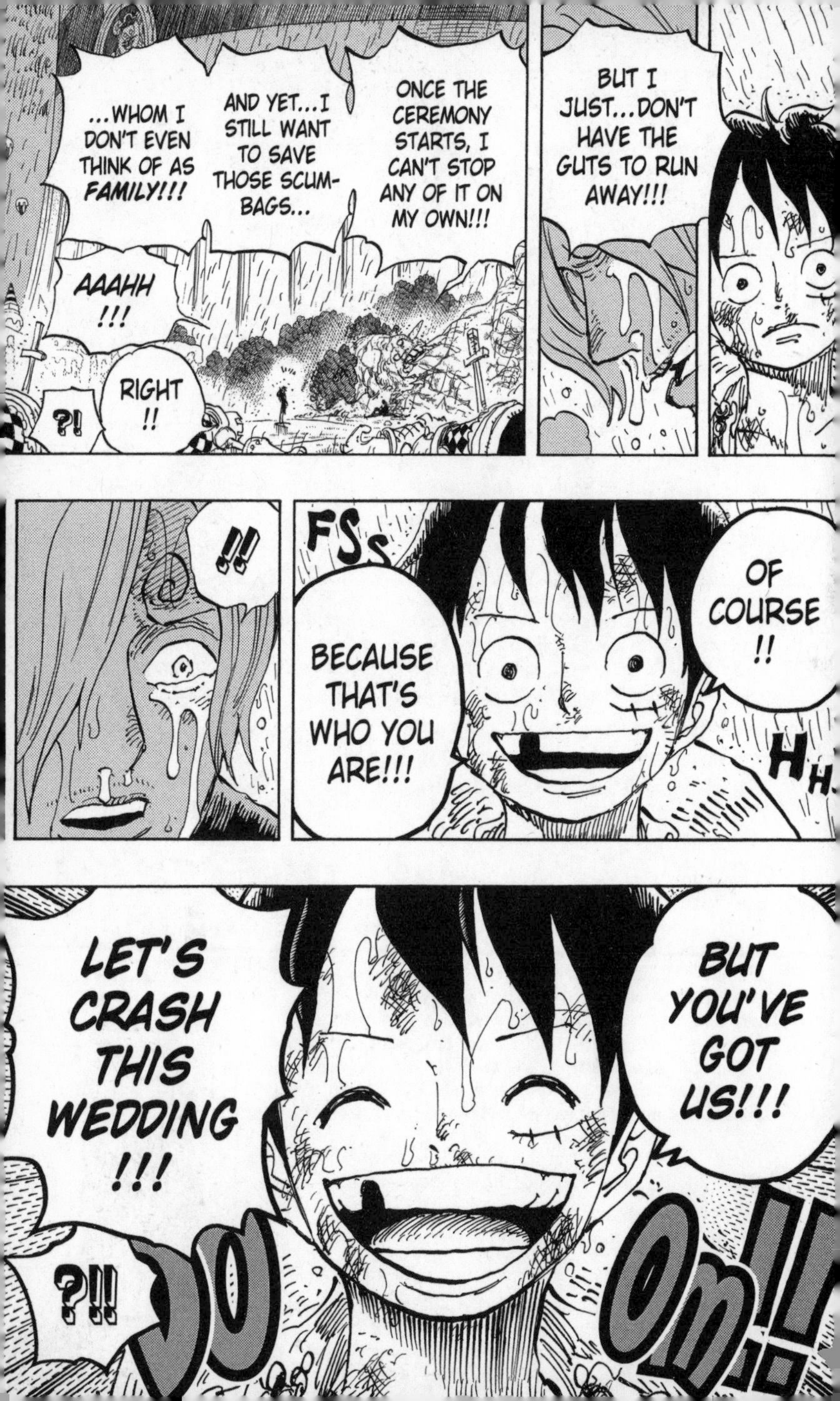
BUT I JUST...DON'T HAVE THE GUTS TO RUN AWAY!!!
ONCE THE CEREMONY STARTS, I CAN'T STOP ANY OF IT ON MY OWN!!!
AND YET...I STILL WANT TO SAVE THOSE SCUM-BAGS...
...WHOM I DON'T EVEN THINK OF AS FAMILY!!!
AAAHH!!!
RIGHT!!
?!
OF COURSE!!
FSS
HH
BECAUSE THAT'S WHO YOU ARE!!!
!!
BUT YOU'VE GOT US!!!
LET'S CRASH THIS WEDDING!!!
DOOM!!
?!!

SBS Question Corner

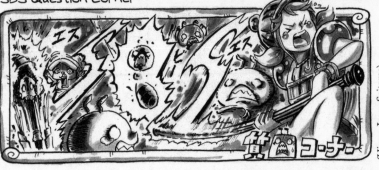

(Hippo Iron, Saitama)

Q: Odacchi! In the SBS of volume 84, you wrote that Zolo is one of the Straw Hats who doesn't chew his ice, but in chapter 701, volume 71, isn't he chewing his ice there?

--Dobbin

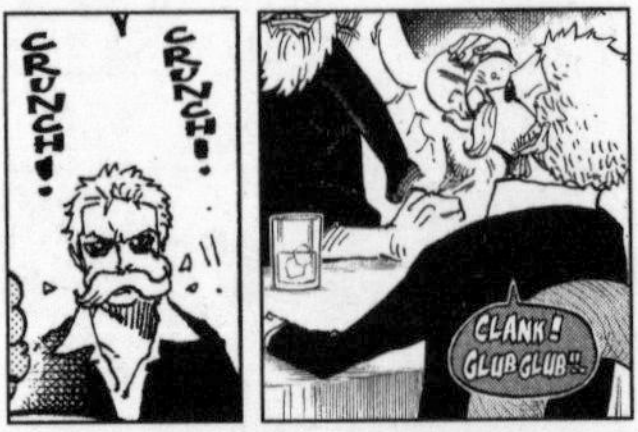

CLANK! GLUB GLUB!!
CRUNCH!
CRUNCH!

A: !!! ....Right... Yeah... It looks that way, right?! Yeah. Well... It only looks like he's eating his ice. Just an impression. But the thing is...Zolo doesn't have a mustache, soooo...I dunno, that might not be Zolo...y'know? So that's probably not him. I mean...is that Zolo? I'm not sure...

Q: In chapter 845, volume 84, I spotted three other characters who look just like Opera. Are they identical quadruplets, just like Sanji and his brothers?

--?

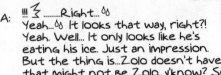

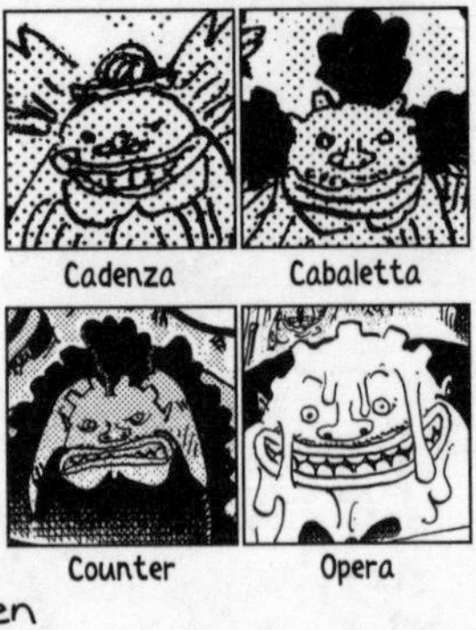

Cabaletta
Cadenza
Opera
Counter

A: Technically, they're quintuplets, but you don't see the last one. There's Opera, fifth son of Charlotte; Counter, the sixth son; Cadenza, the seventh son; Cabaletta, the eighth son; and Gala, the ninth son. Big Mom is currently 68 years old, and for about 42 years, she had children annually. Yet she has 85 children, so there are tons of twins and triplets. The biggest batch is a decuplet bunch who are all 18 years old now--five boys and five girls!! Big Mom, indeed!!

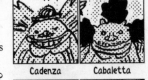

Q: In the corner of page 58 of volume 83, is Nami wearing armor? Is that just a sign of how much she fears an Emperor of the Sea? And the way she takes it off in an instant is super impressive!!

--Kawamacho

AH!!

A: Uh, that was her gear from fighting the sea ants the night before. She changed because they reached the island. And now, we're out of time! See you in the SBS next volume!!

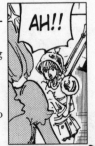

Chapter 857:
ROOK

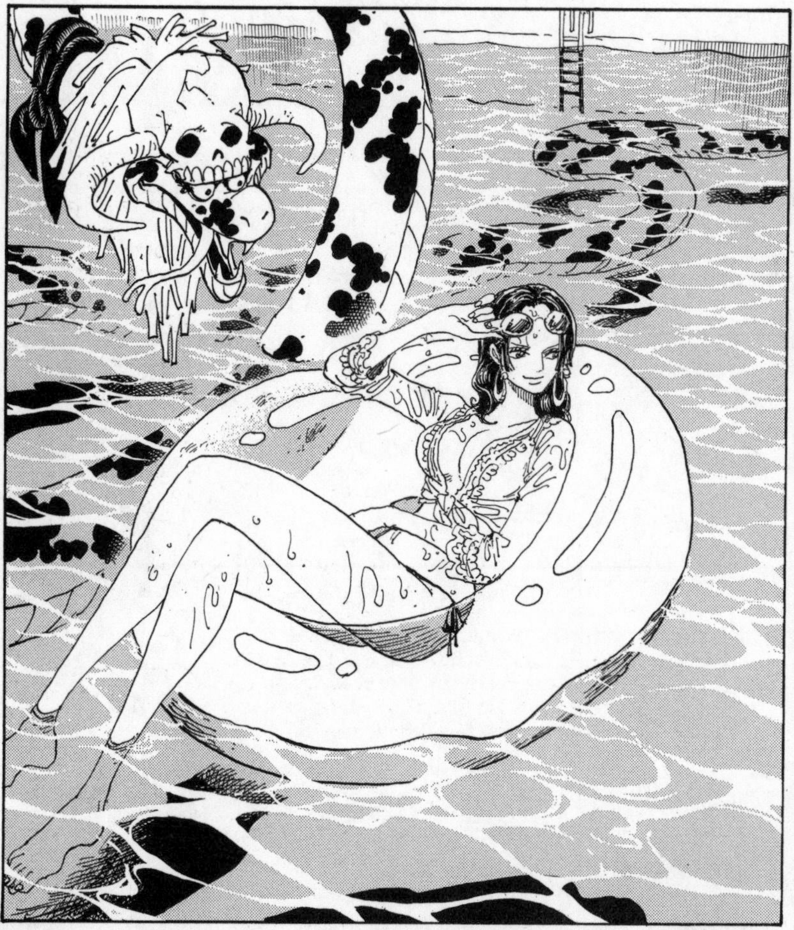

REQUEST: "HANCOCK TAKING A DIP IN THE POOL"
BY ULTRA SEVEN (JUWA!) FROM SAITAMA

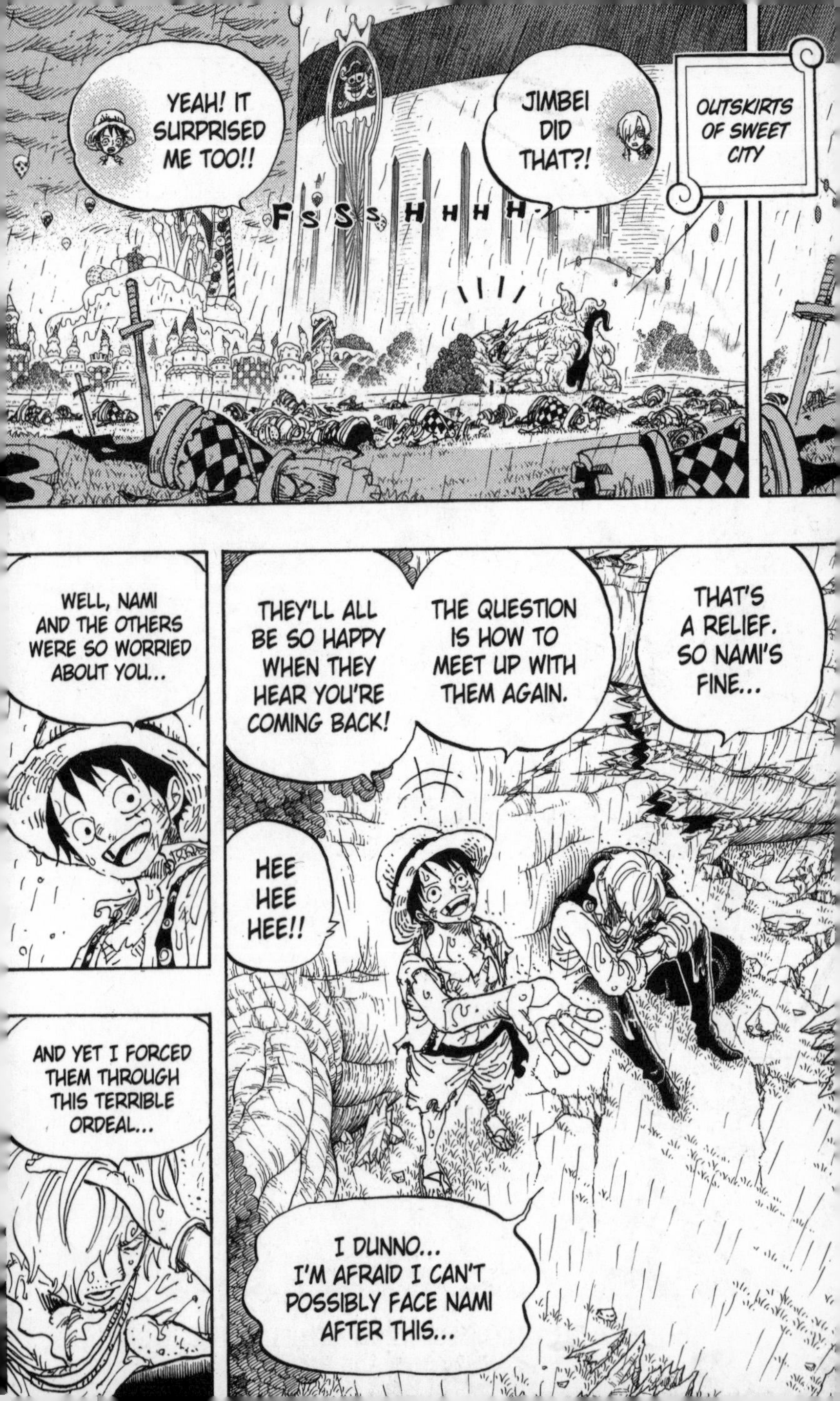
OUTSKIRTS OF SWEET CITY
JIMBEI DID THAT?!
FSSSSHHHH
YEAH! IT SURPRISED ME TOO!!
THAT'S A RELIEF. SO NAMI'S FINE...
THE QUESTION IS HOW TO MEET UP WITH THEM AGAIN.
THEY'LL ALL BE SO HAPPY WHEN THEY HEAR YOU'RE COMING BACK!
HEE HEE HEE!!
I DUNNO... I'M AFRAID I CAN'T POSSIBLY FACE NAMI AFTER THIS...
WELL, NAMI AND THE OTHERS WERE SO WORRIED ABOUT YOU...
AND YET I FORCED THEM THROUGH THIS TERRIBLE ORDEAL...

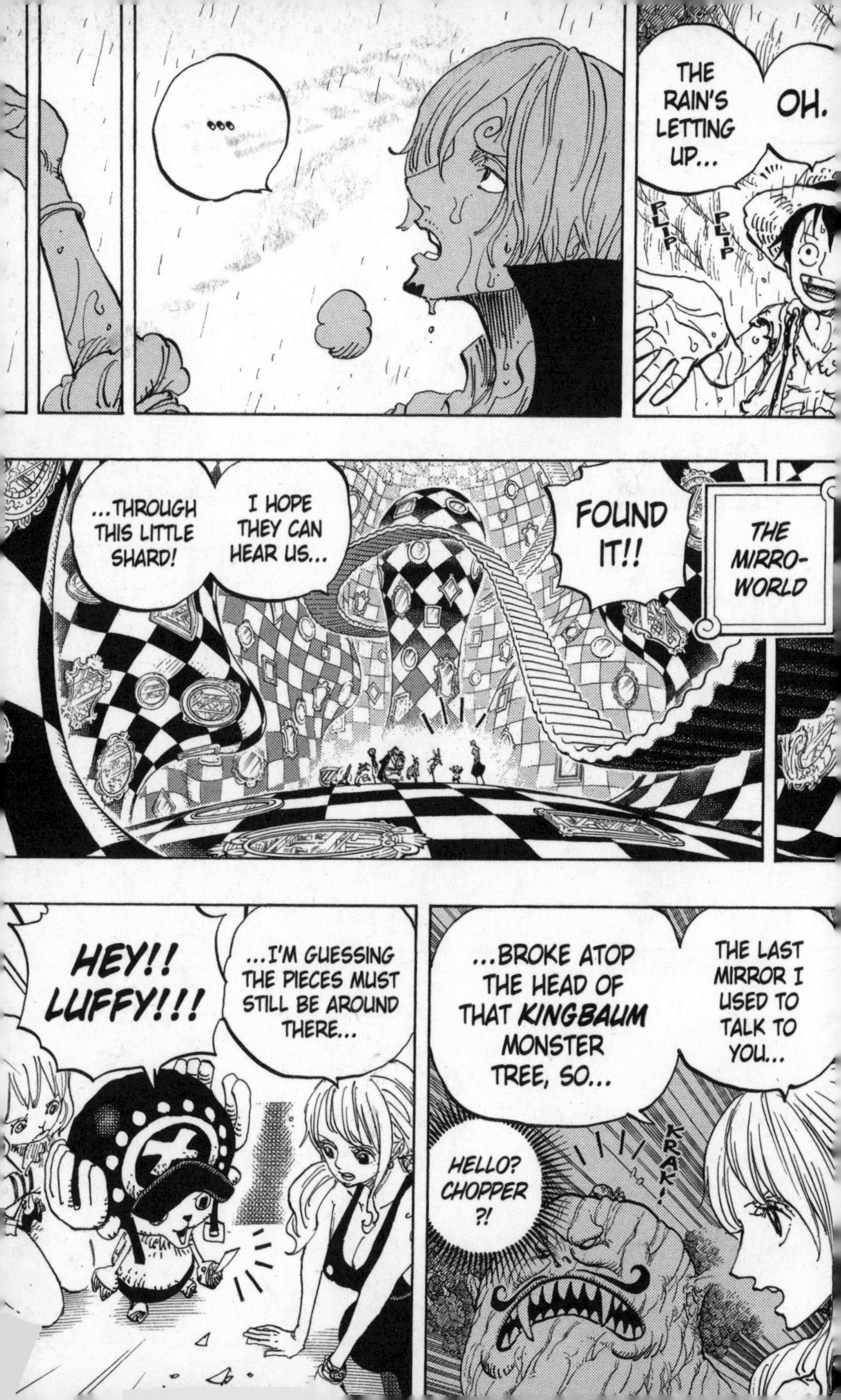
OH.
THE RAIN'S LETTING UP...
FLIP
FLIP
...
THE MIRRO-WORLD
FOUND IT!!
I HOPE THEY CAN HEAR US...
...THROUGH THIS LITTLE SHARD!
THE LAST MIRROR I USED TO TALK TO YOU...
...BROKE ATOP THE HEAD OF THAT KINGBAUM MONSTER TREE, SO...
KRAK!
HELLO? CHOPPER?!
...I'M GUESSING THE PIECES MUST STILL BE AROUND THERE...
HEY!! LUFFY!!!

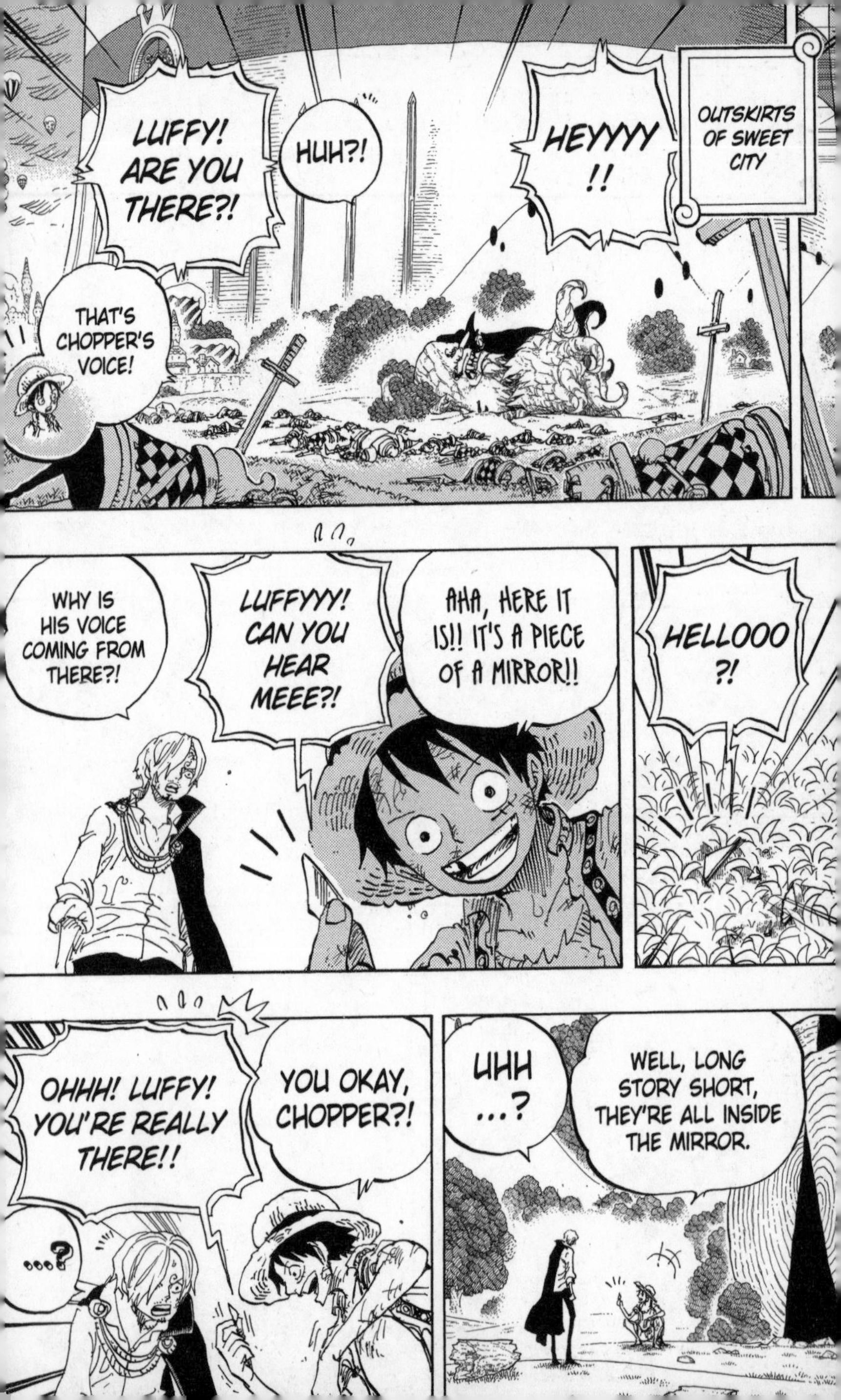
OUTSKIRTS OF SWEET CITY
HEYYYY !!
HUH?!
LUFFY! ARE YOU THERE?!
THAT'S CHOPPER'S VOICE!
HELLOOO ?!
AHA, HERE IT IS!! IT'S A PIECE OF A MIRROR!!
LUFFYYY! CAN YOU HEAR MEEE?!
WHY IS HIS VOICE COMING FROM THERE?!
WELL, LONG STORY SHORT, THEY'RE ALL INSIDE THE MIRROR.
UHH ...?
YOU OKAY, CHOPPER?!
OHHH! LUFFY! YOU'RE REALLY THERE!!
...?

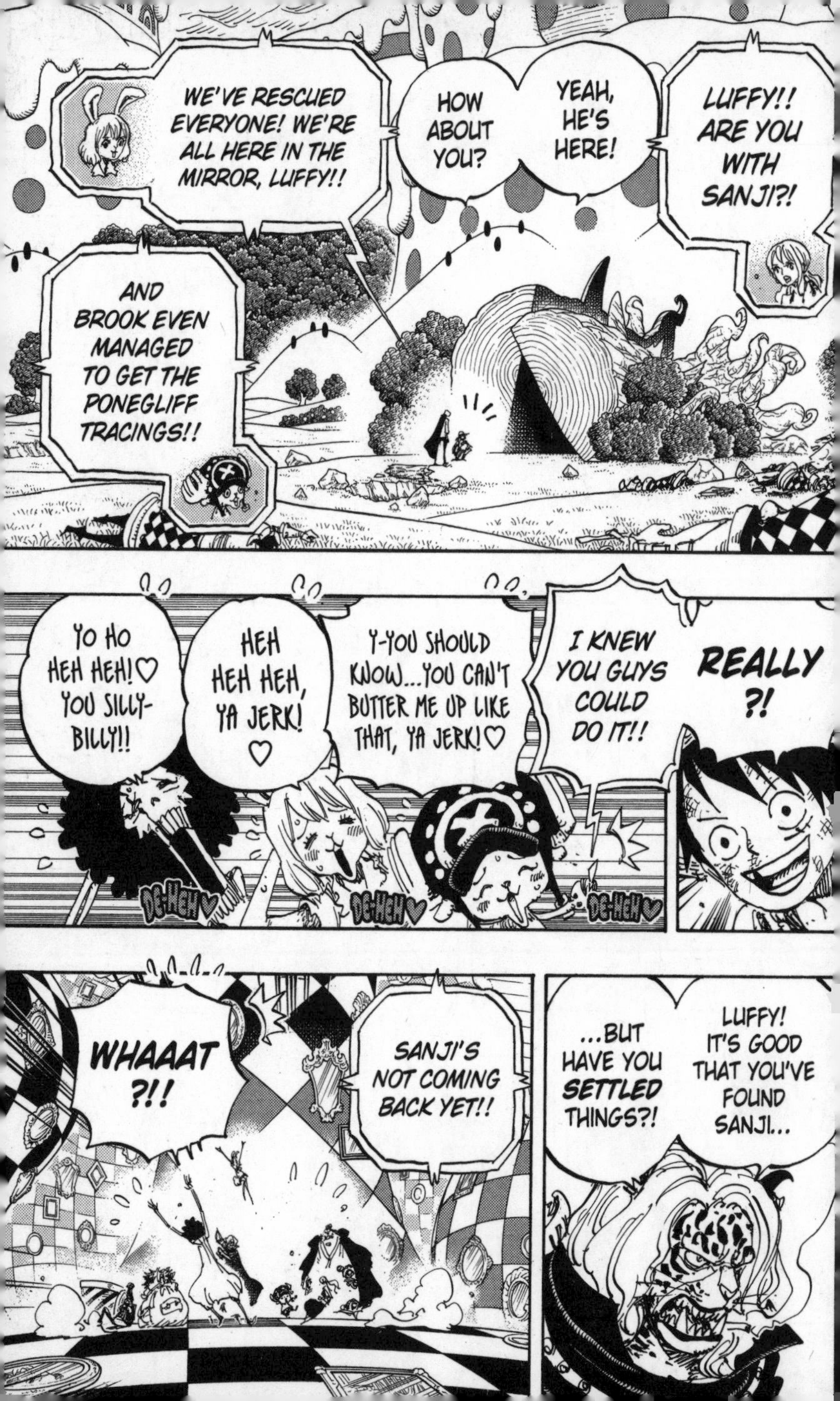
LUFFY!! ARE YOU WITH SANJI?!
YEAH, HE'S HERE!
HOW ABOUT YOU?
WE'VE RESCUED EVERYONE! WE'RE ALL HERE IN THE MIRROR, LUFFY!!
AND BROOK EVEN MANAGED TO GET THE PONEGLIFF TRACINGS!!
REALLY?!
I KNEW YOU GUYS COULD DO IT!!
Y-YOU SHOULD KNOW...YOU CAN'T BUTTER ME UP LIKE THAT, YA JERK!♡
DE-HEH♡
HEH HEH HEH, YA JERK! ♡
DE-HEH♡
YO HO HEH HEH!♡ YOU SILLY-BILLY!!
DE-HEH♡
LUFFY! IT'S GOOD THAT YOU'VE FOUND SANJI...
...BUT HAVE YOU SETTLED THINGS?!
SANJI'S NOT COMING BACK YET!!
WHAAAT?!!

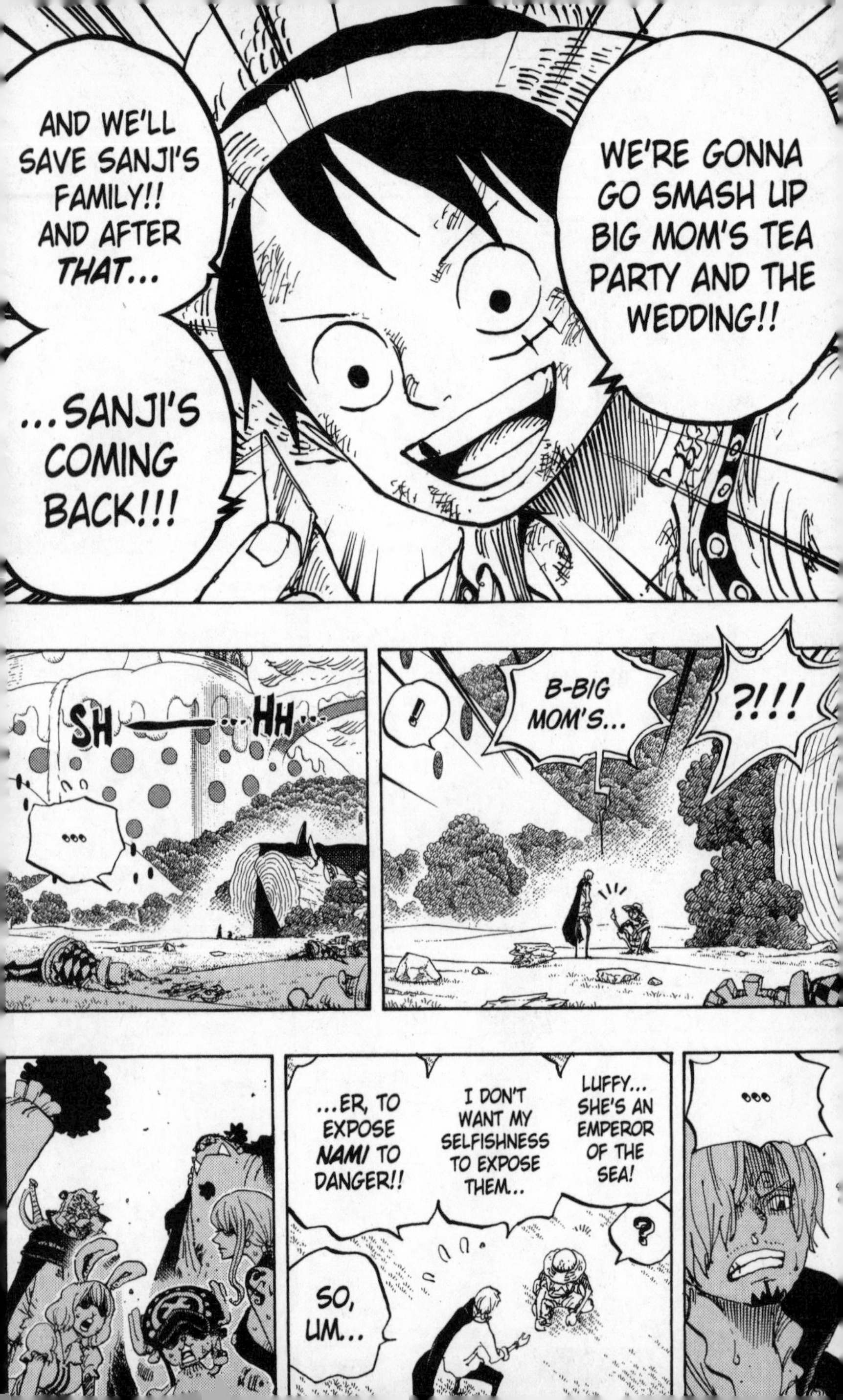
WE'RE GONNA GO SMASH UP BIG MOM'S TEA PARTY AND THE WEDDING!!
AND WE'LL SAVE SANJI'S FAMILY!! AND AFTER *THAT*...
...SANJI'S COMING BACK!!!
?!!!
B-BIG MOM'S...
!
SH——...HH...
...
...
LUFFY... SHE'S AN EMPEROR OF THE SEA!
?
I DON'T WANT MY SELFISHNESS TO EXPOSE THEM..
...ER, TO EXPOSE *NAMI* TO DANGER!!
SO, UM...

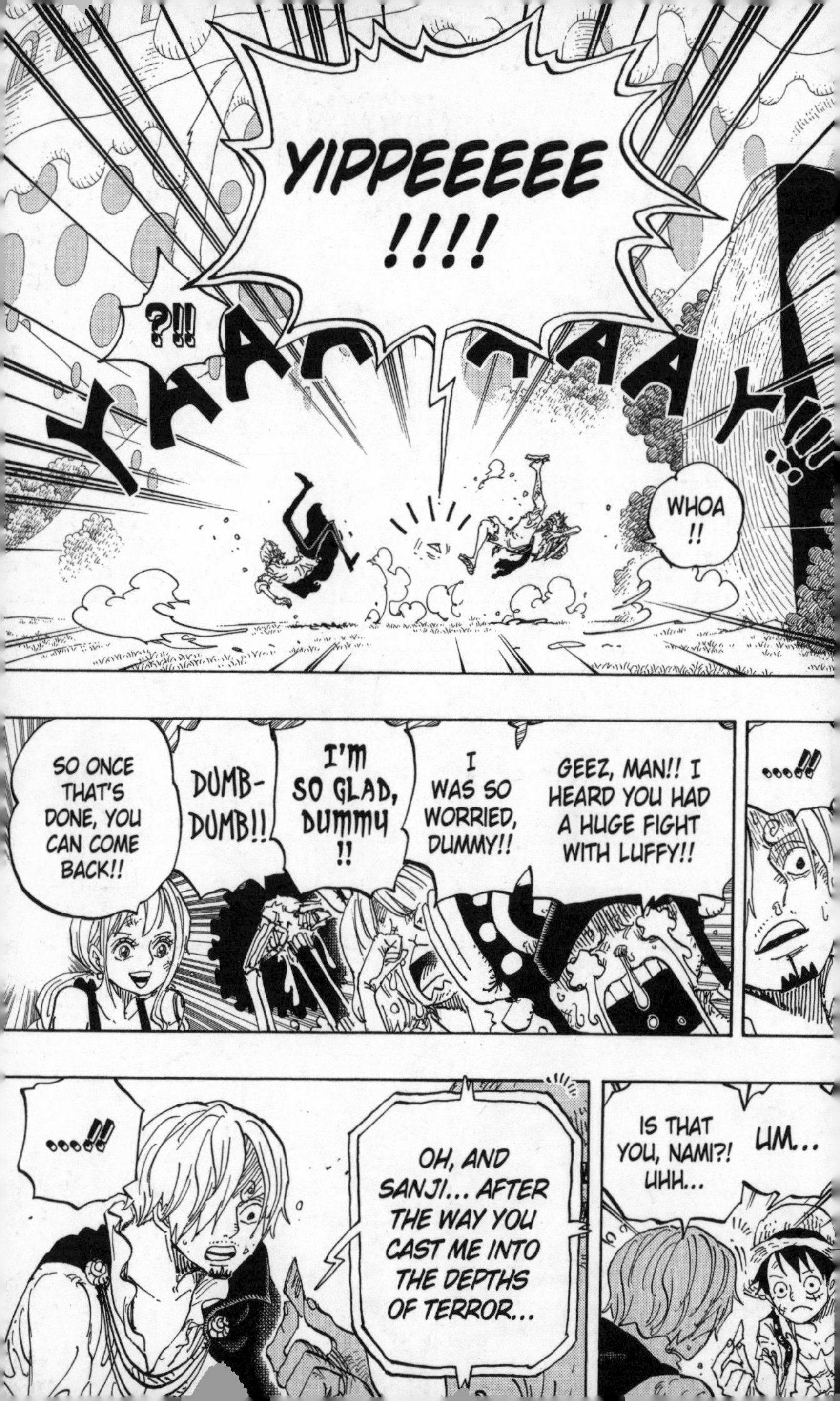
YIPPEEEEE !!!!
WHOA !!
YAAAAAY!!!
?!!
....!!
GEEZ, MAN!! I HEARD YOU HAD A HUGE FIGHT WITH LUFFY!!
I WAS SO WORRIED, DUMMY!!
I'M SO GLAD, DUMMY !!
DUMB-DUMB!!
SO ONCE THAT'S DONE, YOU CAN COME BACK!!
UM...
IS THAT YOU, NAMI?! UHH...
OH, AND SANJI... AFTER THE WAY YOU CAST ME INTO THE DEPTHS OF TERROR...
....!!

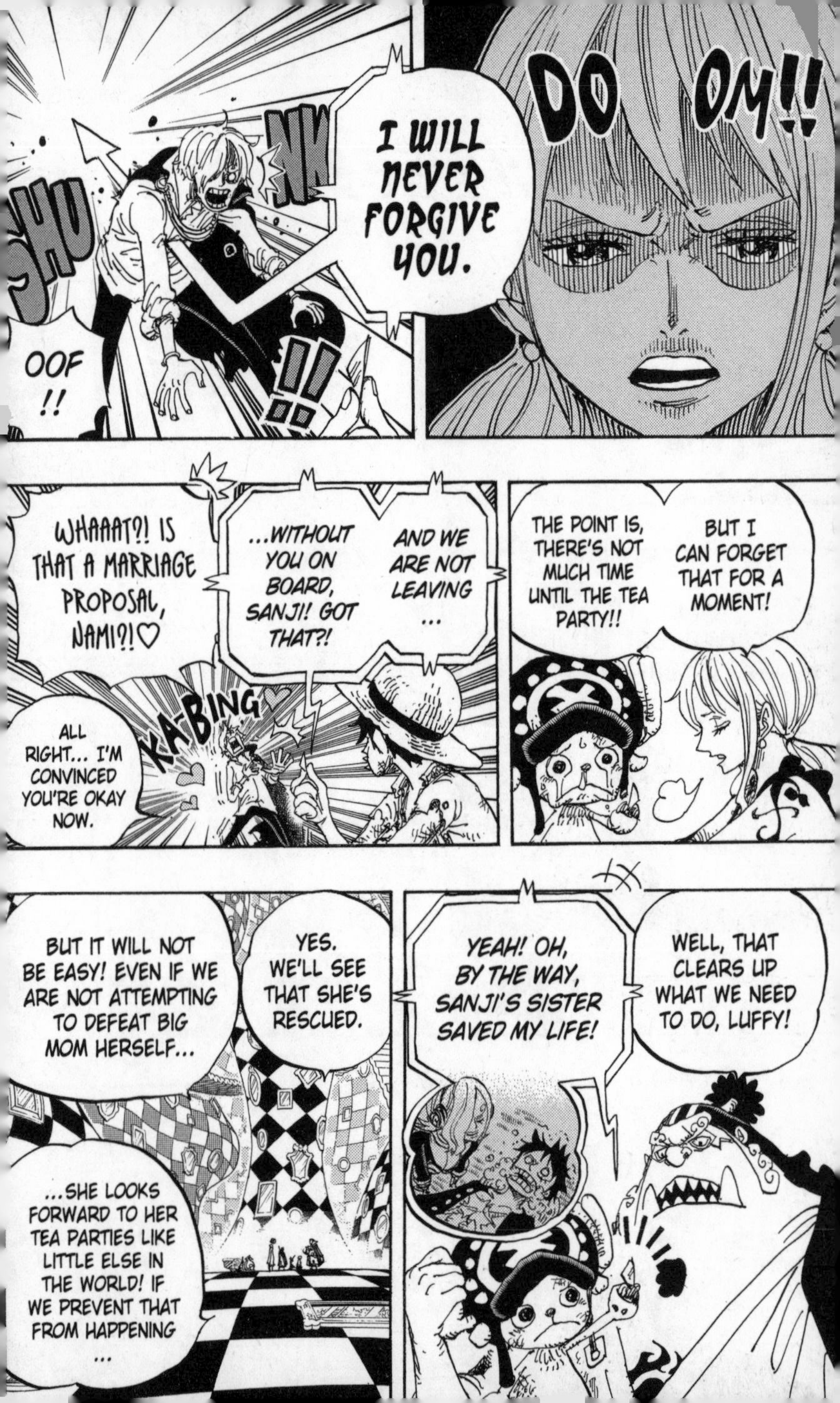
DO OM!!
I WILL NEVER FORGIVE YOU.
SHU
NK
OOF!!
BUT I CAN FORGET THAT FOR A MOMENT!
THE POINT IS, THERE'S NOT MUCH TIME UNTIL THE TEA PARTY!!
AND WE ARE NOT LEAVING...
...WITHOUT YOU ON BOARD, SANJI! GOT THAT?!
WHAAAT?! IS THAT A MARRIAGE PROPOSAL, NAMI?!♡
KA-BING♡
ALL RIGHT... I'M CONVINCED YOU'RE OKAY NOW.
WELL, THAT CLEARS UP WHAT WE NEED TO DO, LUFFY!
YEAH! OH, BY THE WAY, SANJI'S SISTER SAVED MY LIFE!
YES. WE'LL SEE THAT SHE'S RESCUED.
BUT IT WILL NOT BE EASY! EVEN IF WE ARE NOT ATTEMPTING TO DEFEAT BIG MOM HERSELF...
...SHE LOOKS FORWARD TO HER TEA PARTIES LIKE LITTLE ELSE IN THE WORLD! IF WE PREVENT THAT FROM HAPPENING...

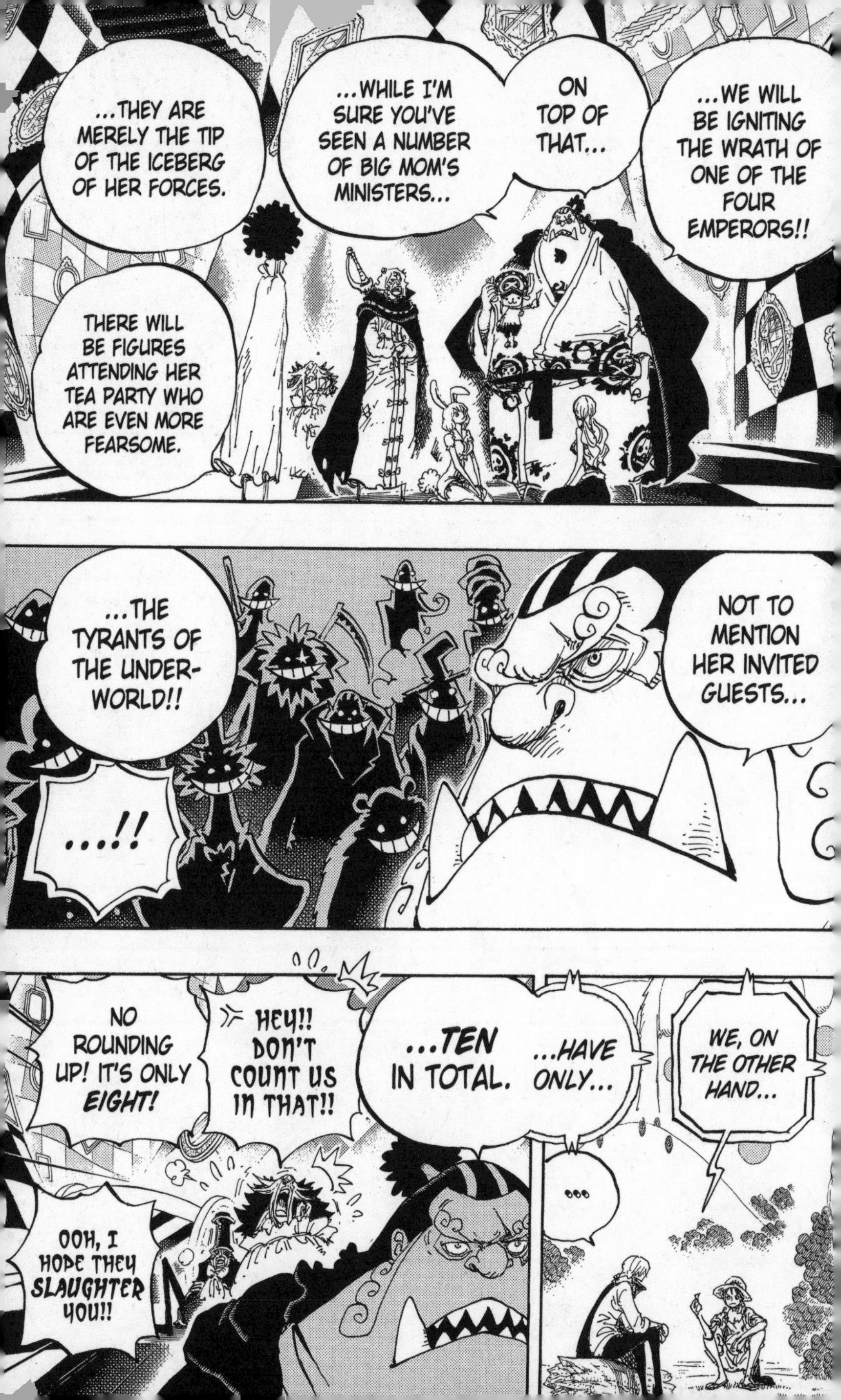
ON TOP OF THAT...
...WE WILL BE IGNITING THE WRATH OF ONE OF THE FOUR EMPERORS!!
...WHILE I'M SURE YOU'VE SEEN A NUMBER OF BIG MOM'S MINISTERS...
...THEY ARE MERELY THE TIP OF THE ICEBERG OF HER FORCES.
THERE WILL BE FIGURES ATTENDING HER TEA PARTY WHO ARE EVEN MORE FEARSOME.
NOT TO MENTION HER INVITED GUESTS...
...THE TYRANTS OF THE UNDER-WORLD!!
...!!
WE, ON THE OTHER HAND...
...HAVE ONLY...
...
...TEN IN TOTAL.
HEY!! DON'T COUNT US IN THAT!!
NO ROUNDING UP! IT'S ONLY EIGHT!
OOH, I HOPE THEY SLAUGHTER YOU!!

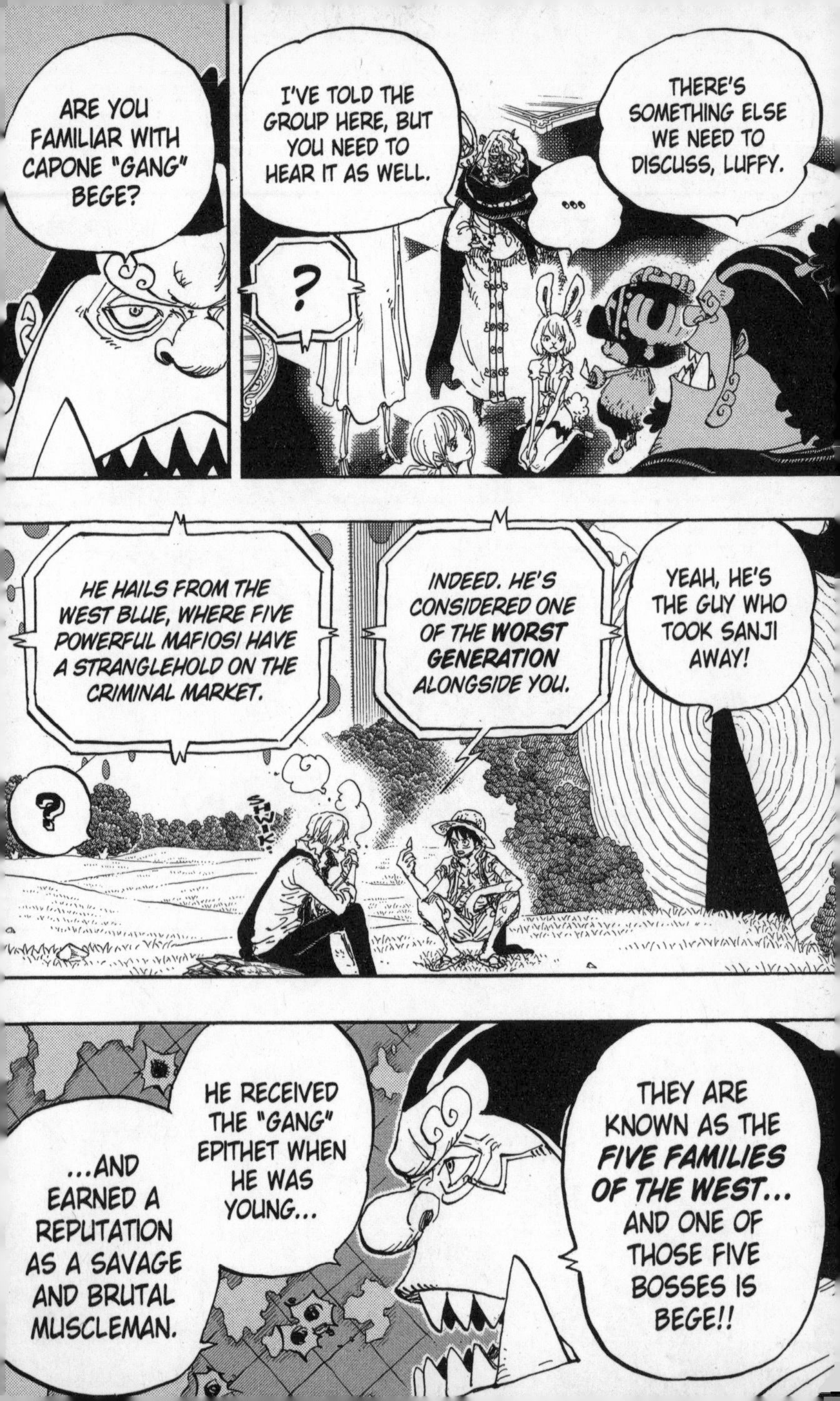
THERE'S SOMETHING ELSE WE NEED TO DISCUSS, LUFFY.
...
I'VE TOLD THE GROUP HERE, BUT YOU NEED TO HEAR IT AS WELL.
?
ARE YOU FAMILIAR WITH CAPONE "GANG" BEGE?
YEAH, HE'S THE GUY WHO TOOK SANJI AWAY!
INDEED. HE'S CONSIDERED ONE OF THE WORST GENERATION ALONGSIDE YOU.
HE HAILS FROM THE WEST BLUE, WHERE FIVE POWERFUL MAFIOSI HAVE A STRANGLEHOLD ON THE CRIMINAL MARKET.
SHWIK
?
THEY ARE KNOWN AS THE FIVE FAMILIES OF THE WEST... AND ONE OF THOSE FIVE BOSSES IS BEGE!!
HE RECEIVED THE "GANG" EPITHET WHEN HE WAS YOUNG...
...AND EARNED A REPUTATION AS A SAVAGE AND BRUTAL MUSCLEMAN.

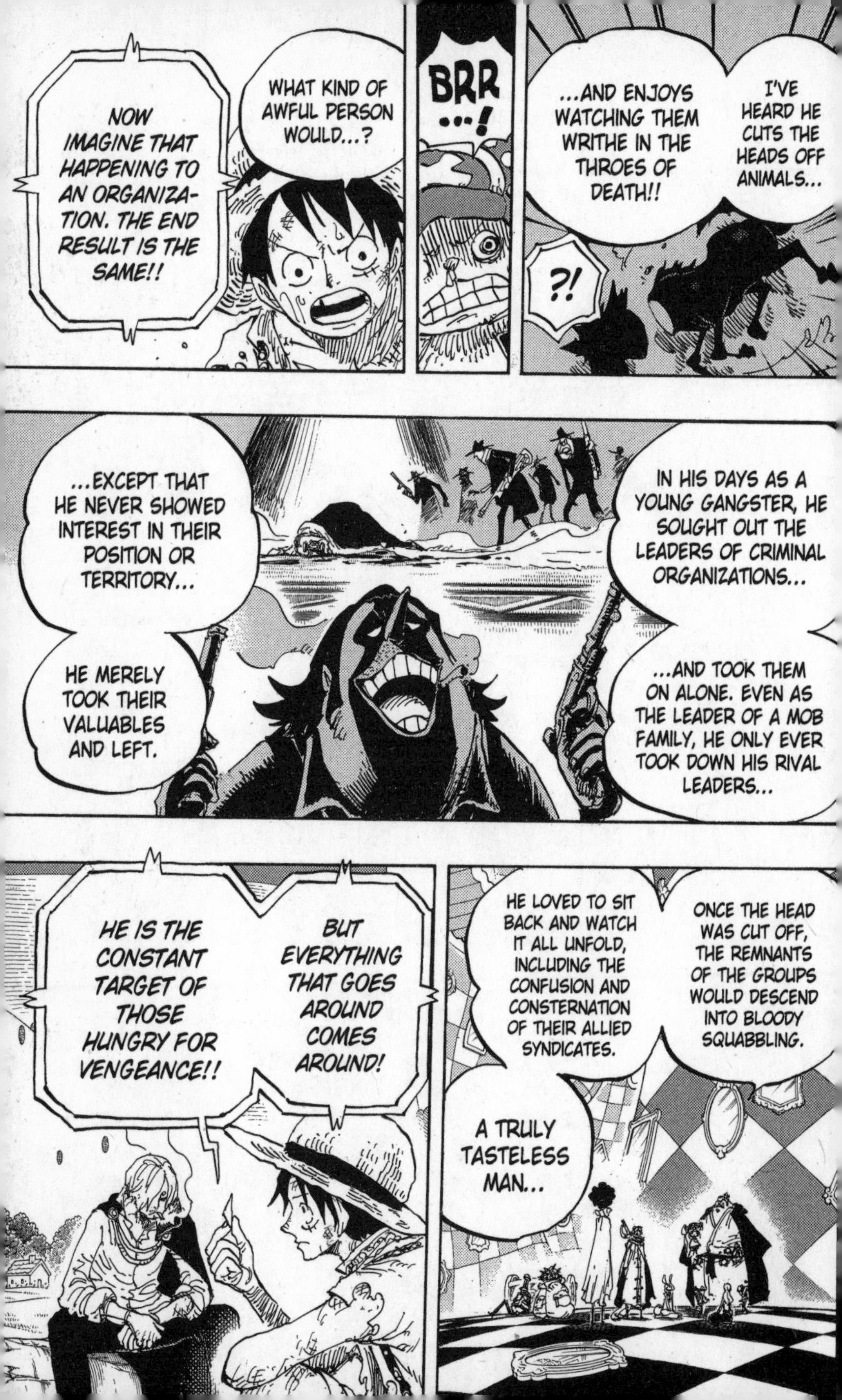
I'VE HEARD HE CUTS THE HEADS OFF ANIMALS...
...AND ENJOYS WATCHING THEM WRITHE IN THE THROES OF DEATH!!
?!
BRR...!
WHAT KIND OF AWFUL PERSON WOULD...?
NOW IMAGINE THAT HAPPENING TO AN ORGANIZATION. THE END RESULT IS THE SAME!!
IN HIS DAYS AS A YOUNG GANGSTER, HE SOUGHT OUT THE LEADERS OF CRIMINAL ORGANIZATIONS...
...AND TOOK THEM ON ALONE. EVEN AS THE LEADER OF A MOB FAMILY, HE ONLY EVER TOOK DOWN HIS RIVAL LEADERS...
...EXCEPT THAT HE NEVER SHOWED INTEREST IN THEIR POSITION OR TERRITORY...
HE MERELY TOOK THEIR VALUABLES AND LEFT.
ONCE THE HEAD WAS CUT OFF, THE REMNANTS OF THE GROUPS WOULD DESCEND INTO BLOODY SQUABBLING.
HE LOVED TO SIT BACK AND WATCH IT ALL UNFOLD, INCLUDING THE CONFUSION AND CONSTERNATION OF THEIR ALLIED SYNDICATES.
A TRULY TASTELESS MAN...
BUT EVERYTHING THAT GOES AROUND COMES AROUND!
HE IS THE CONSTANT TARGET OF THOSE HUNGRY FOR VENGEANCE!!

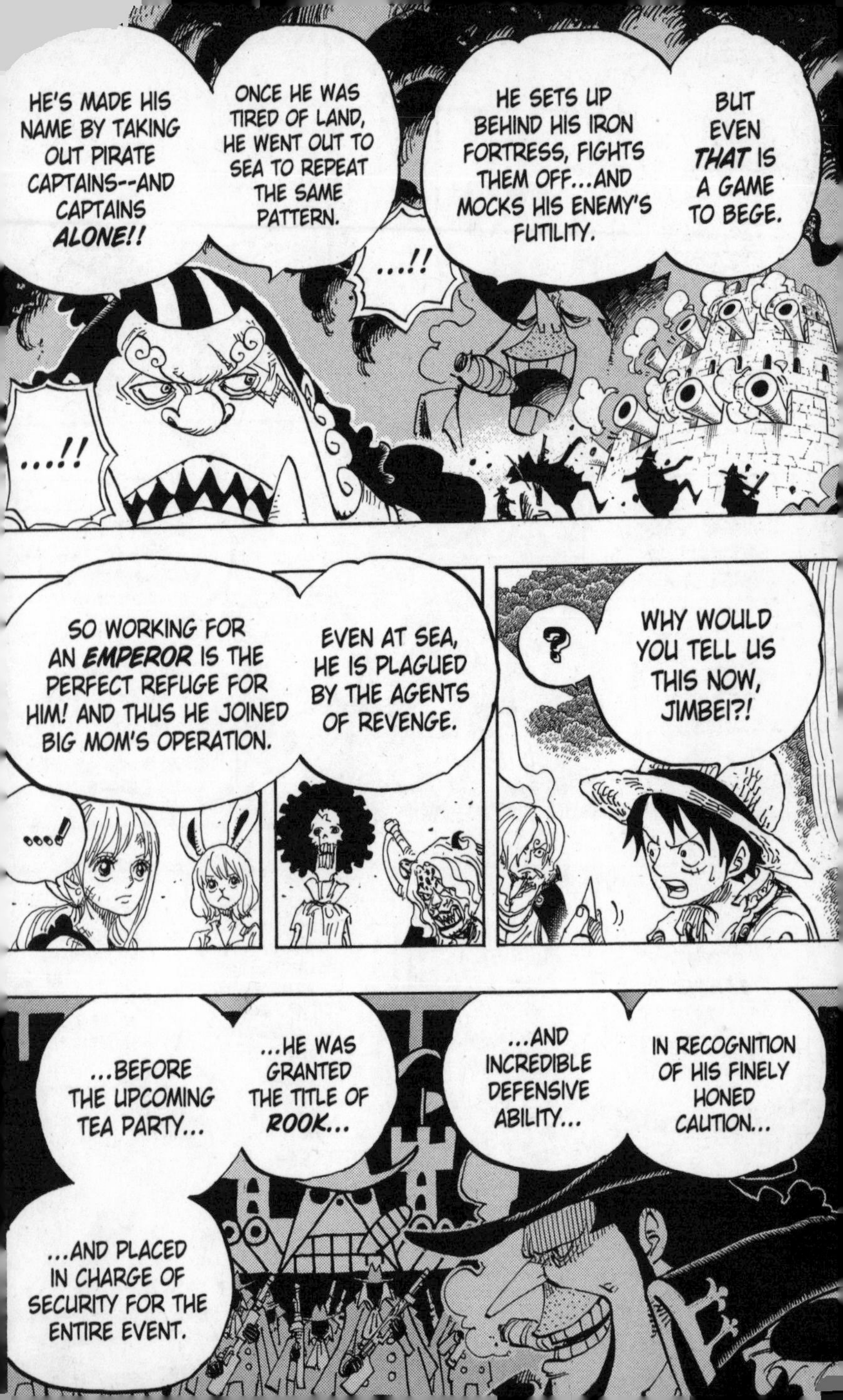
BUT EVEN *THAT* IS A GAME TO BEGE.
HE SETS UP BEHIND HIS IRON FORTRESS, FIGHTS THEM OFF...AND MOCKS HIS ENEMY'S FUTILITY.
ONCE HE WAS TIRED OF LAND, HE WENT OUT TO SEA TO REPEAT THE SAME PATTERN.
HE'S MADE HIS NAME BY TAKING OUT PIRATE CAPTAINS--AND CAPTAINS *ALONE!!*
...!!
...!!
WHY WOULD YOU TELL US THIS NOW, JIMBEI?!
?
EVEN AT SEA, HE IS PLAGUED BY THE AGENTS OF REVENGE.
SO WORKING FOR AN *EMPEROR* IS THE PERFECT REFUGE FOR HIM! AND THUS HE JOINED BIG MOM'S OPERATION.
...!
IN RECOGNITION OF HIS FINELY HONED CAUTION...
...AND INCREDIBLE DEFENSIVE ABILITY...
...HE WAS GRANTED THE TITLE OF *ROOK*...
...BEFORE THE UPCOMING TEA PARTY...
...AND PLACED IN CHARGE OF SECURITY FOR THE ENTIRE EVENT.

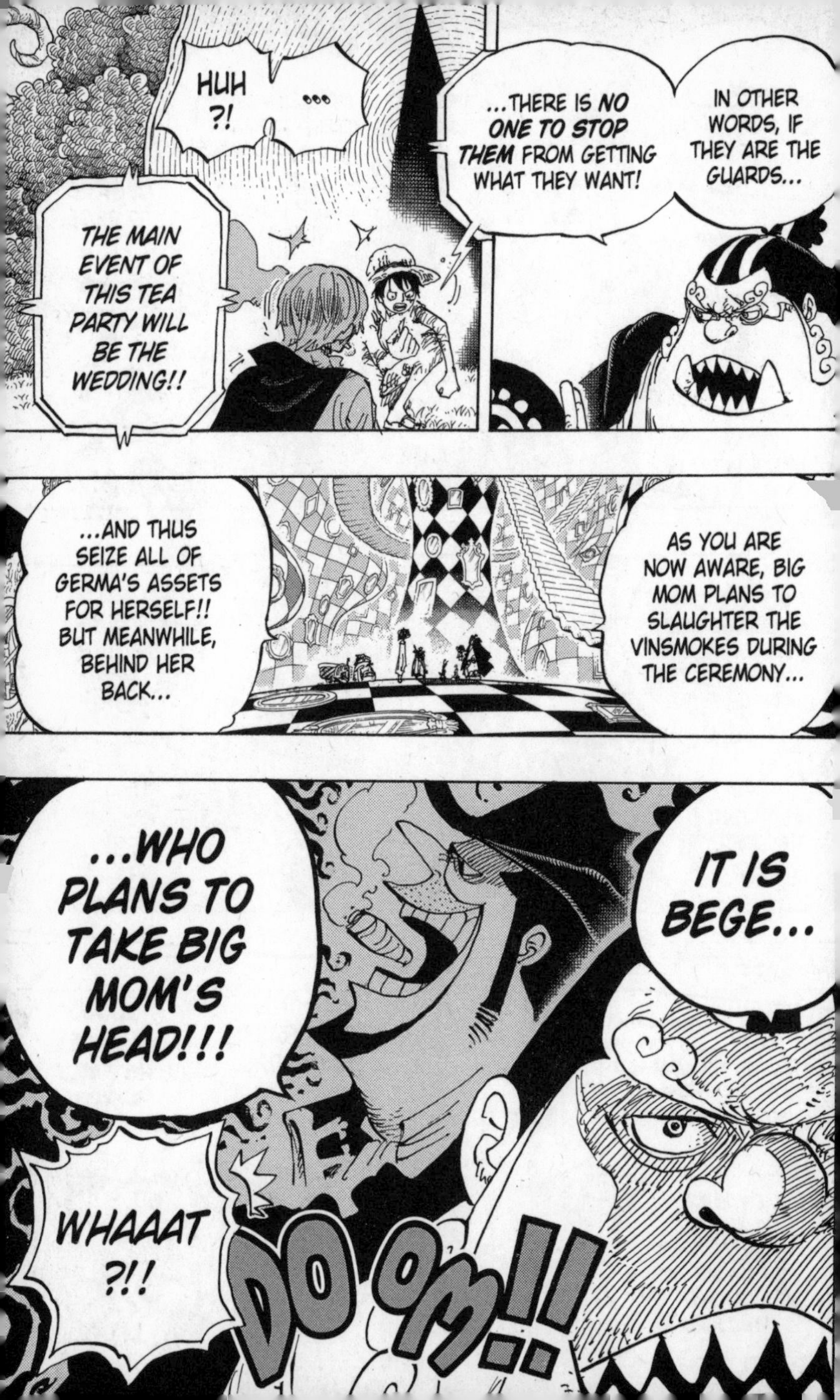
IN OTHER WORDS, IF THEY ARE THE GUARDS...
...THERE IS NO ONE TO STOP THEM FROM GETTING WHAT THEY WANT!
...
HUH ?!
THE MAIN EVENT OF THIS TEA PARTY WILL BE THE WEDDING!!
AS YOU ARE NOW AWARE, BIG MOM PLANS TO SLAUGHTER THE VINSMOKES DURING THE CEREMONY...
...AND THUS SEIZE ALL OF GERMA'S ASSETS FOR HERSELF!! BUT MEANWHILE, BEHIND HER BACK...
IT IS BEGE...
...WHO PLANS TO TAKE BIG MOM'S HEAD!!!
WHAAAT ?!!
DOOM!!

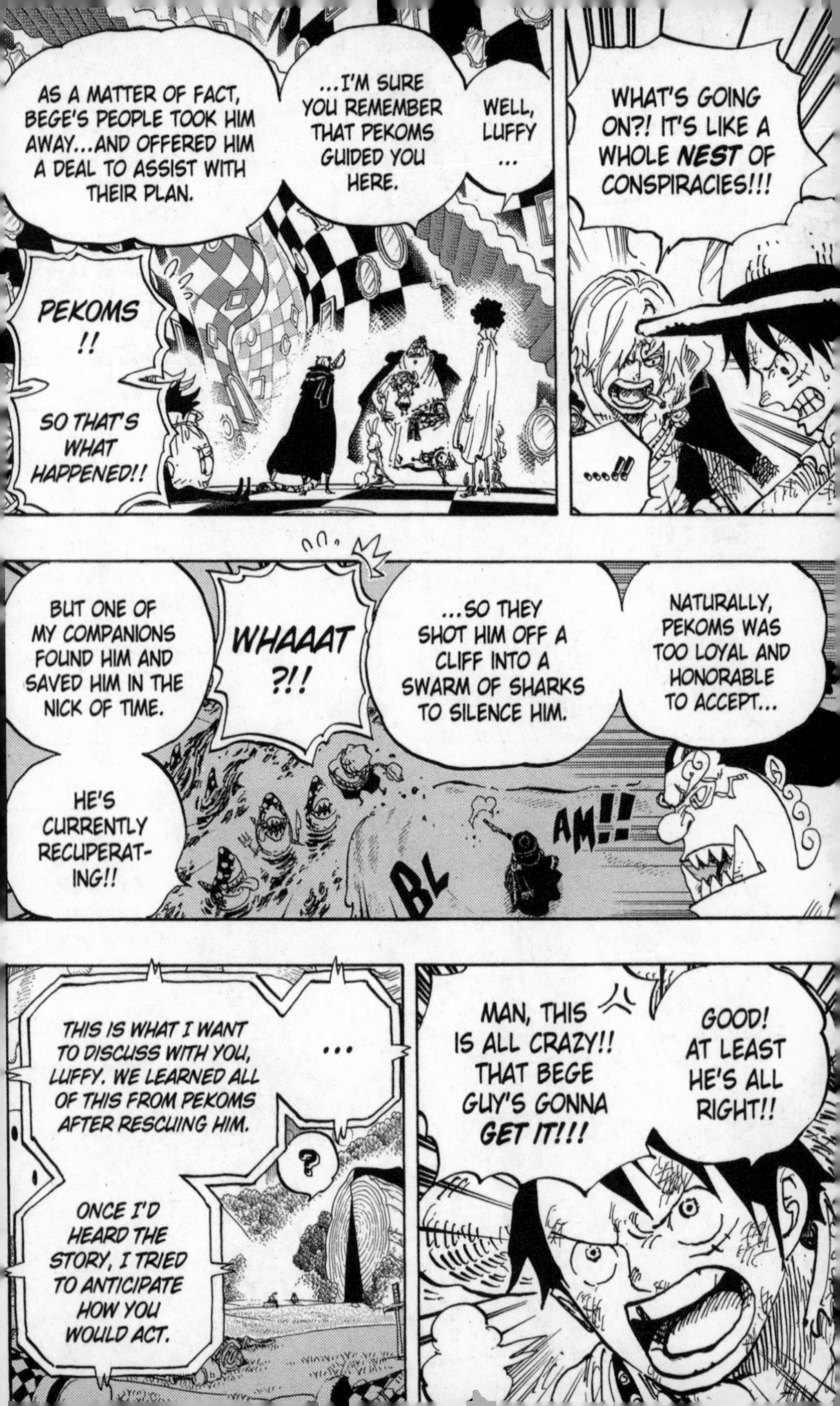
WHAT'S GOING ON?! IT'S LIKE A WHOLE **NEST** OF CONSPIRACIES!!!
...!!
WELL, LUFFY ...
...I'M SURE YOU REMEMBER THAT PEKOMS GUIDED YOU HERE.
AS A MATTER OF FACT, BEGE'S PEOPLE TOOK HIM AWAY...AND OFFERED HIM A DEAL TO ASSIST WITH THEIR PLAN.
PEKOMS !!
SO THAT'S WHAT HAPPENED!!
NATURALLY, PEKOMS WAS TOO LOYAL AND HONORABLE TO ACCEPT...
...SO THEY SHOT HIM OFF A CLIFF INTO A SWARM OF SHARKS TO SILENCE HIM.
WHAAAT ?!!
BUT ONE OF MY COMPANIONS FOUND HIM AND SAVED HIM IN THE NICK OF TIME.
AM!!
BL
HE'S CURRENTLY RECUPERAT-ING!!
GOOD! AT LEAST HE'S ALL RIGHT!!
MAN, THIS IS ALL CRAZY!! THAT BEGE GUY'S GONNA **GET IT!!!**
...
THIS IS WHAT I WANT TO DISCUSS WITH YOU, LUFFY. WE LEARNED ALL OF THIS FROM PEKOMS AFTER RESCUING HIM.
?
ONCE I'D HEARD THE STORY, I TRIED TO ANTICIPATE HOW YOU WOULD ACT.

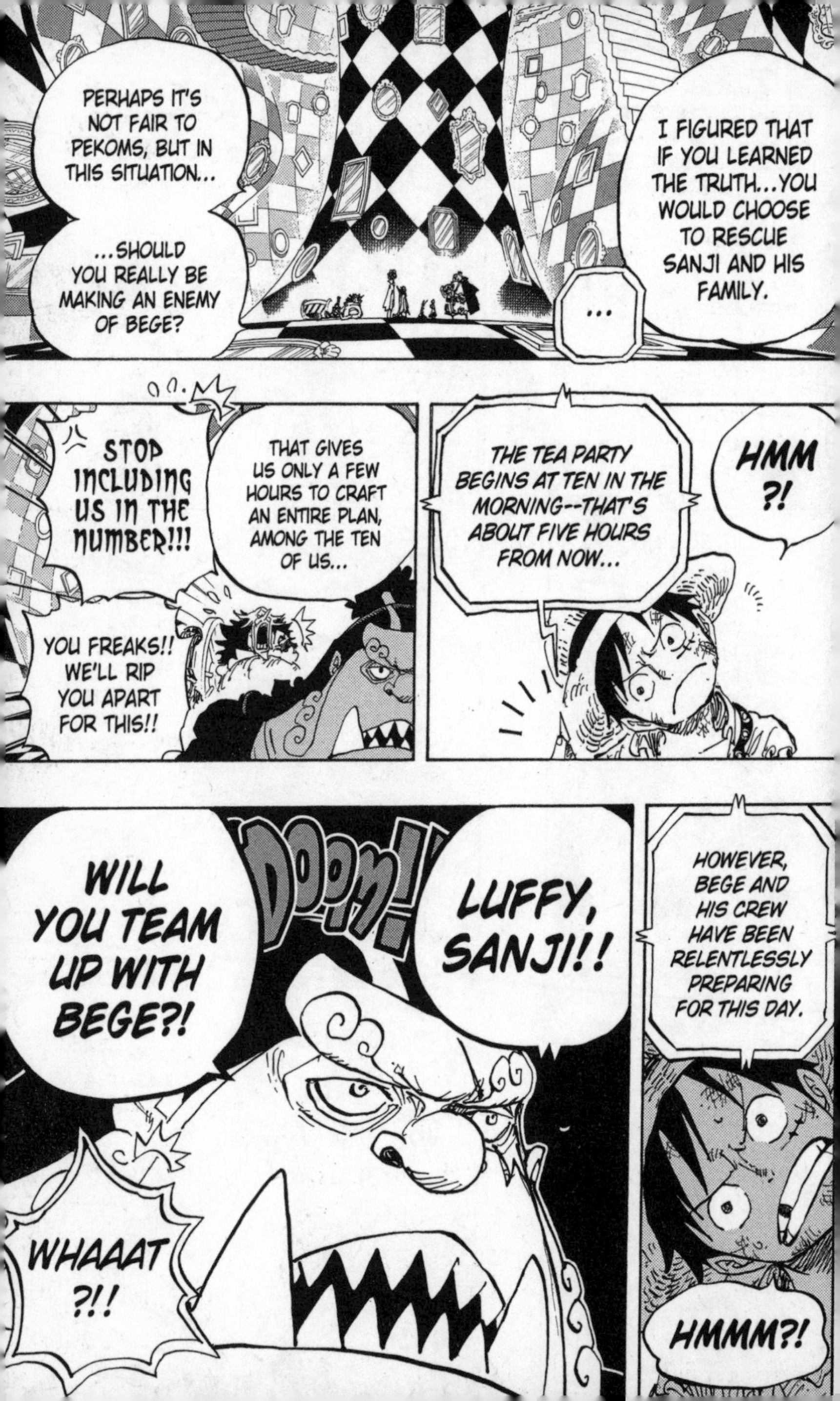
I FIGURED THAT IF YOU LEARNED THE TRUTH...YOU WOULD CHOOSE TO RESCUE SANJI AND HIS FAMILY.
...
PERHAPS IT'S NOT FAIR TO PEKOMS, BUT IN THIS SITUATION...
...SHOULD YOU REALLY BE MAKING AN ENEMY OF BEGE?
HMM ?!
THE TEA PARTY BEGINS AT TEN IN THE MORNING--THAT'S ABOUT FIVE HOURS FROM NOW...
THAT GIVES US ONLY A FEW HOURS TO CRAFT AN ENTIRE PLAN, AMONG THE TEN OF US...
STOP INCLUDING US IN THE NUMBER!!!
YOU FREAKS!! WE'LL RIP YOU APART FOR THIS!!
HOWEVER, BEGE AND HIS CREW HAVE BEEN RELENTLESSLY PREPARING FOR THIS DAY.
HMMM?!
LUFFY, SANJI!!
DOOM!!
WILL YOU TEAM UP WITH BEGE?!
WHAAAT ?!!

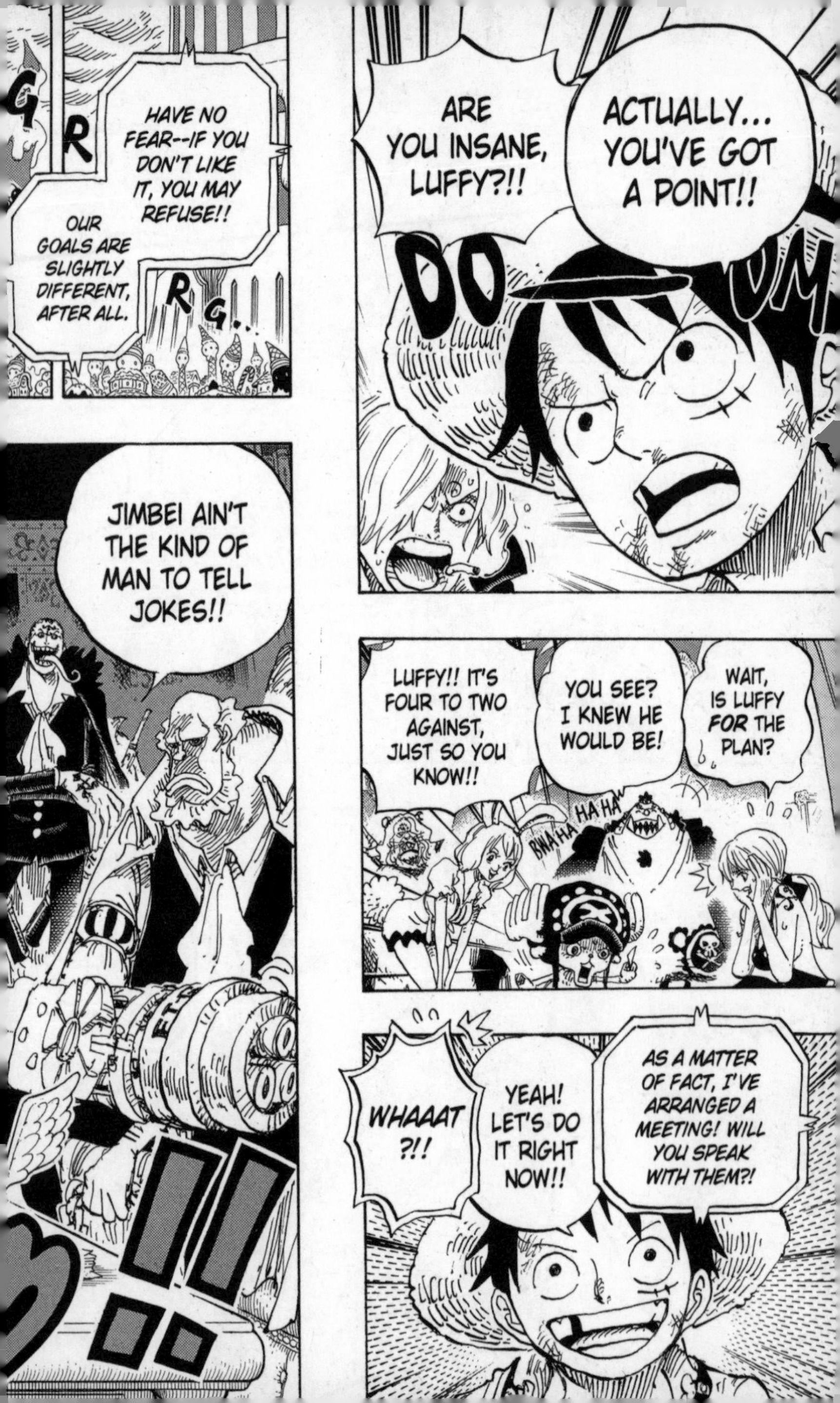

ACTUALLY... YOU'VE GOT A POINT!!
ARE YOU INSANE, LUFFY?!!
DOOM
WAIT, IS LUFFY FOR THE PLAN?
YOU SEE? I KNEW HE WOULD BE!
LUFFY!! IT'S FOUR TO TWO AGAINST, JUST SO YOU KNOW!!
HA HA
BWAHA
AS A MATTER OF FACT, I'VE ARRANGED A MEETING! WILL YOU SPEAK WITH THEM?!
YEAH! LET'S DO IT RIGHT NOW!!
WHAAAT ?!!
GR
HAVE NO FEAR--IF YOU DON'T LIKE IT, YOU MAY REFUSE!!
OUR GOALS ARE SLIGHTLY DIFFERENT, AFTER ALL.
RG...
JIMBEI AIN'T THE KIND OF MAN TO TELL JOKES!!

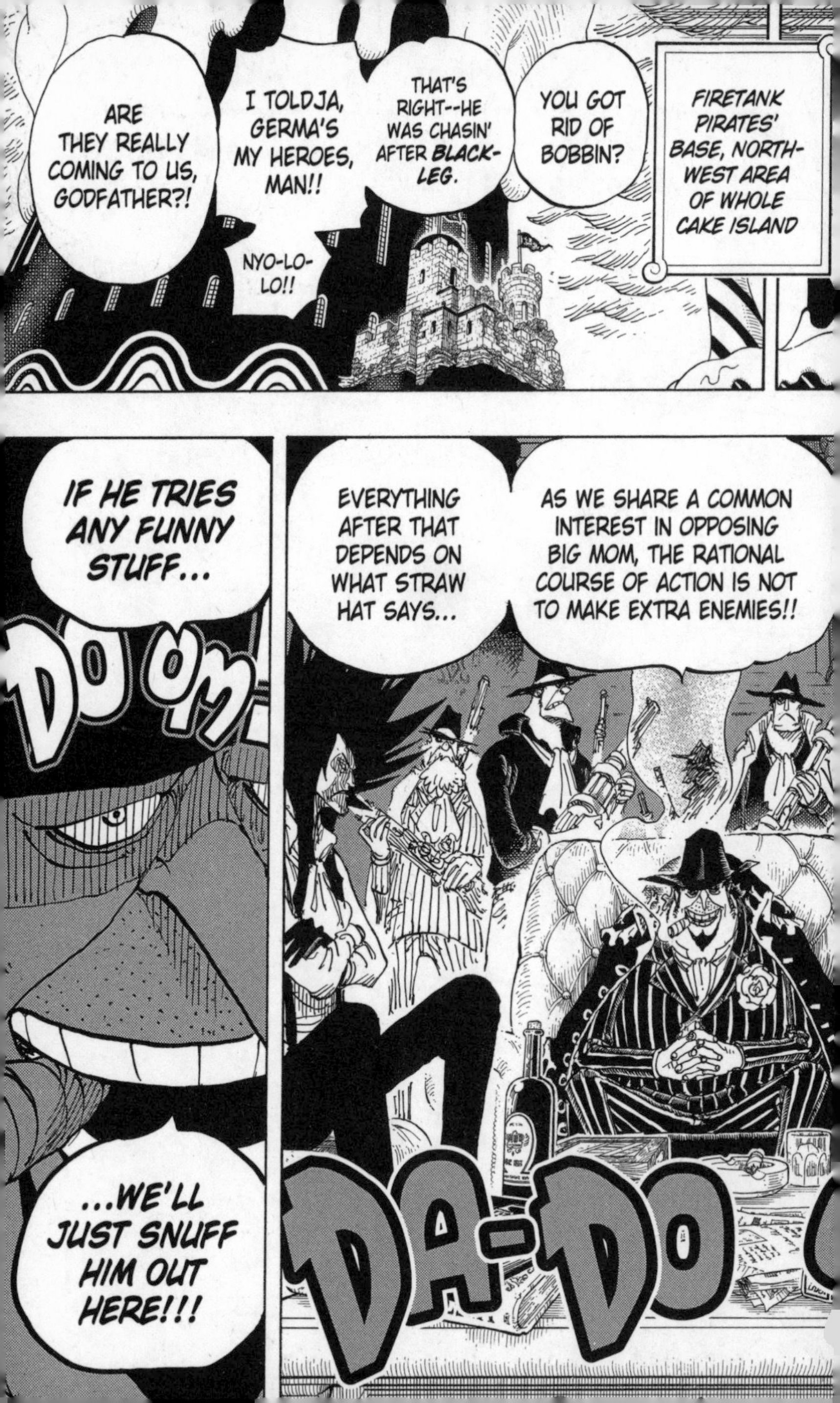
FIRETANK PIRATES' BASE, NORTHWEST AREA OF WHOLE CAKE ISLAND
YOU GOT RID OF BOBBIN?
THAT'S RIGHT--HE WAS CHASIN' AFTER BLACK-LEG.
I TOLDJA, GERMA'S MY HEROES, MAN!!
ARE THEY REALLY COMING TO US, GODFATHER?!
NYO-LO-LO!!
AS WE SHARE A COMMON INTEREST IN OPPOSING BIG MOM, THE RATIONAL COURSE OF ACTION IS NOT TO MAKE EXTRA ENEMIES!!
EVERYTHING AFTER THAT DEPENDS ON WHAT STRAW HAT SAYS...
DA-DO
IF HE TRIES ANY FUNNY STUFF...
DOOM
...WE'LL JUST SNUFF HIM OUT HERE!!!

Chapter 858: MEETING

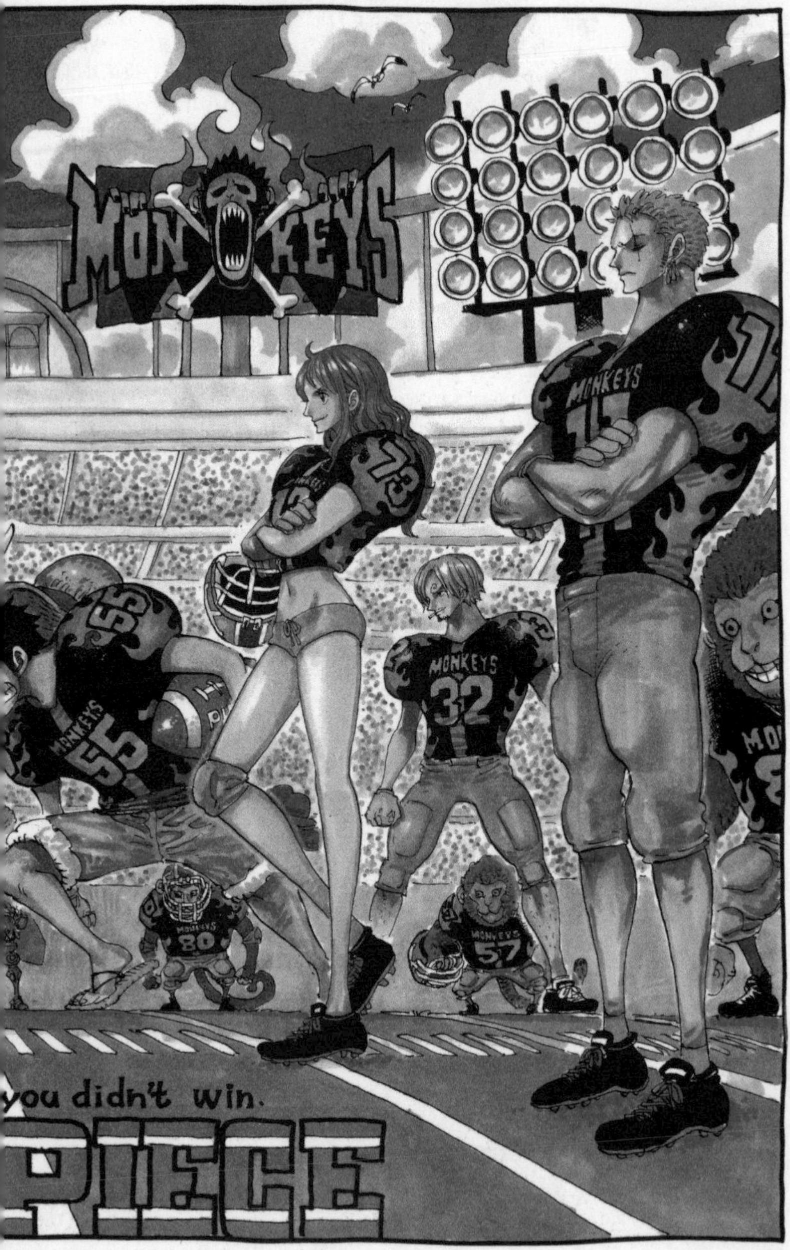
MONKEYS
MONKEYS
MONKEYS
32
MONKEYS
55
MONKEYS
80
MONKEYS
57
you didn't win.
PIECE

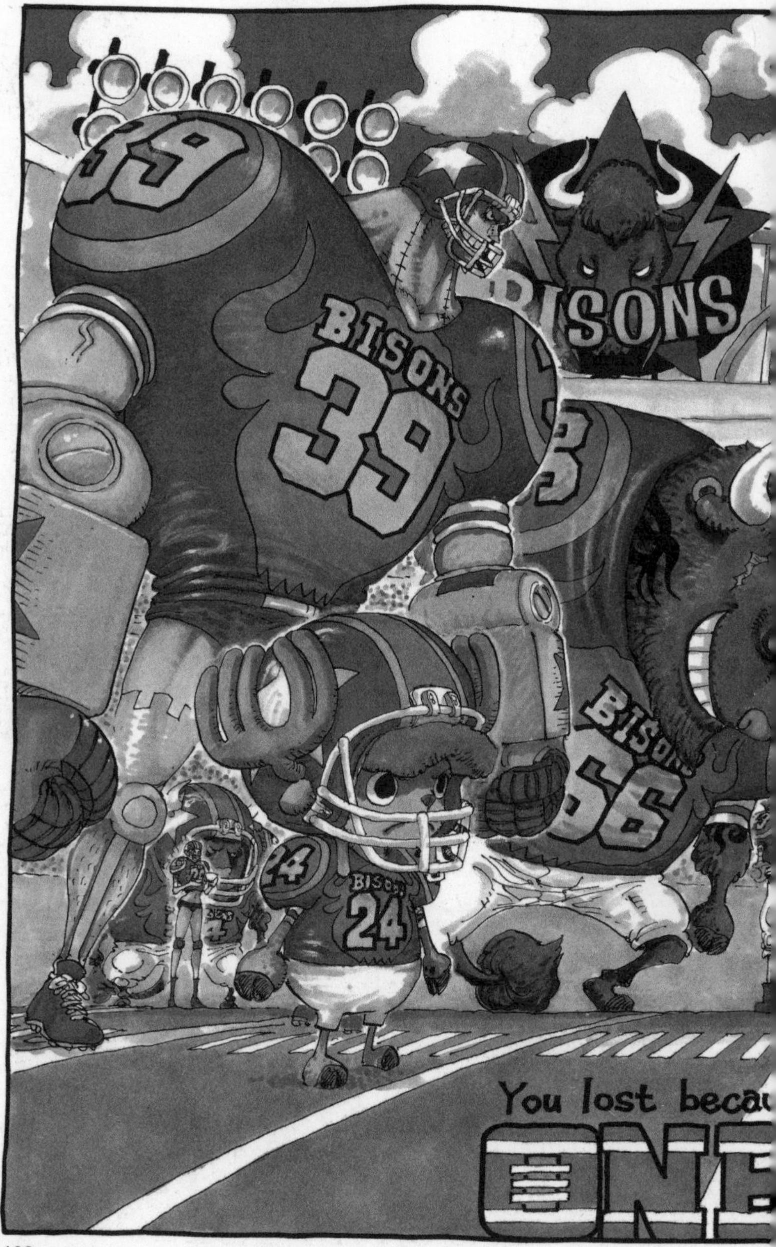
BISONS
You lost becau

vol.85
ONE PIECE

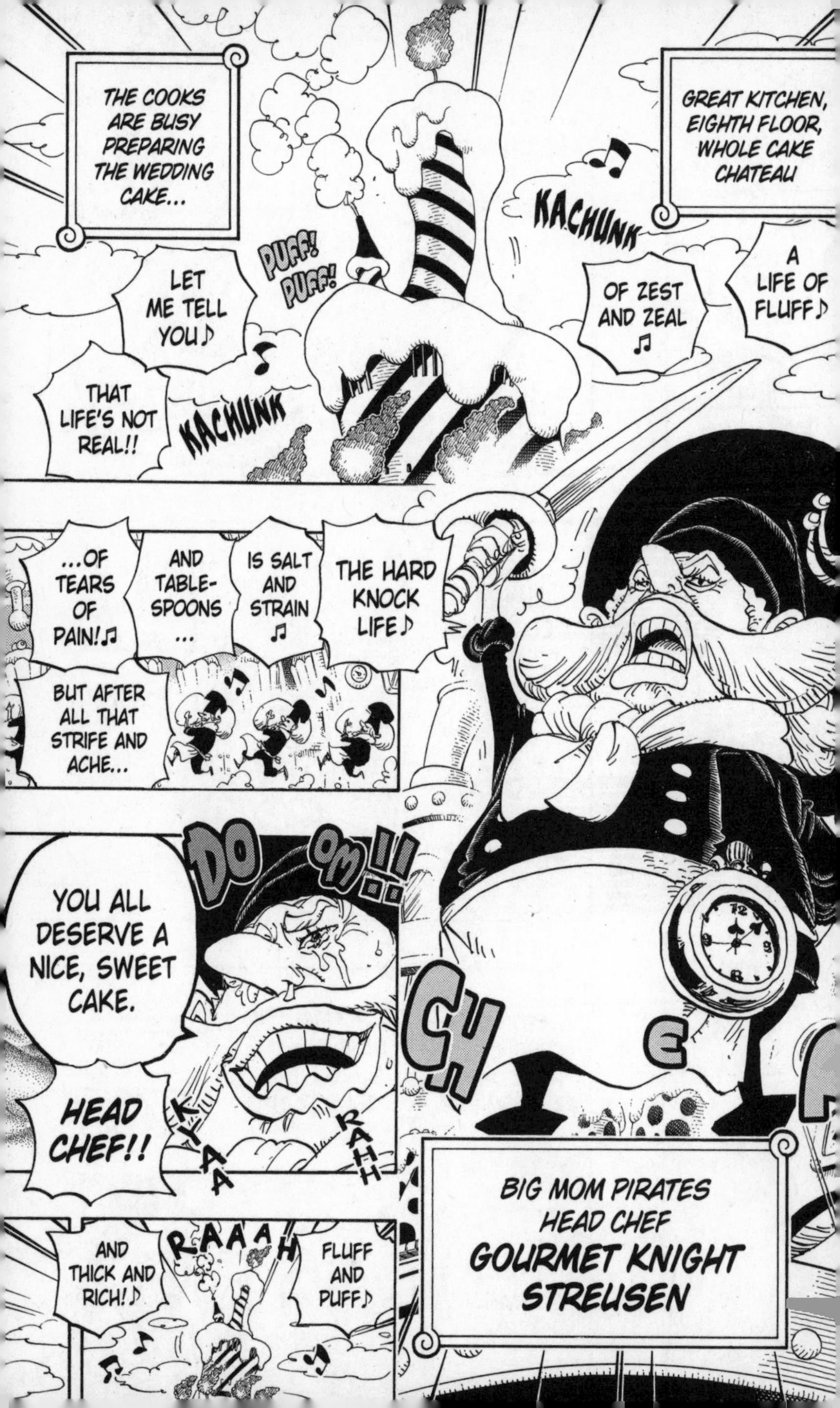

GREAT KITCHEN, EIGHTH FLOOR, WHOLE CAKE CHATEAU
A LIFE OF FLUFF♪
OF ZEST AND ZEAL ♫
KACHUNK
PUFF! PUFF!
THE COOKS ARE BUSY PREPARING THE WEDDING CAKE...
LET ME TELL YOU♪
THAT LIFE'S NOT REAL!!
KACHUNK
THE HARD KNOCK LIFE♪
IS SALT AND STRAIN ♫
AND TABLE-SPOONS ...
...OF TEARS OF PAIN!♫
BUT AFTER ALL THAT STRIFE AND ACHE...
DOOM!!
CHE
BIG MOM PIRATES HEAD CHEF
GOURMET KNIGHT STREUSEN
YOU ALL DESERVE A NICE, SWEET CAKE.
HEAD CHEF!!
KYAA
RAHH
FLUFF AND PUFF♪
RAAAH
AND THICK AND RICH!♪

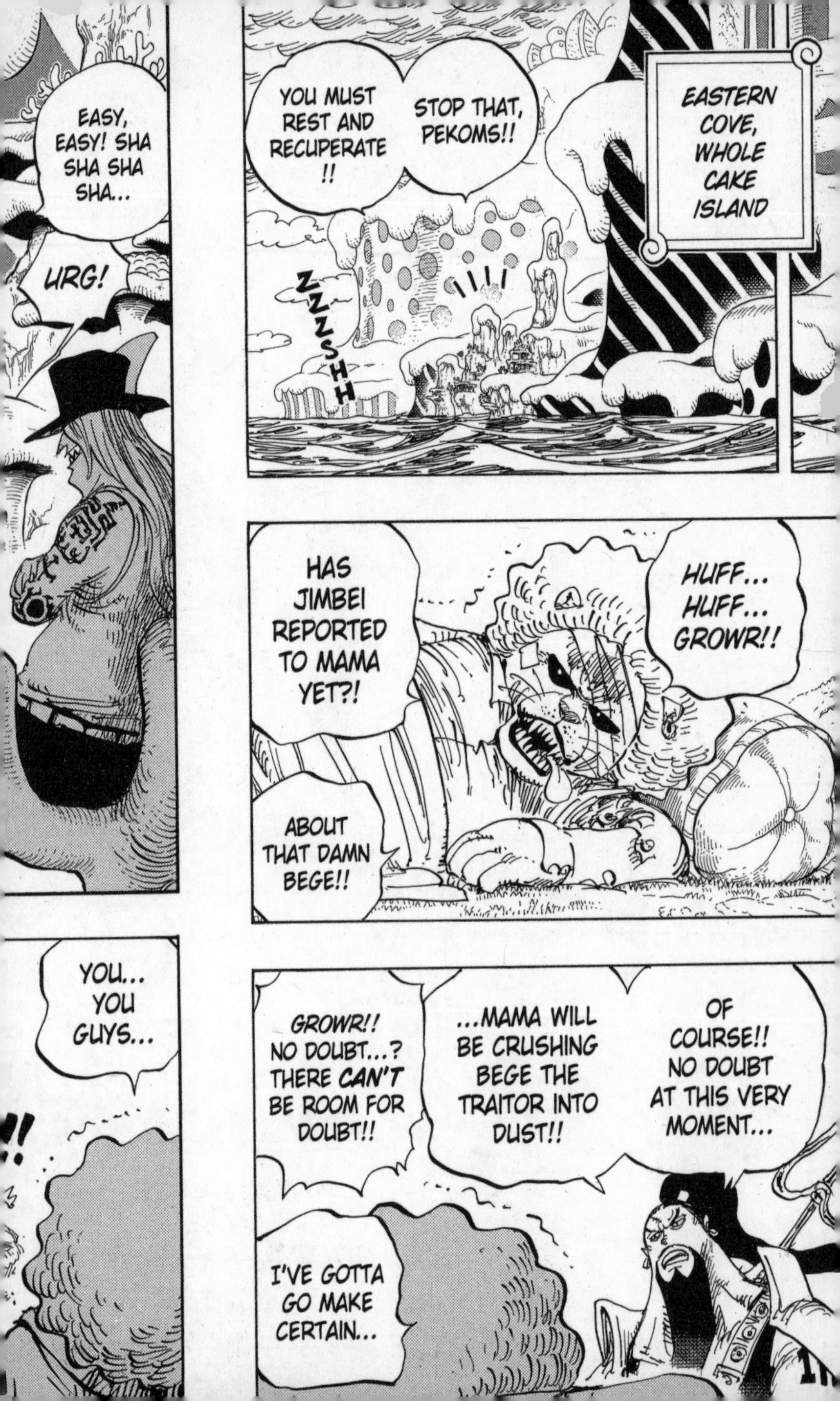
EASTERN COVE, WHOLE CAKE ISLAND
STOP THAT, PEKOMS!!
YOU MUST REST AND RECUPERATE!!
ZZZSHH
HUFF... HUFF... GROWR!!
HAS JIMBEI REPORTED TO MAMA YET?!
ABOUT THAT DAMN BEGE!!
EASY, EASY! SHA SHA SHA SHA...
URG!
OF COURSE!! NO DOUBT AT THIS VERY MOMENT...
...MAMA WILL BE CRUSHING BEGE THE TRAITOR INTO DUST!!
GROWR!! NO DOUBT...? THERE *CAN'T* BE ROOM FOR DOUBT!!
I'VE GOTTA GO MAKE CERTAIN...
YOU... YOU GUYS...

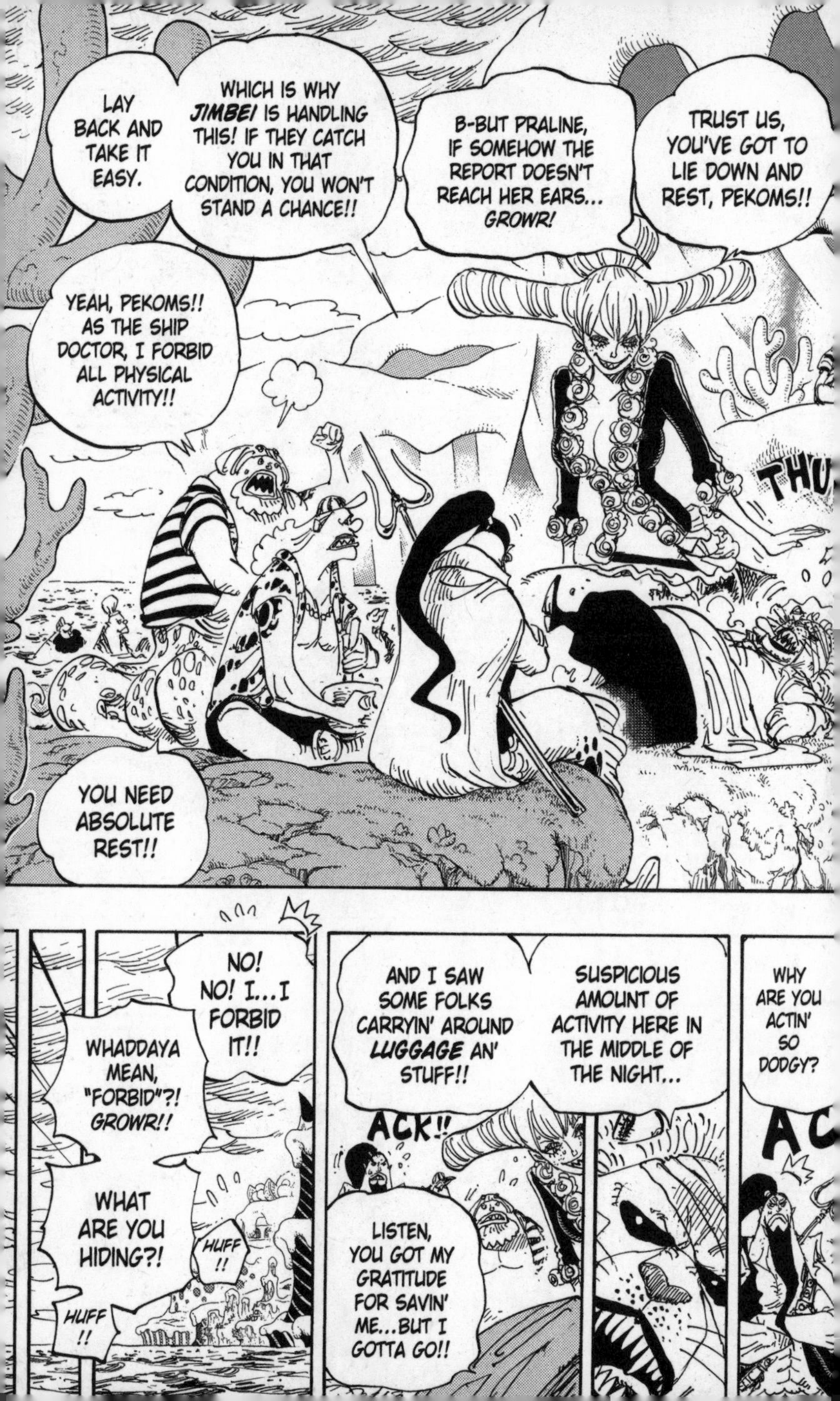
TRUST US, YOU'VE GOT TO LIE DOWN AND REST, PEKOMS!!
B-BUT PRALINE, IF SOMEHOW THE REPORT DOESN'T REACH HER EARS... GROWR!
WHICH IS WHY JIMBEI IS HANDLING THIS! IF THEY CATCH YOU IN THAT CONDITION, YOU WON'T STAND A CHANCE!!
LAY BACK AND TAKE IT EASY.
YEAH, PEKOMS!! AS THE SHIP DOCTOR, I FORBID ALL PHYSICAL ACTIVITY!!
THU
YOU NEED ABSOLUTE REST!!
WHY ARE YOU ACTIN' SO DODGY?
AC
SUSPICIOUS AMOUNT OF ACTIVITY HERE IN THE MIDDLE OF THE NIGHT...
AND I SAW SOME FOLKS CARRYIN' AROUND LUGGAGE AN' STUFF!!
ACK!!
LISTEN, YOU GOT MY GRATITUDE FOR SAVIN' ME...BUT I GOTTA GO!!
NO! NO! I...I FORBID IT!!
WHADDAYA MEAN, "FORBID"?! GROWR!!
WHAT ARE YOU HIDING?!
HUFF !!
HUFF !!

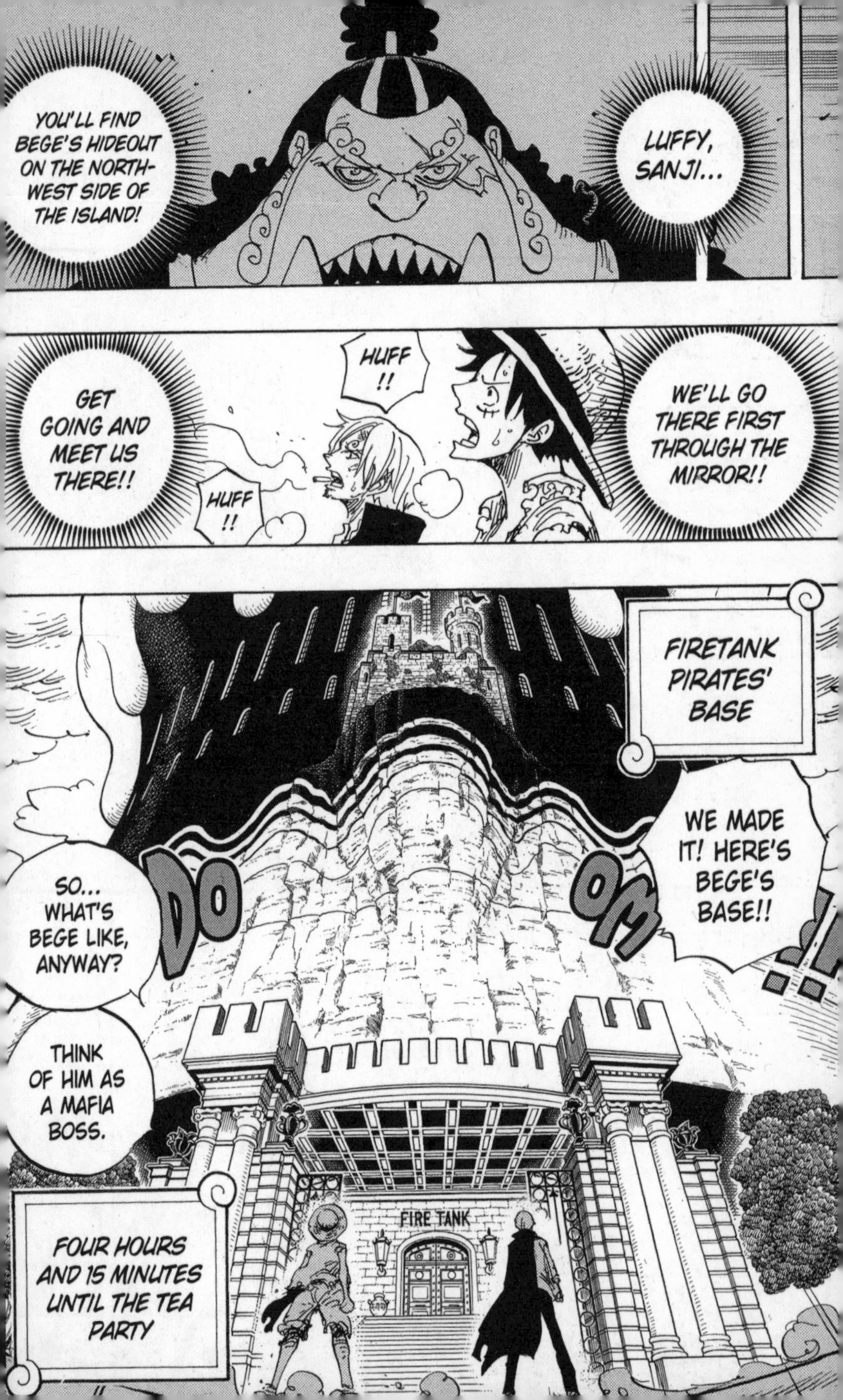

LUFFY, SANJI...
YOU'LL FIND BEGE'S HIDEOUT ON THE NORTH-WEST SIDE OF THE ISLAND!
WE'LL GO THERE FIRST THROUGH THE MIRROR!!
HUFF !!
GET GOING AND MEET US THERE!!
HUFF !!
FIRETANK PIRATES' BASE
WE MADE IT! HERE'S BEGE'S BASE!!
DOOM
SO... WHAT'S BEGE LIKE, ANYWAY?
THINK OF HIM AS A MAFIA BOSS.
FIRE TANK
FOUR HOURS AND 15 MINUTES UNTIL THE TEA PARTY

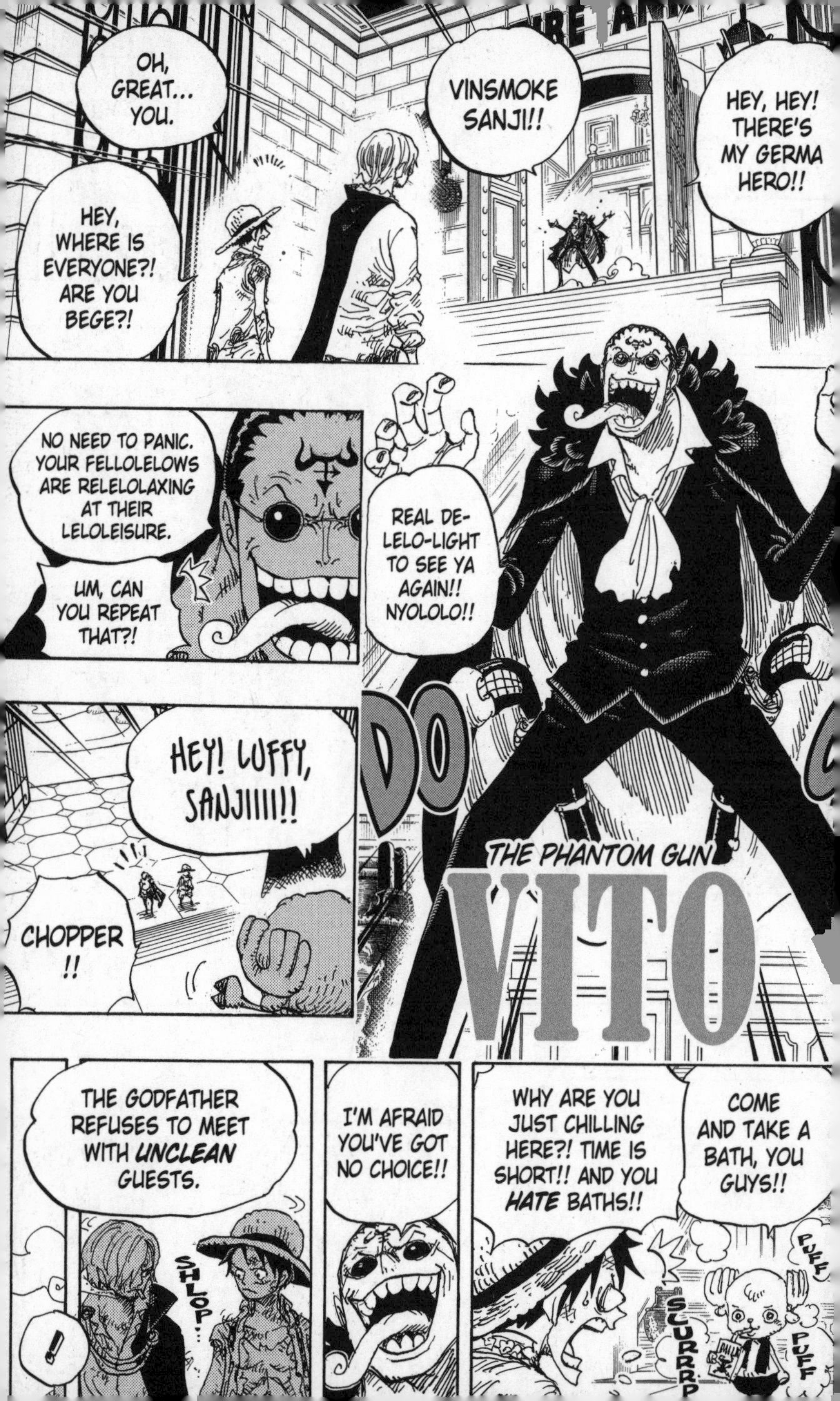
HEY, HEY! THERE'S MY GERMA HERO!!
VINSMOKE SANJI!!
OH, GREAT... YOU.
HEY, WHERE IS EVERYONE?! ARE YOU BEGE?!
REAL DE-LELO-LIGHT TO SEE YA AGAIN!! NYOLOLO!!
DO
THE PHANTOM GUN
VITO
NO NEED TO PANIC. YOUR FELLOLELOWS ARE RELELOLAXING AT THEIR LELOLEISURE.
UM, CAN YOU REPEAT THAT?!
HEY! LUFFY, SANJIIIII!!
CHOPPER !!
COME AND TAKE A BATH, YOU GUYS!!
WHY ARE YOU JUST CHILLING HERE?! TIME IS SHORT!! AND YOU *HATE* BATHS!!
PUFF
PUFF
SCURRRP
I'M AFRAID YOU'VE GOT NO CHOICE!!
THE GODFATHER REFUSES TO MEET WITH *UNCLEAN* GUESTS.
SHLOP...
!

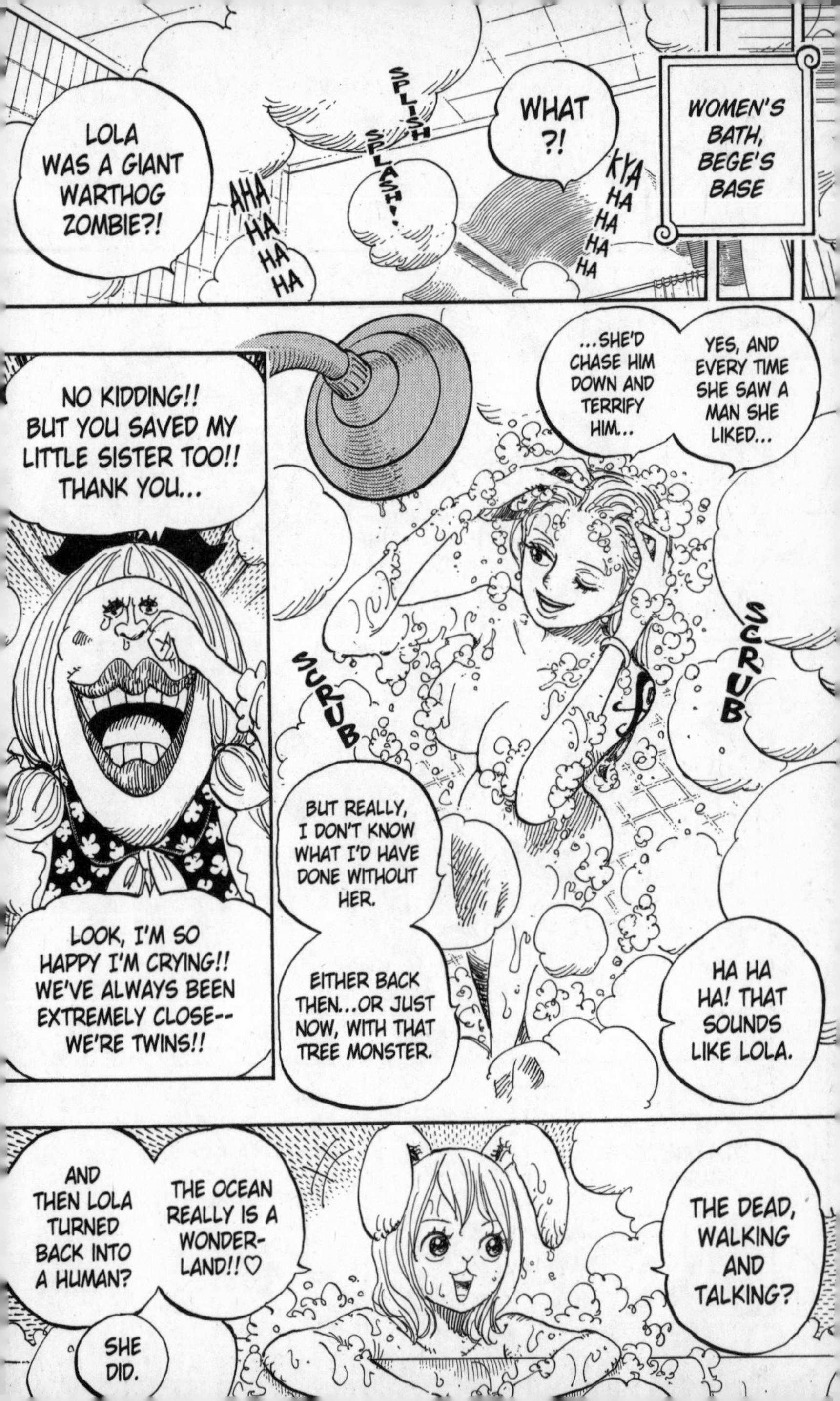
WOMEN'S BATH, BEGE'S BASE
KYA HA HA HA HA
WHAT ?!
SPLISH
SPLASH!
AHA HA HA HA
LOLA WAS A GIANT WARTHOG ZOMBIE?!
YES, AND EVERY TIME SHE SAW A MAN SHE LIKED...
...SHE'D CHASE HIM DOWN AND TERRIFY HIM...
SCRUB
HA HA HA! THAT SOUNDS LIKE LOLA.
SCRUB
BUT REALLY, I DON'T KNOW WHAT I'D HAVE DONE WITHOUT HER.
EITHER BACK THEN...OR JUST NOW, WITH THAT TREE MONSTER.
NO KIDDING!! BUT YOU SAVED MY LITTLE SISTER TOO!! THANK YOU...
LOOK, I'M SO HAPPY I'M CRYING!! WE'VE ALWAYS BEEN EXTREMELY CLOSE-- WE'RE TWINS!!
THE DEAD, WALKING AND TALKING?
THE OCEAN REALLY IS A WONDERLAND!!♡
AND THEN LOLA TURNED BACK INTO A HUMAN?
SHE DID.

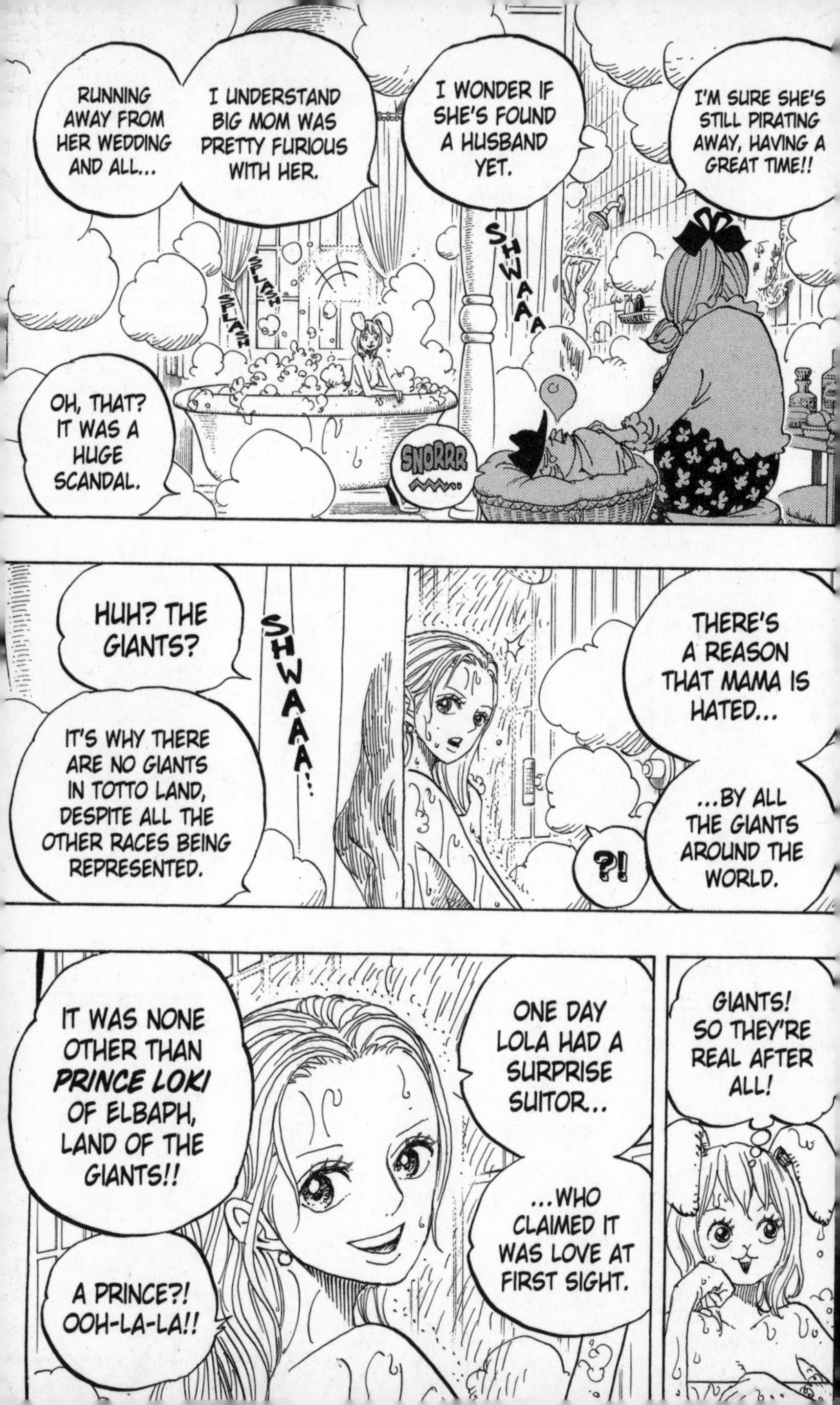
I'M SURE SHE'S STILL PIRATING AWAY, HAVING A GREAT TIME!!
I WONDER IF SHE'S FOUND A HUSBAND YET.
I UNDERSTAND BIG MOM WAS PRETTY FURIOUS WITH HER.
RUNNING AWAY FROM HER WEDDING AND ALL...
SHWAAA
SPLASH SPLASH
OH, THAT? IT WAS A HUGE SCANDAL.
SNORRR
THERE'S A REASON THAT MAMA IS HATED...
...BY ALL THE GIANTS AROUND THE WORLD.
?!
SHWAAA!!
HUH? THE GIANTS?
IT'S WHY THERE ARE NO GIANTS IN TOTTO LAND, DESPITE ALL THE OTHER RACES BEING REPRESENTED.
GIANTS! SO THEY'RE REAL AFTER ALL!
ONE DAY LOLA HAD A SURPRISE SUITOR...
...WHO CLAIMED IT WAS LOVE AT FIRST SIGHT.
IT WAS NONE OTHER THAN *PRINCE LOKI* OF ELBAPH, LAND OF THE GIANTS!!
A PRINCE?! OOH-LA-LA!!

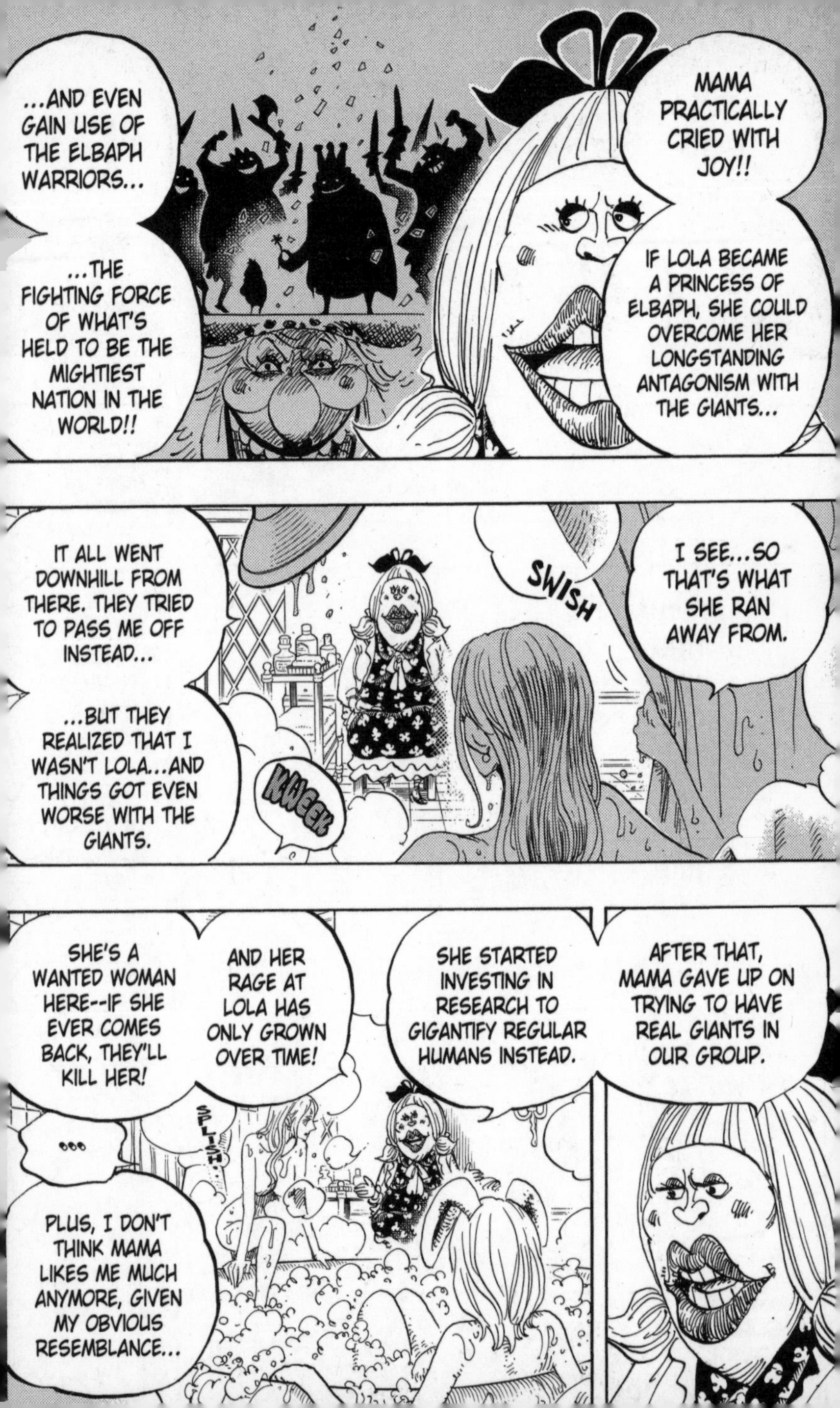
MAMA PRACTICALLY CRIED WITH JOY!!
IF LOLA BECAME A PRINCESS OF ELBAPH, SHE COULD OVERCOME HER LONGSTANDING ANTAGONISM WITH THE GIANTS...
...AND EVEN GAIN USE OF THE ELBAPH WARRIORS...
...THE FIGHTING FORCE OF WHAT'S HELD TO BE THE MIGHTIEST NATION IN THE WORLD!!
I SEE...SO THAT'S WHAT SHE RAN AWAY FROM.
SWISH
IT ALL WENT DOWNHILL FROM THERE. THEY TRIED TO PASS ME OFF INSTEAD...
...BUT THEY REALIZED THAT I WASN'T LOLA...AND THINGS GOT EVEN WORSE WITH THE GIANTS.
KWEEK
AFTER THAT, MAMA GAVE UP ON TRYING TO HAVE REAL GIANTS IN OUR GROUP.
SHE STARTED INVESTING IN RESEARCH TO GIGANTIFY REGULAR HUMANS INSTEAD.
AND HER RAGE AT LOLA HAS ONLY GROWN OVER TIME!
SHE'S A WANTED WOMAN HERE--IF SHE EVER COMES BACK, THEY'LL KILL HER!
SPLISH
...
PLUS, I DON'T THINK MAMA LIKES ME MUCH ANYMORE, GIVEN MY OBVIOUS RESEMBLANCE...

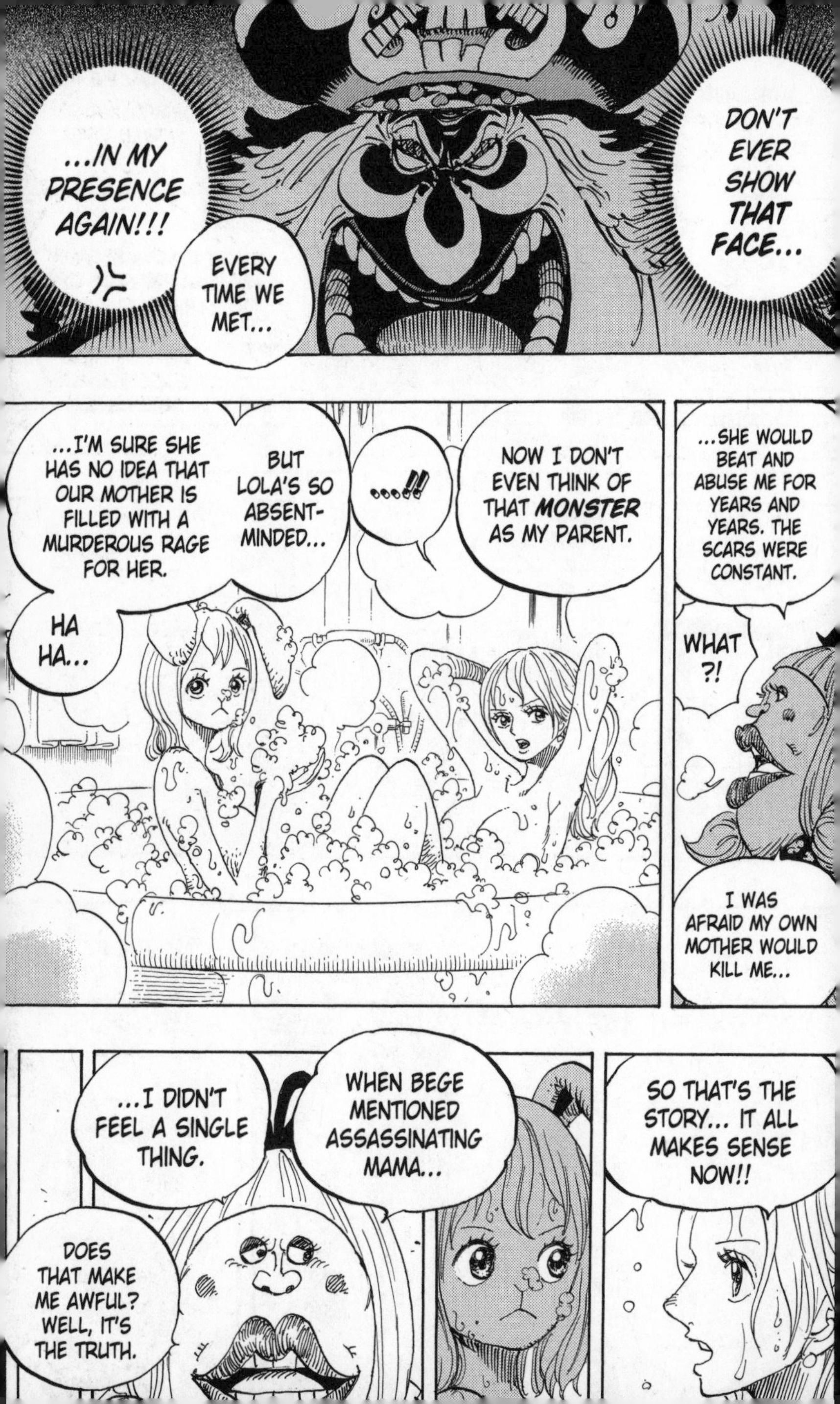
DON'T EVER SHOW THAT FACE...
...IN MY PRESENCE AGAIN!!!
EVERY TIME WE MET...
...SHE WOULD BEAT AND ABUSE ME FOR YEARS AND YEARS. THE SCARS WERE CONSTANT.
WHAT ?!
I WAS AFRAID MY OWN MOTHER WOULD KILL ME...
NOW I DON'T EVEN THINK OF THAT ***MONSTER*** AS MY PARENT.
....!!
BUT LOLA'S SO ABSENT-MINDED...
...I'M SURE SHE HAS NO IDEA THAT OUR MOTHER IS FILLED WITH A MURDEROUS RAGE FOR HER.
HA HA...
SO THAT'S THE STORY... IT ALL MAKES SENSE NOW!!
WHEN BEGE MENTIONED ASSASSINATING MAMA...
...I DIDN'T FEEL A SINGLE THING.
DOES THAT MAKE ME AWFUL? WELL, IT'S THE TRUTH.

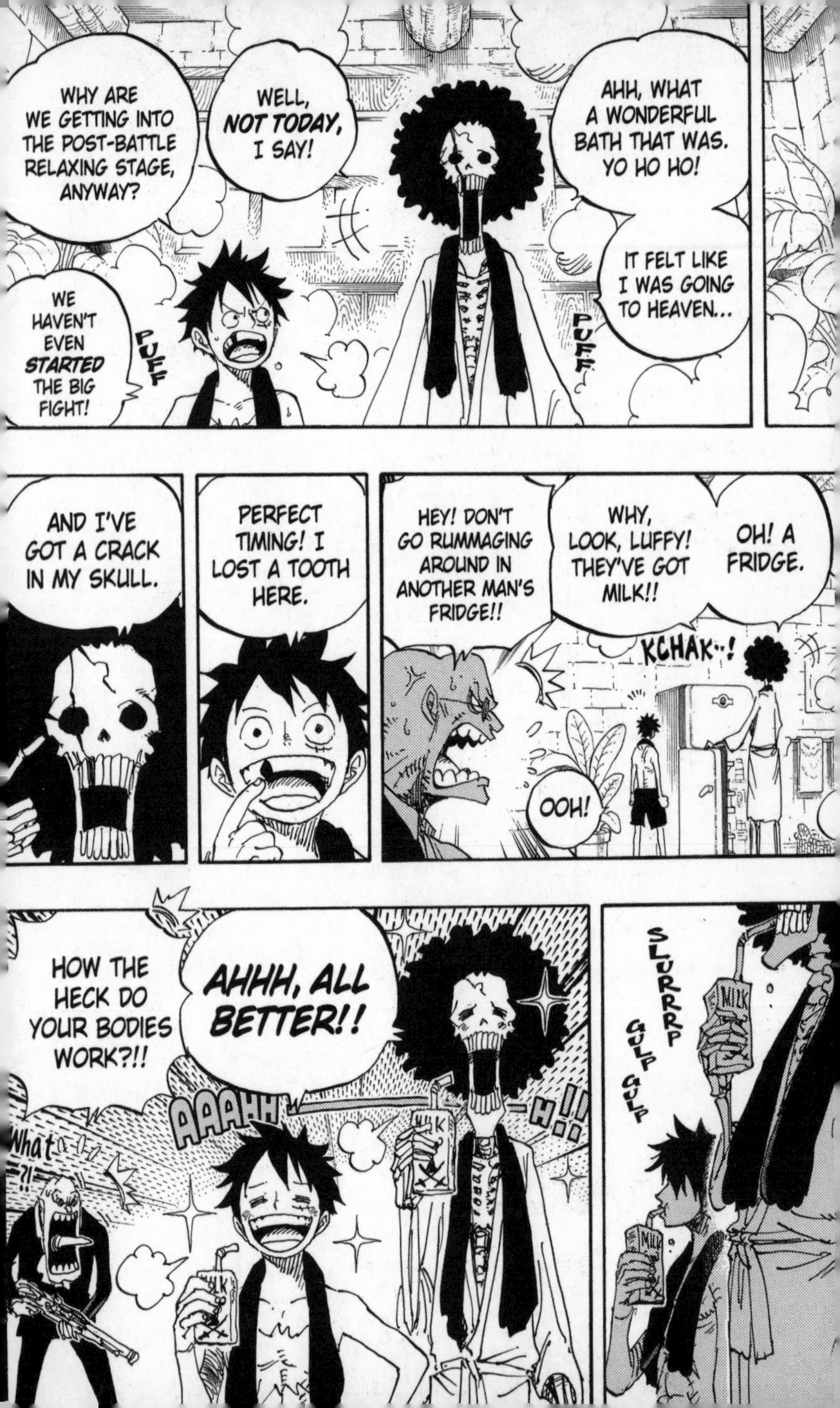
AHH, WHAT A WONDERFUL BATH THAT WAS. YO HO HO!
IT FELT LIKE I WAS GOING TO HEAVEN...
PUFF
WELL, **NOT TODAY,** I SAY!
WHY ARE WE GETTING INTO THE POST-BATTLE RELAXING STAGE, ANYWAY?
PUFF
WE HAVEN'T EVEN **STARTED** THE BIG FIGHT!
OH! A FRIDGE.
WHY, LOOK, LUFFY! THEY'VE GOT MILK!!
KCHAK..!
HEY! DON'T GO RUMMAGING AROUND IN ANOTHER MAN'S FRIDGE!!
OOH!
PERFECT TIMING! I LOST A TOOTH HERE.
AND I'VE GOT A CRACK IN MY SKULL.
MILK
SLURRRP
GULP GULP
MILK
AHHH, ALL BETTER!!
HOW THE HECK DO YOUR BODIES WORK?!!
AAAHH—H!!
What?!
MILK

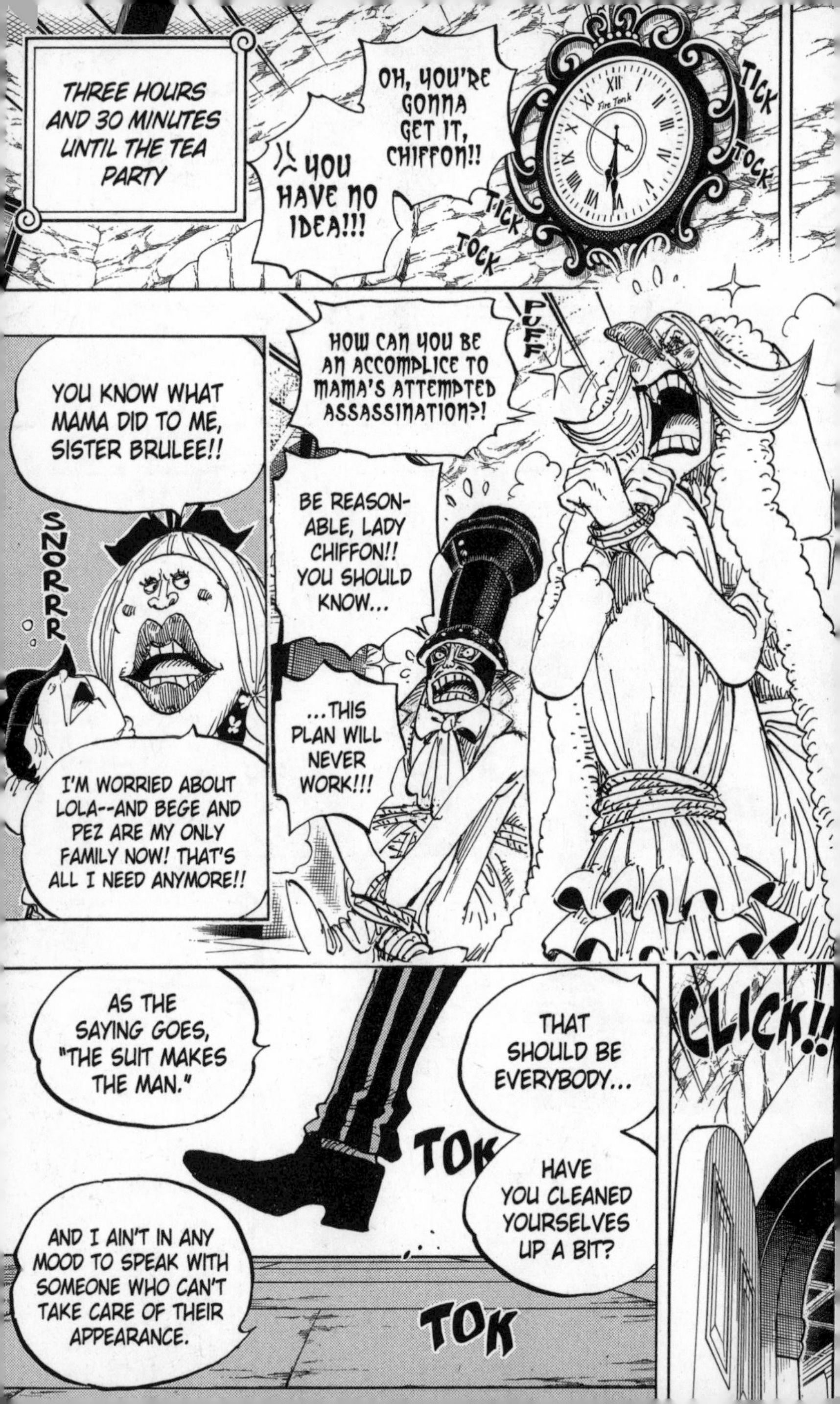
TICK
TOCK
OH, YOU'RE GONNA GET IT, CHIFFON!!
THREE HOURS AND 30 MINUTES UNTIL THE TEA PARTY
YOU HAVE NO IDEA!!!
TICK
TOCK
PUFF
HOW CAN YOU BE AN ACCOMPLICE TO MAMA'S ATTEMPTED ASSASSINATION?!
BE REASON-ABLE, LADY CHIFFON!! YOU SHOULD KNOW...
...THIS PLAN WILL NEVER WORK!!!
YOU KNOW WHAT MAMA DID TO ME, SISTER BRULEE!!
SNORRR
I'M WORRIED ABOUT LOLA--AND BEGE AND PEZ ARE MY ONLY FAMILY NOW! THAT'S ALL I NEED ANYMORE!!
CLICK!!
THAT SHOULD BE EVERYBODY...
AS THE SAYING GOES, "THE SUIT MAKES THE MAN."
TOK
HAVE YOU CLEANED YOURSELVES UP A BIT?
AND I AIN'T IN ANY MOOD TO SPEAK WITH SOMEONE WHO CAN'T TAKE CARE OF THEIR APPEARANCE.
TOK

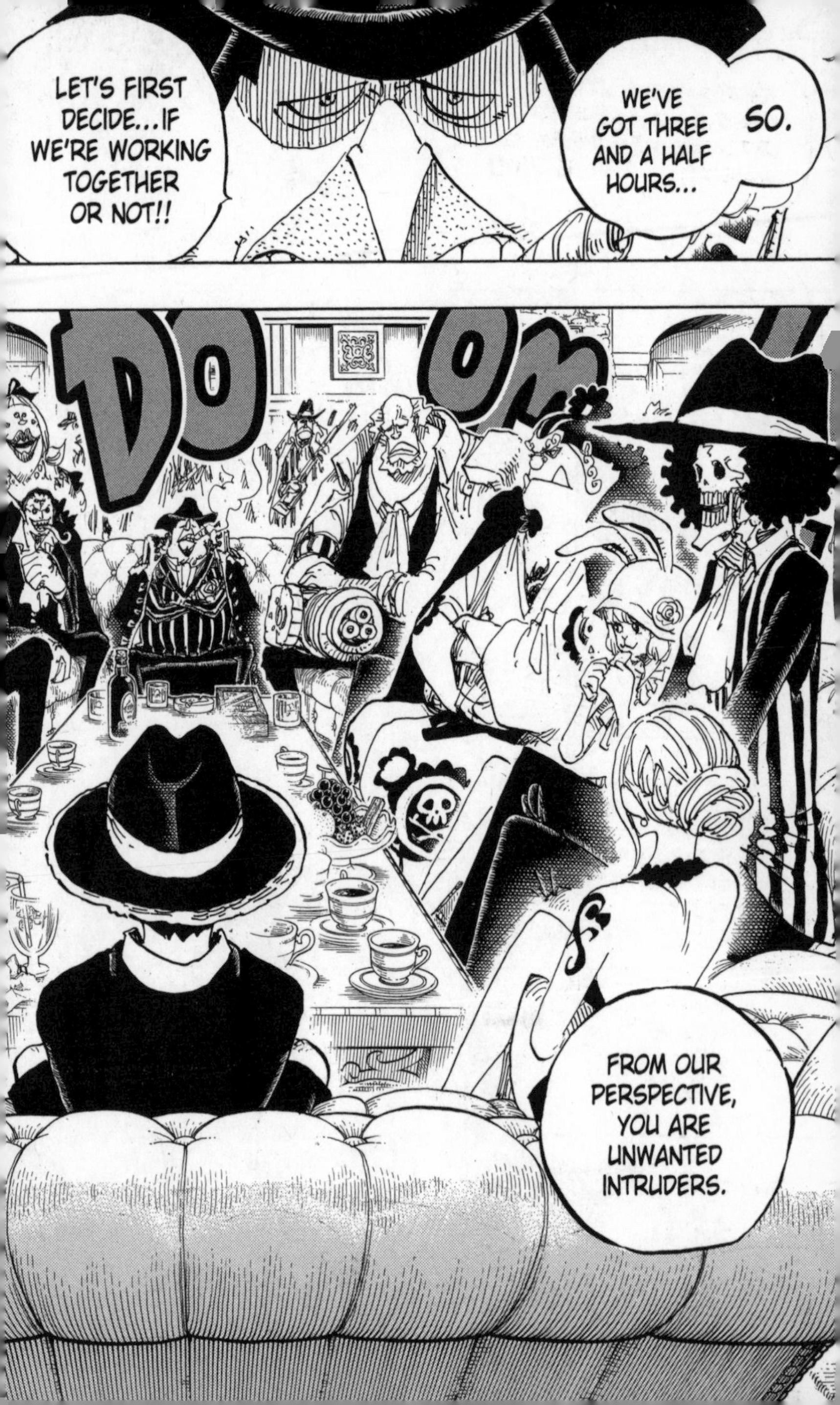
SO.
WE'VE GOT THREE AND A HALF HOURS...
LET'S FIRST DECIDE...IF WE'RE WORKING TOGETHER OR NOT!!
DOOM
FROM OUR PERSPECTIVE, YOU ARE UNWANTED INTRUDERS.

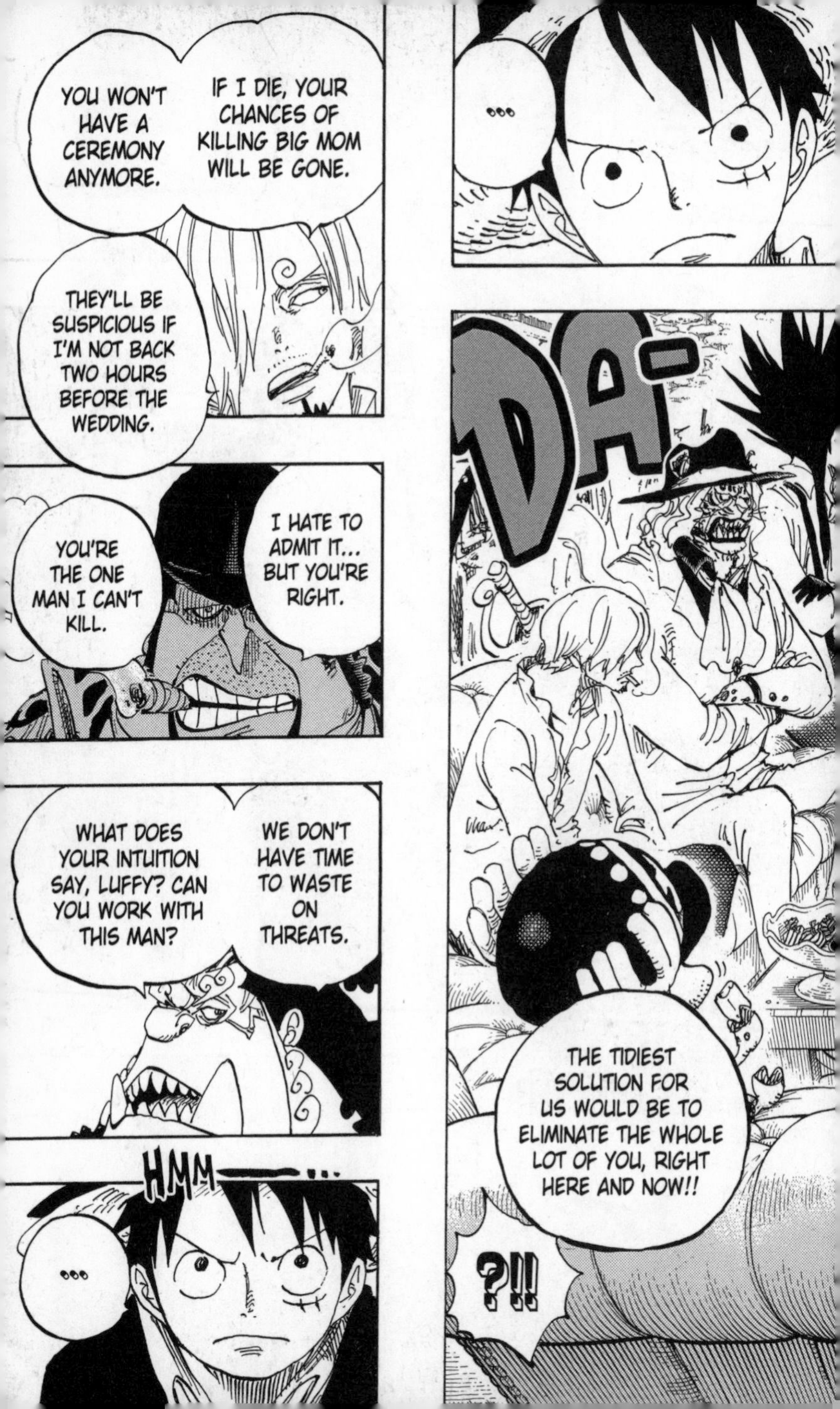
...
DA-
THE TIDIEST SOLUTION FOR US WOULD BE TO ELIMINATE THE WHOLE LOT OF YOU, RIGHT HERE AND NOW!!
?!!
IF I DIE, YOUR CHANCES OF KILLING BIG MOM WILL BE GONE.
YOU WON'T HAVE A CEREMONY ANYMORE.
THEY'LL BE SUSPICIOUS IF I'M NOT BACK TWO HOURS BEFORE THE WEDDING.
I HATE TO ADMIT IT... BUT YOU'RE RIGHT.
YOU'RE THE ONE MAN I CAN'T KILL.
WE DON'T HAVE TIME TO WASTE ON THREATS.
WHAT DOES YOUR INTUITION SAY, LUFFY? CAN YOU WORK WITH THIS MAN?
HMM——...
...

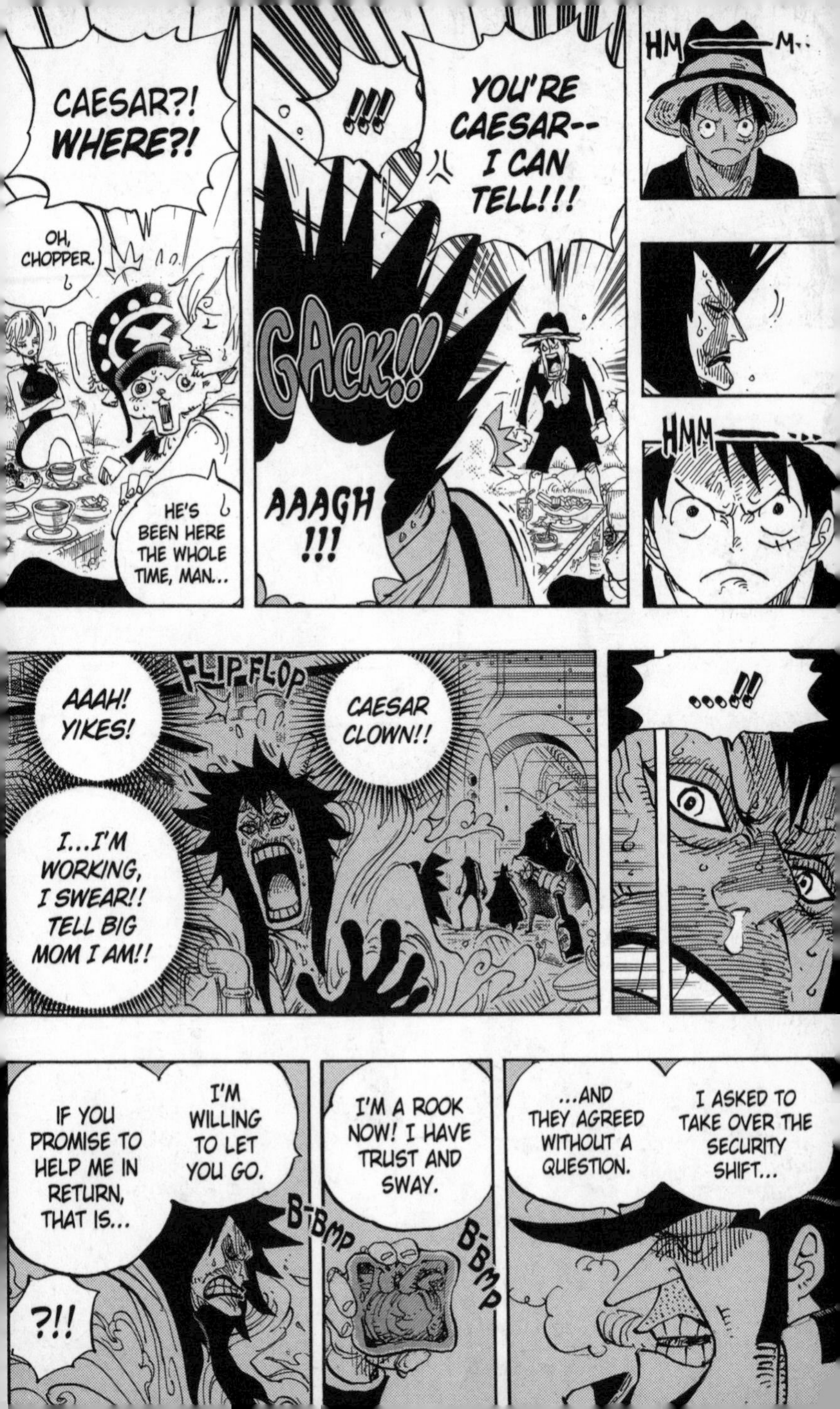
HM——M..
HMM——...
YOU'RE CAESAR-- I CAN TELL!!!
!!!
GACK!!
AAAGH !!!
CAESAR?! WHERE?!
OH, CHOPPER.
HE'S BEEN HERE THE WHOLE TIME, MAN...
....!!
CAESAR CLOWN!!
FLIP FLOP
AAAH! YIKES!
I...I'M WORKING, I SWEAR!! TELL BIG MOM I AM!!
I ASKED TO TAKE OVER THE SECURITY SHIFT...
...AND THEY AGREED WITHOUT A QUESTION.
B-BMP
I'M A ROOK NOW! I HAVE TRUST AND SWAY.
B-BMP
I'M WILLING TO LET YOU GO.
IF YOU PROMISE TO HELP ME IN RETURN, THAT IS...
?!!

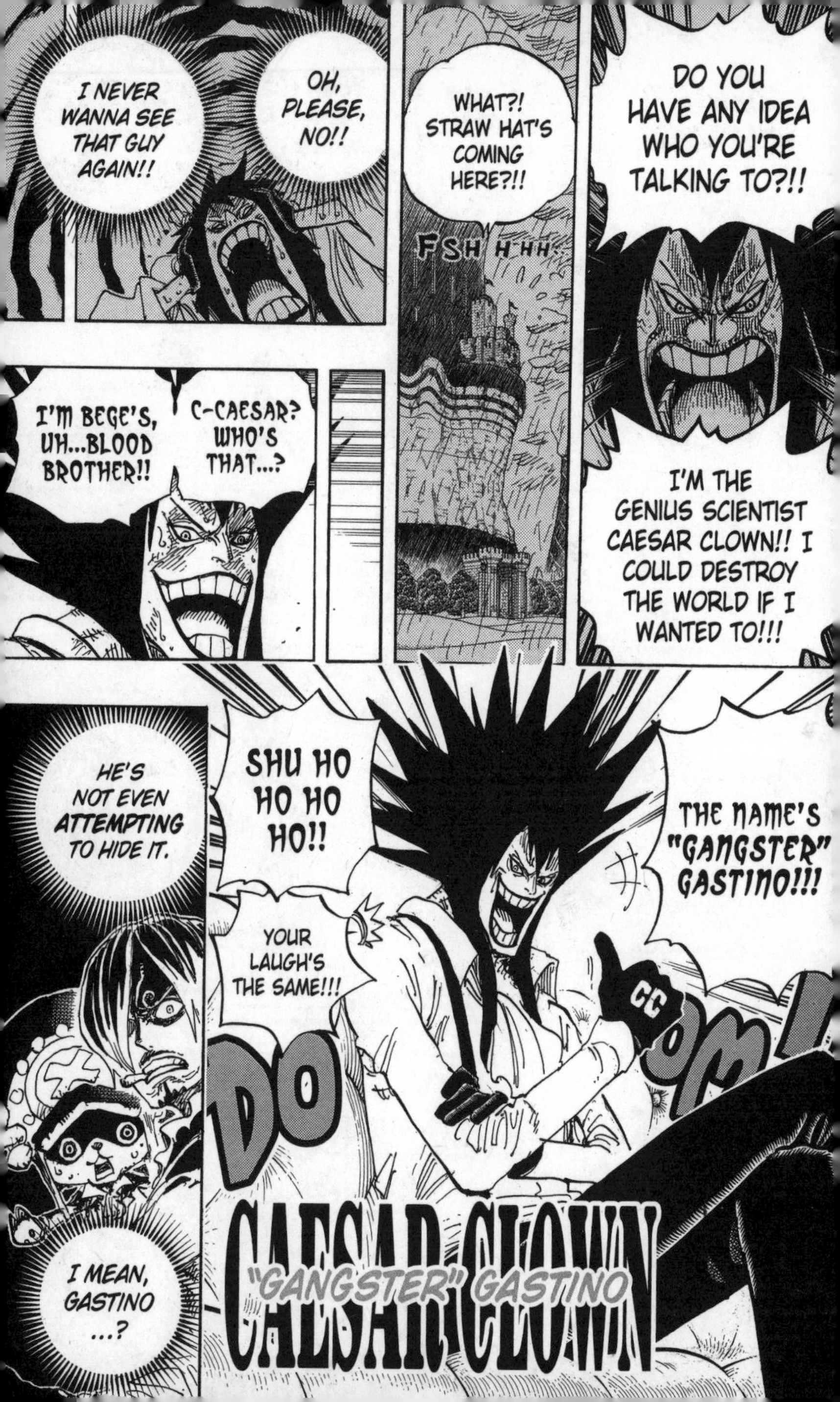
DO YOU HAVE ANY IDEA WHO YOU'RE TALKING TO?!!
I'M THE GENIUS SCIENTIST CAESAR CLOWN!! I COULD DESTROY THE WORLD IF I WANTED TO!!!
WHAT?! STRAW HAT'S COMING HERE?!!
FSHHHH
OH, PLEASE, NO!!
I NEVER WANNA SEE THAT GUY AGAIN!!
C-CAESAR? WHO'S THAT...?
I'M BEGE'S, UH...BLOOD BROTHER!!
THE NAME'S "GANGSTER" GASTINO!!!
SHU HO HO HO HO!!
YOUR LAUGH'S THE SAME!!!
DOOM
CAESAR CLOWN
"GANGSTER" GASTINO
HE'S NOT EVEN ATTEMPTING TO HIDE IT.
I MEAN, GASTINO ...?

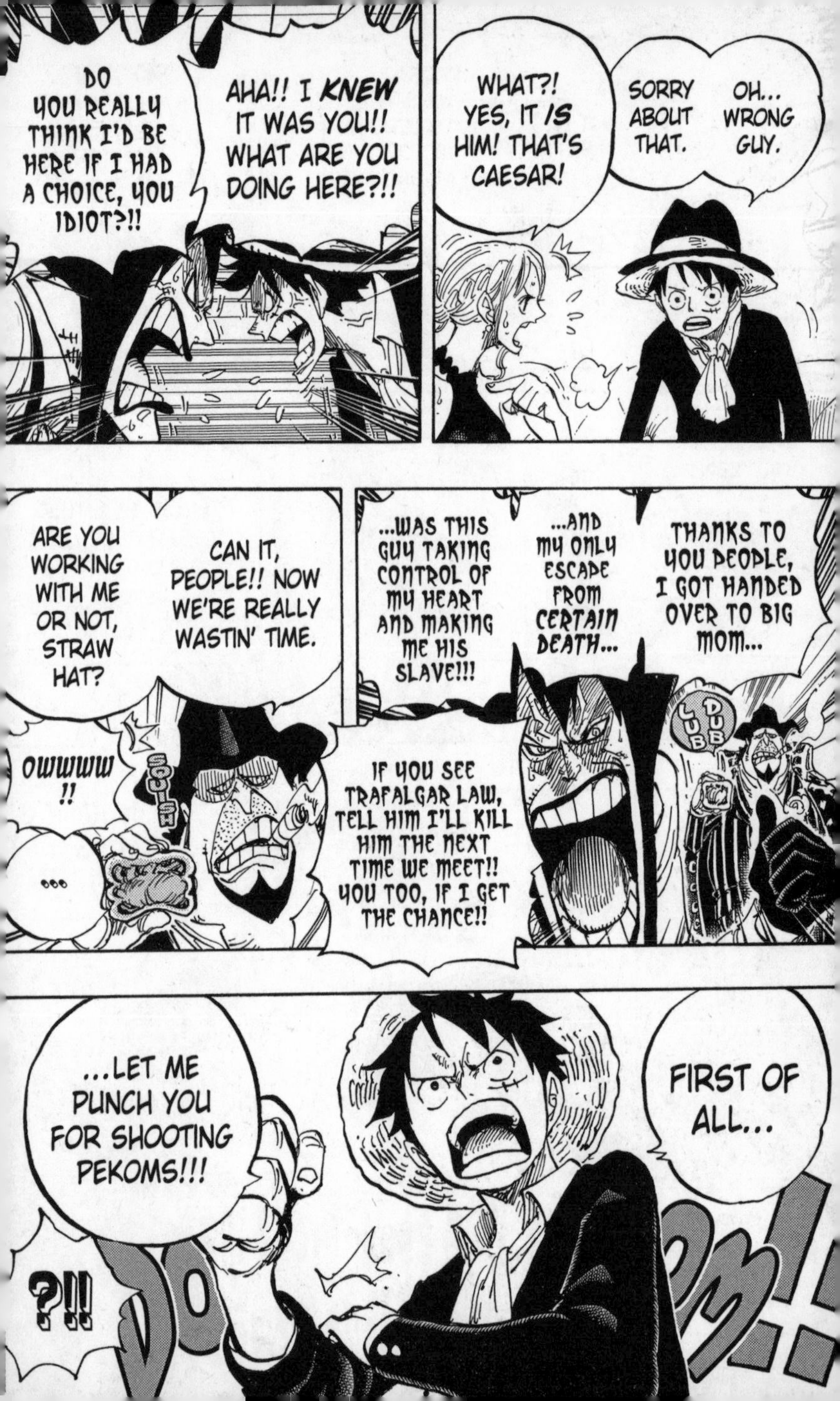
OH... WRONG GUY.
SORRY ABOUT THAT.
WHAT?! YES, IT *IS* HIM! THAT'S CAESAR!
AHA!! I *KNEW* IT WAS YOU!! WHAT ARE YOU DOING HERE?!!
DO YOU REALLY THINK I'D BE HERE IF I HAD A CHOICE, YOU IDIOT?!!
THANKS TO YOU PEOPLE, I GOT HANDED OVER TO BIG MOM...
...AND MY ONLY ESCAPE FROM CERTAIN DEATH...
...WAS THIS GUY TAKING CONTROL OF MY HEART AND MAKING ME HIS SLAVE!!!
DUB
DUB
IF YOU SEE TRAFALGAR LAW, TELL HIM I'LL KILL HIM THE NEXT TIME WE MEET!! YOU TOO, IF I GET THE CHANCE!!
CAN IT, PEOPLE!! NOW WE'RE REALLY WASTIN' TIME.
ARE YOU WORKING WITH ME OR NOT, STRAW HAT?
SQUISH
OWWWW !!
...
FIRST OF ALL...
...LET ME PUNCH YOU FOR SHOOTING PEKOMS!!!
DO
OM!!
?!!

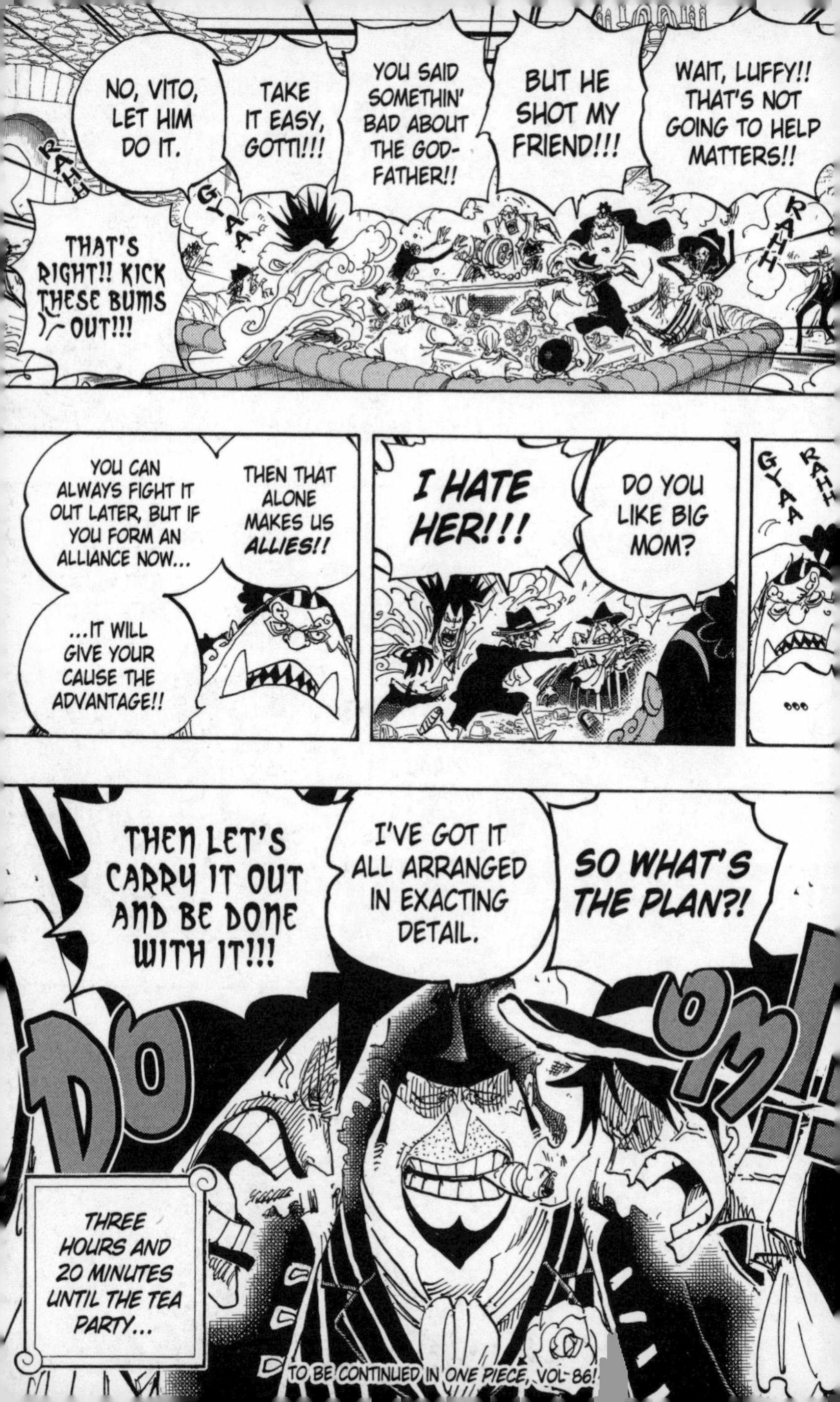
WAIT, LUFFY!! THAT'S NOT GOING TO HELP MATTERS!!
BUT HE SHOT MY FRIEND!!!
YOU SAID SOMETHIN' BAD ABOUT THE GOD-FATHER!!
TAKE IT EASY, GOTTI!!!
NO, VITO, LET HIM DO IT.
RAHH
GYAA
RAHH
THAT'S RIGHT!! KICK THESE BUMS OUT!!!
RAHH
GYAA
...
DO YOU LIKE BIG MOM?
I HATE HER!!!
THEN THAT ALONE MAKES US ALLIES!!
YOU CAN ALWAYS FIGHT IT OUT LATER, BUT IF YOU FORM AN ALLIANCE NOW...
...IT WILL GIVE YOUR CAUSE THE ADVANTAGE!!
SO WHAT'S THE PLAN?!
I'VE GOT IT ALL ARRANGED IN EXACTING DETAIL.
THEN LET'S CARRY IT OUT AND BE DONE WITH IT!!!
DO OM!!
THREE HOURS AND 20 MINUTES UNTIL THE TEA PARTY...
TO BE CONTINUED IN ONE PIECE, VOL. 86!

COMING NEXT VOLUME:

The unlikely alliance between the Straw Hats and Bege's Firetank Pirates prepares to crash Sanji's wedding. But can these two wild groups actually work together? And will it be enough against Big Mom, one of the most powerful pirates in the world?

ON SALE MAY 2018!

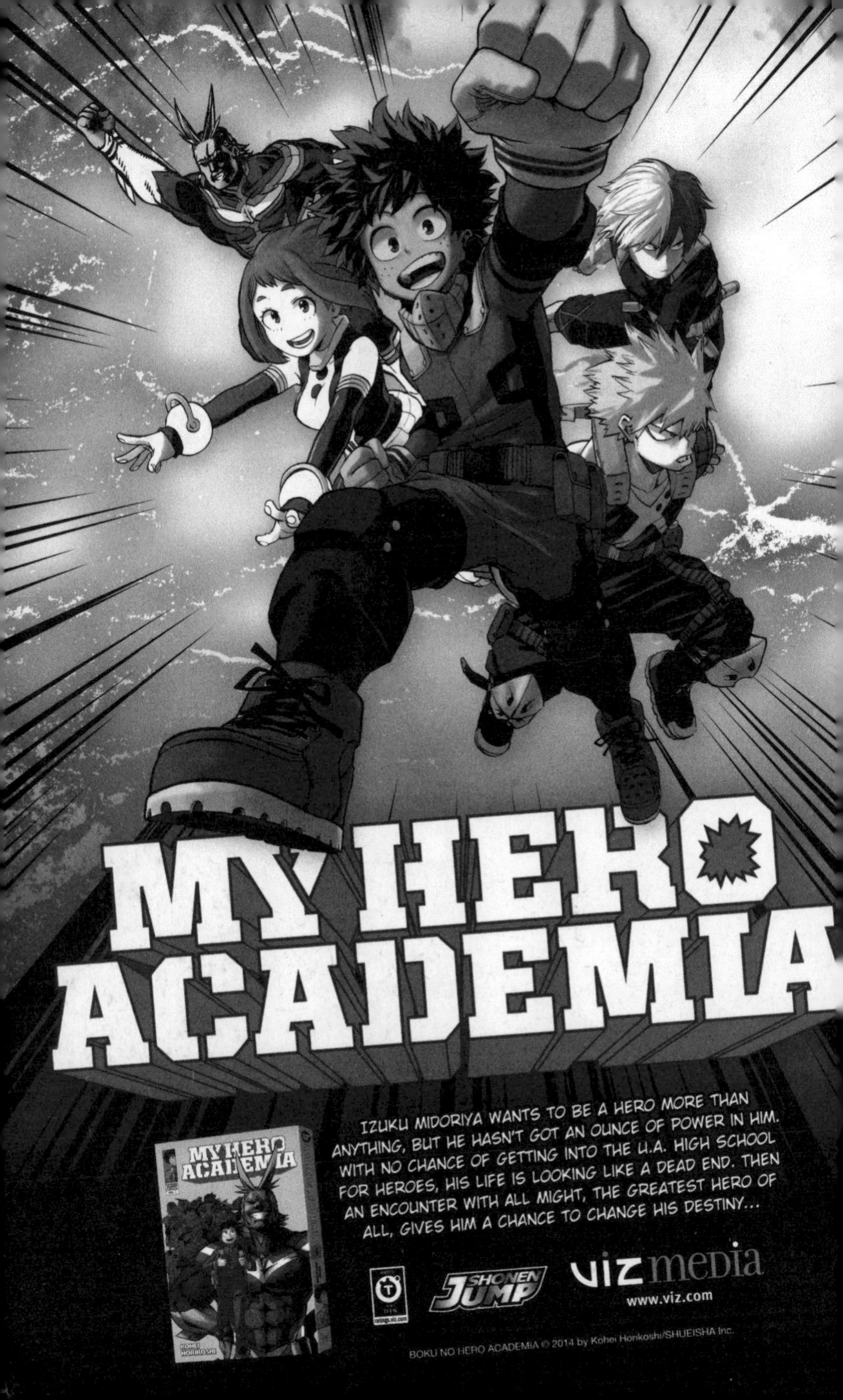

MY HERO ACADEMIA
IZUKU MIDORIYA WANTS TO BE A HERO MORE THAN ANYTHING, BUT HE HASN'T GOT AN OUNCE OF POWER IN HIM. WITH NO CHANCE OF GETTING INTO THE U.A. HIGH SCHOOL FOR HEROES, HIS LIFE IS LOOKING LIKE A DEAD END. THEN AN ENCOUNTER WITH ALL MIGHT, THE GREATEST HERO OF ALL, GIVES HIM A CHANCE TO CHANGE HIS DESTINY...
MY HERO ACADEMIA
KOHEI HORIKOSHI
SHONEN JUMP
viz media
www.viz.com
BOKU NO HERO ACADEMIA © 2014 by Kohei Horikoshi/SHUEISHA Inc.

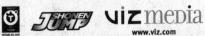

You're Reading in the Wrong Direction!!

Whoops! Guess what? You're starting at the wrong end of the comic!

...It's true! In keeping with the original Japanese format, **One Piece** is meant to be read from right to left, starting in the upper-right corner.

Unlike English, which is read from left to right, Japanese is read from right to left, meaning that action, sound effects and word-balloon order are completely reversed... something which can make readers unfamiliar with Japanese feel pretty backwards themselves. For this reason, manga or Japanese comics published in the U.S. in English have sometimes been published "flopped"—that is, printed in exact reverse order, as though seen from the other side of a mirror.

By flopping pages, U.S. publishers can avoid confusing readers, but the compromise is not without its downside. For one thing, a character in a flopped manga series who once wore in the original Japanese version a T-shirt emblazoned with "M A Y" (as in "the merry month of") now wears one which reads "Y A M"! Additionally, many manga creators in Japan are themselves unhappy with the process, as some feel the mirror-imaging of their art skews their original intentions.

We are proud to bring you Eiichiro Oda's **One Piece** in the original unflopped format. For now, though, turn to the other side of the book and let the journey begin...!

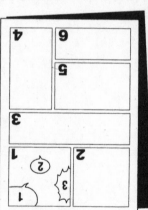

—Editor